Women in Between

Female roles in a male world:
Mount Hagen, New Guinea

Women in Between

Female Roles in a Male World:
Mount Hagen, New Guinea

Marilyn Strathern

*Department of Social Anthropology,
University of Cambridge*

Rowman & Littlefield Publishers, Inc.

ROWMAN & LITTLEFIELD PUBLISHERS, INC.

Published in the United States of America
by Rowman & Littlefield Publishers, Inc.
4720 Boston Way, Lanham, Maryland 20706

3 Henrietta Street, London WC2E 8LU, England

British Cataloging in Publication Information Available

Library of Congress Cataloging-in-Publication Data

Strathern, Marilyn.
Women in between : female roles in a male world : Mount Hagen,
New Guinea / Marilyn Strathern.
      p.   cm.—(Classics in anthropology)
Originally published : London ; New York : Seminar Press, 1972.
Includes bibliographical references (p.   ) and index.
1. Women, Medpla. 2. Medpla (Papua New Guinea people)—Social life
and customs. 3. Sex role—Papua New Guinea—Hagen Mount Region.
4. Ethnology—Papua New Guinea—Hagen Mount Region. 5. Hagen
Mount Region (Papua New Guinea)—Social life and customs. I. Title.
II. Series: Classics in anthropology (Savage, Md.)
[DU740.42.S78 1992]   305.42'09956'5—dc20   92–32785 CIP

ISBN 0–8476–7784–2 (cloth : alk. paper)
ISBN 0–8476–7785–0 (paper : alk. paper)

Printed in the United States of America

 ™ The paper used in this publication meets the minimum requirements of
American National Standard for Information Sciences—Permanence of
Paper for Printed Library Materials, ANSI Z39.48–1984.

Note on orthography

ø — a mid, open, front, rounded vowel, as in German "hören".
raised *e* — a mid, close, central, unrounded vowel (the schwa), as the
   first vowel in English "banana".
y — a high, close, front, rounded vowel, as in French "mûr".

Not all phonemically relevant distinctions are indicated in my
transcription.

Note on case histories

Since one of my fieldwork interests was disputes and the way these are
settled, during the course of my stay in Hagen I witnessed several
quarrels and enquired into others. Some of these were quite open and
made public within the local community; others were affairs which
people expected only a few would know about. In neither case, however, would those concerned necessarily invite the participation of a
wider audience. I therefore use pseudonyms throughout in all references
to particular individuals. My thanks are to the people of Kawelka,
Elti and other groups for their generosity in discussing such matters
with me; I hope the fact that I tend to concentrate on quarrels and
disputes, and use these to illustrate points at several junctures, will give
them no offence.

   "Cases" based on informants' accounts alone are distinguished by an
asterisk. I take these as revealing about attitudes even if they are not
accurate as to behaviour.

Preface   The case of the good wife

In 1967 I was told about a young girl who had recently married a youth from one of the Northern Hagen tribes. Her kin were said to be dissatisfied with the bridewealth they had received, and with hopes of finding better elsewhere, had tried to persuade the new wife to leave her husband. But, so the account went, she protested that this would harm her reputation, make her name bad: they had taken her bridewealth in the first place and now they wanted to throw it back at the husband! Her husband's relatives were full of praise for her desire to stay; she had proved herself a good wife indeed, with their interests at heart, and in resisting the influence of her parents had really become one of them. "She has come inside us," they said, *tin-tin-kin rukrung onom*.

At marriage, Hagen women usually go to live on their husband's clan territory. However, they by no means automatically "go inside" their husband's group—it is expected that strong ties will be maintained with the wife's own kin. Hagen society fits Barnes' characterization of New Guinea Highlands systems in which "a married woman neither remains fully affiliated to her natal group nor is completely transferred to her husband's group but rather sustains an interest in both", and where "the division of rights in and responsibilities towards the woman is not exclusive" (1962: 6). In examining such systems, one can talk of the degree to which women become incorporated into their husband's group, and their jural status vis-à-vis this and their natal group.

Aspects of female incorporation have been considered important variables in general discussions of such topics as marital stability, concepts of mystical power and descent principles.[1] The quality of women's attachment to groups with descent ideologies has bearing on the whole nature of group formation, and the significance of male

---

[1] See for example, Fallers (1957), Leach (1961), Douglas (1966), Middleton and Winter (1963), Lewis and Goody E. N. and J. R. (1967).

membership. A principal focus of New Guinea Highlands ethnographies has been comparative analysis of group structure, and in a
sense this book touches on the same theme. My main interest, however,
is the rather narrower one of women's roles and the way aspects of group
membership from women's point of view compare with men's involvement, loyalties and values.

Women's affiliations to corporate groups are sometimes discussed in
either/or terms, as though the more rights the husband's group acquires
in respect of a wife, the fewer her natal group can hold; as though
loyalty to the husband must be proportionately detrimental to sibling
solidarity. The woman's position is thus seen as an outcome of the way
rights in her are distributed or of the balance of influences over her. She
is "interstitial" between groups, "peripheral" in terms of the power
structure. These concepts have limitations if they imply entirely passive
roles on the part of women themselves. In common with other High-
landers, Hageners operate an elaborate system of ceremonial exchange.
Relations between groups may be expressed through prestations as well
as through confrontation in warfare. Indeed, the nature of descent
groups in the Highlands cannot be understood without considering
also the kinds of alliances set up between them (cf. Strathern, A. J.,
1969a). Hagen women traditionally had little part to play in warfare,
although their transference between clans sometimes signified friendly
intentions; in the exchange system, however, their participation is more
active. It is because of this that my analysis stresses not only women's
dual and partial group affiliations but their positive mediatory roles. It
is not the simple fact of alliance at issue here. Groups may be linked in
ways which concern men only (e.g. by circulating male cults); and even
where marriages are used as the basis for a link, the wife or sister herself
may be no more than an object of transfer. The point is that Hagen
ceremonial exchange makes certain requirements of women as actors
in the system. These in turn assume a degree of personal commitment
to men's interests, so that women are seen as having loyalties to distribute.
The young girl who "came inside" was praised for aligning herself with
her husband's kin.

Although Hageners are using an idiom of incorporation when they
refer to a wife having "come inside" her husband's clan, parallel
idioms put the emphasis on alliance. A married woman may be
described as "in between" (*ruk ile morom*), that is, between two sets of
in-laws. From the viewpoint of the men on each side the woman

between them is their link, their "road" (*nombokla*), as it is put, for mutual transactions. She will act as a go-between, and is referred to as bearing valuables from one side to the other. Her own prestige derives in part from this.

But women's prestige is not quite the same as men's. Men are always the major public actors in an exchange transaction, and the phrase, "in between", carries a further derogatory connotation. Brothers-in-law may assert their own joint interests against the wife/sister, for between them they control the woman, who is powerless to act on her own accord, and has no "road" of her own. Unlike a man, a woman has limited contacts; she serves men, and what prestige she has derives from her dependence on males. By herself she is nothing. These are statements men quite openly make about women.

Nevertheless, the fact that women are seen as intermediaries perhaps leads them to put more emphasis on, to seek more from, their active participation in transactions than men admit is the case. A Hagen man analyzing the power structure of his own society might well categorize females as peripheral, maintaining that women are really irrelevant to the important processes of decision-making. Women, however, not only see things a little differently but sometimes behave as though they were rather more important than men usually allow. For in some contexts it is in men's interests to foster if not exploit women's involvement, and they sometimes find themselves being taken literally. Indeed, women are able to claim, and to achieve, a degree of autonomy.

* * *

Two major accounts of traditional Hagen society have been written by missionary-anthropologists whose knowledge of Hagen dates from the early years of contact (cf. Vicedom and Tischner, 1943–8 and Strauss, 1962). Vicedom's impression of Hagen women was that they "occupy a higher status than elsewhere in Melanesia" (Vicedom and Tischner, 1943–8; 2: 232). He notes that (*ibid*, 227f) women did not participate in religious activities, that a "woman's task is merely to help the male blood of a new generation come into life" since it is through men that clans have continuity, and that it is men who decide the life of the clan and tribe: "they wage wars and bring success or failure to the clan . . . the women have no influence in these public matters but must endure what men impose on them". Yet for all this, "the relationship between the sexes is easy and natural. The woman . . . is considered a full member of society. She is expected to be reserved in the company of men, but she nevertheless sits and talks quietly with them. By this fact alone, the women at Mount Hagen occupy a far superior position to that of the women of the Gulf and the Huon Peninsula."

Within the New Guinea Highlands alone, the reported tenor of relations between the sexes differs from society to society. Meggitt's article (1964), *Male-female relationships in the Highlands of Australian New Guinea*, deals with just such differences. He suggests that the social status of women in everyday life is a factor to be considered in the overall assessment of relations between the sexes. A certain amount of antagonism or opposition marks such relations throughout the Highlands; this intersexual conflict can be divided into at least two types. The one is found among the Mae-Enga, western neighbours of Hagen, the other in Kuma, neighbours to the east. Hagen (Medlpa) itself Meggitt ascribes to those with the "Kuma syndrome". He remarks that women's status is highest among societies of this cluster.

The hypotheses Meggitt set up were primarily intended as a basis for comparisons between several Highlands societies. I do not take up the issue in detail here. It is, nevertheless, illuminating to contrast the situation of Mae-Enga and Hagen women; Hagen also differs to some degree from Kuma, and if Hagen women are of as high status as their Kuma counterparts it would seem to be for very different reasons. The topic in fact raises the whole question of whether one can usefully gloss women as having an overall "high" or "low" status. In making his assessment Vicedom had to use dialectic, alternately weighing up positive and negative factors. What women do or think, what men do or think about them, is as complex a sphere as any other domain of social life. The bulk of the following account is an attempt to sketch some of the complexities for Hagen; in the final chapter I return to the question of whether, even if one does not think in terms of an overall status, it is possible to characterize features of female roles as distinctive to Hagen by comparison with other Highlands societies. It is here that I specifically turn again to Meggitt's hypotheses and suggest some of the ways in which Hagen differs from both Enga and Kuma.

The book falls into two parts. In the first I describe aspects of the formal relations a married woman has with her clan of origin and with her husband's clan. These include her position as a resident on her husband's clan territory, her domestic duties and the reciprocal dependence of husband and wife on each other; and also the consideration a woman claims from her own clansmen, and the influences they retain over her. In dealing with the relationship which marriage sets up between groups, I touch on the implications of marital alliances for political relations and the exchange system. Finally, I show how values associated with the exchange system contribute to attitudes which men and women hold about their major spheres of activity, and special attitudes towards women's intermediary roles. The second part examines certain situations to illustrate the autonomy of action which women's intermediary status precipitates, in particular, marital disputes and the circumstances of divorce. The same situations also reveal constraints limiting women's action, and allow us to assess their jural status.

I concentrate on marital relations for several reasons. In the first place this echoes a prevalent way of thinking: many Hagen stereotypes about "women" in general touch on their specific role as wives. It is also true that a large part of a woman's activities are directed towards caring for her husband and children, and that relations between affines are important for her. Marriage transforms a woman's ties with her kin; indeed it is as a married person that she in a way helps her own kin most. Finally, the emphasis must be on interaction between the sexes. Although women may have different views and different interests from men, they rarely combine together simply on the basis of their sex. They neither participate in a subculture of their own nor form exclusive associations. Rather, they subscribe to public values that derive from politics, religion and exchange: spheres in which males play the key roles.

*   *   *   *

The study is based on sixteen months' work spent in Hagen in 1964–5, and an additional two months in 1967. The ethnographic present refers to the whole period 1964–7.

The fieldwork of 1964–5 was supported by grants from the Emslie Horniman Anthropological Scholarship Fund, the Smuts Memorial Fund and the Anthony Wilkin Fund in the University of Cambridge, and the Mount Everest Foundation. I held a J.E. Cairnes Scholarship, subsequently Studentship, from Girton College, Cambridge, and a Bartle Frere Exhibition (University of Cambridge). Five months were spent under the hospitality of the Department of Anthropology and Sociology at the Australian National University, during which time I held an Ida Smedley Maclean Junior British Scholarship from the British Federation of University Women. In 1967 I received further assistance from Girton College, from Cambridge University and from the Royal Anthropological Institute of Great Britain and Ireland; and was awarded a Winifred Cullis grant by the International Federation of University Women. For all this help I am most grateful.

My thanks to people in New Guinea are first to the Hageners. Komitis Kont, Nøring and Køya helped me especially with court cases. Accounts of conditions before the arrival of Europeans were given in detail by Tetep and Wundake, and the latter's wife, Wanmba. I was made to feel welcome in many households both among the Kawelka, Tipuka and Minembi tribes at Buk and the Elti and Ndika at Kelua, and our own household over time included Puklum, Køi, Moka and Moet. Nykint and Rongnda helped me on their clan territories; above all I was dependent on the assistance and companionship of Ru, Oke and Yakomb and of Yarop who enabled me to see things with a woman's eye.

The then Department of Native Affairs allowed access to records, and through its District and Sub-district Offices in Mt. Hagen aided me in many ways. I especially thank Mr M. Allwood and the Officers stationed from time to time at Dei Local Government Council. I am also grateful to Mr and Mrs G. Broomhead, then of Baglaga Plantation, and to the Rev. and Mrs F. Doering and the Rev. and Mrs R. Jamieson of the Lutheran Mission, for their kind hospitality and practical help; and in Port Moresby to Mr and Mrs Nigel Oram. Dr Paula Brown Glick supervised the initial fieldwork, and I owe much to her encouragement throughout this period, as I do to the stimulating and detailed criticism of Dr Esther Goody while I was preparing the material for a thesis (with the title, *Women's status in the Mt. Hagen area*). Behind this lies my more general gratitude to Professor Meyer Fortes, Drs Edmund Leach and Jack Goody, and members of the Department of Archaeology and Anthropology in Cambridge. I was considerably helped by discussions with Dr Elizabeth Kennedy in Cambridge; Dr Marie Reay and Professor John Barnes in Canberra; and with Dr Phyllis Kaberry and Professors Ralph Bulmer and Mervyn Meggitt; and in New Guinea, Father Ernest Brandewie, who was working among Western Melpa in 1964. I have benefited from conversations with the Rev. H. Strauss, as well as from being able to draw on his and the works of Dr G. Vicedom.

Miss Pamela Morris aided me in the statistical analysis of some of my material.

The person from whom I have received most, both in terms of specific criticism and of general stimulus and encouragement, is my husband, Andrew. This book is intended to complement his own material on group structure and ceremonial exchange, but my debt to him goes far beyond the particular references I make to his work.

June, 1971   Marilyn Strathern

Contents

For Mother and Father

PART 1

Producers and Transactors

"When we are thirsty, women go to fetch water. We want a cigarette and tell them to roll one for us. We are hungry, and tell the women to cook food. Every day women do this, and we call them our *kintmant amb*, our female servants."

A young family man (Northern Melpa)

"Women think that the pigs they rear will be theirs to eat later."

Central Melpa wife

1

Hagen Society

Mount Hagen gives its name to the administrative centre of the Western Highlands District in the Territory of New Guinea. The area of forested mountain slopes and grassy plainland which spreads out eastward from its foothills is inhabited by some seventy tribes whom I speak of as the Hageners. It was from the east, travelling up the Wahgi valley, that the first Europeans came in 1933. An airstrip was established on the Ogelbeng plain near the site of the present Mt. Hagen township, and reconnaissance journeys from it included one over the mountainous Sepik-Wahgi Divide, some twenty miles to the north. While the Ogelbeng and Mt. Hagen area quickly came under effective control, the Sepik-Wahgi Divide was not opened up till after the Second World War. Roads, rest houses, resident policemen and medical orderlies became established here at the same time (1951–2) as Lutheran missionaries from Ogelbeng set up Kotna station at the foot of the Divide. In 1964 Mt. Hagen was a flourishing town catering for an expanding expatriate population; Kotna had a secondary school, a large hospital and permanent fabric church.

I have concentrated on these two localities, most of the time in the field being spent either at Buk (or Mbukl), on the Sepik-Wahgi Divide, or at Kelua, on the Ogelbeng plain.

The people at Buk and Kelua regard the Gumant river which separates them as a rough boundary, and specify small details of custom to distinguish the two regions. North of the Gumant people speak Melpa ("Hagen", Wurm 1964) almost exclusively, while to the south many understand both Melpa and the closely related Temboka (a dialect of Gawigl, Wurm 1964), whose speakers extend into the Nebilyer valley.

Warfare, group expansions and migrations in the recent past had led to the intermingling of Temboka and Melpa groups in the immediate vicinity of the present town. Melpa and Temboka speakers together number perhaps 75 000. These are the Hageners. Within Melpa, I call the people north of the Gumant Northern Melpa, and those to the south Central Melpa. Regional and dialect variations also differentiate tribes living towards the eastern border who have contacts with their Wahgi valley neighbours (Eastern Melpa), and those on the slopes of Mount Hagen, the boundary with Enga speakers (Western Melpa). At Buk live the Kawelka, Tipuka and Minembi tribes who thus fall into the category of Northern Melpa; Elti associated with clans of Ndika and Yamka tribes at Kelua, are Central Melpa. While my specific material derives in the main from these groups, the conclusions probably have a general applicability throughout the Hagen area.[1]

Traditionally, the inhabitants of Kelua and Buk were in little direct contact, although they traded through intermediaries on the Gumant river. Northern Melpa had access to the Jimi valley, from which came stone axes, prized foods, cassowaries and plumes, while Central Melpa traded salt and tree oil obtained from groups to their west and south-west. Different types of shell, along with pigs, were exchanged in both directions. Occasional marriages were made in the past[2] to foster these trading links. Pacification, road building and the spread of motor vehicles have facilitated much more frequent contact since the advent of Europeans.

Pacification was one of the first tasks of the Australian administration and warfare has been banned since 1945–50. Nevertheless, old military enmities and alliances still form a framework on which groups organize their external relations. Although open warfare has been suppressed, people continue to feel threatened by the poisoning activities of their old enemies. In 1964–5 compensation payments for deaths inflicted twenty years earlier were the focus of intensive ceremonial exchange sequences round Buk, while in 1967 groups at Kelua were beginning to prepare for a set of ally-payments. These payments in turn further contribute to the way in which groups regard themselves as in confrontation

------

[1] Vicedom, who termed the Hageners as Mbowamb, from their phrase meaning "human beings", was stationed among the Central Melpa (1934–9). Strauss was with Vicedom before the war; after 1945 he was able to travel more extensively over the Hagen region.
[2] i.e. before the arrival of Europeans.

or alliance with one another. Pacification and the development of transport has increased the number of tribes with which a single group has contact, both marriages and exchanges in general being made further afield.

Europeans are seen as having brought wealth to the area, initially in the form of large quantities of shell valuables, from which the Central Melpa were first to profit. These today are probably the wealthiest Hageners in terms of Australian currency. At the time of fieldwork, coffee was the most important cash crop, many Central Melpa men having coffee gardens of long-standing; women were able to take vegetables twice-weekly to a market in the township; and it was from this area that young men in the more highly paid jobs (clerks, truck-drivers) tended to be drawn. There is perhaps rather less money among Northern Melpa; in 1964–5 people still looked to casual labour on European-owned plantations to meet their needs, although many individuals also had coffee. Boys often spent a few months away from home on contract to plantations in the Wahgi valley. Until the weekly market was established at the Dei Local Government Council in 1966, only local planters or Kotna mission occasionally bought the women's produce.

Cash has entered into a wide range of transactions, including bridewealth and compensation payments. In ceremonial exchange, however, it is no more than an "extra" to the main valuables, shells and pigs. Of all the types of shell valuable in currency when Europeans first entered Hagen, only the goldlip pearl shell is still used regularly, although other kinds are worn as ornaments. While it has taken over many of their functions, money is not quite comparable to the traditional shell valuables; for example, shells were strictly owned only by men, while women today may both earn and keep the money they earn.[1]

People think of themselves as gradually becoming more and more involved in the cash economy. The new regime is summed up in the notion that the government has brought "law"; this covers both the positive inducements associated with making money and the injunctions that fighting and self-help should be abandoned as instruments in the settling of disputes. Since the early 1960's, most of the Hagen tribes have been incorporated into Local Government Councils; the Central Melpa form an amalgamated Hagen Council (31 000 people),[2] the Northern

[1] For further material on trade, ceremonial exchange and traditional economics see Strathern A.J., 1971.
[2] Since expanded to include expatriates and residents in the Nebilyer valley.

Melpa, Dei Council (14300 in 1964). Councillors appoint helpers, originally known as *Komiti* ("Committee man") and since given official recognition under the title *Memba* ("Member"). Although without official magisterial powers, it is the Councillors and their Komitis who, as elsewhere (Barnett, 1967), settle the majority of local disputes. In this they perform some of the functions of the former administration-appointed Bosbois, Tultuls and Luluais.

Both Roman Catholic and Lutheran missions have stations in Hagen; my work was done in areas mainly under Lutheran influence. Outstations are supervised by native evangelists who encourage the converted to live together in villages. Mission teaching has led to general abandonment by the people at large of certain religious customs, notably public prayers and the protracted mourning duties which widows used to observe. Attempts to eliminate polygyny, however, affect only those who decide to become baptised. Converts also publicly disclaim traditional fears of the polluting power of females, although taboos concerning these are firmly adhered to by the majority of the population. While the missions present a model of European-style family life, and while many people envisage that in the end they will become baptised, for the most part values which Vicedom (Vicedom and Tischner, 1943-8) and Strauss (1962) ascribe to pre-contact Hagen society still have currency.

Group Structure

Prominent in Hagen are segmentary hierarchies of named groups, of which the highest level is generally the tribe; these are paired and sometimes further clustered into named congeries. Tribes vary in size from 6000 people to below 500, with an average in the region of 1000. Small tribes may be attached to larger ones, while still preserving their identity; some inhabit a continuous segment of land, others are scattered. Details concerning the size and territories of certain tribes are given in Appendix I.

Although tribes are conceptualized as political units which take joint action, the clan (200-300 people, size range 50-450) could act independently in war. Alliances between neighbouring clans often crossed tribal boundaries. Clans divide into those feared as traditional, perpetual enemies (*el parka wamb*, "fighters in full war regalia") and those who conduct only "minor wars" (*el øninga*). The largest tribes may be split into sections which are *el parka* to each other, but usually tribe-sections wage only minor wars between themselves. The importance of this distinction is that allies were regularly drawn only from a clan's minor enemies, and it is these people who intermarry most and between whom interpersonal ties are strongest.

Whole tribes or tribe-sections may be exogamous, but the typical exogamous unit is the clan, a level of group at which emphatic assertions of common descent are made. Within the clan, lethal fighting is forbidden and its members have joint responsibility for war compensation payments. Clans are divided into further named groups, sub-clans and sub-sub-clans. There may be no comprehensive genealogical framework for the whole clan, although the charter for co-operation is putative common brotherhood, and it is the ghosts of dead clan members who look after the living. The same is true for the clan's subdivisions. But at the lowest level are groups focused on an eponymous male ancestor usually one or two generations senior to living men. These are "father–son sets" (*tepam-kang^emal*). Here, complete genealogies are known; the sets can be called "lineages". In spite of this agnatic model, under certain circumstances members may be recruited to lineages through females as well as males. Their non-agnatic status is irrelevant for most clan or sub-clan activities, although it is important in the application of marriage rules. Men attached through women suffer no formal inferiority; they may form 20–50% of a clan's adult males.[1]

The analytical ascription of any one named group to a structural category (such as clan) depends on the kinds of functions which cluster around it and its interaction with other groups. Some of the functions which apply to different levels, and associated dogmas, are presented in a rough synopsis (Fig. 1) based largely on the analysis given in Strathern, A. J. (1965, 1966b). Levels 2, 5, 7 and 9 are most frequently found in any single hierarchy; some of the functions (such as responsibility for ally payments) may hold at several different levels, but others (such as the rule that one may marry sisters' daughters from one's opposite clansection) relate to specific structural positions (thus sub-clans not grouped into sections do not observe this rule). In the case of exchange activities, the type of occasion (war compensation, funeral payment, bridewealth) often determines the span of group participating.

---

[1] The status of non-agnates and an examination of the reasons for which men become attached to other clans is the subject of Strathern, A. J. To be published.

Fig. 1. Synopsis of dogmas and functions of named groups

| DOGMA | FUNCTIONS | | |
	Warfare	Marriage rules	Exchange
1. *Tribe pair* Sometimes origin myth of association	May or may not be allies		
2. *Tribe* Origin place; creation myth; common *mi^a*; "one name", *mbi tenda*	May combine against traditional enemies	Occasionally exogamous	May hold common Pig Feast
3. *Tribe-section* Origin myth	Usually allies/ minor enemies	Occasionally exogamous	May combine for war compensation
4. *Clan pair* Sometimes "genealogical" link (half-brothers)	Ideally always allies; no lethal fighting internally; ally payments between clans of a pair	Closely intermarried or else single exogamous unit	May combine for war compensation
5. *Clan* Assertions of patrilineal descent ("one father", *tepam tenda*) or common territory ("one garden ditch", *pana ru tenda*); *mbi tenda*	Fights as corporate gp; no lethal fighting internally; common responsibility for starting wars	Usually exogamous; widow inheritance within clan if no clan-sections	Responsible for both blood-revenge and ally payments[b], thus often *moka*-making unit
6. *Clan-section*	As allies, two sections may compensate each other for help	May marry ZD of opposite section; widow inheritance within section	Responsible for blood-revenge and ally payments

DOGMA	FUNCTIONS		
	Warfare	Marriage rules	Exchange
7. Sub-clan "One men's house", rapa tenda	Automatic allies, no ally compens. paid internally	Classif. extension of rules often includes whole sub-clan	Independent moka unit in context; makes common funeral payments
8. Sub-sub-clan "Little men's house", rapa kel	Automatic allies, no ally compens. paid internally	Classif. extension of rules often includes whole sub-sub-clan	Internal unit for distribution and consumption of pork
9. Lineage Comprehensive genealogical framework: F–S (tepam-kang^e mal) group	Automatic allies, no ally compens. paid internally	Classif. extension of rules often includes whole lineage; ego continues to observe marriage prohibitions of lineage even if attached elsewhere	Provides most of members' bridewealth; some co-operation in garden work

^a Mi is a substance used in divination (cf. Strauss, 1962), and functions as an inward-facing tribal "totem" (Fortes, 1967).

^b Groups above sub-clan level have a liability towards one another as allies: those who started the fight must compensate their allies for losses incurred on their behalf. These are the focus for large scale moka payments between friendly groups. Minor enemies may also compensate each other for deaths inflicted. Payments of this nature between traditional enemies are rare.

The named subdivisions of two tribes are given in Appendix I— Northern Melpa Kawelka and Central Melpa Elti.

People thinking of themselves as a unit in negotiations are designated "one rapa", after the men's house (manga rapa) where they meet. Sub-clans each have their own big-men or leaders (Strathern, A. J., 1966a). Big-men (wu^e nyim) coordinate activities which involve group participation, act as spokesmen in settling disputes, and from pursuit of their own interests and reputation as wealthy men also bring prestige to those associated with them. Such individuals do not, however, hold offices; it is their own ability which brings them prominence. In the past they were important in warfare, but as diplomats in the securing of peace-terms rather than as fight-leaders. Peace settlement involved wealth exchanges, and it is largely through ceremonial exchange (*moka*) that big-men build their reputations today.

Moka transactions with pig and shell valuables follow standardized forms and may accompany performance of religious cults, payment of war indemnities, and funeral and childbirth gifts; bridewealth is a precursor of *moka* exchanges between affinal kin. *Moka* can be conducted quite privately between individual partners; or a clan, divisions or combinations of clans, may come together in public display, each man giving to his own partner, but jointly celebrating the whole wealth of the group. Public transactions take place at ceremonial grounds and are often accompanied by dancing. They are a vehicle for the expression of competition between groups, assertions of strength and prosperity, and claims to prestige.

Settlement Patterns

Clan lands are likely to be compact and bounded. Clansmen cannot alienate such land, but readily grant rights of gardening and co-residence if extra-clan kin wish to associate with their hosts. Within a clan territory, gardens and settlements may be intermingled, although members of a clan-section tend to live near one another. Individual garden claims are inherited within the lineage.

Residence is dispersed; ceremonial grounds, "*moka* places", provide a focus for clans and sub-clans. At the head of such a ground usually stands the men's house where major discussions are held. This may in addition be the private house of a big-man who has his homestead nearby. At the men's houses of less important individuals plans for bridewealth and minor occasions are made. Here a man keeps his shell valuables, although he may also decide to secrete them in the depths of his wife's house, away from the prying eyes of visitors.

Men and women generally sleep in separate dwellings; pigs are stalled in the woman's house. Sometimes they share a single "sleeping house", and erect rough pig shelters, or an extra woman's house, in the pastures. Men's houses with their associated women's houses, or the sleeping house, may form isolated homesteads from a few minutes' to up to half an hour's walk away from neighbours, or else be grouped with others into larger units (settlements). Settlements and homesteads are not distinguished terminologically by Hageners, who have a single designation, *mangkona*, "house place" or "home", for both.

Homesteads are typically occupied by one married man, his wife (or wives) and dependants (children, widowed parent, unmarried siblings). Settlements include two or more married men. These may have a single senior member, as when father and son live together, or comprise brothers along with their married and unmarried children. Married sons tend to stay with their father till his death, but may afterwards separate, to establish independent homesteads or set up residence with distant brothers or other kinsmen. A few men (5% in the Buk area) live with their wife's kin. In brief, people of a homestead tend to comprise a nuclear or compound family,[1] while those of a settlement approximate to the nucleus of a lineage.

Members of one residential group (homestead or settlement) can be distinguished from those of another by their tendency to co-operate in clearing gardens, building houses and cooking small feasts. A desire for privacy, however, opposes the advantages of co-operation, and the larger settlements rarely contain more than 25–30 persons. Even here, houses will form clusters screened from one another by trees. It is said of large units that it becomes impossible for people to entertain their individual sets of matrilateral and affinal kin properly. Smoke from cooking preparations may be visible for miles, but people do not like to intrude uninvited on the hospitality of others.

Men's and women's houses are very different in appearance, the former round, with a cone-shaped roof; the latter long and low lying. They are not rigidly exclusive to either sex, men and women on occasion being able to sleep and eat in both. It is not unusual for a whole family to sleep temporarily in one kind while waiting for another house to be built. Wives in a homestead, however, are much more likely to make use of the men's house than wives living in a settlement where there are several male residents; here the men's house is left to the men. The oblong joint "sleeping house" was a traditional house-style (Vicedom and Tischner, 1943–8: 1: 168); nowadays it is often built in what is thought of as a European manner.

Certain rules stem from the fact that females are regarded as having a polluting or weakening influence on males; men do not enter the rear sleeping compartment of a woman's house; women should not leave personal items such as pubic aprons in the men's house. A special hut is used by females in seclusion during menstruation or after childbirth,

---

[1] There is no category term for this apart from *mangkona wamb*, "home people".

although (particularly among Central Melpa) they may simply retire to the rear compartment of their ordinary house, especially if this is built away from the main areas of settlement in the pig pastures.

Hageners say that husbands and wives tend to associate together more closely nowadays than they did in the past. Then men had to be on constant guard for night attacks. Nevertheless, Vicedom's account (1943–8:1:169f) would suggest that in the past there was almost as much casual toing and froing between the men's and women's houses of a family group as there is today.

The Agricultural Background

Kelua lies in a quite heavily populated region (118 persons per square mile);[1] the land is comparatively flat, with gentle hills, at about 5250 ft above sea level though Mount Hagen itself rises to within 13 000 ft. The natural vegetation is dominated by the grasses and "wild sugar cane" known in Pidgin English as *kunai* (Imperata) and *pitpit* (e.g. Miscanthus). Some of the land is too wet to be cultivated. Settlements near Kelua tend to be built on ridges, the main gardens being made on the slopes of these or other dryish ground. Gardens and settlements together are enclosed by deep ditches. Sweet potato is the Hagen staple crop. Pigs, the chief domestic animal, forage outside the enclosed area.

Buk people are envious of the Ogelbeng grasslands, which is good pig pasture. Conversely, Kelua people envy the range of crops which Northern Melpa can grow on their hill soils or obtain from the Jimi valley; they have plenty of European vegetables but complain of the poor quality of their sugarcane, bananas, taro and yams, prized crops which flourish at Buk. Buk itself lies at 6500 ft, at the head of the Meka river, which flows into the Gumant. The valley flanks are settled and cultivated between 5300 ft and above 7000 ft. They are steep and heavily wooded, but the steel axe has pushed back the timber line. Long-used sweet potato gardens may lie under grass fallow, while people encourage secondary woodland growth and plant casuarina trees in plots which they plan to use for mixed-vegetable gardens (greens, bananas, cane, taro, yams). Gardens are scattered, often on quite steep slopes (15–35°), and are individually fenced with stout wooden stakes.

---

[1] The Dei Council area, 67 per square mile, although the density in the vicinity of Buk must be much higher. These figures, kindly supplied by T. Downs, A.D.O., are computed from the entire Hagen and Dei Council areas, which include large tracts of unpopulated country.

Gardens can be cleared all the year round, except when the weather is very wet. April to September tend to be the drier months, October to March somewhat wetter, but there are no marked seasons or a specific horticultural calendar. Men clear and fence or ditch gardenland, women being responsible for the planting, tending and daily harvesting of the staple. Food is normally harvested afresh each day and is sometimes the work of several hours if the gardens are far away from the homestead. Women thus spend a greater part of their time in the gardens than do men, whose activities include frequent visiting connected with arrangements for private and public exchange transactions. The introduction of steel has further cut down the length of time men need spend on agricultural work. Apart from minor jobs, such as chopping firewood, women do not use the axe, for this is the most important single implement belonging to men. Like its stone counterpart, the modern steel axe is carried about on the person by men, and is an object of display (Strathern, A.M., 1969). The wooden digging stick is women's major tool, and Hagen women are also ordinarily never seen without netbags over their heads—in which they carry garden produce, young children, gifts of meat and shell valuables. The netbag is suspended from the forehead, and lies down over the back. In the past men used to have small bags in which they kept scraps of tobacco and other articles, but these were never worn on the head; a man carrying his own sweet potatoes slings his bag over the shoulder.

This difference is of some significance. A man's head is an object of ornament, the hair usually being bound into a wig which is decorated with feathers, fur, leaves and grasses. But women, Hagen men say, have no reason for decorating themselves as often as men do. "When men walk about it is to conduct business, to visit exchange partners, to take part in political discussions. When women walk about it is to bring produce home from the gardens or to carry some share of a food distribution made by their kin. If women put feathers in their hair, where would they carry sweet potatoes?"

2

Residence and Work: the Woman with her Husband's Kin

The netbag is important as a receptacle in which produce and gifts are carried; in some contexts it symbolizes the womb.

A bride comes to her husband's kin with a dowry from her parents, and this includes breeding sows, netbags, and personal items such as aprons and flasks of cosmetic oil. The netbags (and sometimes extra aprons) she distributes to her new sisters-in-law: her husband's married and unmarried sisters and his brothers' wives. The gift signifies the friendly relations she hopes to establish with these women.[1]

Apart from these ordinary netbags, the new wife will also have a specially fine one (*wal kupin*), with long tying strings, that she has been wearing on special occasions since she was of marriageable age. This she may give to her husband's younger sister, who will wear it in turn till she is married. Or she may follow the custom of cutting it up, continuing to use part as a bag, but converting the tying strings into a pubic apron for her husband (or sometimes her father-in-law). Although I have not heard it put as explicitly, we may see this as a symbol of the interest her husband and her father-in-law now have in her.

It is up to the bride to allocate the bags as she wishes. They both mark her relations with her husband's womenfolk and represent con-

---

[1] With the mother-in-law her relationship is more formal, and only occasionally does a bride offer such a gift.

cern on the part of her own kinswomen. They are made specifically for her marriage by father's and mother's sisters, and other wives married into her own lineage, as well as by her mother. All these women hope to receive a bridewealth portion in recognition of their support.

Women's things are divided among women; men are not particularly interested in the netbags and aprons. A breeding pig, on the other hand, is a concrete start to the contribution the young wife will make to the prosperity of the husband and his clansmen. It also indicates the involvement of her own clansmen in the marriage, for it reflects badly on both the girl and her father and brothers if they do not provide one. People say that a girl sent to her husband without pigs is so upset she may run away. From her point of view the dowry is a reward for the way she cared and worked for her kin at home.

The new bride is thought to be particularly sensitive to slights from her husband's folk, which she will interpret also as slights on her own family. Even after the formal marriage transactions are over, the groom should be assiduous in soliciting the enduring goodwill of her kin by sending them gifts of pork at every possible opportunity. She should also be made to feel at home. Her parents-in-law, especially, must not only provide her with shelter and food, but be tolerant of her ways in the early months. Above all, they must involve her in their affairs, meticulously including her in any food distributions in which they may participate.

Residence

At marriage, women leave their home[1] territory to take up residence with their husbands, whether these are with their agnatic clansmen or not. There is a high chance that a woman will be in one of the larger settlements rather than in a homestead; some 70% of women currently married to Kawelka men live in settlements. In 1965, Kawelka in the vicinity of Buk were distributed over three clan territories in 45 homesteads and 41 settlements; the average number of people in homesteads was 4.68 (range 2–12) and in settlements 14.3 (7–28). Almost certainly in the early years of marriage the young wife is likely to be residing with other women, for few men marrying for the first time have already

---

[1] A term I use for the people with whom a woman has been associating prior to her marriage, on whom she calls for support, etc., "home" here not being synonymous with birth ("natal") place, though usually these overlap.

established independent homesteads.[1] The bride is instructed to look after her husband, so that he will think highly of her and send gifts back to her kin; but she is also told by them to care for the parents-in-law, since they provided the bridewealth, and her duties here are phrased in terms of co-residence. She must sleep in the same house as her husband's mother, and thus keep her company at night, and attend to her parents-in-law's household comforts—ensuring that there is water to drink, collecting firewood, and so on.

Indeed, the focus of a woman's attachment to her husband's community is her mother-in-law, in whose house she sleeps and stalls her pigs. This may be felt quite keenly by the younger woman, as the following reveals.

> Pa, who is married into the Mokei tribe, complained bitterly about how angry (*popokl*) she is when her husband's mother shares food with other people and neglects her. The mother-in-law is generous to everyone else— Pa's husband and all his brothers and sisters and all their children and all the wives of these brothers. The old lady takes more notice of her numerous grandchildren by other women than she does of Pa herself; and there are so many of them that they finish any special preparation of food, leaving none for the adults. Pa is also annoyed when visitors come to the house, and they are offered food, herself by implication being left out.

Although other women of the residential group may give her occasional gifts of tubers to cook, in the early months it is the mother-in-law who "shows" the bride a strip of already cultivated garden which she is allowed to harvest until allocated her own plot. She should accompany her mother-in-law in the garden work. This applies particularly in the case of a girl marrying a youth who himself has not been married before. It is by no means expected that boys will make gardens prior to marriage, and the wife's first plot is likely to be one cleared by her father-in-law. Pigs the boy may have been given from his father's herd, however, will have been used for the bridewealth, and the nucleus of his new herd will be the stock his wife brings with her. Only occasionally at this stage would his parents add to these. The groom is likely to sleep in the men's house. In the case of a girl marrying a man already with a wife, the senior cowife may take on some of the duties of a mother-in-law, such as looking after the junior woman's pigs when she goes home for a visit.

---

[1] Strathern, A.J. (1965) includes an examination of the developmental cycle of domestic groups.

The wider the age-gap between the two wives, the more likely this becomes.

The following table summarizes the situation of 24 newly married Northern Melpa brides. They divide into (a) those whose husbands were not previously married; and (b) those whose husbands already had at least one wife with them. Mothers-in-law (ML) include the husband's actual or foster mother[1].

TABLE I

The situation of the newly married bride

A	Bride shares house with:				
	ML only	ML + bride's cowife	ML + others (HBW, etc.)	Other women, not ML	Total
a	14	—	4	1	19
b	1	3	0	1	5

B	Before new gardens are made, bride is allocated strip by:				
	ML only	ML + bride's cowife	ML + others including her cowives	Other women, not ML	Total
a	14	—	3	1	18[a]
b	1	2	2	0	5

C	Pigs with which new herd begun:			
	Dowry from wife's kin	Dowry + help from husband's kin	Help from husband's kin only	Total
a	14	0	1	15[b]
b	3	1	0	4[b]

[a] No allocation in one instance where bride had been married for only a few weeks.

[b] Dowry pigs may be omitted from the bridewealth transactions if the bride has been married previously: this was so in one case; in two cases endowment had not been made at time of enquiry; for the rest I have no information. At least 16 of the husbands of category (a) had had pigs prior to the marriage, but only two retained any to contribute to the new herd; 6 had made and 10 had not made gardens themselves.

---

[1] If a boy's mother dies, the woman who takes care of him acts as "mother-in-law" to his bride. This may be his own mother's cowife or a further wife his father marries afterwards. In all the cases considered in Table I there was a "mother-in-law" alive at the time of marriage.

As her husband's mother becomes older, the daughter-in-law assumes responsibility for her. Many old women continue with a little gardening although they cease to contribute to their son's supplies. Widows are cared for by their children and children's spouses; once past the age of re-marriage, they may choose to live with a married daughter rather than remain with their sons. A woman with no children of her own must depend on the thoughtfulness of others from her husband's lineage for firewood and occasional supplies. Responsibilities of this nature are not diffuse. A young woman expects help from her immediate mother-in-law, receiving no more than occasional assistance from others in the residential group; an old woman in turn can only expect automatic and continuous support from those who used to be her dependants. Support is tied to specific relationships, as between mother and son, and is based on reciprocity: "When I was small my mother cared for me, and now I care for her." On her immediate dependants, a woman who feels neglected can bring pressure to bear by hinting of the disasters that might befall her survivors were she to die with anger in her heart (and thus want to take revenge as a ghost). All old people expect solicitude from their children in view of their impending death, particularly requesting that they should be fed well with pork, a gesture that is seen to foreshadow the sacrifices their ghosts will later demand.

With growing families of their own, wives may establish independent houses; or when the mother-in-law dies, join a sister-in-law (husband's brother's wife). Wives of polygynists, however, are not often found together in the same house.

Pigs and Gardens

Having a house of her own is of little importance to a woman's status by comparison with the acquisition of rights in gardening land and the establishment of a pig herd.

During the daytime pigs roam the bush for food, but at night they are stalled and fed small sweet potato tubers. Each wife feeds only her own stock, and one who regularly gives food to another's pigs may regard herself as having some claim on them. This may be a point of ambiguity between mother- and daughter-in-law. The older woman has been accustomed to feeding her son's pigs, and although these have usually all been given away at his marriage, she still takes a supervisory interest in his herd, and may manage them till his wife becomes fully capable. But if their total care is left to her, and her services are unacknowledged, she will grumble about having to feed "someone else's" pigs, complaining that neither her son nor his wife appreciate her.

The daily jobs associated with stock-keeping are mainly in the hands of women; men sometimes lead pigs out to forage, and because of the physical danger involved it is their task to fetch piglets from the bush where sows are allowed to litter. But women do most of the feeding, care for pigs when they are sick and conventionally become very attached to them. The theft of a cherished beast may make a woman distraught with anxiety and, as Hageners interpret it, with grief. The intimate attention they receive is displayed when pigs are the object of a public transaction such as bridewealth; then women may be seen scooping up the droppings that threaten to soil the ceremonial ground, and when they are to be given away in *moka*, it is women who stripe the pigs' backs with decorative clay.

For a woman to raise a large herd, she must have access to adequate gardenland, and rueful comments may be made by the wife of a would-be big-man whose ambitions in pig-*moka* are not matched by an enthusiasm for horticulture. There is a crucial difference in the way pigs and gardens are initially acquired. As we have already seen, the groom's parents do not normally expect to provide the pigs; it is up to the couple to obtain them, which means in this case from the wife's kin. Pigs come in from the outside. The fact that the groom is seen as having to "find" them is related to their importance as valuables in exchanges. Wealth is not inherited in any significant amount, and this is as true of stock as of shell valuables; each man must acquire his own. Hence there is a very specific value attached to the endowment sows a bride brings. Through his herd a man is distinguished from his brothers, in the same way as his affinal connections are unique. By contrast, gardenland is his patrimony. Claims to particular tracts of the clan territory are inherited from one's father or from close lineage ancestors who die without immediate heirs. Whereas the young husband and wife establish an independent pig herd at the start of their marriage, a man only gradually builds up personal claims to areas of gardenland, although he may have begun doing so long before marriage.

We have seen that a woman is first given gardens in crop by her mother-in-law, and this holds even if the groom himself had made gardens: those given to his mother would be transferred by her, not him, to his wife. Moreover, the fact that he may have made gardens for the wife of an elder brother or another of his father's wives does not in any way compel these women to show his new wife a strip. This is a duty encumbent on the mother-in-law (or senior cowife in her absence) and it operates whether the son has made his mother gardens or not. The daughter-in-law, however, only has usufruct of the already growing crops, and the plots may later revert to the senior woman. On rare occasions a woman may refuse to show her daughter-in-law gardens because of grievances against her menfolk. This is likely to happen only in the case of a polygynist's wife. As soon as it is time to clear new land the son will be encouraged by his father to take an active part and prepare a plot for his wife, although if he is particularly lazy the father will assume this responsibility. But once the man takes his full share in gardening, the father ceases to provide for the daughter-in-law, even though the son will continue to allocate his mother plots. This is consistent with the fact that mothers carry on sending portions of food to their adult sons after marriage, whereas such an intimate relationship exists between a man and his daughter-in-law only if the former is widowed.

The father-in-law, who sees himself as having obtained his son's wife for him, may also look on himself as a more general support for her. One Central Melpa man commented that a woman's father-in-law is really her security—if a new bride quarrels with her husband's brothers' wives she is supposed to retort, "My *kulpam* (husband's father) is here; I have all I want." He is particularly willing and anxious to respond to her needs when she is newly married (so that the marriage will not founder); others of her husband's clansmen are not represented as so concerned in her welfare.

A family has several gardens in different stages of cultivation at a time, and the tenure system is such that these can be added to as required: land is not regarded as a fixed, bounded resource which must be permanently divided up, as between the wives of a polygynist and his sons. Women simply receive shares in each new field brought into cultivation. Thus a young man with a new wife to support will give a proportionately larger share of his next garden to his wife than to his mother. Occasionally this may be the cause of a dispute:

> Nøngi, a widow living at Kelua, complained about her son: he was working a garden that had belonged to her deceased husband, and she had hoped to plant it and give some to her daughter-in-law. But her son had himself taken it all for this woman, and given none to his mother. Nøngi

was very angry about this, and later when she suspected the son's wife of having used some of her cabbages to plant in the garden, she went into it and pulled up not only the cabbages but other crops that the younger woman had there.

A contributing factor here is the way women see themselves as looking after and promoting the fertility of the soil with careful gardening; this investment often makes them anxious to be reallocated the same plots when fields come back into cultivation after lying fallow—a point I discuss below.

Women are directly dependent on men for the preparation of garden-land. Only once a garden is under way can a woman dig it herself and keep it in cultivation. Wives may help in the final stages of clearing and in turning over the topsoil, but men are expected to cut down the bush and dig ditches (Central Melpa) or erect and maintain fencing (Northern Melpa). Several men from a single residential group, or from the lineage to which the area belongs may co-operate when the garden to be cleared is large. They allocate portions to their own wives to plant. Other men and women may come to help, not because they have claims on the land but because of their ties with the gardener(s), and each will be given a plot or strip. Women plant coloured cordylines along the boundaries of their sections.

If a garden has been cleared for sweet potato, then the major part will be handed over to women; but a few men like to keep a little patch of sweet potato for themselves. A man may ask his wife to plant this for him, which he can then use when she is away or in menstrual seclusion; the rest of the garden which the wife plants she tends and harvests herself. A mixed-vegetable garden (*pana*) is inter-planted by both sexes. While women's main crop is sweet potato, they also plant maize, most types of green vegetable, yams and *Colocasia* taro; men plant *Xanthosoma* taro, bananas, sugarcane and certain other vegetables. There is no definite rule which prevents females from growing bananas and sugarcane, although these are not regarded as "their" crops. "I am only a woman!" was the protest to my questioning on more than one occasion. Nevertheless, some women use up odd patches of ground and plant small clumps—of 37 wives questioned in the Buk area, 20 said they had planted bananas recently, and most of these (in all 18) also had sugarcane growing. Women who do this may be admired by men for their strength. It is generally reckoned, however, that male help is needed in the final stages, which involve tying up the cane or banana fruit.

A mixed-vegetable garden develops over a two year period; in the first year it produces greens, maize and the tubers; bananas and sugarcane ripen in the second, and sweet potatoes may be planted while these are standing. Subsequently, the garden may be turned over completely to sweet potato, or carry only a single scrop before reverting to fallow. Young casuarina trees are planted during the second year if the latter course is taken. Occasionally clumps of banana and cane are planted in what is otherwise a sweet potato field. Thus, although people think in terms of a contrast between men's and women's crops, they are not spatially segregated. A married man makes the major portion of a prepared area over to his wife or wives—cowives sometimes being given alternating strips to avoid quarrels over differences in soil quality. Other women likely to receive shares are his mother, married sisters, daughters and wife's sisters, and perhaps other wives of a settlement if he is a member of one. Where these women are supported by their own husbands, their claims are likely to be quantitatively slight; women themselves may give further sub-divisions to their children, or invite a mother or sister to plant a plot in their strip. Non-residential women—married sisters and daughters, and more distant connections—are especially likely to be invited to share in the planting of mixed-vegetable gardens; both because the planting and harvesting of these may be made into something of a special occasion, and because they are not in production so regularly as sweet potato gardens are. It is worth noting that sometimes a man gives a share to a woman because of the tie between him and her husband, as in the case of a brother or friend; but when he allocates gardens to a married sister or daughter then this is in the first place to the kinswoman herself; he separately invites her husband to plant taro or sugarcane with him. The woman may make a small gift in appreciation to her kinsman, but does not contribute substantially to his household; the bulk of the produce she carries away for her husband and children.

Wives can thus have claims outside the garden areas of their husband's residential group. Of 33 wives living virilocally near Buk in 1964, 18 had gardens elsewhere, allocated by their kin. Women value highly being able to visit different kinsfolk, and it is partly through such claims that they activate their links. The kin a woman particularly looks to for gardens are her own father and brothers; these men will have made gardens for her before she married, and in the early years of marriage the girl may go home to collect the produce even if she can no longer be bothered to maintain her plots in further cultivation. Plots that she may have had when she accompanied her mother to *her* home, she usually abandons completely.

Irrespective of whether help was given in the initial preparation of a garden, assertions of crop ownership rest on who planted them. Women plant their own shares, the exceptions to this being that a daughter might help an aged mother, or (as we have seen) a wife might plant a plot for her husband's special use. Cowives do not plant for each other. A woman has near absolute rights of control over her crops, which she may regard as holding even against her husband and children. They may go into her garden, but strictly should not harvest any of the produce without permission. A mother encourages her young children to plant sections themselves so that they will neither be tempted to steal from nor in the process ruin her own plants; the mother, in turn, does not take from these little patches till the child loses interest. Children are trained not to steal from the gardens of their father's brothers or of other wives of their own father. The same holds for a woman herself; a wife does not take food planted by her husband without his permission, and a mother-in-law shows her son's wife an already planted strip precisely so the younger woman shall be independent of her, and not have random access to her own gardens.[1] This exclusiveness shows up in the licence which allows a person to take without asking food from the gardens of a mother's brother, father's sister, mother's sister or the children of these. But one should take only crops actually planted by one's relative: bananas and sugarcane from a mother's brother garden but not sweet potatoes belonging to the mother's brother's wife; sweet potatoes planted by a father's sister, but not her husband's bananas or sugarcane.

The actual observance of these rules depends on the personal relations of those involved. In describing their attitudes towards husbands helping themselves without notification to bananas and cane which the wife happens to have planted, women vary between saying that they would be angry since the crops are theirs, and pointing out that as husband and wife they do things together, and how could one have anger? Again, a woman visiting her married daughter digs up sweet potatoes for herself, because she knows that the daughter would in any case in-

---

[1] Accusations of thieving from gardens are not uncommon between mother- and daughter-in-law. A mother-in-law who removed the wife's personal property (netbags, ornaments), however, would be suspected of wanting to get rid of the younger woman.

tend to feed her old mother; and vice versa. But on one occasion, a daughter helping herself to food quarrelled so severely with her irate mother that a court had to be held to settle compensation for the wounds inflicted.

These differences in attitudes underline the fact that it is not wholly satisfactory to gloss the generalizations just enumerated as "rules". Women make strenuous complaints on discovering that someone has been in their gardens. Petty thieving between wives of a settlement or of neighbouring homesteads is not uncommon, and the assertions of a woman in such a case are usually regarded as justified, the husband frequently coming to his wife's support. When it is a husband or child the woman is accusing, reactions are more varied. It may be agreed that the person concerned should have asked her first, but it is pointed out that it was on the strength of their ties with her that the food was taken. Thus, while a woman's claims are recognized there are situations where it is not appropriate to push them. This is particularly true between parents and young children: the mother has a general obligation to provide for her children from her gardens, and other people would tend to regard the claims of the children as dependants stronger than the right of the owner to be asked first. A child who is unlikely to be punished for taking from his mother's garden may be if he takes from the gardens of other women, including her cowives.

Between husband and wife, statements of norms concerning rights to produce and gardenland tend to be of a rhetorical order (Scheffler, 1965); set in the general context of conjugal interdependency, they are made an issue only when quarrels lead to each party defining his or her position. I deal with some aspects of this in Chapter 3.

I conclude these details with a brief account of the way women see their claims to land, including the gardenland they cultivate in their home territory.

A women has claims on her husband to keep her supplied with gardens, rather than claims to the land itself. Nevertheless, when old fallow comes to be reworked, wives usually maintain that they should be given gardens where they had planted crops before. A woman is particularly sensitive if a husband tries to give such an area to her cowife. In the case of other men, a husband's brother or sister's husband, it rests with the generosity of the donor to make a temporary gift, although women may hope that once invited they will be invited again. Claims a woman has on her home kin fall between these two extremes. It is not the brother's duty to support his sister[1] in the same way as it is the husband's, and a refusal to grant land is not (as it would be in the case of the husband) a challenge to the total relationship. A sister may be living too far away for her even to want to have gardens at home. Nevertheless, she has strong claims on her brother's pity and affection (*kaemb*), and since it is often of value to the brother to keep on good terms with his sister, he is likely to be responsive to her requests. Men appreciate women's sentimental attachment to their home land, the place where they may have gardened in their youth. A woman can stabilize her claims to some extent if she improves the land by planting casuarina trees (a job done regularly by men); and about a third of the Buk women seem to do this. Their trees are mainly at their husband's place or at home.

Since women are not seen as having perpetual rights over land, the planting of trees gives rise to conflicting attitudes similar to those that surround female cultivation of male crops, banana and sugarcane. One wife of a big-man commented that "it is the work of men to plant casuarinas", and on my noting that two elderly women of a nearby settlement regularly grew casuarinas in mixed-vegetable gardens, she expostulated, "We do not plant casuarinas here. Those two women of X! Are they really women! They have become strong (*rondokl*)." A Central Melpa woman laughingly admitted that she had not only casuarina trees at her home but some pandanus as well—but she had not been serious about it, they were planted as a joke (*na kol rop rør*). She was nevertheless quite adamant about her expectations that her father and brothers would continue to allocate to her the plots of both mixed-vegetable and sweet potato gardens which she had cultivated in the past. There would be a quarrel with them if they did not. She added that her father makes a garden for each of his married daughters so they will not take from their mother. One Northern Melpa wife referred more solemnly to trees she had planted at her father's place; she did so because that was where she had grown up, and had she been a man then she and her brother would have worked gardens together; it is only because she is a woman that she has come to garden away from her home. At her home place, then, a woman would like to be given shares in the garden where she has planted trees, although it is recognized that, in fact, her father or brother may allocate the land afresh as he thinks fit. This being the case,

---

[1] The situation is more complicated when a married woman decides to take up residence with her brother (Chapter 3).

a woman cannot pass on claims to these shares to her children, unless they become permanently attached to her home clan. A son hoping for temporary use of his mother's fields without joining the group has to approach the mother's brother, and if his mother failed to plant casuarinas this man might point out, "Your mother took away the fertility (*kopong*, "grease") of the soil and did not replenish it."

Casuarinas planted at her husband's place also strengthen a woman's hopes of being reallocated her original plots. She may in addition establish them as shade trees around her own house.

> *In one case these proved of unexpected value. A patch of land formerly a house-site was given by a man to his brother for use as a coffee garden. When the coffee began to bear, the former's wife demanded some share of the proceeds in recognition of the fact that she had improved the soil by planting trees there. Before the land had been of little use, and now, with the trees growing on it, had proved productive. Since it was the woman and not her husband who had done the planting, the Komiti of the husband's clan to whom she went with her grievance (and who afterwards told me of it) said that it was to her that the coffee-grower should pay compensation.

As far as ownership of the timber goes, some women say they hope their sons will eventually have the trees planted at their home, others expect that as a matter of course their brothers will take them over. If in need, a husband may ask to cut down his wife's trees at her place. Normally the husband also owns the timber she planted on his land, but a brother may ask the husband for these trees after the sister's death. A woman may or may not expect to be notified of the use to which her menfolk put the trees she has planted. At the other end of the scale are her sweet potatoes and vegetables which should never be taken without her knowing, and which she prefers to gather herself anyway. Between these fall the male crops (bananas, sugarcane); a woman likes to be told, but also recognizes the right of certain men to help themselves. A woman's brother should really inform his sister if he cuts any of the bananas or sugarcane she has at his place, though if she fails to harvest them before they turn rotten he may take them without saying anything. At her death, the brother takes the crops over and the brother's wives use her sweet potato gardens, although if her children are still little the bereaved husband may beg some of the food for them.

A widow normally stays with her husband's brothers at least till the end of her mourning, and she subsists off her old gardens during this time. If she re-marries elsewhere she loses all claim to them. A woman who leaves her husband in divorce forfeits not only her interest in the land but also in the standing crops she has planted.

I have entered into some detail over garden rights because these illustrate an important aspect of a woman's relations with other members of her residential group; and also something of the balance that exists between the claims she has on her husband and on her own kin. From a woman's point of view, her ties with both sets of people are publicized in the way these rights are defined. Thus, it is said, "A man may help himself to sweet potato planted by his wife on her home ground, although it is polite to notify the wife's brother first; similarly, a wife's brother will be given permission when he visits his sister at her husband's place." Although affines cannot take these things freely, they hope to be given because of their ties with her. Further, "If a woman has planted bananas and sugarcane, she grumbles when her husband cuts them to give his friends, but she should have no cause for complaint if the recipients are her own kin."

The pattern of rights over pigs is a little different; to a greater extent than garden plots and produce, in women's eyes, the distribution of pigs demarcates various aspects of their status. Pigs are much more a focus for dispute between men and women. Cowives may quarrel over the allocation of rights in a garden, and thieving of produce may arouse animosities between the women of a residential group, but such matters are not nearly so often the object of major disputes between husband and wife[1] or between brother and sister as are pigs. This is because gardens are not wealth in the same way; transactions in land do not enter ceremonial exchange. Rights in pigs, however, cannot be properly analyzed before something has been said of the exchange system.

The woman's Affines: inter-personal Relations

Although men of a residential group may co-operate in clearing heavy fallow, gardens can be made single-handed. To an even greater extent, women's horticultural jobs—planting, weeding, harvesting—are undertaken singly. No women's tasks technologically require regular co-operation and few are made the social focus of it.[2] Women with shares

---

[1] A husband sometimes refuses to make his wife's gardens as a sanction of the same order as the wife refusing to cook for him. Quarrels also turn on the amount of work one or other does.
[2] When large mixed-vegetable gardens are prepared an effort will be made by the women to synchronize their planting; all the garden will then be ready for harvesting at once, and an occasion is made of it.

in the same garden may work side by side for company, but they might equally well work at opposite ends of the field. Once allocated, a plot thus receives the exclusive attention of its owner; because of this a co-wife takes care not even to be seen in another woman's garden area lest she arouse suspicions of thieving. A cowife may, however, be delegated to feed pigs if a woman is away for the night. She may also assist at childbirth, as may husbands' brother's wives (who are the most frequent attendants) or a mother-in-law. Cowives of a polygynist sometimes decide to rotate the preparation of his meals, a casual not a stipulated arrangement.

There are a few occasions for which the several married woman of a settlement combine together. One is house-building. Women are responsible for the tedious gathering of grass for thatch, and it is expected that all female residents will help, along with various neighbours and others who come because of their ties with the builder. Outside women may assist on such occasions through their own links, or accompany their husbands. (A total of 46 men and 35 women were involved in building 6 houses near Buk in 1964–5. Of those who were married, there were 22 husband-wife pairs, while 20 men and 9 women came by themselves, 11 of all the women being from outside the builder's residential group.)

A second is communal cooking. Most cooking is done over individual fires inside a woman's house; but sometimes external ovens in the courtyard or on a ceremonial ground are used, and several women help prepare the food. Such occasions celebrate the clearing of a new garden, preparations for a dancing display, and so on. Men always take charge of cooking pork; they say women lack the intelligence to judge when it is ready to be removed from the steam oven, a false judgement in such a matter being a bad omen.[1] Women are responsible for scraping and cooking vegetables. Although female guests may help with all stages of preparation, only the wives of the residential group where the cooking is held are likely to contribute raw food. Often the pretext for such a cooking itself determines the span of participants. Thus, if it is to repay those who have loaned feathers for dance decorations, the donors and their families (wives and children) are invited; again, food cooked at a house-building repays the help of the workers. But sometimes the har-

---

[1] Men also kill pigs and butcher the meat, dividing the carcass into the right cuts for later distribution. Women are given the unpleasant job of washing out the stomach and intestines.

vesting of special vegetables (bananas, taro, yams, the first picking of greens) is a simple pretext for feasting. An examination of eleven such occasions (at Buk and Kelua) suggests that while the cooked food is likely to be distributed to everyone of the residential group as well as to visitors, in cases where there are several married women in a settlement, only a few from the potentially larger number in fact collect and prepare the food together. Co-operation in this sphere is thus by no means automatic.

On rare occasions wives married into a single sub-clan or clan may dance as a group when their husbands celebrate *moka*. But they do not combine for any festive or ritual activities of their own. This relative absence of co-operation between women is of some importance to the ways in which men and women interact. Yet it would be false to give the impression that females never associate with one another. Many functions, such as bridewealth, courting parties, *moka* festivals and funerals, see them gather in large numbers. Such functions often require their participation precisely as wives of their husband's clan—thus at funerals it is women's duty to wail and cry, and wives of a dead man's sub-clan will be in attendance. Joint participation, however, does not necessarily imply mutual interdependence.

Although a wife is bound to few other women of her husband's residential group through requirements for domestic co-operation, the hope is nevertheless that she will be friendly with them. The extent to which casual help is given is largely a matter of personal inclination. She may also have friends in nearby settlements. The informal nature of a woman's ties with most of her female co-residents is pointed up by the extreme dependence of the new bride on the one mother-in-law.

Personal friends often mark their relationship by dividing a piece of food between themselves and thenceforth addressing each other by its name (e.g. "Corn", "Liver"). Women often call some of their husband's brothers' wives by food names, but rarely a mother-in-law. It is never done, as far as I know, with cowives (whose special relationship is discussed in Chapter 3). A degree of formality in a woman's relationship with her mother-in-law glosses over the competition which exists between them, in spite of the early dependence of the younger upon the older woman which has put the latter into a superior position. Hageners see the relationship as one of potential strain and the idiom used to described the jealousy of cowives (*amb wølik*) may on occasion be applied to mother- and daughter-in-law. Aside from conflicts over caring for pigs or using gardens, in a wider sense the two are competing in the support they give to the son/husband. The following incident shows how explicit this can be:

*The wife of a young Kawelka man [it was he who related the incident] accused his mother of taking some green vegetables from a part of a garden which the husband had allocated to her, the wife. The mother denied she had done any such thing, and flounced off—if her daughter-in-law was going to accuse her of stealing, then she would rather live elsewhere. She removed all her household possessions and went to sleep with a husband's sister who lived nearby and with whom she was on very good terms, later staying a few days at her Tipuka home. While she was away, her sow littered, and the daughter-in-law went into the mother-in-law's garden to harvest sweet potatoes to feed the hungry pig. The older woman was furious when she returned to find that her gardens had been touched and erected a *mi*-sign (swathes of cane grass tied together) which indicated that the theft had been discovered and action would be taken a second time. The young wife was insulted by this, and arguing that the administration had "forbidden" such advertisements of revenge complained to a local Komiti. He made the mother pay her nine shillings compensation, for people living together should not erect such signs against each other.

After this, the mother went into her son's house and took out his personal things—towels, clothes—and said that she would look after them for him; he was her son and why should the wife use them. The wife protested that the man wasn't the old woman's husband but hers—she was his wife, and his things were for her to look after.

A wife may also share food-names with her husband's brothers (but not the husband himself). She has no specific duties towards these men, although she is supposed to show them good humour by occasionally offering food, and to demonstrate a general loyalty to her husband's lineage and clan. Senior men, including her husband's father, should be accorded some respect.

A woman's relations with her husband's male kin are seen largely through her attachment to the husband—assisting a husband's brother to build a house, for example, will be because of her husband's links with this man.[1] Conversely, a woman has no independent claim on such men (apart from her father-in-law); if she is neglected by her husband she

---

[1] We may contrast relations between male brothers-in-law; although structurally the two men are linked by a woman, as sister's husband and wife's brother to each other, once established the relationship can to some extent endure in its own right.

cannot necessarily expect their support.[1] Nevertheless, insofar as her work is seen to contribute to their general prosperity, the husband's lineage-mates have an interest in her, expressed through reference to their contributions to her bridewealth. On this ground, they may reproach her if she is lazy or sexually promiscuous, and should she run away may join with the husband in retrieving her. At his death, the husband's clansmen have claims to marry the wife.

Affines: terminological Categories

I touch briefly on terms for cognatic and affinal kin, commenting on women's usages from the point of view of their double group membership.

Cousin terminology is Iroquois (FBS = MZS ≠ FZS = MBS) and cognatic terms are bifurcate-merging in the first ascending generation (F = FB ≠ MB).[2] Distinctions are not made between patri-, matrilateral or affinal kin in the second ascending or descending generations, the sex of the senior speaker/referent being the sole discriminator.[3] I give reference forms; in address all terms are reciprocal, except those for "husband" (*wu^e*) and "wife" (*amb*). *Wu^e* and *amb*, when meaning "man" and "woman", along with *kang* ("boy") and *ambokla* ("girl") in address, may be used as sex-markers where the terms do not otherwise indicate sex (e.g. *amb ape*, *wu^e ape*, female grandchild, male grandchild, woman speaking; *amb kulpam*, *wu^e kulpam*, senior female affine, senior male affine).

The relevance of the speaker's sex in certain contexts gives rise to the different range of usages men and women have. With a single exception,[4]

---

1 When, nowadays, a husband leaves home to find work, his brothers may take care of his wife, giving her gardens, and so on. If the man is away too long, however, or they think he has lost interest in home affairs, they may impatiently withdraw the gardens and send the wife back to her kin.

2 F for father, FB for father's brother, Z for sister, etc. I also use BL (brother-in-law) etc. where precise relationship (whether WB, ZH) is irrelevant.

3 Old people are *kouwa* (grandfather), *apom* (grandmother), and for such persons on their husband's side, women say they simply copy the usage of their husband.

4 *Mønin* (opposite-sex sibling's spouse, spouse's opposite-sex sibling, woman-speaking). A parallel term used by men (*koklom*) can also refer to the affinal connection in general (*koklomal*, the affines) and occasionally a woman may call a category of male affine (see Table II) *wu^e koklom*, the reciprocal being *amb koklom*. *Koklom* may also be used by women (not shown in Table II) for remoter male affines otherwise called *kulpam* e.g. BWF, HBDH; also HBWF. Vicedom (1943–8:2:63f) reports ZH (woman-speaking) as *koklom*, but adds this might be a mistake in recording (he gives WZ (man-speaking) as *kimøn*). This use of *koklom* by women may be a mainly Central Melpa idiom. There are small differences in the terms reported for Central and Northern Melpa, but I do not consider them here.

men and women employ identical terms, but in partially different distribution. This must be to some extent related to their respective clan
statuses. Thus, a woman shares with her male clansmen their usages for
senior members of her natal clan, and with her husband's clansmen
their usages for junior members of her husband's clan. Clearly this marks
a switch in a woman's affiliations.[1] In her own generation, same-sex and
opposite-sex siblings are differentiated as are same-sex and opposite-
sex contemporary affines. In the first descending generation a woman's
brother's children (children of her natal clan) form a discrete category,
while her sister's children (her sister also having married out), are
terminologically linked to her own.

The following tables summarize these points with some examples.
Table II shows the areas in which women's usage coincides with men's;
Table III where the sex of the speaker is relevant and hence the distri-
bution of terms is unique to women.

TABLE II

Reference terms: examples of common usages between the sexes[a]

	WOMAN SHARES TERMS WITH BROTHER FOR HER				HUSBAND FOR HER	Generation
"Cognates"						
tepam	F	FB	MZH			
mam	M	FBW	MZ			
pam	MB					
apom	MBW	MBWZ			HMBW	+1
øtin	FZ					
pelpam	FZS	FZD	MBS	MBD		0
kangᵉm					S HBS ZS HBWZS	
mboklam					D HBD ZD HBWZD	−1
"Affines"						
kulpam	HF	HFB	BWF	BWM	HZHp(arents)	+1
kulpam	HZH	ZHZH	BWBW		DHp SWp	
koklom	BWB					0
kulpam	BDH	ZDH			DH DHZ HBDH HZDH	−1

[1] I draw attention to this because is not standard throughout the Highlands. Among the
Eastern Highlands Siane, for example, a newly married bride uses for members of her husband's village the kin terms her own brothers would, her husband and true parents-in-law
excepted; after the birth of children, as a mark of her increasing absorption into her husband's
community, she uses instead for these people terms her husband himself applies to his village-
mates. The only exception here is the sex-marked sibling. (Salisbury, 1962:20.)

TABLE III

Reference terms: examples of usages exclusive to females[a]

	USED BY WOMEN FOR LINKS THROUGH		
	BROTHER (OR OWN CLAN) FOR HER	HUSBAND FOR HER	Generation
tepam		HBWF	
mam		HBWM	
apom	MMBD FMBD	HM HMZ HFZ	+1
kulpam		HMB HMZH HFZH[b]	
angin or *əngin*	Z FBD MZD	cowife HBW HMBSW HMZSW HFZSW	
mənin	BW BWZ MZSW MBSW FZSW ZHZ	HZ HFZD HMBD HMZD HBWBW	0
kimun	B FBS MZS	HBWB	
kiməm[c]	ZH ZHB BWB FZDH MBDH MZDH	HB HFZS HMBS HMZS HBWZH	
kulpam	BWZH	HFZDH HMBDH[d] HMZDH	
wam		H	
ətin	Bch MZSch BWZch		
kang[e]m(m) ⎱ & *mboklam*(f) ⎰	MBSch[e] MZDch MBDch ZHBch	HFZSch[e]	−1
apom	ZSW BSW FZSch FZDch[f] ZHZch	SW HBSW HZSW HZch HMZSch HMBSch HMZDch HMBDch HFZDch	

[a] Although the tables are set out in the form /term + denotata/ there is a range of kin categories whose designations depend upon context; these are usually categories defined by an indirect link with ego, and ego determines the term according to how the intermediate link is seen by her. An example is given in note *d*.

[b] If addressed by the woman's brother, he probably also says *kulpam* (cf. ZHF, man-speaking).

[c] *Kiməm* may also think of themselves as "like husband and wife" (*wam/ambom*).

[d] We may note that husband's cousins can be equated with husband's siblings, the spouses of these being termed accordingly (e.g. HMBD = HZ; HMBDH = HZH, cf. Table II). Similarly, the spouses of cousins are designated like spouses of siblings (MBSW = BW). However, FZDH (*kiməm* cf. ZH) may also be designated *kulpam* (cf. "DH") and MBSW (*mənin* cf. BW) may be designated *apom* (cf. BSW). Thinking of her FZS as a "B" a woman may also call her FZSch *ətin* (cf. "Bch"); see note *f*.

[e] A man may sometimes use *kang[e]m* and *mboklam* for his FZSch and MBSch, so that a woman here shares these terms with her brother and husband.

[f] FZSch may also be classed as *ətin* (see note d); FZDch may be classed as "own children" (cf. "Zch"). (Presumably similar permutations hold for MBSch, though I have no record of such.)

A comment on the meaning of "affine" is in place. I have been using it to refer to relatives connected through marriage. There is a distinctive set of terms which fall under this rubric—thus (man-speaking) *kulpam* (e.g. WF), *koklom* (e.g. WB), *kimøm* (e.g. WZ). Spouses of certain cognates (whom we might distinguish from affines as "step-kin") fall under different rubrics, such as that for parent (e.g. FBW = M *mam*). The FBW is seen not from the point of view of her connections with other clans but of her affiliation to the speaker's clan as a mother. By contrast, a distinctive "affinal" term (*kimøm*) is used for the brother's wife. It is only over time that women are regarded as being absorbed into their husband's clan, becoming mothers (*mam*) instead of in-married wives (*kimøm*). This is not to say that the clans of origin of mothers become less important, but that vis-à-vis their husband's clan older women acquire a role as incorporated members, important in its own right, where younger wives are still marginal.

This, however, takes terms simply from a man's viewpoint. Women, like men, use "affinal" terms for persons to whom they are linked through marriage (e.g. DH, ZHZ), but in the case of their own marriage they use "cognatic" terms as well for some members of their husband's community. It is significant that these apply mainly to other women. A woman's own mother-in-law may be addressed as *ma* ("mother"), other senior women of her husband's clan as *ape*. *Ape* is the addressive form of *apom* (also used in reference for own ML), which includes in its denotata "grandmother/grandchild, woman-speaking".[1] Cowives and other wives of the husband's lineage are *angin* (cf. "same-sex sibling"). A woman is identified with these (HBWs) to the extent that she calls their parents *mam*, *tepam* ("mother", "father"), their brothers *kimun* ("opposite-sex sibling") and the wife of *this* man *mønin* (here "brother's wife"). In the same way as the rule of same-sex sibling equivalence equates mother's sister's children with own siblings although they are members of another clan, so here a rule of equivalence between wives married into the same clan[2] terminologically links persons originating from a number of groups. But although women call one another sister, these terms do not imply that their natal clans are seen as linked, in the way that two clans, from the point of view of men, may indeed be linked

---

[1] ML may also be addressed as *amb wenda* ("old woman") another term commonly used for "grandmother". *Apom* has a range of usages which I do not analyze here.

[2] Women call all wives of their husband's clan *angin*—beyond the clan in some cases as when the solidarity of a tribe is stressed. The logical extension of the associated set (for parents, brothers, etc.) is not, on the other hand, normally made beyond the wives of the husband's immediate lineage. The frequency with which the addressive form of *angin* ("sister") is applied usually depends on the degree of cordiality between the women.

as *koklomal*) ("men related by marriage") to each other (cf. page 31, footnote 4). They apply only to women themselves from their common association with their husband's group.

Affines: constraints of Conduct

The relationship of *kulpam* carries with it constraints of conduct.[1] Some men also observe similar constraints (speaking the kinsman's name, see infra) towards *koklom* (WB, ZH) although others say that one can be quite free with people of this category. There are differing degrees in the constraints; but women overall apply these to a narrower range of persons than do men. A woman is not marked off in formal terms from her husband's kin to the extent that he is from hers. Thus both a man's parents-in-law are *kulpam* and he has to be reserved towards them; but we have already noted that a woman's mother-in-law falls outside this category, and although her father-in-law is referred to as *kulpam*, she may address him as *anda kouwa* ("grandfather") and her actual observation of formal constraints seems largely a personal matter.

Women's *kulpam* fall into four main classes. First, fathers and classificatory fathers (e.g. MZH) of her husband; second, her brother's parents-in-law (and his WBW); third, husbands of daughters (*mboklam*, including ZD, HBD) and of brother's daughters (*øtin*); fourth, in her own generation, husbands of sisters-in-law whom she calls *mønin* (thus, HZH, BWZH, HFZDH). Constraints apply chiefly to the last three categories.

Constraints are graded. (1) One should not walk behind the affine's back for it is here that lie the threads (*polkan*) connecting him to his clan ancestors. This is true also for women; the ghosts of her natal clan throng at her back (*tipu wamb mburlung oronga moromen*)—if an affine were to walk there, it is said, the ghosts would flee in shame and fear. (2) The ordinary form of the affine's name is forbidden; every personal name has an alternative, and it is this which should be used, not only in the affine's presence, but in any context. (3) The ordinary name may be avoided in his presence, although used in other contexts, and he would be addressed as *kopa* (addressive form of *kulpam*). (4) *Kopa* may also be used to the face of classificatory *kulpam*, but as a matter of courtesy, and not because there is any shame felt in their presence or strong

---

[1] The phrase is from Firth (1957: 314).

requirements for name-avoidance as in the cases above. Finally, (5) distant affines may be known in reference as *kulpam*, but there are no effective constraints and the person's name can be used freely. Where observed, constraints are usually reciprocal.

A man observes (1) and (2) towards his wife's mother and wife's father, his wife's brother's wife, and his own daughter's husband. Like her husband, a woman similarly observes (1) and (2) towards her daughter's husband, and reciprocally towards her husband's immediate sister's husband. She and her brother both call this person *kulpam*; he is *koklom* to her husband. Table II shows that a woman's brother, like herself, calls her own father-in-law *kulpam*, and a woman reciprocally calls her brother's parents-in-law *kulpam*. She has to observe constraints (1) and (2) towards them also.

Hageners explain these customs in two ways. From the point of view of a man and his parents-in-law, stress is put on his intimate relationship with the woman (his wife). In the face of her parents, who through their own sexual relations with each other bore her, he is ashamed (*pipil*). The reciprocal holds for attitudes towards the DH. But another kind of explanation is needed for the constraints between WBW—HZH. A woman's reserve towards her *kulpam* is related generally by Hageners to bridewealth; either these are persons who would have a share in the bridewealth paid for her, or else she would have had a share herself in bridewealth paid by them person, which is the origin of the shame felt in their presence.[1] The bridewealth a brother receives for a sister is seen as enabling him to obtain a wife; thus a woman's HZH provided the wealth paid for her own marriage.

It is interesting that Hageners associate these constraints, which emphasize distance in terms of the discrete ancestral origins of affines, with the institution of bridewealth, which brings them together in transactions. Once a marriage is contracted between two groups further intermarriage between close relatives of the bride and groom is forbidden;[2] the range of relatives is symbolically demarcated by those who contribute to or receive from the bridewealth. Thus, at a woman's own marriage her husband's sister will be a recipient, and an entailment of

---

[1] There seems to be a negative equation here between sexual relations and "eating bridewealth": thus one eats one's sister's bridewealth in the place of having a sexual relationship with her. There are, of course, affines other than *kulpam* who share in bridewealth and in relation to whom no constraints are observed.

[2] Details of marriage rules are given in a later chapter.

this is that her own immediate lineage cannot marry into the husband's sister's husband's lineage. Members of the two lineages are brought into contact with one another through her marriage, yet are prevented from establishing a direct alliance. The constraints between the two individuals most closely related emphasize the continuing linkage and distance between them.[1]

A woman observes modified constraints (3 and 4) towards others she calls *kulpam*. These include brothers or lineage relatives of the kin towards whom she observes stricter constraints, i.e. (1) and (2); for example, the lineage brothers of her DH and the husbands of her lineage daughters. For more distant connections of these the immediate relative may be known as *kulpam*, but the term is not further extended, and no name taboo (*mbi mawa*) is followed (5); the MZS ("brother") of the DH falls into this category.

Among her husband's kin a woman's most prominent *kulpam* is her father-in-law. She may call all senior men of her husband's clan by this term but only towards her husband's father and other members of her husband's lineage does she use the respectful alternative name (2,3).[2] This seems, however, to be partly a matter of personal choice: some say that the HF's actual name may be used with impunity; in any case she does not avoid his back, and we may remember that the HF can also be a kindly "protector" to his SW (see page 20). It is appropriate however, that of all persons it is the senior males who are *kulpam*, same generation males being *kimøm* (cf. "husband") and junior males *kangᵉm* ("son") for, *kulpam* carries with it the greatest implications of distance. To the senior generation, the recently married wives of the younger men are still "affines". The focus is on their external origins rather than on their incorporation. Of all in-married women the commitments of a young wife are least proved and she is the least trusted.

The terms a woman uses for her husband's kin are thus an amalgam of cognatic and affinal ones, which follows from her own attachment to this group; except towards her father-in-law, she observes no formal constraints. This contrast markedly with her husband's relations with

---

1 The classificatory extensions of the constraints are as follows:
    (1) and (2) towards HZH and his full B
    (3) towards HZH seminal B
    (4)towards HZH lineage B,
      H lineage Z actual H.
2 I have no evidence of the asymmetrical taboos between FL and DL reported by Vicedom (1943–8:2:73).

her own kin. The respect he owes her parents in particular a woman interprets for herself as well. A huband should not only refrain from using the ordinary names of his parents-in-law to their face, they having a right to demand compensation if he does, but out of consideration for his wife should never speak their name in her company. As is true of all *mbi mawa* (forbidden name) situations, it is polite to avoid the names of other people's *kulpam* in their presence. Similarly a wife may try not to speak her father-in-law's name in her husband's company (but see above). This holds whether the parents are alive or dead. Although there is no specific taboo (*mawa*) involved, out of delicacy spouses may also prefer not to use their personal names for each other.

Studied insults can utilize this: a husband roused to anger against his wife may refer to her parents by their ordinary names. Since this is in the context of a quarrel, such an act does not normally lead to demands for compensation. However, should the wife go home and report the matter to her kin the husband is ashamed (*pipil*) and may make them a gift. It is especially insulting to remind anyone of the death of a close kinsman— thus a mother-in-law deliberately insults her daughter's husband by referring to his dead parents, although she herself observes no name taboo towards such persons. The following case is interesting from a number of points of view.

> The little daughter of Ant, an Elti man, was sick. The immediate cause was said to be a recent quarrel between Ant and his wife's mother, Kng. Ant had wanted to pay back a debt of pork to an Elti brother of his but was prevailed on by his wife to send pork he had received in *moka* (ceremonial exchange) to his wife's sister. This was only after a bitter altercation between the two, in which Ant had struck her. The wife went home with her complaints and her father came to Ant to see what the matter was. Her father is a big-man, and a close lineage-mate of Ant paid him a pearl shell in compensation on Ant's behalf. The father was said to be dis-pleased with the shell (a pig is often demanded in such circumstances, and would have been insisted upon if blood had been drawn). These were the public issues, and the child's sickness was put down to ghostly disapproval of the quarrelling.
>
> In private to me, however, Ant said there was another reason. He suspected that his dead father was making his daughter sick because of his own anger (*popokl*) against his mother-in-law. This woman had (taking her daughter's part) abused him in public, calling him names which she had shouted out along a path near the settlement—and most heinous of all had mentioned the name of his dead father. This particularly upset Ant because his father had died when he was a tiny child, and he had hardly known him. This father was now "helping" his outraged son by making the girl sick.

Such insults between husband and wife belong to a wider class of accusations in which they may refer disparagingly to each other's parents. They comment, for example, that it is just as well that the other's mother or father is dead, since they were rubbish (*korpa*) anyway. Thus a husband to his wife: "Too true your father is dead—you have no pigs or pearl shells to your name! Where are the pigs and valuables your father could have given you—he was a rubbish man!" The import of such vilifications are to be understood within the context of expectations affines have of one another and the way these react on husband and wife, topics I turn to in the following chapters.

3

The Household

A man and his wife regard themselves as being in an economically reciprocal position. The one prepares gardens which the other tends and harvests; the one brings pigs into the house through his transactions,[1] while the other looks after them. Hageners lay particular emphasis on the exclusiveness of this provisioning unit. It is a punishment for the ghosts to remove a man's wife. For if the widower then sets to and harvests food, who is there to chop firewood for the evening? And if he chops firewood, who is there to fetch in the food?

Within a large residential group such as a settlement, men may, to a certain extent, choose with whom they are going to eat or where to sleep, but responsibilities for cooking and providing food on the part of the womenfolk are not diffuse. A man has a right to expect food daily from his wife, for it is his duty to clear gardenland for her. He may hope that his mother will sometimes cook for him, yet can say little if she does not. He cannot expect this of other women in the settlement. Even when his wife is in menstrual seclusion, and prohibited from preparing his meals, he must, if he has no other wives, depend on his mother's willingness, or else upon young daughters. The exception here is the brother who has a married sister, separated from her husband, living in his settlement; if he makes gardens for her she will feed him, though not necessarily all the time.

In this sense, husband and wife, with their dependent children, comprise a household. In his analysis of Kyaka Enga domestic organization, Bulmer (1960) comments that arrangements such as co-residence,

---

[1] This is true subsequent to the initial endowment.

sharing of meals, and gardening, involve overlapping sets of participants and he questions how useful the notion of a "household" is to
describe such a situation. His suggested definition of a "domestic
group" is one "acknowledging common authority in domestic matters"
(1960:112). For Hagen, I would emphasize the perception of mutual
responsibilities for the production and provisioning of food, which hold
typically between spouses, but may also link other categories of persons.
This isolates the husband-wife unit (a household) from wider groupings comprising perhaps a man's co-residential fathers or brothers and
their families. My designation also separates out the husband-wife dyads
of a polygynous family, which is thus composed of several households.

Each household has its own herd of pigs. A son, married or unmarried,
may establish a "quasi-household" with a widowed mother who tends
pigs on his behalf and provides food for him in return for gardens.
Reciprocity is in any case set up between an adult son and his ageing
mother, the latter becoming increasingly dependent on him for garden
services. But if the older woman's husband is still alive, even though she
may send food to her son, she herds pigs only for her husband and her
first responsibilities are to him. Rights between husband and wife are of a
jural order in that failure to acknowledge them may threaten the relationship; but between mother and son, this is heavily overlaid by the
son's moral obligations to support the former in her old age.

The kinds of claims women have on other males to give them garden
shares (pp. 24–25) could also be called moral ones. To a certain extent
moral obligations develop between spouses as a marriage endures, but
at the outset contractual elements of the relationship are prominent. I
turn to a consideration of the reciprocities by which husband and wife
define their relations to each other.

The Rights of Marital Partners

Bridewealth is exchanged between the bride's and groom's kin at marriage, although individual components of it are not tied to the transfer
of specific rights. It is true that different items explicitly stand for particular aspects of the new relationship, yet it would be impossible to make a
partial payment and bring but some facets of the relationship into operation. The exchange as a whole demarcates the exclusive rights which
husband and wife have in each other, and establishes rapport between
the affinal kin on both sides. This last is so important that a bride may

refuse to have intercourse with her husband or cook his food till she is satisfied that her kin have received the final payments. Shyness is in any case expected of a couple marrying for the first time, and it may be six months or so before the marriage is consummated. No particular cere- mony marks this, although in the past the husband was said to remove the knee-band his bride would be wearing (Vicedom and Tischner, 1943–8:2:213).

Husband and wife should be attentive to each other's needs, and be good company. The woman who is sullen, who "looks down her nose" (*koembketa enem*), and never laughs with her husband, and the man who is constantly on the road, too preoccupied to stay and chat, are equally criticised. At marriage a boy is told that he must "sit down" with his wife, and one of the complaints women may make against husbands is that they just do not spend enough time in their company. Couples differ in the extent to which they work or go on visits together; often different activities take them separate ways, but it is not true in Hagen that "man and wife are rarely seen together unless they are quarrelling or eating", as is the case among their Kuma neighbours (Reay 1959:83).

A wife is obliged to ensure that her husband does not have intercourse with her while she is menstruating, for this will harm him.[1] The re- sponsibility is partly on the husband's shoulders as well: it is recognized to be his own fault if he forces his wife against her will in such circum- stances, as women sometimes claim happens. The couple should also avoid intercourse while the wife is suckling a child, since her milk would become contaminated and the child suffer. Adultery is a wrong for which the lover must compensate the husband. Responsibility is com- monly laid on the wife for having enticed the unfortunate man; her husband may or may not beat her. Sometimes, however, a lover may be charged with seduction, especially if the wife shouts out or reports the matter to her husband afterwards. Women have no formal claims against their husband's "adultery"; it is my impression that they tend to show concern over this only when it is accompanied by blatant neglect of themselves.

Several acts of intercourse are thought necessary to conceive and then mould a foetus, and even where a wife has been adulterous it is assumed that her husband alone has had frequent enough sexual relations with her to cause a successful pregnancy. It is from the mother's womb blood

---

[1] See Chapter 7; compensations payable between spouses are considered in Chapter 10.

(*mema*) and the father's semen (*kopong*) that the child is formed. In reference to the procreative substance, the term *kopong* ("grease") may be used for both; if the emphasis is on the general physical tie between child and parent (either parent) the link is said to be one of "blood", *mema*. The *pater* of a child should be its *genitor*. In scandals involving frequent adulteries, it may be rumoured that the woman's child has been formed from the contributions of several men, but if she has a husband he is undisputed *pater*, and for all intents and purposes *genitor*. Thus, for reckoning marriage rules the child will regard himself as of the "blood" of his mother's husband. If the husband dies while the child is a baby and the mother re-marries, the child subsequently observes prohibitions as though the new husband were his *pater*. He still remembers his *genitor*, however, and cannot take a wife from his *genitor*'s clan.

Fatherless children are born in two circumstances: to a widow who has affairs with several men before settling down again, and to *amb wapra* ("promiscuous women") who pass from man to man in a series of short unions. Such offspring have no clear *genitor* or *pater* ("they have no name") and may lack firm clan affiliation. The subsequent marriage of their mother may provide them with this; but a man cannot lay claim to his mistress's children unless he has at some stage been married to her. Pre-marital motherhood in girls was, until very recently, almost unheard-of.

Fewer than 20% of divorces involve women with children. Men try hard to persuade their offspring to stay with them or return when they are older, but cannot coerce them to do so; should they remain with their mother they may become affiliated to her new husband's clan.

A child's animation (*min* or *mini*) is derived from the ancestral ghosts of both parents, although there are no firm dogmas here, and people have conflicting ideas about the origin of the *min*. Some say it comes through the *genitor*, others that ancestors on either side send it. The clan ghosts of an unmarried *wapra* woman may animate a child in her to teach her to settle down and assume some responsibility as a mother. Here only her own clan ancestors are involved. If a married woman is promiscuous then these, along with the ghosts of her husband's clan, supposedly disagree as to whether to send her a child, and either set may act independently. The process of childbirth itself and the subsequent health of the children are also susceptible to ghostly influence from either side.

Husbands are not in attendance at birth, and, like abortion, infanticide (which occurs only immediately after birth) is a woman's matter.

Motives on the part of the mother in such circumstances include anger against the husband, or at the pain of giving birth; there is no discrimination according to the baby's sex, the act being directed against other persons and not the child itself. Wives of a polygynist are said to effect abortions in order to avoid the sexual abstinence of the *post partum* taboo and accompanying loss of favour with the husband. Such an action, it is pointed out, rebounds on the wife herself, for she thereby deprives her own kin of childbirth payments. A woman tries to hide the fact from her husband, telling him she has had a miscarriage or that the child was still-born, but if he finds out he may demand compensation from his wife's kin, or he may get rid of the wife. Since the woman is likely to deny the incident, the husband has to take the initiative in making her go, and he thereby forfeits return of the bridewealth he gave for her.

Some women are specialists in helping with difficult births, and there are also women known to assist abortions. The following incidents happened before the arrival of Europeans.

> *A pregnant woman quarrelled with her husband. She already had a boy and a girl, and this would be her third child. (She bore another subsequently.) She was angry with her husband for not having made good the debt of a pearl shell he had with her brother, and the two came to blows. So she hired a woman expert in abortion, and went down to a river where the expert pummelled her abdomen. The grateful wife gave her a fine quality netbag and some salt in payment. She lied to her husband, saying the child had died in her womb, and she did not know why—was it her own ancestors or the husband's ancestors who killed it?[1]
>
> *A specialist (the story-teller in both these incidents) was called in to help save a woman who had hired the same expert to abort her four-month old foetus, and had fallen dangerously ill. The husband was grateful to the specialist, who had managed to remove the foetus, and gave her a pig; but he accused the abortion expert of killing his child and demanded compensation. The woman paid him two pigs. The wife herself had been angry with the husband for giving a pearl shell to his own sister's husband instead of her brother, which was why she had acted as she did; he took no steps against her.

Husband and wife should both care for their children. Parents have the right of punishment and should protect them from too severe punishment by the other parent. The right to punish is not shared with others, e.g. grandparents or maternal kin of the child or the father's brothers.

---

[1] If the child had in any case died after such a quarrel, the wife would let the husband draw the conclusion that her own ancestral ghosts had killed it because of the bad debt.

The wife sees to the child's food, carries it about till it can walk, clears up after it; but a father is considered necessary for a balanced upbringing, both to provide the child with little luxuries and to teach it obedience. Husband and wife also owe it to each other to care for any other children brought to the marriage, but step-parents are notoriously neglectful.[1] (A husband may drive away a second wife who fails to care for the children of his first wife.) This fits with the exclusiveness of the parent-child tie. A baby being breast-fed is suckled by one woman only —its own mother, or, if she is dead, her surrogate; and an older child is taught to expect food from her alone, not from female relatives in general. Children eat occasionally at the houses of their father's brothers within the sub-clan, but are made to feel ashamed to do so often. A father may berate a child: "There are so many pigs in our house, are there, that they finish up the sweet potatoes and leave none for you? No, there is plenty of food in our house!" In the company of playmates a child goes to other homesteads or settlements and hopes for a share in the meals being cooked there, but in this case as a friend of the local children; he would not have the temerity to go by himself. A parent sees his disciplining of the child threatened if the latter spends too much time at the houses of other people, even its own mother's brother or father's sister. Parents are also afraid that a child who wanders too far away and eats in stranger's houses is a target for poisoning.

A husband protects his wife from outside physical attack, but in the past their respective political affiliations might modify this: indeed, a man (it is said) would concur in the execution of his wife if it were proved she had poisoned his clansmen.

Women have a right to their husband's help in provisioning the house with water and firewood, although in fact they often do these jobs themselves or delegate them to children. Men spend a considerable amount of time away visiting or on *moka* business, and often come home too late at night to see to these tasks. Their major agricultural contribution is seasonal and women cannot rely on daily help from them. A provident husband would see his wife was left with a good stack of firewood; but otherwise women continue to do these chores till their annoyance feeds into some other complaint and they accuse their spouse of neglect.

A wife may show her grievances by refusing to cook for her husband,

---

[1] That is, by repute. Where the subsequent parent looks after the child adequately, the fact of step-parentage is not commented on.

so that when he comes home tired at night he finds everybody else has eaten and there is nothing left out for him. Such an action threatens to repudiate the relationship, for cooking food is also an important symbol of the wife's total position. In addition, the offering of the staple, sweet potato, may be jokingly referred to as a metaphor for sexual relations. Courting songs speak of the young nubile girl who during the day harvests sweet potatoes, and in the evening sits peeling them, wondering to whom she will offer them. In fact, one insult a husband can level at his wife is that she is *kng oka*, sweet potato fit only for pigs to eat (by contrast with *wamb oka*, suitable for human consumption).[1] Aside from the sexual connotations, providing food signifies, for women, their total care for the husband or children. A woman takes offence if the meal is refused ("What! does my food have a bad odour that you spurn it?").

For his part, a husband may beat a lazy wife who does not prepare his meals properly. This has only limited effectiveness since it often provokes the woman into running home to her kin. But a wife who fails to see to her husband's food incurs general censure.

> *Waemon is married to a Kawelka man, Nil. She stayed in the house one afternoon and did not bother to rouse herself to harvest sweet potatoes for the evening meal. Nil himself dug out some tubers and then went to cut firewood. When he came back he found Waemon cooking some of them. He was angry: why was she eating *his* sweet potatoes? She stayed in the house and dug out none of her own and now was finishing his—had she turned into a man?—it is women's job to fetch in the food! She hit at him for this with a stick. At a subsequent hearing, the court decided in favour of Nil; she had struck him for no reason—Nil had been reasonably provoked into what he had said; it was her fault since she had not harvested the sweet potatoes as she should have done. Her kin provided a compensation pig which Nil cooked and shared with those who heard the court along with members of his settlement. This happened in 1966; the account is from a man of Nil's sub-clan.

We have seen that in return for cooking food women expect reciprocity in the allocation of cleared land, from their husband (always) and sons (sometimes), the adults for whom they cook. Towards evening each woman individually collects tubers in her netbag from her own planted gardens. If she shares a house with other women they may all cook over a common fire, but she alone will be responsible for putting aside portions

---

[1] The smallest, stringiest tubers, without much *kopong* ("juice") are set aside for pigs. Women may retaliate (calling their husbands *kng oka*), and the phrase can also be used disparagingly by a mother of her son's wife.

for her husband and children. Two cowives cooking at the same fire each present the husband with a meal. All those sleeping in the women's house, or in one partition of it,[1] will eat together. Men and boys who later retire to a men's house may eat with the women, or else the food is sent directly to them at the men's house. Several men may put their tubers together, but each individual regards himself as being fed only by his wife (or mother) and not by the wives of other men present. If one gives some of his food to another, the latter sees this as because of his relationship with the man, and not with the man's wife. A man sleeps in a joint men's house with others, or in a brother's men's house, but never in the women's houses of his male kin; nor do women move between their own houses and those of cowives or husband's brothers' wives, partly because they must care for the pigs stalled in their own.

While rights to labour and produce do operate reciprocally they are not, from men's point of view, entirely symmetrical. On the whole a woman's claims to the crops she has planted are respected. A husband does not dispute her disposal so long as he is provided for adequately. Women are thus free to make small gifts of sweet potatoes to others or to keep the proceeds from selling them. Between spouses, the interpretation of an encroachment by the one on the garden rights of the other rests on the context of the deed, and may or may not be made into an issue. A wife who decides to fuss over a husband digging up some of her tubers may provoke him by her vituperations[2] into declarations on his part that since he owns the land and worked it, the garden and the crops in it are his to do as he wants with. In the abstract men may also say that since they clear land, and the land is their clan land, they are the real "owners" of a garden: *wu^e okapana pukl wu^e morom* ("the husband is the root-man of the sweet potato garden"), and women simply "look after"

---

[1] Women's houses may be divided into two partitions, each with its sitting room, sleeping room and pig stalls; though often there is a common set of pig stalls. Mother- and daughter-in-law or cowives may live in separate partitions.

[2] A woman may represent her husband's intrusion into her gardens as a more general violation. With heavy humour, an old Kelua man gave the following as a typical interchange: The husband (H) digs out sweet potatoes during the day from his wife's (W) garden. W: "You dig out my sweet potatoes! Isn't it my genitals you are really after?" H: "It is my garden and I cut it from the bush. I can do as I want". He continued: the wife may threaten to run home; the husband remarks that it is too bad, and makes a show of killing a pig, excluding her from the distribution. The woman stays at her home, so the husband has to come and fetch her. He pleads that he was just hungry and ate some tubers, and then his wife insulted him; so her father sympathetically despatches her back.

(*nokopa iti*) the crops grown there. This is a rhetorical norm being brought up in a situation where the wife ignores her role as provider by being so ungenerous; it is also a more general dogma which men hold in relation to women. Litigation over planted gardens ruined by pigs is frequently concluded with compensation payments; and while sometimes the wife receives all or a share of the payment because of the spoiled crops, on occasion the husband may claim it entirely, under the rubric that he is the "owner".

A wife's control over the pig herd is more restricted. Although she tends them, the amount of say she has in their disposal rests largely on the husband's willingness to treat her as an equal.

Pigs are important items in ceremonial exchange (*moka*), and stemming partly from joint interests in the herd are joint interests in exchange relations between the wife's and husband's kin. Thus, a husband should not only, after the initial endowment from her people, provide his wife with further pigs to rear, but should make *moka* with her kin. This is not obligatory in that the wife's kin would not formally remove her if the husband fails in this, but it may become an important element in the eventual stability of the conjugal relationship.

Most women would like the situation to be such that (i) they were consulted over every decision made about the herd; (ii) in any case that the decision should be either to kill and eat the pigs (so that they taste the fruits of their labours) or else (iii) reserve them for transactions with their own kin. Women dislike men using "their" pigs for exchanges with other partners or with a cowife's people. A polygynist sometimes counts up all the pigs he has as a single herd, but each wife sees her share as discrete. Thus if "her" pigs are contributed to a bridewealth, then she expects return to be made to herself, and not to another. A wife stands some chance of having her independent contribution recognized if pigs are involved on both sides of the transaction. But she has even less control over shell valuables, and if her pigs are converted into these she may lose track of her claims. This lies behind objections women often make that their pigs are being given away for shell-*moka* (the immediate return for pigs being shells) and not in pig-*moka* (to solicit more pigs).

I do not, however, wish to overemphasize the effort a woman has to make in staking her claims. Sometimes a husband specifically allocates shells to his wife to keep, earmarking them for her kin. A polygynist who upsets his various wives by not keeping their claims discrete may receive little sympathy from other men at his bad management. If a husband uses pigs to gain shells (as in one of the standard *moka* transactions) it is wise of him to put the shells in the house of the wife who supplied the pigs. Many women are not too concerned about the shells themselves; pearl shells are like money, they do not stay with one but "just walk around" (*kin andepa mint morom*), though some assert, "the man goes and gets the shells, but we look after them" (on analogy with pigs). Pigs are the chief object of care and devotion, and women wait to see what happens to the animals which eventually come in return for these shells. But the principle that a polygynist should allocate the eventual return to the wife concerned in the initial transaction may clash with other principles, for example that cowives should receive equal shares from the husband's enterprises, or that a woman is entitled to look after the proceeds of exchanges with her own kin. I cite two instances of recent disputes on these grounds.

*A Tipuka man, Nami, had two wives, one from Minembi and one from Maplke. He made *moka* with the brother of his Minembi wife, receiving two sets of pearl shells for two pigs, which he took from the Mapike woman's stalls. Later he sent the shells off and made *moka* with another man; the two pigs gained from this he divided equally between his wives. Then the Maplke wife protested that she had provided two pigs in the first place, and why had she received only one now? Nami promised her another later, but she maintained that the second pig belonged to her, pulled at the pig rope and lashed out at her cowife. The quarrelling was broken up by a big-man who said that the husband was wrong: the Maplke woman should receive both pigs, since she provided them in the first place, although it was true that the shells were from the Minembi brother-in-law. The Minembi wife was not at all pleased but had to acquiesce. Later comment on the case was that Nami's initial error was to make *moka* from the pigs of one wife with the brother of another.

*Another Tipuka man, Wena, made *moka* with a fellow clansman using a pig looked after by one wife, a Kendipi woman, but the return gift of eight shells he put in the house of his other wife (who was from his own tribe, Tipuka). Later he used them to give to his Tipuka father-in-law. The Kendipi woman had kept her own counsel till the father-in-law's returned pig was put in his daughter's house, i.e. was given to her cowife. It was then that she quarrelled with her husband, demanding that the pig go to her. In the ensuing fight the husband drew blood. A court was held: Wena was told to pay compensation for the blood he had spilt and he turned the pig over to her.

The extent to which wives can depend on support for their claims from others of their husband's group, or from their own kin, is not a simple matter. Rights and duties are certainly seen to exist between husband and wife in a very specific way. Default on any of the points outlined may cause grievances but these do not necessarily find automatic appeasement in courts or other means of settlement. I would argue that this is not because such grievances are considered unjustified; rather, it arises from the relationship of marriage to other institutions. The nature of domestic ties between spouses cannot, in fact, be understood without reference to the political domain.

Some of the issues I have been discussing illustrate aspects of relations between cowives, and I consider now the facts of polygyny.

Polygyny and Relations Between Cowives

Nearly all females are likely to marry, but this is by no means true of males. Aside from physical and mental disabilities, some men have no close sponsors to raise bridewealth for them. A youth can depend on his own father (or own mother's brother if he is living with him), but if this man dies, claims on classificatory relatives can prove too weak. Even an elder brother, concerned with the establishment of his own affinal exchanges may shirk the responsibility. Some bachelors (*wu^e wangen*) attach themselves to related big-men in the hope that these will provide them with bridewealth in return for services, or they may marry widowed or divorced women late in life.

Details of the marital status of men from Kawelka and Elti tribes are given in Strathern, A.J. and A.M. (1969). Appendix II comments on some differences between the tribes. I reproduce information (Strathern, A.J. and A.M., 1969) (Table 4, Glasse and Meggitt, 1969; with permission of Prentice-Hall), on the range of wives currently married. Here Elti and Kawelka are somewhat similar.

TABLE IV

Range of wives currently married

Number of wives married	0	1	2	3	4	5	Number of men married at least once
KAWELKA	20	150	24	8	2	—	204
ELTI	18	64	5	7	—	—	94

Among the Kawelka five men have successively married 5, 6 or 7 wives; the maximum number of wives any of them has had at any one time is four. One Elti man married a total of eight wives, while four men have had five in their life-time. Among other Hagen tribes, especially in Central Melpa, much larger numbers have been recorded. A few big-men of the larger Northern Melpa tribes, such as Tipuka, claim to have married as many as "ten" women in their time. There is no statistical difference between the two samples in the percentage of polygynists to others among married men, which is 18·5% for Kawelka and 15·8% for Elti.[1] From a third to a half of the wedded man of the various Kawelka clans who are now over 35 have had experience of more than one marriage, although not all have been polygynists.

Much of the quality of relations between cowives depends on their personal friendliness or animosity. I have noted that they owe few specific duties to one another. Thus, during menstrual seclusion it is her daughter or her mother-in-law rather than a cowife on whom a woman frequently relies to feed her children. Nevertheless, one informant (male) said that a cowife may suckle a motherless child whereas the wives of its father's brothers would be reluctant to do so: they are *amb elpa*, "other women".[2]

A polygynist cannot make eating, sleeping, stock-raising and gardening arrangements simply as suits his convenience, for it is through these activities that each wife establishes her own relationship with him. The wife of a polygynist not only has the general right to gardens, pigs and so forth, but in addition has a right against her cowives for an equal share of these things and for an equal share of her husband's attention. A successful husband must be scrupulously fair. In particular, he should apportion his hours so that he eats and spends time in the house of each one.

Among the wives of polygynists, then, the claims which women make

---

[1] Vicedom notes that in the past "four to five women used to be the most a man could afford economically", but that with the inflow of wealth into Hagen general prosperity increased so that "up to 40% of the married men today are polygamous" (Vicedom and Tischner, 1943–8:2:217). The figure is taken from his census of the Ndika tribe. However, the Ndika figures he gives in detail (an earlier census?) show about 18% (187/1011) of currently married men as polygynous (cf. my 15–19%) and the average number of wives for polygynists as 2·6. My figures are 2·35 for Kawelka, 2·58 for Elti.

[2] However, in 10 cases for which I have details, motherless babies were suckled by a FBW in 4, by a FZ and MM in 2 each, by a FM in 1, and in 1 case by an outside agent (a Hagen hospital nurse); but in no instance by a cowife.

on their husbands are sharpened to the point of competition. Hageners regard the cowife relationship as typically characterized by *wølik* ("jealousy"). *Wølik rop amb tembokl rop iti*, a cowife "is a jealous woman and fights". *Wølik* is also found between siblings or between mother- and daughter-in-law; but between the wives of one man it is stereotype.

Cowives are seen as rivals, competing for favour, a view which men perhaps overstress, for it flatters themselves. An Elti man made caustic remarks about the constant friction which existed between two wives of a brother of his. But the women in question claimed to be on the best of terms, saying they were only *wølik* about very specific issues, such as the allocation of valuables to their respective kin; anyway, they said, it all belonged to the time when they were newly married. Older women usually claim they have abandoned *wølik*. *Wølik* also refers to a wife's efforts to get rid of her rival. Cowives "make *wølik*" against each other through spells and magical devices. A central component of the concept is sexual jealousy, and brides were traditionally given magic stones to make them attractive to their new husbands. These, or similar stones would also bring them success in pig breeding, for sexual attraction and economic success are seen to go together. A skilful manager is thought to endear herself to her spouse, and conversely the favourite wife is given preferential treatment in the allocation of valuables.

The situation of a second wife can make her an object of pathos as well as a target for aggression. If she is a much younger woman, the first often suspects her husband's preference for her; yet the second wife may also be depicted as standing in wistful envy of the original couple. Women's songs, with their themes of courting and love, also touch on *wølik* between cowives. Allusions are made to the ugliness or immodesty of the other woman, and the contrast of the singer's own beauty which she wonders will not rather hold the husband's admiring glances. But songs are not always in a fighting mood. One recounts the realization of a second wife that a man does not forget the woman he married first. She goes up to the house where they are having a meal together; her hand on the doorpost, she hesitates, but turns away. The pair were sharing things before she ever came and there is no place for her.

The first wife a man marries is his *peng amb* ("head woman"), and it is she who is expected to devote herself most fully to his affairs. In fact most polygynists have favourite wives (no special term) with whom they are most often seen. A Kawelka big-man who had had seven wives spoke of his second as the *peng amb* (the first having left him soon after marriage); but the wife with whom he most closely associated was the fifth. Not only would he spend more of his time at her woman's house, but when he went visiting, it would be she who accompanied him. She reared more pigs for him than the other wives, and on public occasions would be seen bustling around the tethered animals or in consultation with him. In spite of these notions, cowives are not formally ranked and the senior woman expects no mandatory privileges. Rather, every effort should be made to maintain formal equality. A second or third wife inherited as a widow has no special position, though she is more likely than the others to have a house of her own (especially if she has children). But the matricentral unit is not necessarily marked off in this way. Widow inheritance is discussed in chapter 8.

Personal relations between cowives may be very unequal. The following brief history refers to the households of a prominent Northern Melpa man.

Unt has at the moment three wives. The first two were said to have got on well with each other and initially shared a house, before the second of the pair moved a short distance away to a large settlement where she lived with the wife of one of Unt's lineage brothers. Trouble followed, Unt suspecting his second wife of adultery with a man from a neighbouring clan; about the same time he began to make plans to marry again. Both his wives were upset at the thought of someone else and the second wife left him.[1] Bridewealth was returned, and the woman re-married, leaving behind her two children. Unt's third wife came to live in a separate settlement from the first. This was in the late 1950s; in the early 1960s men from Unt's tribe began settling in the Gumant river area, renowned for its good pig pasture, and his former second wife also went there to stay for a while with her old mother. She was said to have had a yearning to be with her children again, and Unt persuaded her to come back to him. Reinstated, she set up house at the Gumant, and Unt maintains dual residence between it and Buk. She visits Buk for special occasions but has not since resided or gardened there. While she looks after Unt's *bisnis* (Pidgin English, "business") at the Gumant, his third wife manages his affairs at Buk. The natal kin of the latter are particularly important exchange partners. The second and the third wife have now settled down with each other, to the exclusion of the first.

The first wife comes from a Tipuka group living in the Jimi valley, and was married at a time when several Buk people maintained Jimi contacts.

---

[1] In addition to the *wølik* the two wives had towards the third, the second claimed a specific grievance: she had helped Unt make a prestation to the third woman's kin but received none of the return-gift herself; an additional reason for feeling *popokl* (angry) was that Unt and the new wife shared a "joint sleeping house", while she was relegated to a woman's house. What rankled was the fact that the new woman was a divorcee whereas she herself had come to Unt as a young girl, never before married.

Her kin are relatively insignificant as exchange partners. She herself has withdrawn from interest in her husband's *moka* affairs, living apart in a dilapidated men's house with no pigs to care for. She no longer regularly provides food for Unt, and other people describe her as lazy. She feeds herself and her children from old gardens she manages to keep in cultivation, with occasional help from neighbours. Unt's policy, which he carries out with the support of his other two wives, is to make her take up residence at the Gumant, where her labour would be useful. Till she does, he says, he will not provide her with any pigs to look after and will not make her new gardens. (In 1964 she allocated her small tubers (sweet potatoes fit for pigs) to the wife of a neighbour with whom she was friendly, in the hope that the latter would give her a piglet in return.) Though obstinate, she is a weak woman; others under similar pressure would be driven away.

Open friction between cowives is alleviated by two residential arrangements; one ensuring the presence of other women, the other separating the wives in question.

Polygynists tend to live in settlements rather than homesteads. By definition, a homestead could comprise a polygynist living by himself along with his wives, but in fact such men show a preference for settlements.[1] In Kawelka Mandembo clan, for example, all polygynists reside in settlements with the exception of one man whose second wife is rarely with him, and another who had inherited the widow of a big-man—but the woman left him after spending most of her time at her former husband's settlement.[2] Of the adult women living on Kawelka Membo clan territory at Buk in 1965, 68% were residing in (13) settlements, and 32% in (approximately 20) homesteads. The latter figures, however, include homesteads clustered together in a mission village; if these are omitted only 17% of the women were residing in (10) homesteads. I tabulate the average number of women living in homesteads or settlements, indicating (a) where only women of the same generation are found, and (b) where there are two generations of women. (Residential groups with two generations of married *men* are by definition settlements; the usual type of homestead with married women of more than one generation comprises a couple and the widowed mother of one of them.)

---

[1] This does not appear to be a simple function of age (e.g. an older man acquiring second and third wives as his sons also marry) since men tend to marry most of their wives while they are fairly young; it is rare for a father to marry afresh when his own sons or brother's sons are ready to find wives, although an older man may inherit a widow late in life.

[2] A polygynist may allow a former widow and her children to live away from his settlement, but other husbands expect a more positive demonstration of association after their re-marriage. One widow is included in the figures for "separated" wives in Appendix III.

TABLE V
Number of wives in homesteads and settlements
(Northern Melpa clan)

| | Homestead | | Settlement | | Totals |
	(a)	(b)	(a)	(b)	
Number of wives	11	0	8	45	64
Number of residential groups	10	0	4	9	23
Average number of wives/residential group	1.1	0	2	5	

We thus see that two-thirds (45/64) of the married women live in settlements with an average of five married females (including themselves). Of the 11 wives who live in (one-generational) homesteads, 9 are the only wives of their monogamous husbands. In one case a homestead contains a pair of cowives; all other polygynists are in settlements. This means that men with more than one wife are living with them *along with* their fathers and/or brothers and the wives of these men. The result is that wives married polygynously usually reside in groups where there are women married to other men. Although it has not been stated to me in quite this way, we can see that this prevents cowives from being forced exclusively on their own company.

The second arrangement has the more explicit purpose of separating cowives from one another. This is achieved in two ways: dispersal in several residential groups, or the establishment of quasi-households, making their wives partly independent of the husband. Typically, they then live with their home kin.

Dispersal and Separation

A. Dispersal

There seems to be a limit on the number of cowives who can live in close residential association; a husband may be able to keep three or four women attached to him, but will probably only have two living in any one residential group. The following table show the residential arrangements of 25 of the Kawelka polygynists, whose wives all live on their (the men's) clan territory.[1]

TABLE VI

Marital status of 25 Kawelka polygynists with wives dispersed
in different residential groups (RG)

Number of wives married	Men with wives in 1 RG	Men with wives in 2 RG	Men with wives in 3 RG
2	13	5	—
3	1	2	3
4	0	1	0
TOTALS 14	14	8	3

Where cowives do live in the same settlement they often have different houses. A woman with a mother- or daughter-in-law alive is much more likely to share a house with such a person than are a pair of cowives. I consider the situation of the 64 women described in Table V. Some have both cowives and an in-law alive, but I separate out the categories and do not therefore give an overall total.

TABLE VII

Sharing of houses with categories of women
(Northern Melpa clan)

Categories of person alive	By themselves	Number of women residing With this category alone	Number of women residing With this category + others	Number of women residing With others only	Sub total
Cowives	11	0	2	6	19
ML / DL	7	7	8	4	26
Neither[a]	16	—	—	24	40

[a] No information for two women.

The table includes cases where wives of polygynists are dispersed in different residential groups. I do not differentiate situations where one of the wives may have been a former widow. From it we can see that of 19

[1] Information on a further case is uncertain. Eight men, some of whose wives reside in different clan territories, are considered under "separation".

women with cowives, only two shared a house with each other, and this was along with a third woman. Of the 26 with a mother-in-law or daughter-in-law, 15 shared a house with this person, although in 8 of the cases further women were also present. I might note that of the women who shared their house with no-one, 5 could have chosen to live with either a cowife or an in-law. In the only case of two cowives sharing a house this was a divided one (see footnote on p. 47), each wife furthermore having her own separate pig stalls. Of ML/DL sharing, at least 4 pairs were together in an undivided house or the single compartment of a divided one; one pair was separated into different compartments; for 5 women I do not know the situation.

Consideration of internal changes within a settlement suggests that new houses are sometimes built and house membership altered, not to provide every woman with her own dwelling, but to keep cowives apart.

Near Buk lives a Tipuka Kitepi big-man with three wives, one of whom resides with her lineage brothers several miles away. The other two, Wapil and Porongk, are (to the outside world) *wølik*. Wapil is both *peng amb* and favourite wife; Porongk has a reputation for laziness. They had separate women's houses, A and B. When Wapil's son married the new wife slept with her in A; but at the time of the marriage of Porongk's son, the latter quarrelled with her son for neglecting her gardens and Porongk moved to sleep also in A, leaving her son and daughter-in-law in B. About this time the senior husband built a new "joint sleeping house" and Wapil went to sleep there; she left A to Porongk and her own daughter-in-law. With the coming of two more young wives to Wapil's sons, who all slept in A, the women's house A was felt to be overcrowded and Porongk moved back to B and her own daughter-in-law. We may note that Wapil had originally moved out of A, which had the effect of avoiding the incoming Porongk, but she did not relinquish it; she stalled her pigs in it and her daughters-in-law slept there. Wapil now sleeps sometimes in A and sometimes in the "joint house" with her husband. Of the younger generation of women, the two wives of one of Wapil's sons originally shared a common house (A); but when the second wife bore her first child she moved away to a newly built house of her own. The other continues to reside in A along with the wife of Wapil's other son. The split was not between the wives of two brothers, but between the two cowives of one man.

Women's jobs are not dependent on specific teamwork with other women. The crucial interdependence is between husband and wife, and a husband can maintain almost full domestic relations with wives living away from his main settlement. The situation is a little different in the arrangements I term separation.

B. Separation

By this I refer not to an informal dissolution of marital ties (in Hagen such a situation is unlikely to persist; it rapidly develops into divorce) but to arrangements made whereby husband and wife no longer form a full household, although they are still considered married. They live apart; but this is distinct from divorce in that the spouses still have certain rights in each other, and full exchange relations between the affines on both sides can be maintained.

It is a diminution of the total rights and responsibilities held between husband and wife which is involved in separation. The wife herself may take the initiative to live with her parents or brothers or with a married daughter, away from the husband's clan territory. She is given garden land at her new residence, and ceases to support her husband in his everyday needs. She may retain varying degrees of involvement in his affairs, but is still considered married to him and to no-one else. It is always possible for such a woman to return and resume full marital relations. Usually she cohabits with him, brings up their children and rears his pigs; she may, however, set up a quasi-household with her brother or with whomever she resides, the latter cutting gardens for her and she reciprocally cooking for him. Most importantly, her kin are still potential exchange partners for her husband. For a big-man this may be one of the most crucial aspects of his continuing relations with his wife. He has other women to rely upon for daily sustenance; but such separated wives add to his stock of pigs and help in his maintenance of a wide affinal network. What he loses is partial control over the pig herd, for the wife is likely to insist that he use the stock in exchange with the kin she is living with; he also runs the risk of his children electing to stay at their mother's domicile, and perhaps even of his wife eventually divorcing him altogether, though divorce after prolonged separation of this kind is rare.

Women of all ages may establish themselves apart from their husbands; there is no regular pattern of "terminal separation" (i.e. effective divorce) of the kind Goody, E. N. (1962) has described. Only wives of polygynists are likely to do so for any length of time. In 1965 there were no cases of Kawelka monogamists with separated wives, although two had wives who had left them for several months in the preceding year. Of the total of 80 wives married polygynously to Kawelka men, 9 (11·2%) were separated (these are married to the eight polygynists mentioned on page 56 footnote [13]). Details of the current household arrangements and some of the circumstances of their separation for these nine women are given in Appendix III.

If both arrangements are considered, at least 19 of the 34 Kawelka polygynists either had some wives living separated from them or else had wives dispersed in different residential groups. I have drawn my data in the main from Kawelka; to point the argument I cite the example of a Ndika Councillor who lives near Kelua. He currently has 9 wives; 5 live in the vicinity of his main men's house, but are divided among three homestead-like clusters, each hidden some minutes' walk away from the others; 2 share a house on the borders of Ndika and Elti territories, Elti being the home area of one of them; another wife lives with her home kin and looks after his pigs there; while the last, inherited from a deceased brother, spends her time at the place of her married daughter and with her own matrilateral kin.

It should be noted that a marriage can be maintained in separation only when husband and wife are not living too far apart (within a half-day's journey or so). As well as spouses, affines should be able to visit one another. But this is an ideal women hold for all marriages; they cannot maintain garden claims at home where it is too far for them to carry produce back. Women in any case place a high value on being able to see their home kin from time to time. For such reasons there are preferences for marrying nearby.

As women look on it, separation may be more than a negative response to marital difficulties. It may be accompanied on the wife's part with a positive desire to return to her home kin and care for them, especially if her parents are old or her brother unmarried. She has sympathy (*kaemb*) for them. Such a feeling may be precipitated as much by the plight of a relative (e.g. a brother unable to marry or keep a wife) as by an upsetting experience of her own. Whereas the wife of a polygynist feels free to live apart from him, a monogamously married woman who is drawn towards her own kin may try to induce her husband to accompany her back and take up uxorilocal residence.

The actual number of married women living at their brother's place, or of couples residing uxorilocally does not, however, yield a high "ratio of sibling residence" (Goody, E. N. and J. R., 1967). Nevertheless, there is a strong bond between brothers and sisters, and the weight given to examples of such residential arrangements is as illuminating as their statistical frequency. Cases of sisters taking up domicile with their brothers are conspicuous in that they are felt to fall into an acceptable pattern: "Women are like that; she is sorry for her brother". In other words, an ideological provision is made for this kind of residence. Whatever the disputes that led to the woman going off in the first place, her behaviour is justifiable in terms of the affection women are supposed to feel for their home.

Husband and Wife: the Supernatural Dimension

Although a wife participates in the affairs of her husband's residential group, the focus of her interests is the household. The exclusive claims a woman has on her husband are challenged in a polygynous marriage, where each woman tries to exert an influence over the husband which will exclude the others. Much of the sentiment attached to the marital relationship indeed assumes it is an exclusive one, an aspect expressed more by women more than by men.

There is a popular supposition that attachments formed between young girls and youths at courting parties last throughout life. A girl made to marry someone against her wishes allegedly harbours secret longings to run away to the youth who had earlier courted her. This is akin to the feeling that a first marriage is the most important (which in fact contradicts what must be most people's knowledge of divorce patterns). Occasionally a rejected first husband actually takes revenge on a runaway wife, although more often pride leads to statements of indifference.

Women say that after death the spirits (*min*)[1] of husband and wife find each other again. As in her lifetime, a woman's *min* may wander around and visit her clansmen, but it always returns to the abode of her husband's *min*. And some say that in the case of a woman with several husbands, her *min* returns to the first man she married, however short a time she was with him. But this goes against the feeling that the spirits are joined together because of the affection (*kaemb*) between them which has grown up over the years. The same sentiment shows in the supposition that when one partner dies his or her spirit, impatient of waiting, kills the survivor. The ghost is said to act this way out of tender feelings (*kaemb*) towards the spouse whose company it pines for; but the act may also stem from frustration (*popokl*)—the ghost, angry at having died,

---

[1] *Min* is used specifically for the spirit of a recently dead person; sacrifices eventually establish the person as one among all the other ghosts (*kor* or *tipu wamb*).

takes revenge on the living. Claims spouses have over each other thus persist after death. Indeed, such an exclusive interest may be over-asserted; an Elti widower lamented the difficulty he had had in finding another woman to replace his former wife, and blamed his trouble on interference from the jealous (*wølik*) ghost of the dead woman. He commented also that she probably wanted to see that he kept his wealth for their children rather than expend it on another wife for himself.

If someone related to a widow's deceased husband marries her (see Chapter 8), he must provide a sacrifice allotting a pig to the former husband's agnates, which is killed with the prayer that the dead man join his brothers and share the pig with them. It is regarded as a kind of bridewealth (*kuimø*); the analogy with bridewealth is extended so far that the close brothers of the dead man may make a return-gift of a small pig. If children are involved, the second husband may hand over a few shells, for which return is also made, so he will "feel good" (i.e. not resent the payment). The new husband and wife partake of a further pig themselves, and the husband signifies the responsibility he now assumes of sacrificing to the woman's ancestral ghosts, as her former husband once also did. The widow's children may share in this second sacrifice if they are very small, but otherwise they eat of the first pig as children of their father; they will look to his ghost for future support and do not wish to cut themselves off from him. The new marital unit is thus explicitly demarcated.

The giving of the first pig (*amb wøy^e pol kng*, "the bridge pig of the widow") marks the status of the new husband vis-à-vis others of the deceased's clansmen. The second pig (*kng kaemb* "pig liver," after the most important sacrificial organ) focuses on the new marriage. Sometimes only one is killed, in which case the widow and her new husband eat its liver, while the rest is consumed by the clansmen. But some kind of sacrifice has to be made or else the dead man will send sickness to his survivors. The ghost is asked to leave the widow, her husband and the children alone; if it is a relative of his the widow has married, any of these persons can succumb to his attacks. The inimical spirit may be more summarily despatched by a ritual expert who enunciates rejection spells. When the widow marries a close brother, the ghost is thought to be particularly jealous. Full brothers may inherit one another's wives, but are often reluctant to do so. This is out of delicacy to the uniqueness of the husband-wife tie: the survivor fears the avenging ghost of the first husband who had such an intimate relationship with the widow, a fear which is intensified by his own close tie with the dead man. Moreover, the equality that once existed between the brothers has been upset by the living taking the dead man's wife. In such a case the expert beats the backs of the new couple with a switch to brush off the lingering ghost. If no sacrifices are made, the former husband's ghost may kill off-spring born to the second marriage, or simply prevent the couple from having further children; but his over-riding jealousy can bring these things about even if sacrifices are made.

During the period of mourning, the spirit of the dead man sits on the widow. This used to be symbolized by the widow's blackened face, the burden of netbags which bowed her head, and the covering up of her body in swathes of mourning beads. These are not to protect her from the spirit[1] but rather signify its presence; she is particularly vulnerable to attack at this time. (If she caused her husband's death through poison the angry spirit attacks her at once; her own spirit does not then join him but goes wild (*rakra*).) Pigs are killed, perhaps six months to a year after the death, to establish the man's ghost among his clan ances-tors; if proper revenge for the death has been taken, the widow is freed from mourning at this time. Nevertheless, as we have seen, the occasion of her re-marriage will excite the ghost's attention; it will kill her should she rush too precipitately into another union, especially if there is any hint of her having previously philandered with the second man. Only if she leaves the dead man's clan altogether does his influence over her weaken, although he can still visit sickness on his children by her. A man loses this mystical control over his biological offspring if he dies before having seen them; or if before his death he himself got rid of his wife and children. It is not often, however, that a man with children initiates divorce; and if it is the wife who left him, he retains his influence.

"Re-marriage" for a widower is a much less dangerous matter; he may in any case have a second wife. Nevertheless, a dead woman can send sickness to her surviving husband and her children. Some say that she can visit sickness on her cowife or the woman a husband marries after her own death; others deny the possibility of this, and she cannot in any case attack her cowife's children. Neglect during her lifetime,

---

[1] Cf. Goody, J.R. (1962: 89–90); Heider notes that Dani men drape women's netbags over their heads to conceal themselves from ghosts (Heider, 1969: 385). Here there is a reversal in the wearing of sex-linked clothing. But the Hagen widow is clothed in an excess of female garments.

especially if her husband favoured other wives over her, may be avenged by ghostly attacks.

The husband-wife tie is thus given special emphasis: outside it, only the ghosts of cognatic kin are usually thought capable of directly influencing the living. In the same way as cognatic ghosts take revenge on the offending kinsmen if they die with anger (*popokl*) in their hearts or if the cause of their death lies with such persons, spouses may also kill or make ill their survivor.

There is more to such mystical interaction between them than jealousy and revenge. A dead spouse also helps an angry (*popokl*) person in the same way as cognatic ghosts do. A widow herself may be upset that her second husband has not made the proper sacrifice, so the ghost of the first carries her off. If a man dies after losing a former wife through divorce, and the latter is unhappy in her second marriage, angry perhaps that proper payments have not been made to her kin, the dead husband, one is told, might kill her so that she returns to live with him as a ghost. The attire of a bereaved widow is supposed to reflect her feelings; she disfigures herself in her own *popokl* (anger) at the death. In the past the wife of a man killed by his enemies would wear his hair on her breast until revenge had been taken. At the news his clansmen brought of this, she rejoiced. Her feelings are seen to parallel sentiments held by the deceased's clansmen.

Women's deaths are not the subject of revenge to the same extent; and although husband and wife may both influence each other after death, and are supposed finally to live together, their deaths receive different treatment from society at large. Here, their wider status as men and women intervenes.

A widower does not observe the elaborate mourning incumbent upon a widow. The beads (*kokla wøyᵉ*), which give the widow her special designation (*amb wøyᵉ*, "woman of the mourning beads") were also worn in the past by female relatives for the deaths of brothers or sons, youngish men cut off in their prime. The emphasis is on female bereavement at the deaths of certain males, and not vice versa. It is also on females that general duties of public mourning fall most heavily (whatever the sex of the deceased). When a man dies, wives of his clansmen as well as sisters and daughters who have married elsewhere congregate to wail for him; in the case of a woman it is wives of her husband's clan, perhaps female agnates of this clan as well, and sisters and brothers' wives from her own clan. At the end of the first intensive mourning period (about a week), the initial sacrifices are referred to as releasing the women who can then resume their domestic duties. The more elaborate mourning by women (by comparison with men), and by widows in particular for their dead husbands, is not bound up so much with the ease with which the services of a spouse can be replaced, widows in fact finding it easier to re-marry than widowers, but (I suggest) the imputation that women are helpless without the support of males, comments to this effect being made by both sexes.

We have seen that the ghost of a dead man may threaten his widow, and also attack her second husband. Others of his clan are not threatened in this way. But when a woman dies it is not only her husband who fears attack. His clansmen in general are said to be afraid.[1] At a final sacrifice, her spirit is despatched by a ritual expert so that she will not harm her husband, and in addition will not bring trouble to his clan. The woman, it is explained, comes to her husband's clan from elsewhere to marry him, and they are afraid of her lingering spirit: they banish it lest it plague them. But they would never expel the ghost of a male clansman in this way; rather it must remain with them to look after the living as all clan ghosts do.

_____

[1] Although specific misfortunes other than those suffered by her husband are usually not attributed to her. Here it is the status of a woman as wife, not mother, being commented upon: in other contexts, people speak of being helped equally by the protection of their dead mothers and fathers. (This account of funeral behaviour and sacrifice is drawn largely from informants' statements, overt religious activity being drastically curtailed under mission influence.)

4

The Roads of Marriage

Marriages create the "roads" (*nombokla, mon*) which give an individual important connections with groups other than his own. One's mother's kin are thought of as "behind" one, while from the point of view of her home clan a sister or father's sister who has married out "goes away". These are the roads pursued in making *moka*, attending feasts, visiting friends or collecting bridewealth.

But once a marriage has established a road, further unions between those already closely linked by it are not possible. Where one has already "eaten" bridewealth, one would be ashamed to contract a marriage for oneself. Notions of sexual intimacy are involved. Sexual intercourse with a maternal cross cousin is described as turning back to where one originated from; with a paternal cross cousin, as running in the direction already taken by a clanswoman. Direct brother–sister exchange is wrong, one woman commented, for it would mean that instead of using his sister's bridewealth to marry a wife from elsewhere (make a new road), the groom's wealth would come back on itself. Consonant with the notion, then, that roads created by marriage provide channels for wealth, is the desirability of maximizing them, fresh marriages providing opportunities for new channels. At the same time, profitable exchanges (which in Hagen are based largely on individual partnerships) can only be conducted between persons who are on friendly terms and with whom credit is thus secure. This leads to a preference for contracting marriages with known and relatively friendly groups. On the one hand, then, marriage rules are concerned with negative prohibitions on unions with persons already related; on the other hand, there is a preference for marriage with groups with whom prior contacts exist. Such groups are in "alliance" with one another, for intermarriage should ideally be accompanied by positive, friendly relations and carries, among other things, an expectation of military help in times of stress.

Alliances affect individual choices, not through demarcating marriageable categories of kin but by defining where, for political reasons, it is best to marry. In replication of group alliance, affines are also seen as allied to each other. Marriage choices further involve personal preferences. Thus, the advantages which a particular affinal connection may offer perhaps lead to an alliance quite independent of group political relations. The feelings of the prospective husband and wife must be given some weight. These may coincide with other preferences; or they may, on the contrary, lead to decisions which run counter not only to political alliances but also to the desired connections their respective kin would like to make.

Patterns of Intermarriage

The majority of marriages made by men at Buk are with women living within a radius of about two hours' walk (perhaps eight to ten miles). At Kelua a more extensive network of government roads and the existence of Hagen market, a centre of communication, have resulted in a wider spread of marriages. The recent migration of Elti themselves from the Temboka area, and their maintenance of links there, contribute to the fact that living Elti men have contracted marriages with 35 different Melpa and Temboka tribes; twice as many Kawelka having married into only 27 tribes. It is to the Kawelka and other Northern Melpa groups that the following discussion mainly refers.

In the past marriages might be made far afield for the purpose of establishing specific trade connections, but these were not common. Vicedom (1943–8:2:201) describes how unpopular this sometimes was with women. Occasionally marriages are arranged nowadays with coastal workers and Europeans in Hagen town, in the hopes of gaining access to large amounts of Australian currency.

Of marriages made by Kawelka men, 15% are within Kawelka, and a further 58% with neighbouring tribes.[1] In larger tribes (where more

---

[1] i.e. those sharing a common border. Figures are given in Strathern, J. M. & A. A. (1969). They are based on all the wives ever married by living Kawelka men (328) together with the wives of their dead contemporaries (full total, 380 wives).

neighbouring clans may also be members of the single tribe) the proportion of intra-tribal marriages can be much higher. Because of the wide geographical sprawl of some tribal territories, a more meaningful unit of analysis is the clan. The first impression that propinquity is an overriding factor in the placement of marriages has to be modified.

The three clans of Kawelka tribe at Buk live within a compact area, so that the neighbours of one clan are near-neighbours of the other two. Yet there are internal differences between them in the proportions of intra- and extra-tribal marriages.[1] This is also so of the larger Tipuka tribe (population 2419, with eight exogamous units); some clans have contracted some 30–40% of their marriages within Tipuka, while one exogamous clan pairs show as many as 50% intra-tribal marriages. The latter borders on clans of the W^{e}lyi tribe, which themselves have even more (55%) intra-tribal unions. Although the size of the tribe and the number of its exogamous units is relevant to contrasts in rates between Kawelka and Tipuka as a whole, demography alone cannot explain differences in the internal rates between separate clans of a single tribe. We may note in addition that the population size of W^{e}lyi (1224) is nearer to Kawelka (860) than to Tipuka (2419).

A significant contributory factor is the quality of political relations between groups, and here all clans have their own unique configurations. Nearby clans are classed either as traditional enemies (*el parka wamb*) or as being sometimes in an enemy and sometimes in an ally relation (*el øninga wamb*). The parameters of *el parka* relations are fairly stable, in that particular groups acquire an enduring reputation as the traditional enemies of others. The preference is for marriage not with these but with *el øninga wamb*, minor enemies. In the past, the tenor of relations with *el øninga* was variable. Such groups might be associated for periods of time with the kind of hostility expected of *el parka* enemies (e.g. between hostile clans of a single tribe); while with others of this category the relationship alternated between minor bickering and emphatic alliance against outsiders. But enmities were not expected to persist, and hostilities could usually be terminated with peace-making ceremonies. This was not possible between major enemies. While groups are no longer

---

[1] Kundmbo clan has the smallest number of intra-tribal unions (11·5% of its total) and the largest number of marriages with bordering tribes (nearly 62%). The same proportions for Membo are 14·5% and 54·8%; for Mandembo 19% and 56·5%.

mobilized as enemies or allies in warfare, they are still thought of in terms of these categories.[1]

Marriages made by two Kawelka clans show the preferences quite clearly. They are near-neighbours of four tribes, Minembi, Kombukla, Tipuka and Klamakae. Over the last two generations they have taken three times as many wives from Tipuka and Klamakae (combined population 2660), their allies and minor enemies, as from their major enemies, Minembi and Kombukla (whose combined total is appreciably greater, 4355).

Although Hageners often talk about major and minor enemy relations as though tribes were involved, alliances established by individual clans may run counter to the supposed orientation of their tribe. It is this which distinguishes the marriage patterns of the individual Kawelka clans. Kawelka as a whole are spoken of as major enemies to the Minembi–Kombukla pair, and as minor enemies/allies of Tipuka. At a lower level this ideology holds for only two of the three clans;[2] the third has established its own alliances. Its lower rate of intermarriage with the other two, and its concentration of marriages with clans of bordering tribes (such as Minembi), stem from this. At the other end of the Meka valley, the Welyi were, in the recent past, involved in protracted warfare with neighbours on both sides, and thus tended to find wives from within their own tribe. The Tipuka clan pair with the highest ratio of within-tribe marriage borders directly on Welyi: it was the antagonism between neighbours here which made it turn to women from other Tipuka groups. By contrast, those clans sharing a long boundary with Kawelka, their allies and minor enemies, as well as with a friendly clan from an otherwise major enemy tribe (Minembi Yelipi), have contracted a higher proportion of extra-tribal marriages, the majority being with these friendly groups. The desirability of marrying minor rather than major enemies is an explicit dogma; if they are neighbours, such a choice is also advantageous to the individual affines who do not have to pass through hostile territory on their visits, and especially to the wives who like to marry near home. Hostility between neighbours reduces inter-marriage, although it is likely to be higher between them than between *el parka* enemies who also live some distance apart. It is important to

---

[1] I use both past and present tenses in my account here. References to fighting (and to overt accusations of poisoning) all refer to a time prior to pacification. The structure of warfare is treated in detail in Strathern, A. J. (1971).

[2] Membo and Mandembo as opposed to Kundmbo. (See footnote on p. 67).

reiterate, however, that political alliances are complex. We have seen that individual clans may establish independently friendly relations with clans of otherwise major enemy tribes. Individuals are also free to marry into hostile groups. Here their clansmen are not involved in the alliance, friendly relations being restricted to the immediate affines linked by the marriage. Such unions may prove brittle with the outbreak of fighting, becoming immediately vulnerable to dissolution through suspicions of poisoning. Intensive intermarriage is thus discouraged. On the other hand, marriages with groups that have been fighting as minor enemies can lead to a diminishing of previous hostility, which in turn encourages further marriages.

Intermarriage with people who are relatively friendly (i.e. allies cum minor enemies) means several things. Alliance in the past entailed mutual aid in warfare against outsiders, limited fighting between themselves; nowadays, alternating superiority and inferiority in ceremonial exchange. These aspects are duplicated at the personal level in relations between affines. Affinal kin should give one another aid and protection, may expect to give and receive *moka* and are involved in certain specific transactions. When a clan is given refuge by a sponsor on the strength of a marriage tie, it is likely to consolidate its position by making further marriages; the same phenomenon occurs if an individual family finds refuge with an affine. Thus an original marriage between Elti and Ndika Opramb clan led to the Elti seeking protection from Ndika; since then there have been ten unions with the same clan. Similarly, two Tipuka sons of a Kawelka Membo woman living on Kawelka land near Buk have themselves taken a wife from two Kawelka Mandembo clan-sections. The daughter of one of them and the son of the other have also made Kawelka marriages. At the back of such arrangements is the expectation that it is only where multiple marriages link groups that true friendliness exists, for the interests of individual affines can modify the clan relationship (cf. Brown, 1964).

When fighting broke out, affinal and matrilateral kin might come to their kinsmen's aid. Support in such circumstances was more likely to be forthcoming when they were from minor and not major enemy groups. Affinal and matrilateral or sororilateral kin could expect protection from their immediate relatives.[1] However, individuals sometimes

---

[1] Vicedom (1943–8:2:82) describes how in the midst of fighting a man might run to the side of his affine in the opposite party, protecting him from attack and his fields and houses from ruin. "This often happens under protest (from his clansmen), but the protection is recognised".

cut across group alignments in giving such support. In the case of marriage with a major enemy, the wife's brother and sister's husband would refrain from direct conflict, although they might not stop their clansmen attacking. A man whose affine had been killed in such a bout was said not to hold it against his clansmen, for the affine had after all belonged to a major enemy group. For in actuality, the friendliness of affines is tinged with hostility, being itself partly modified by intergroup relations, and where major enemies come unambiguously into conflict, the hostile element may be overt.

The amicable and profitable transactions which should typify affinal relations, and the sentiments felt towards sisters' children, are incompatible with sustained hostilities. Thus the network of interpersonal relations between minor enemies would be used to encourage pacification. Between major enemies marriages are rare and the concept of making peace is for the most part inapplicable. Where minor enemies were anxious for peace, individual big-men who were prominent in encouraging a settlement might be looked on as prompted by a consideration of their own affinal links with one or other side. Marriages were contracted after a bout of fighting, specifically to mark the disputants' desire for peace. Both sides might provide women, the exchange of bridewealths being a basis for future financial transactions. Even between groups who were not major enemies, however, fear of reprisals might dominate desire for marital alliance.

*An elderly Elti woman described how as a young girl she had been courted by a Maninga man. She was oiled and sent to his house, with an initial gift of cooked pig, once his immediate kin had indicated that the bridewealth was ready. But the bridal party was accosted on the way by other Maninga who said they could not allow the marriage to proceed: they were afraid of poison from the Elti—the groom's father had been killed by the bride's mother's brother in a past encounter between Maninga and the Elti-Penambe pair. Traditionally, there was little fear of poisoning between the two tribes, who were minor enemies; it was the context of the particular marriage following recent hostilities which led to suspicions. The groom was said to have followed the bridal party as it turned home, and, from grief and anger, like a mourner at the death of a close relative, cut off a finger joint with his axe.

Enmities and alliances which sprang from warfare relations in the past, and values associated with the intermarriage of allies, are still pertinent today. Traditional coalitions and confrontations are re-created in the war payments which provide pretexts for much modern exchange activity between clans. Reciprocal exchanges between ex-allies pay both for past help which had involved losses on the part of the helpers, and for killings inflicted directly on one another as ex-minor enemies. These exchanges, falling under the rubric *moka*, all involve heavy financial investment between the clans concerned, and pre-existing affinal and matrilateral links are vehicles for the transactions and provide some surety that a return will be made. When in 1964 the Tipuka Kitepi were trying to raise resources for a *moka* with their Kawelka allies, outsiders commented on the safety of the investment: Kawelka are Kitepi *pamal* (matri- and sororilateral kin), "they drink from one breast". One observer referred to the Kitepi as "wanting to pay for the breast-milk of the Kawelka"—they were giving war payments to clans from which they had obtained wives. Political reasons for such payments can thus be charged with notions about the appropriateness of making gifts to people with whom kinship is shared, people who, from the point of view of the investors, will be reliable partners. The desire to honour the debts lies in the fact that it is not only group prestige at stake but the personal reputation of in-laws and maternal relatives with their kin.

Since ex-allies/minor enemies are most involved in such exchanges with one another, continuing intermarriage with these groups is politically advantageous. A comparison of marriages made by senior and junior generations of Kawelka shows that on the whole, younger people continue to marry traditional allies and to avoid traditional enemies. That the pattern is not completely replicated in the junior generation is due partly to the functioning of rules which, as I describe later, militate against close consanguines repeating marriages. At the same time, the cessation of warfare has brought with it a gradual trend towards marrying further afield. This is consistent with plans that envisage large-scale group exchanges with more distant tribes, with whom contacts in the past would have been slight. A persistently inhibiting barrier against contracting marriages with ex-major enemies is the fear of poison (*kopna* or *konga*). It was particularly major enemies who used poison as a weapon of revenge, and the ban on open warfare has not removed this fear. While minor enemies may employ poison on occasion, major enemies are habitual poisoners. Although public accusations are not often made nowadays, deaths are still attributed to these groups.

Poison is thought of as a lethal substance typically administered in food. It is passed from hand to hand, from avenger to victim through intermediaries. People can avoid associating directly with major enemies who might poison them, but they cannot avoid having indirect links with them. Everyone is vulnerable through the marriages they and their clan-mates contract. While one's affines may be allies, the affines of one's affines quite probably have contacts with major enemies. Affinal ties are roads to productive exchanges, but the same interpersonal links can also become roads for poison. This is especially likely in the ambiguous situations of warfare between allies or marriage with major enemies; but it is a threat which any marriage indirectly brings. Women are suspected as agents in these chains.

Exchange Marriage

Close intermarriage between groups becomes a charter for their friendship. Two intermarried clans may speak of themselves as being *pamal* (matrilateral kin) to each other. Occasionally intermarriage is so intensive that further marriages are felt to be inappropriate, and the groups agree to intermarry no more. They set up a bond of "antigamy",[1] and henceforth regard each other as "brothers". This has happened between Elti and one of the clans of its pair tribe, Penambe (some people even saying the relationship now exists with the whole Penambe tribe). Two groups migrating into a common area may establish antigamy between them as a basis for friendship, as Elti have done with a Kombukla clan. This practice reveals an interesting contrast between the alliance of intermarrying groups and the solidarity shared by clan brothers. For although intermarriage does create amicable relations, the greater solidarity is between those whose ties are not disturbed by the transfer of women. Ties between affines are marked by a degree of tension; thus when people are referring to friendly groups they tend to stress the matrilateral rather than the affinal aspects of the link.[2] There is, how-

---

[1] "Antigamy" is used by Ryan (1969:163) for the bond established between two Mendi (Southern Highlands) lineages, after a single marriage has taken place which precludes further unions. I use it here to contrast the relationship of "non-marrying" which results from an accumulation of previous marriages ("antigamy") with that resulting from descent or common name ties ("exogamy"); solidarity may be expressed in the idiom of "brotherhood" in both cases.

[2] The *pam* (MB-ZS) tie is stressed particularly when the friendliness of the group is at issue; following serious fighting a clan may stop referring to its now enemy as *pamal*, only the immediate MB or ZS continuing to use this term for each other. The same groups can also be thought of as *koklomal* (*koklom* = WB − ZH). A man uses *pam* for all the members of his immediate mother's brother's clan, and his half-brothers follow him in this. But others of his clansmen will use *pam* (MB) or *koklom* (WB) according to their own generation relationship with individuals.

ever, one set of idioms applicable to inter-group relations which draws directly on the fact of transfer; the concept that clans "exchange" women. Although details of this have appeared elsewhere (Strathern, A. J. and A. M., 1969), the relevance of the institution to my theme warrants its further description.

Such an exchange comes about when a clan has both given to and received women from another. The phrase *amb rop rui* means a "bartering" of women; *amb timb ak^ek ngui* refers to the way a reciprocating marriage retraces (literally, "harvests") the footsteps taken at the first transaction. The advantages of a double link are stated clearly. "People who fight us, they poison us. If we just take their women as wives they will bring us poison, but if we give them our sisters as well then they will be our friends and we will no longer poison each other." The speaker (an old man who remembered the days of fighting) indicated that sisters are to be trusted, even if wives are not.[1] But such statements are not made simply in reference to practical gains. As elsewhere in the Highlands (e.g. Brown, 1964:338; Glasse and Meggitt, 1969:10), the notion of a reciprocal transfer of women symbolizes alliance.

The exchange of women is likened to an exchange of pigs or shell valuables. *Amb ngoklngena amb ngond, kng ngoklngena kng ngond*: "I give women as I am given them, and give pig as I am given pig". In *moka*, pigs and shells are exchanged for each other, but ideally a reversal of the initial transaction should effect an eventual transfer of pigs for pigs and shells for shells. In the same way, while at each marriage bridewealth is given for a woman, a second woman should ultimately be given in return for the first, and thus a bridewealth for a bridewealth.[2] But unlike *moka* transactions, receiving or giving a bride does not in reality create debt or credit. A marriage puts no individual or group under the specific obligation to find a woman in return. Particular exchanges of women, in other words, have little to do directly with the *arrangements* of marriages, although they symbolize the preference for marrying where links already exist. To this extent, Hagen exchange marriage is in no way comparable to institutions resulting from prescriptive or preferential rules that specify certain kin categories as desirable marriage partners. Among the Southern Highlands Huli (Glasse, 1968:53), and among the

---

[1] i.e. sisters would not succumb to persuasion from their husband's group to poison their own brothers, as a wife may be persuaded by her kin to poison her husband's clansmen.

[2] "Indirect exchange" ("circulation of women by means of a bride-price") is a possible stage in transactions which, on completion, are seen as "direct exchange" (cf. Pouwer, 1966:283).

Kuma (Reay, 1959a:60), marriages may actually be organized according to the dictum, "We exchange sisters". When a Hagener refers to two clans exchanging their sisters he is using a figure of speech: lineages or (sub-) sub-clans are the units which negotiate marriages and they cannot exchange women with units of comparable order. A Hagener is forbidden by marriage rules to send his own sister to the lineage from which he acquired a wife; nor does his acquiring a wife place him in a position of having to supply a woman to his wife's clan at large. What is meant by "women exchange" is that, *post facto*, the sum of independently arranged marriages between two clans puts them into a relationship analogous to the alliance created by the exchange of *moka* goods: it is an evaluation of this relationship.

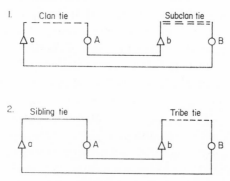

Fig. 2. How exchange marriages may be reckoned. In both cases the clans or tribes to which A and B belong may be seen as exchanging women.

After the event, two specific marriages may be cited as reciprocating each other. This is a systematization of the concept of exchange, rather than a reference to factors which determined the choice of spouses. Thus, "We sent our woman A over there, and they returned their woman B whom we married". People tend to mention marriages with which they are best acquainted: if a person's own clan has given to and received women from a single sub-clan he will cite this as an exchange; on the other hand he may consider marriages with people who are related only as members of one tribe if on his own side a brother–sister pair is involved. (See Fig. 2.)

Appendix IV indicates the manner in which men from Elti and Kawelka described 153 exchange marriages their respective tribes had made. Here I note that in only five cases did two informants ever cite precisely the same combination of marriages as comprising an exchange.[1] While individuals may link exchange marriages with the generalized good relations between two groups, their statements can also refer to their personal cross-cutting ties with perhaps otherwise hostile groups. In the recent past Elti have contracted 339 marriages (including those of men now dead) with 51 different tribes. With 22 they have both given and received wives, but exchange marriages were cited to me for only eleven of these. These eleven tribes represent the locus of nearly two-thirds of all marriages. Six are groups with whom they have become friendly after the move to Kelua; another is their ally and pair tribe, Penambe; but the remaining four are enemy groups, including some *el parka* major enemies with whom individuals have contracted independently friendly ties not shared by their clansmen. The Kawelka pattern is rather different. I take the instance of Mandembo clan, who have given women to, and received women from, eleven other tribes, but clans from only four of these were designated as exchanging with them. One recent exchange (1963–4) involves a Kombukla (*el parka*) clan, but all others are between Mandembo and Membo or with clans of the ally/minor enemy category.

The concept of exchanging women is used particularly to typify relations between ally/minor enemy groups, being both drawn from an analogy with *moka* and used where *moka* or alliance relations exist in actuality. A completed exchange implies equality; but as in *moka*, and as in warfare with one's allies, an incomplete exchange brings inequality. A Hagener may enumerate the total number of women who have passed between two groups and add the balance of wives *not* exchanged for. Thus: "We have sent them two and they sent us six". The definition of "we" clearly lays such statements open to different arithmetical interpretations. In enumerating marriages for which there has been no return people are making assertions of superiority. The superior are not those who have provided women, but those who have had the wealth to gain the most brides from the other side.[2] "We could raise the resources to buy six of their women, but they are so poor they could take only two

---

[1] Several of the same marriages were paired in different combinations (153 exchanges being derived from 236 marriages).

[2] Individual affines are not formally superior or inferior to one another, although their respective successes in wealth exchanges may point up relative prestige. A husband does, however feel something of an enduring obligation to his wife's kin, the initiative for making exchanges, lying with him.

of ours." Jokingly, it may be added that those who had the bridewealth to "buy" more than others could "buy" from them have "won" (*kuk mondop tinimon*, "we take the flower").

"We say to the other group, 'We have daughters: you come and take our children.' But the big-men of the other group admit, 'We have no shells and pigs.' So we say we have won over them." (Elti)

"We win them all when we have given a prestation and our partners cannot find the valuables to return to us. In the same way we win when we have married off all our young men and another group has not been able to match this." (Kawelka)

In the face of claims to superiority because of the number of women a group has obtained from another, the wife-givers may refer to a different set of values.

In 1964, the most recent of several marriages which a small refugee group (X) had made with its host clan (Y) was transacted. In the bridewealth speeches, a big-man from the groom's side (the refugee group) jibed at their hosts, saying how superior they themselves were for snatching all the latter's girls away—the hosts obviously felt they could not compete because they were unable to raise the bridewealth to marry their (X's) girls in return. The leader on the hosts' side, who was also the bride's father, retaliated that it was patent that he should draw to himself all the valuables (i.e. in the form of bridewealth) of the refugees, since they could never repay him enough for having been rescued when they were near the point of extermination.

The bride's father had begun by referring to the fact that the refugee group (X) was due to make *moka* to them (Y), and he was collecting in their shells and pigs all the time in *moka* as well as in bridewealth. To the groom's father he said how pleased he was to be "eating" this wealth, and he enumerated all the marriages for which his group had received bridewealth. Another man of the bride's clan (Y) then referred to the fact that the groom's side (X) had "won" by taking so many of their girls but insinuated that it was only through the children these girls had borne that they had any strength. All this was delivered in what seemed a quite moderate manner, and in a speech in which the groom's father countered that of course it was they, X, who were the strong ones to be able to buy all Y's wives, he also thanked Y for the generosity with which they returned part of the bridewealth. The big-man of Y then began commanding X to make their pig-*moka* quickly, saying that the whole group should "work" for him. This sparked off the vituperative speech from the X big-man (of a related but not the same sub-clan as the groom) which I quote above. The big-men on both sides shouted wildly at each other. Subsequent speeches turned to the matter of the bridewealth distribution and were more conciliatory in tone, although another important man from X, while commenting favourably on the return the bride's kin were making, also said with some sullenness that they would find their *moka* pigs in their own good time: what right had the Y leader to shout at them? It seems to have been this resentment at the latter's peremptory *moka* demands which led to the competitiveness displayed on this occasion.

The friendship of intermarriage, then, entails both reciprocity and competition.

Marriage Prohibitions

From the point of view of the individual, replication of marriages with neighbouring, friendly clans means that he (or she) is likely to marry into a clan with which his own is already related. But it is not simply that marriage follows alliance. Each union also generates its own relatively exclusive ties between the immediate kinsmen of the spouses; and in this sense, marriage creates alliance. From the generalized friendly relations between clans, a new marriage sets up specific affinal bonds between their component lineages. Moreover, some marriages are made with distant or major enemy clans. In the past Tipuka and Kawelka maintained links with tribes on the Jimi side of the Sepik-Wahgi Divide; although these were not regularly called on as allies to help fighting in the M^eka valley, their territories could be used as refuge if clans were under severe stress. Nowadays a clan engaged in *moka* with its ex-allies needs some access to outside resources in order to raise finance. As well as having affines in the groups with whom *moka* is contemplated it is advantageous to seek connections outside this network. The intensive concentration of marriage ties in some directions is thus countered by dispersion in others (cf. Barnes, 1962:8).

Statements that persons should not marry where they trace kin connections encourage a spread of marriages, in the same way as statements that one should marry into familiar groups support the concentration of ties with allies. Superficially, these appear contradictory. But when people comment that they "marry their *pamal*", the reference is taken to mean a group related by matrilateral ties, rather than the individual's own matrilateral kin. Indeed, it is quite inappropriate to interpret the generalised tie as specifying a precise kin relationship. Whenever I suggested that such statements must mean that a person is therefore marrying a cross-cousin (*pelpam*), I was rebuked. When the point of reference is the individual it is quite wrong to think of people as marrying kinsmen. It is the existing obligations between specific kinsmen that Hageners see as a bar to marriage. "When we kill pigs, we invite our relatives and all eat together. If we married them, how could we distribute pig?". These are supported also in the sentiment that it is a good thing when a lineage spreads its ties. Each marriage provides contact with a range of people, and may be used as the basis for transactions between classificatory affines. Affines not only have obligations to one another but also enjoy the privilege of utilising such connections (as in ceremonial exchange). Mae-Enga say that it wastes bridewealth to re-affirm existing links (Meggitt, 1965:95); the Hagen view is rather that a second marriage would diminish the exchange potential of the first.

To marry where one already has relatives shows disrespect for these people. A man who took a wife from his mother's brother's sub-clan would have to ignore the close tie he already has with these people through his mother's brother. One sanction against such an act is the anger (*popokl*) of the affronted kinsman, which may bring ghostly vengeance on the guilty pair. Again, for a man to marry his cross cousin's wife's sister would be to ignore the cross cousin, through whom he has already an indirect link with her group. One can, however, avoid the anger of such a relative by consulting him and asking him to act as an intermediary in negotiations. If the kinsman supplies a woman in this way, he clearly concurs in the union. On the other hand, a kinsman who is by-passed may claim compensation: "I am here, and you went over my head; now you can pay me!" The typical gesture is for the offended person to light a fire in the path of the bridal party (*amb ndip mon*, "woman fire road") and demand a pig or shell from the bridewealth given for the woman. Usually the groom's side (occasionally the bride's kin) provide this. Although it is mainly men who claim compensation, the woman whose marriage created the link may also be looked upon as injured, and in some cases receives payment. In other cases, the woman may press her son or brother to make claims.

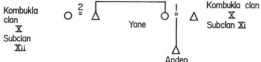

Fig. 3. Relationships in a "wrong-marriage" compensation case.

*A Kawelka woman, Yane, married into a Kombukla clan some forty years ago. Her younger (full) brother then took a wife from a different sub-clan (*rapa*) but from the same clan, although Yane already had a son, Andep, to whom he was mother's brother. In the account (from a member of Yane's clan) the son was described as demanding compensation although he was only a young lad (estimated 14 or 15 years old), and in fact it was Yane who put pressure on her brother to make recompense. Yane's husband is not mentioned. The brother handed over a pig and a pearl shell; Yane took the pig and Andep kept the shell.

The brother here married his full sister's clan daughter. In fact statements reveal some ambiguity towards this category of women, as they also do towards marriage with a full father's sister's clan daughter, which some say is permissible. Marriage with a full FZ *sub-clan*, D on the other hand, is not (see Strathern, A.J. and A.M., 1969: Table 1A). Such cases depend on whether the person making a claim can get it recognized. There is also a slight ideological sympathy (cf. the idiom of "exchanging women") for taking a wife from a group to which a clans woman has gone by contrast with repeating the direction from which a wife has already been taken, so that a "close" marriage with a patrilateral cross cousin may be excused for this reason, where a similarly close marriage with a matrilateral cross cousin will lead to requests for compensation payments.[1]

The following table is based on 15 cases, both past and recent, in which claims for compensation were successfully made. I heard about other cases (19) in which such claims were unsuccessful or which from the point of view of some of my informants merited compensation, although information was lacking as to whether this was paid; the totals of these are indicated in brackets.

TABLE VIII

Claims for compensation made by women and men affronted at a "close" marriage

Type of classificatory relation of bride to groom	Man	Number of cases in which compensation paid to Woman	Man and Woman	Total
MBD	2		1	3 (5)[a]
MZD		1		1 (1)
BWZ	3	1	1	5 (7)
FZD	1			1 (2)
ZD			1	1 (0)
ZHZ	3			3 (1)
MZ	1			1 (1)
Other				(2)
Total	10	2	3	15 (19)

[a] For explanation, see text.

[1] Cf. the large number of claims for marriages with a BWZ in Table VIII (repeating a brother's marriage) by comparison with ZHZ (taking from where a sister has gone).

Once, depending on context, a clan's or sub-clan's lower level units (sub-sub-clans, lineages) have each made a marriage with those of another sub-clan, no further unions can be contracted between the two groups.[1] A man cannot marry the sub-clan sisters of his own wife (though he may marry a clan sister, and others of his sub-clan may take women from outside his wife's lineage) nor may he marry the immediate (lineage) sisters of his own sub-clan brothers' wives. Direct sister-exchange is precluded, two siblings being unable to marry into the same sub-clan (*rapa*). *Rapa*, however, is a term applicable to various levels of grouping, and since there is also variety in clan segmentation patterns, the span relevant to a particular situation is open to manipulation. Persuasive definitions can make a marriage seem less close than others might assert. A duplication of marriages thus may or may not be defined as trespass. Nevertheless, the dogma remains that kinsmen should not be marriage partners. The notion exists that members of a *rapa* share blood (*mema*). It is hoped that every marriage will produce children who will become blood kin to the two *rapa* themselves related affinally. The expectation of this is perhaps asociated with *rapa* prohibitions between affines; in the case of a childless marriage terminated in death, divorce or long-standing childlessness the rule is waived and further intermarriage is possible.

It would be misleading to overemphasise the injunctions contained in people's statements about where one may or may not marry. Supernatural sanctions inhibit marriage with close consanguines, genealogically related kin who are reckoned to share blood, but beyond this the definition of an improper situation is open to bargaining. When it said that marriages should not be made with a particular category of kin, this is as much a symbol of the closeness of the relationship as a rule. Thus, it may be said that a man should not marry his own mother's sister's own daughter (MZD) nor any of her (the daughter's) *rapa* (here sub-clan) sisters. In the case of the MZHZ, however, the prohibition includes also her half-sisters but not her sub-clan sisters, who are marriageable. If we were to take these statements as absolute rules, we should have to admit they are contradictory. The MZD (=MZHD) and MZHZ belong to the same sub-clan, only a generation line distinguishing them, an incomplete criterion since generation equiva-

---

[1] A more accurate formulation than the truncated version which appears in Strathern, A. J. and A. M. (1969:140–1).

lences cannot be estimated with any accuracy outside the lineage. Clearly, there will be females of this sub-clan who might be defined as either. The same is true also for prohibitions on a ZD by contrast with ZHZ; for FMBDD and FMBDHZ, and so on. The point is that an individual may see the quality of his ties with the sub-clan in question in two ways. To take the example of "MZD": the women of this group thought of as daughters of one's MZ are seen as cognates ("blood kin" in a wide sense) and thus it is appropriate that the whole *rapa* should fall under the prohibition. On the other hand, seen as sisters of the MZH the women are affines, and the prohibition has only a narrow extension. In such cases it would rest with the intermediary MZ (and her husband) to define the propriety of a marriage.

For different reasons, not because relations are already too close for further intermarriage, but because intermarriage would bring too close persons in a hostile relationship, it is dangerous to marry into a *rapa* whose members have been killed by one's own clansmen. Women do not forget their dead brothers. The fear here is that such marriages would provide roads for poison. Rules of this nature are clearly aspects of the more general preference to avoid marriage with major enemies or minor enemies with whom relations are worsening.

We may note that the quite considerable restriction on a duplication of marriage ties with already related persons makes remarkable the very extent to which allied groups are in fact intermarried. Where many marriages already exist, further unions may be justified by reference to the strict agnatic status of the spouses. Clansmen of different patrifilial origins are technically able to contract marriages their fellow-clansmen are prohibited from making. In the eleven marriages Elti have made with Ndika Opramb, (see p. 69), three of the spouses on the Elti side can be reckoned as "non-agnates".

A further entailment is that women do not marry into the same lineages as their close sisters. Settlements usually focus on a lineage rather than on wider groups, so it is thus made unlikely that two sisters residing virilocally would be living at the same place.[1] Depending on the location of settlements in relation to clan or tribe boundaries, women may have sisters in the vicinity or more distant (e.g. clan) sisters or father's sisters married nearby. The chances are, however, that girls from a single lineage will be geographically dispersed.

---

[1] Not all women do reside virilocally; but it is not very usual for one married sister to take up residence with another sister (with or without her husband).

Courting and Negotiations

Prohibitions which forbid kinsfolk to marry also forbid sexual relations between them. This applies equally to courting. Courting parties (*amb kanan*) are attended by nubile girls and by married and unmarried men (a once-married woman can no longer participate). While the rest of the company sing love songs, another of the men "turns head" (as in the Pidgin English phrase),[1] perhaps fifteen or twenty crowded into the women's house where two or three girls are seated. Strictly, a pair who would be forbidden as marriage partners because of a too-close kin relationship cannot turn head with each other. Courting parties are frequently held the night following a large *moka* festival which has brought many visitors—and it is new girls from other clans, staying with their relatives, who attract the local men. In mid-August 1964 Kawelka Membo and Mandembo gave their final solicitory *moka* to Tipuka Kitepi and Oklembo; there were 19 courting parties held near Buk between August 4th and 17th over the time of the festival, and a total of 25 in the two months between July and September.

The climax of such a season of courting parties comes when girls who have turned head with particular men on more than one occasion accompany them back to their settlements, where they spend the day and the following night. This is known as *amb keaka* ("temporary woman"). They are then returned to their own kin, oiled and decorated by the men, with small presents for their fathers or brothers. If several girls from one clan, along with visitors, have gone *keaka* with men of another, one of the more energetic of their senior kinswomen may take it on herself to round them up. Her presence also makes it more likely that gifts will be given. Once this has happened, the courting parties finish.

Although it is expected that *amb kanan* and *keaka* may lead to more lasting relationships, they can also be entered into by people with no further intentions in mind. Overt sexual advances, and sexual intercourse, are excluded, girls at courting parties being chaperoned by older women, and a man who acquires a reputation for being too adventurous in his style of turning head may find himself the object of public ridicule. Any suggestion that a girl is dispensing sexual favours is thought by her kin to prejudice her later chances of a good match; nevertheless, at the

---

[1] The pair kneel with their foreheads pressed together, and sway backwards and forwards and from side to side. A description is given in Vicedom and Tischner (1943–8:2:190f) and Strathern A. J. and A. M. (1971:ch. 3).

time there are romantic hopes that more lasting affairs will come of such encounters. Young men boast that they so win over the girls they have courted they are able to conduct clandestine affairs with them after their marriage to someone else. A woman who becomes particularly enamoured of a young man may, on her own initiative, "sit down" at his mother's house. If she has not gone away of her own accord within about two weeks, the embarrassed parents of the boy try to persuade her to go or else are forced to think about raising a bridewealth. This dramatic public action on the part of the girl can embarrass the man she has so openly confronted with her expressed desires. At the same time, in retrospect, men take pride in having girls flock to them. One of the indices of a festival's success is the large number of young women who run to the houses of the irresistably handsome dancers afterwards.

Girls of nubile age enjoy a degree of freedom. Daughters help their mothers in garden work and with other household chores from the time they are able to carry things in the netbag over their heads. This is especially so in the case of an only child; members of large polygynous families are more often to be found, even when young, with their peers in play-groups. But at adolescence much time is spent in the company of contemporaries and away on visits with kinsfolk, over the period of courting, which is at the most a brief two or three years. A girl who visits an elder sister married to a fairly remote group becomes an object of local interest, not only to distant clansmen of the sister's husband, but to men of neighbouring clans, and *amb kanan* sessions are held for her. Long absence from home makes the parents anxious. Visits may end abruptly with the mother briskly removing an unwilling daughter. Girls differ considerably, however, in the extent of their enthusiasms. Some turn head rarely, if at all, while others take a flamboyant pride in the number of men with whom they have attended parties—men sometimes drawn from as many as 13 or 14 different clans.

While a young man himself enthusiastically courts the prettiest girls, he is likely to be more cautious than they are about making positive moves towards marriage. The girl's general character becomes an issue when she is thought of as a potential wife. Moreover, in the case of a first marriage a youth is aware of his dependence on the approval of his seniors for help with bridewealth. There is more to it than that she should be known to be hardworking and knowledgeable in household matters; the very qualities of vivacity and independence which make someone popular at courting parties do not necessarily auger well for the faithfulness Hagen husbands look for in their wives. The reputation of *amb kanan* girls actually rests on their eagerness to join in the parties, their skills at turning head and their general high spiritedness, rather than on sexual forwardness. On the whole, the discouragement of pre-marital sexual relations is effective; if anyone does acquire a reputation for promiscuity, their kin try to marry them far away. Where she is known, the parents of such a daughter cannot expect a good bridewealth. Even the attraction of having to pay only a negligible amount on the groom's part does not offset the undesirability of a promiscuous wife, and only a poor man regards such women as potential brides. A few individuals, often those who have had such a reputation in their youth, remain permanently independent (*amb epta*, "spinster").

A poor man who has been disappointed in his hopes of support for bridewealth from kinsmen, and is doubtful of his brothers' repeated promises, may try to press claims through *amb kanan*. One youngish Tipuka third in a family with his own father dead, attempted in 1964–5 to do just this. He was the local leader of a band of youths who participated vigorously in several seasons of courting parties, and turned head with a variety of girls. He put claims on one girl from a pair clan on the grounds that her parents had invited him to teach her how to turn head in the first place. He attempted to consolidate this by labouring in her parents' garden for one day—but the understanding he thought he had gained with them came to nothing. Although a woman may "go to" a man's house, forcible abduction by men is practically unknown; it occurred in the past only in the context of warfare, when fighters seized nubile women or the wives of their enemies as part of the spoils of war. Sometimes an enemy girl fleeing home to her kin would be taken by men through whose territory she was passing.

A young couple may establish a friendship through the exchange of small gifts; this is quite informal, and neither party has any claim to their return should the other marry elsewhere. The gifts are known as *kuimø* ("bridewealth"); nowadays they include money, cloth, beads, talcum powder and soap, and in the past consisted of small shell ornaments, perhaps a special catch of marsupials, and such like. A more certain suitor may make presents directly to the girl's father, but if she is sent to someone else will only be able to claim back any major valuable he had managed to raise.[1] The Hagen system allows individual spouses-

[1] Strauss (1962:322) and Vicedom (1943–8:2:187) describe formal bethrothal gifts in the past; Strauss notes that they were occasional arrangements made with exceptionally friendly groups.

to-be some, though not entire, choice in whom they marry. The theme of thwarted sweethearts contributes to the romance that surrounds courting sessions. Parents come between the would-be lovers—a drama illustrated by the speaker pressing two fingers together in an inverted V (Λ) and then moving them apart (II). Personal choice is almost invariably exercised in the re-marriage of women once divorced or widowed, unless the first marriage has been very brief and the girl is still young. Otherwise "improper" unions are tolerated for widows or divorcees when the responsibility for negotiation does not rest on their kinsmen, and "it is a matter up to the woman herself". A girl's first marriage, however, is more often arranged by her elders.

It is the fathers or male guardians on either side who make the initial move; if mothers have different preferences, then they try to influence the child rather than oppose (and probably be contradicted by) their husband outright. Men sometimes complain that a bride has been persuaded by her mother or a female kins woman to marry only where it pleases the women. (It is typically women who act as go-between for sweethearts.) The kinds of considerations which influence the choices of the parents include: the capability of the prospective spouse, especially that of the bride, who, parents-in-law hope, will be hard working and obedient; the general wealth of the spouses' near kin; whether these live near or far; and whether they belong to groups with which marriages have been previously made by clansmen. Some of these points require comment.

In addition to the general preference for marrying into nearby friendly clans, the particular circumstances of a bride's parents may encourage them to look for a nearby son-in-law, who does not live too distant—typically if they have no sons of their own, and hope that the daughter will be able to visit them frequently. If marriages have previously been contracted with groups of one locality—particularly if the bride's clan have already sent a woman there—further marriages are thought to have more chance of being stable. Unions cannot of course be replicated between the identical lineages involved in the original union, but it is thought that if an older kinswoman is living near she will be a good influence on the young bride, in encouraging her to settle down. When a new marriage is made with a distant and otherwise relatively stranger

---

Such gifts also took the form of exchanges between the parents of prospective spouses, and there has been some administration pressure against this as an institution likely to foster "child marriage".

group, the first woman married there sometimes negotiates for another
from her clan to marry nearby: far from home, she feels estranged and
lonely—"Who will look after me when I am sick?"—and seeks the
company of a clan sister in this way .

To the bride's parents in particular, the wealth of the prospective
groom and/or his father is important, especially their ability to make a
good bridewealth payment. They are interested in overall financial
standing, but the crucial factor at the point of choosing between more
than one suitor will be a specific offer of bridewealth. Admittedly, generosity in this indicates adequate general resources, but Hageners stress
that it is the bridewealth exchanges themselves which above all must be
carried through honourably. This value may even outweigh other considerations, such as long term exchange prospects between the groups
concerned, or the desirability of further links with an ally.

> *About fifteen years ago, Kawelka Membo were negotiating for a girl from
> their pair clan, Mandembo. Membo youths had courted her at *amb kanan*
> parties, and it was understood that she was "marked" for one of them,
> although a specific groom had not been named and no bridewealth yet dis-
> played. Then bridewealth was offered to her father by a man from the
> enemy group, Kombukla Mongkopokae; Mandembo were said to have
> looked at the pigs and the shells and "shaken with excitement". While
> Mongkopokae were neighbours living on the borders of Mandembo terri-
> tory, they were by no means allies of Mandembo in the same way as Membo
> staunchly were; indeed Membo and Mandembo had together expanded
> their own territories at the expense of Mongkopokae. Membo were clearly
> disappointed at the arrangement, and arrived on the scene when the bride's
> people were distributing cooked pig (*penal kng*); they were given a leg in
> compensation. (Account from Mandembo.)

Compensation paid in this way is known by the same term (*amb ndip
mon*) as payments made at a too-close marriage; it may also be demanded by men of a clan neighbouring the bride's clan if her parents negotiate for marriage with *their* neighbours on the other side without
consulting them as intermediaries. In such cases, then, allied groups may
feel they have a claim on each other's women, either to take them as
wives for themselves, or else to negotiate for the marriages of these women
when the marriage road goes through their territory. There are also
bound to be individual kinsmen who will be affronted that they were not
asked to act as go-betweens.

Sometimes the immediate parents of the prospective spouses have
interests which clash with arrangements others would like to make.

Two Mandembo men living with their mother's agnates on Membo Oyambo clan territory, wanted a younger half-brother of theirs (by a different mother) to marry a girl from another Membo sub-clan (Roklambo). They had more or less promised (*ol ik nitinggil*) her father the good bridewealth he would receive from them all. Their own father, however, was willing to pay bridewealth for a girl who had come to his son's house from the distant R*e*mndi tribe, and the cheated Membo turned on the two brothers in anger. They themselves were angry that the marriage with R*e*mndi meant that they could not keep their word, and refused to contribute any bridewealth. The boy's father was helped by other men from their sub-sub-clan (1964–5).

The value put on bridewealth at the expense of other factors clearly facilitates a spread of marriages, as does visiting between distant kinsmen and the courting of female visitors. At the same time, the volume of visiting is greatest where there are several already existing connections between groups, and it would be wrong to give the impression that it is only foreign girls who are courted. In fact, *amb kanan* parties are regularly held between neighbours. At the time of the Tipuka-Kawelka *moka*, men who were precluded from possible marriage into the ally clans turned head with visitors, but there were others for whom marriage was still feasible, and sessions included ones between these men and local girls. There is a congruence between the tendency for prospective parents-in-law to look first to local, friendly clans and the fact that it is the young men and girls of these clans who are most likely to have participated in courting together.

If his father has a particular bride in mind, the young groom marrying for the first time will probably accept his choice with a show of passivity, and lack of interest marks his public pose in the subsequent proceedings. He may, after all, look forward to a wife of his own choice in later years, and must be careful not to lose the present support of his seniors. Occasionally, however, this hides a helpless anger (*popokl*); he allows his kin to display and hand over the bridewealth, and not till the bride has established herself at his settlement does he make it clear he does not want her as a wife. His revenge is a suicidal one, for if his kin have to go to the humiliating lengths of sending back the girl, and, since the fault lies with them, forfeiting some of the bridewealth return, they may be less willing to support the groom a second time.

To girls, marriage looms as an important event. "When young girls talk among themselves", I was told, "the only topic they are interested in is where they are going to marry." Arrangements for marriage are usually not made before they are old enough to have started courting, travelling, attending market, and visiting friends and relatives. But while some embark on friendships of their own and refuse to comply with their parents' wishes, others say they are quite content to marry wherever they are sent. If a girl baulks at all the suggestions which her parents make, they try to persuade her by cooking a pig (*waltepa pili kng*, "the asking to find out pig") and giving her a large portion of it to distribute as she pleases. If she is still obstinate, she may be accused of already having given a secret promise to some man.

> Such a case was that of Rimbi, the daughter of an Elti man who had had several tentative offers for her. She refused to agree to any of them. In a final rage the father forbade her and her mother to harvest food from their own gardens, because he said that all they did was to take it off to sell in Hagen market where they obviously met up with other men. The mother (who supported Rimbi) was just encouraging her waywardness. In the ensuing quarrel, Rimbi flung back a shell the father had recently given her (a gift to persuade her to change her mind). She came complaining to an Elti Komiti that her father had beaten her and had broken some of her beads— ones she had bought for herself with her own money; but was given little sympathy either from the Komiti or from other men and women of her sub-clan. They were all of the opinion that she should marry: she was getting old, and it was high time that she brought in bridewealth for her kin to eat (1965).

The case is interesting in that it shows that the father's efforts were to make his daughter *agree* to a proposal. On the whole parents are unwilling to force marriage on their daughters, for fear that they will only run away afterwards. Divorce is commonly attributed to the original disposition of the bride, who had never wanted to marry the groom anyway (*wu⁰ pi nø pimb nitim*, "I am not going to (marry) the man, she kept saying"). Usually there is some attempt at compromise, as also seems to have happened in the past—an impression supported by Vicedom (1943–8:2:145, 199) and Strauss (1962:322f.). There are accounts of women in the past being beaten into compliance, but also many stories of parents having to let the girl have her way because she was "strong" (*rondokl*) and they "could do nothing about it".

Twelve fairly reliable versions given by women of how their marriages were arranged have the following pattern:

Woman's choice with parents' agreement	4 cases
Parents' choice with woman's agreement	4 cases

Woman's choice, parents' objection and woman's
    temporary estrangement from them   2 cases
Parents' choice, woman's objection and forced
    compliance, with subsequent divorce   2 cases

Personal choice is to be distinguished from the negotiations between
kin on both sides which must follow in the case of a bride's first marriage.
These negotiations take place whether the groom has been chosen by the
bride herself or not. To this extent, all first marriages are arranged. The
two sets of potential affines, have to be brought together in communication over the amount of bridewealth to be given. They do not open negotiations (*amb ol* or *ol ik*, "wife discussion", "discussion talk") directly
between themselves, but commonly employ an intermediary (*ol ik
amb/wu*^{e}), either a man or woman, to carry their messages. This person is
typically a close kinsman of one side who has more distant links with the
other. He may, for example, be a lineage FZ own S (patrilateral cross
cousin) who finds a bride from a group into which a clan sister has married (Fig. 4(a)). Sometimes a husband-wife or a brother-sister pair

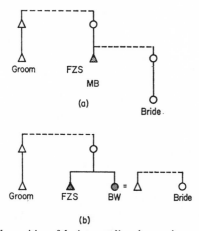

Fig. 4. The position of the intermediary in marriage negotiations.

(Fig. 4(b)) are intermediaries. Table IX analyzes the negotiations for
some 39 Kawelka Kurupmbo marriages, and places these into the context of other Kurupmbo marriages.

    In this table, the "status of the intermediary" does not of course
necessarily represent the bride's or groom's relationship to their group of
marriage, the intermediary being a third party who negotiates between

TABLE IX

Marriage arrangements

A. *How the current wives of men of Kawelka Kurupmbo clan-section were obtained*

	Number of cases
Wife came as widow	8
Negotiations conducted[1]	39
Negotiations not conducted	11
Arrangements not known	5
Total	63

B. *Where negotiations conducted, incidence of the relationship of intermediaries to bride and groom*

Status of intermediary, classificatory or full			His (her) relationship to	
			bride	groom
M	MB	MBS	3 ⎫	4 ⎫
			⎬ 20	⎬ 13
B	BW	BWF	17 ⎭	9 ⎭
FZ, FZDS	FZH	FZS	7 ⎫	11 ⎫
	FZDH		⎬ 13	⎬ 21
Z	ZH	ZS	6 ⎭	10 ⎭
Other kin (including MZH)			4	3
Neighbour			2	2
Total			39	39

[1] In 11 of the 39 cases bride and groom had attended courting parties together; in 7 had not; rest not known.

two groups (although he may be acting in some cases on behalf of a distant agnate). Marriage arrangements are thus triadic. The table suggests that men tend to look towards those groups to which a woman has already been sent; they turn to a married sister or father's sister, or the sons of such persons, to find a distant husband's sister or sister's daughter. The initiative in negotiations is taken often by the groom's lineage, and where a man would hesitate to approach another man's mothers' brother, he might approach a distant sub-clan or clan sister. If he went to a distant "mother", then he would do so through her son, his brother. The intermediary is no more than a go-between; he exercises no rights of bestowal[1] over the bride. If the bridewealth of which he brings news does not meet the original promises, or if the marriage subsequently breaks up, he is not held responsible. While he may have found the bride or groom for the prospective affines seeking marriage in a particular direction, his own part in the ensuing bridewealth transactions is limited to his kinship links with either side. Of the 39 cases listed in Table IX, the intermediary received a bridewealth share in 11, contributed wealth in 7, both contributed and received in 3, did neither in 8; the rest are uncertain.

In summary, Hagen courting parties may be a realistic preliminary to serious marriage plans and, within certain limits, women are allowed a genuine latitude of choice in the partners they marry. However, parents also exert their own influence and arrange marriages for their children, since marriages are important roads for exchanges. The overall pattern reveals a balance between the concentration of the majority of a clan's marriages with allied groups, and a dispersal of others over a wider range. An inhibition against too wide a dispersal lies in the fear that roads for exchanges can also be roads for poison. The idiom of exchange marriage is modelled on an analogy with *moka*, and the reciprocal transfer of women actually facilitates alliance and *moka* transactions; but this is a manner of speaking about group relations. Exchange marriage pinpoints the mixed attitudes of reciprocity and competitiveness which Hagen men hold towards their affines.

---

[1] Cf. Hiatt (1965), Maddock (1969).

5

Kin at her Back

Distance between certain affines finds expression in the taboos that prevent one from disturbing the ghosts thronging at an affine's back. Ghosts control the welfare of their living kin. A woman remains similarly under the influence of her living clansmen and Hageners use the same idiom to express this; a woman's home kin are *mburlung oronga wamb*, "people on the back side".[1] From these she turns away, at marriage, leaving them behind her to "face" her husband (*koembket' oronga*, "on the face side"). This refers to the shift in residence which marriage brings, and to a shift in the quality of relations. A woman's kin recede, she is no longer in daily "face to face" contact with them; but they have not abandoned her —on the contrary they tug at her from behind, exercising an influence which, like the influence of ghosts, may be unseen.

On the rare occasions when women are invited by their husbands to dance at a pig-*moka*, they are decorated profusely at both back and front, and as they dance, gradually turn round to present both sides to the spectators. Men's ornaments, by contrast, are designed to be viewed from the front only. Some husbands place over their wife's back a mounted pearl shell valuable. When the dancers remove their decorations this shell is presented to the wife's kin. It compensates them for the fact that the once-decorated woman must now return to the drudgery of her daily household tasks, as well as being part of the payment given for the ornament her kin contributed on the occasion. More generally,

---

[1] Her children use the same phrase for them (i.e. their maternal kin).

the shell symbolizes the woman's role as bearer of valuables between spouse and kin.[1]

The wife's kin are particularly thought to influence her on the matter of exchanges between them and her husband. Both sides may in fact put pressure on the woman, who through her loyalties to each becomes involved in the exchange system. It is her own ties with her home kin which help keep open the affinal road.

A corollary of this lies in the strong attachment which many women profess to maintain with their kin after marriage. One of the most poignant threats parents or brothers can make is to say they will cut themselves off. Men suspect that mothers continue to wield influence over their daughters long after the latter are married and the tools of persuasion include the threat never to see the daughter again: "If you do not obey my words, then I shall no longer come to your house; you can stay alone with your husband. No, I shall not feel sorry for you and come to see you. I shall not bring presents of food your husband can feed you now!" The abandoned daughter is thus visualized as thrown back on her husband's care. Women who disobey their parents and "go their own way" subsequently express remorse and a wish to see them again. Someone unfortunate enough to have no surviving close relatives is to be pitied; she is known by a special term (*amb pokndame*). If a woman in fact has no close kin, her husband is expected to become "like a father and brother" to her. In the past, conditions of warfare exacerbated the chances of this: not only might her close fathers and brothers be killed in enemy attack, but male survivors taking refuge among various distant kin would lose contact with sisters married elsewhere. Visiting was more difficult during times of fighting. The effective ties a woman retains with her home kin are usually limited to her own lineage-mates (or the lineage of an adopting father). Except in special circumstances, more distant kin are of less importance.

A woman sees her lineage kin as a source of support: these are the people who will come to her aid. When a woman has no kin her entire identification must be with her husband, which is why, it is said, the husband in such circumstances should be particularly understanding and tolerant. If he strikes her, where will she go? She has no-one else to

---

[1] Unless qualified, "kin" here refers primarily to members of a woman's lineage (and clan), her "home kin", also to her other cognatic kinsfolk and spouses of these, by contrast with her "affines" = her husband's relatives.

turn to. A man who forgets himself may afterwards show remorse by making her a gift. In one case, a husband who had struck his kinless wife for her lack of care while she was menstruating, found the weeping woman in the men's house, and (so the account goes) being overcome with pity obtained a pig from his sister which he gave her. In ordinary circumstances, as I discuss later, compensation would be paid to the woman's brother or father.

Much of the sentiment women are supposed to feel towards their home kin is specified as affection for brothers. The tie between brother and sister is ideally a close, friendly one. (Brothers as well as sisters and brothers' wives may be given food-names as a mark of friendship.) It is an insult to remind a spouse that he or she has no cross-sex sibling. The imputation is that there is no-one whom they can visit. Visiting is important, not only as a direct way of maintaining contact, but as a demonstration of the numerous roads for exchanges which exist. Thus women may see an advantage in the fact that their immediate sisters are all dispersed in marriage, for there will be invitations "to eat pork" from a wide range of places. Since clans in different areas are likely to hold *moka* and cult festivals at different times, their chances of sharing in several distributions are increased.

Most frequent visits are made to the home kin (parents and brothers). Sisters may travel home for small occasions (a special food cooking), or for more important ones concerning her clan (such as funeral or bride-wealth), and frequently during the early months of a first marriage. Visits away which become too prolonged however, cause the anxious young husband to follow in pursuit. Her kin may use the occasion to demand settlement of some bridewealth claim about which they are dissatisfied, or the husband may in any case bring a gift for his wife's kin. Occasionally they give him a valuable as a sign that they have no intention of holding back their daughter. A husband who fails to make enquiries after his wife risks losing her altogether, for it is a test of his interest in whether she remain with him or not. When a woman is married fairly near her home she will expect to go there often, especially if she has gardens to look after; sisters also allocate strips to one another at their husband's homes. Once she has borne children and assumed her full household responsibilities, however, a wife is unlikely to be away for more than the daytime from her husband's place, except over a festival period. Sometimes a woman spends the day with her brothers simply because she is "feeling bad"—as did an elderly wife, four of whose pigs had suddenly succumbed to disease. A few days previously she and her husband had tearfully cooked and distributed the meat of animals they would otherwise have had no intention of killing. She had lost heart for her ordinary jobs and leaving her daughter to harvest food, spent time with her sympathetic brother who lived a short forty minutes' walk away.

Whether or not they live near by, married women make the effort to attend funerals at the death of parents or close brothers, or members of their sub-clan. Mourning songs may even touch on the pathos of the meaningless visit: the woman travels to see her kinsman, but actually it is the kinsman's funeral she has come to. The following lament was sung by a lineage sister (immediate FBD)[1] of a youngish Minembi big-man who died in 1965. She did not arrive in time for the first day's mourning, when the corpse had been displayed on a trestle.

> Thinking I would see my light-skinned man[2] I came,
> My light-skinned man, when shall I later see him?
> My brother, my brother,
> You did not send word you were going away and I should come.
> If I had seen you first, then you could have gone.
> My brother, where are you that I can come and see you?
> Brother, my brother, all the men have collected around you,[3]
> My one man. Has he turned his back on us and gone?
> What man was I thinking to see when I came on my visit,
> My brother, who is it I have come to see?

Over thirty married sisters from the dead man's clan-section were present to wail for him. These included three-quarters of all the female members of his own sub-clan.[4] The husbands of the majority of these women attended for at least one of the days during the first week of mourning.

In the past, women severed their fingers at the joint for the death or prolonged sickness of close relatives. Of some 61 instances recorded among Northern Melpa women, the object of this display of grief was said in seven cases to be an immediate brother. The other major categories were: own son 7, own husband 5, husband's brother 9. This demonstrativeness on the part of females is paralleled in their reputation as more easily given to tears than males. A woman married far away who

---

[1] She was not the dead man's only "sister"; he had three living half-sisters (seminal) as well as others of his lineage like herself. I give an extremely abbreviated rendering of the lament.
[2] An epithet given to people with fair (reddish) skin.
[3] i.e. in mourning.
[4] Wives married into his sub-clan and clan-section (total 40) also attended, as did several brothers and other relatives of sub-clan wives.

sees her kin only rarely is said to cry when they visit her, both out of her feelings for them (*kaemb*) and her resentment (*popokl*) that they had not come before. She cries again when they leave. In the same way a bride is expected to feel tearful at the last stages of the bridewealth ceremony when she takes leave of her kin and the companions with whom she used to work in the gardens of her home. It is pointed out that whereas boys will grow up and die in the one place, girls cannot. When girls refuse at first to marry, a common assumption is simply that they are reluctant to leave home.

The groups of origin of wives married to apical ancestors (not always themselves remembered) are said to provide some of the names for the issuing groups. Thus, Kawelka Kurupmbo Romalkembo, Kurup being a small Jimi tribe, and Romalke a section of the Wᵉlyi tribe: the particular woman from Kurup who gave her name to the clan-section cannot in this case be recalled; in the case of the sub-sub-clan Romalkembo, an ancestor two generations from living men is remembered as having had a Romalke wife. Living women are often called after their clan of origin, particularly by members of their husband's tribe. Thus *Oklembo amb*;. "Woman from (Tipuka) Oklembo clan". Tribe names can be used in the same way. The epithet is frequently heard at food distributions, when the host calls out to the assembled women to come forward for their portions. These designations avoid the use of personal names which might afford offence to anyone with affines present or with affines of the same names.

Formal distributions of food follow a meticulous routine, especially if the division is of pork. The allocation is decided upon by men, while boys crowd round the opened oven with them. The women, with young children and girls, sit back and wait for their names to be called. Women always receive first, and then the individual children. Depending on the occasion, they may be given small pieces for themselves to consume on the spot or later share privately with their husbands. Or they may be handed substantial cuts intended for their kin or their husband to whom they will carry the gift. Inclusion in such distribution acknowledges the woman's status: gifts to her kin or husband, she interprets as to some extent gifts to herself, and the reverse also holds.

Exchanges between Affines

Affinal relations are established in the context of an obligatory prestation: bridewealth. Bridewealth also affords scope for generosity and display. Ideally, as the marriage matures, the flow of gifts between affines should develop into *moka*, although engagement in it always remains optional. There is not the same obligation on them to become *moka* partners as there is to make bridewealth and then later childbirth or mortuary payments. Women may feel more strongly about this than men, and act in some instances as though *moka* exchanges with their kin were a duty the husband owed them. Most men, however, by no means restrict their *moka* partnerships to affines, but also make exchanges with their own clansmen, with other cognates and with friends, who may be distantly related or not at all.

Where *moka* partners are related by marriage to each other, exchange relations become imbued with obligations peculiar to the kin relationship, while at the same time the fulfilment of these obligations tends to be transformed into *moka*. Child-growth payments (*maepkla kng*, Central Melpa; *wakl te kng*, Northern Melpa) consisting of one or several cooked pigs, are typical of this. They are made by the child's father to his wife's kin when the baby begins to eat solid food,[1] to enlist their and their ancestors' benevolent interest in the child. They are mandatory, at least for the first-born, omission angering the matrilateral ghosts who can cause the child to fall ill. The gifts may acquire a *moka* character, the wife's kin sending return gifts to the husband, which he further reciprocates, and so on.

That child-growth payments should be a springboard for *moka* is consistent with the transition in relationships which the birth of children brings about. Until she has a child, Hageners realize that there is a greater chance of a new wife running away, and few affines commit themselves wholeheartedly to exchange before this. Suspicion that a marriage may break up inhibits investment in it (this in turn to some extent weakening concern in its maintenance). If a man has married a previously divorced woman for whom he gave no bridewealth, the birth of children becomes the occasion for gifts to her kin. Not only is it important for the child's health that connections with its matrilateral kin should be recognized, but the husband who before may have wondered whether

---

[1] Any one of several stages in the child's early development may be the pretext for gifts, e.g. when its hair is first cut, or when it is finally weaned. See Vicedom and Tischner (1943–8: 2:240–3).

his wife might not run away as she had from previous men is now more certain that she will stay. A husband who is not sure himself whether he cares for his wife tries to avoid making her pregnant. There are one or two old men alive in each of the Kawelka clans whose wives were captured in warfare from enemies, to whom they were formerly married. In some cases the new husbands later handed bridewealth over to the women's kin; in others they made substantial child payments.

Barrenness is not grounds for divorce, but if a childless union is subsequently annulled, it has no further consequences for the groups previously related by it. Indeed, a fresh marriage may be deliberately contracted between the same husband and his ex-wife's actual or lineage sister. During her lifetime the barren woman may also arrange that a "daughter" from her husband's lineage is sent to her own. This potentially too-close union is admissable since her own connections will have no continuity. In the case of a marriage with the wife's sister, the second woman is regarded as a replacement of the first. She may come from the wife's sub-clan and/or be married to a sub-clan mate of the first husband. The arrangement affects only the sub-clans (not groups of higher span) of the original pair. It is known as *ombil* (or *mongal*) *wal rakenem*: "(the sub-clan) fills up the netbag with bones (or a jawbone)". The meaning is that new strength is sent to the groom's group .

There is a linguistic analogy here with exchanges of war compensation payments. When the group of a man killed in warfare solicits compensation for the death, the gifts are known as *wu^e ombil* ("man bone"). One explanation (cf. Strathern, A.J., 1971: 94 for another) is that the victim's kin metaphorically hand over the bones of the dead man (solicitory gift) in order that the enemy will pay for them. In the same way the woman's kin return the dead woman's "bones" (in the shape of the second wife)[1] to solicit a new bridewealth. The analogy with war payments is expanded further: reparations made to the victim's kin in return for *wu^e ombil* are called *wu^e peng* ("man head"), for they are paying for his life (symbolized by the head). Bridewealth payments in general

---

[1] The first bridewealth "died" (*kukli*) with the death of the wife. An interpretation given by one Northern Melpa informant was both that the second wife herself represented the bones (body, strength) of the first, and that the solicitory gift she carried in her netbag (*wal*) (a gift of pork or shells from the bride's to the groom's kin which precedes the main bridewealth) was the *amb ombil* ("woman bone"). The netbag is specified here as the distinctive dress of women, in which they put the gifts to be carried for their brothers or husbands.

are known as *amb peng iti*, "to pay for the head of the woman". Accounts of *ombil wal rakenem* make it explicit that the husband (or his sub-clan) will "feel good" now that a replacement has been found for the dead woman, and this in turn encourages a generous bridewealth. Thus, from the outset marriage ties afford roads for exchanges: sending a bride solicits wealth. "Women are like tradestores", it was once said, and *amb mbø mel kakna etek mek anderemen*, "women walk about and bring in plenty of valuables".

Bridewealth transactions themselves are frequently a source of friction. Either side may be disappointed in their outcome. One well known ploy arises from a "misunderstanding" between the new affines as to the status of their gifts: subsequent gifts to the wife's kin may be interpreted by them as a continuation of the bridewealth (*kuimø*), it therefore being up to their goodwill whether they make a return, whereas the sister's husband is hoping for reciprocation as though he had given *moka*. The early months of marriage are a time of strain, for the potentialities of the new relationship are considerable but uncertain.

This affects the position of the new bride, especially in relation to her childless state. In the past, young and childless women would be those specifically invited to witness and take warning from the torture of female poisoners, for (Hagen men say), "Women who do not bear children quickly are the ones who poison us". The corpse of a childless woman was not given a quiet burial by her husband's kin, but the bones were smashed and the eyes blocked up lest the spirit, frustrated (*popokl*) at an unfulfilled life, should plague the living. These practices were said to have been kept secret from other women, burying being the work of men alone. (Ross gives an account in 1936:362.) While all widowers may be troubled by the spirits of their jealous wives, the surviving husband of a childless wife is in particular danger, which is why special precautions have to be taken. It is not having had the chance to marry and bear children which also makes a dead younger sibling likely to take revenge on his survivors. Childlessness in a married couple may be attributed to an attack from ghosts affronted for some reason by the union. In the case of killings in the past between two groups now contracting an alliance, the angry ghosts of the dead men ensure the alliance is not fruitful.

Childbirth can thus be a time of anxiety. Difficult labour is often attributed to anger on the part of the woman's kin (helped by clan ghosts) at some outstanding debt the husband owes them—the debt jeopardizes the kind of friendship which should exist between groups to be related cognatically. Difficulties in childbirth may also be attributed to the husband's kin and their ghosts: if, for example, the wife's people press the young husband too hard, these ghosts may feel sorry for him and make the labour difficult in order to demonstrate his resentment (*popokl*). The mother herself may suffer on account of her own *popokl* (e.g. if she is angry with her husband for marrying a cowife); or her clan ghosts may be punishing her for showing anger she ought to control, as towards her mother-in-law. There is concern that children should make the alliance a reality, and difficulties in giving birth draw attention to existing disputes between the affines, or between the wife and members of her husband's community.

Bridewealth

It is, then, in the context of uncertainty that bridewealth is negotiated, the first of a potential series of exchanges between people who by definition are unlikely to have made exchanges with one another before. The bride's parents have the special attitude that the payments are primarily an acknowledgement of their own contribution to her up-bringing. Account is taken of omens to ascertain whether the bridewealth her kin are about to be offered will be adequate.

The idiom of exchange marriage indicates the competitive prestige bound up with raising high bridewealths for the sons of a lineage. Similarly, a family hopes for good settlement on their daughters. Having ugly daughters may be interpreted as a curse to prevent just this.

*About 15 years ago, Elti Muntr defaulted on *moka* payments he should have made his father-in-law. Returning from a visit to him, the old man drowned, and his angry spirit came and killed Muntr's son. The dead child thought, "Oh my mother and my father! You wronged my maternal kin so that my grandfather drowned and then came for me. All right, I have a sister and she can stay small and ugly (*wangen*). However much pork her parents feed her, she will never grow up properly, and they can never eat good bridewealth for her!" The girl in question, past the normal age for marriage, is stunted and retarded in growth.

While a bride is often supposed to be reluctant to leave home, the suggestion that fathers might cry at their daughter's wedding, as Kuma and Chimbu fathers are said to do (Reay and Criper: personal communications) was met with incredulity. They would only "feel bad" if the bridewealth were inadequate. The attitudes of Hagen mothers, however, are admitted to be more mixed.

I describe details of the actual transactions at some length, for the light they throw on attitudes and expectations surrounding this exchange in which, of all exchanges, women are crucially involved. Not only the bride but kinswomen on both sides are to some extent participants.

The main components of bridewealth nowadays are live and cooked pigs, pearlshells and Australian money. Cassowaries and such prized items as bamboo tubes of decorating oil may be added as "extras". Accounts of bridewealths a generation or so ago suggest that shells were too scarce to be given away in more than small numbers, and the gifts consisted mainly of cooked meat and a few live pigs.

Bridewealth is an exchange of goods between the bride's and groom's kin, the main gift passing from the latter to the former. As with the number of items given, the precise sequence of events can differ, and there may also be some variation in the categories of items transferred. The following account is therefore a generalized one, of the kind held for a bride's first marriage; transactions at subsequent marriages may be truncated, consisting perhaps of stages 2, 3, 4 and 5. The supposition is that once a girl has left her kin her ties with them will have been partly weakened; it is at her first marriage that they are particularly vulnerable to "feeling bad".

Gifts fall into several named categories. These break down the total prestation into various components. The components enumerate not so much specific rights in the bride which are under transfer, but aspects of the whole relationship between the two sides. Many of the names summarize features of the relationship in neat metaphor. They also structure the bridewealth into two main elements: items which are exchanged and those for which no direct return is expected. The proportion of goods falling into one or other class may give rise to disputes. Different interpretations on which categories of valuables have or have not been returned are responsible for much of the conflict which surrounds the handing back of outstanding items at divorce.

Stages in a Bridewealth Transaction

1. The bride is sent to the groom's place with solicitory gifts: a pearl shell (*rumndi kin*, "the ornamental pearl shell", in reference to its being

tied round the bride's neck) and cooked meat (*røkndi kng*, "pig put in a bag"), are carried in her netbag. The meat is intended for those who will contribute to the main bridewealth gift on the groom's side, to encourage them to put on a generous display. If the bride is accompanied by close lineage kin, the groom sometimes cooks a small pig for the guests but otherwise no direct return is made. Some people, however, regard a later portion of pork which is put aside specifically for the bride's parents by the groom as being a return for the initial solicitory gift. It is called *kanan ndip kng* ("courting fire pig"), referring to the way the bride's mother stoked the fire at her daughter's courting parties, and is given as a token for this "work"; it may also be known (in Central Melpa) as *keral ngomong kng* ("*keral* leaves pig"). Fibres from the *keral* plant are used for women's aprons; no etymology could be supplied by Hageners, but a guess might connect the gift with a recognition of the mother's labours in making her daughter's clothes. One example of variations in procedure is that cooked *keral* pig may also be given when the bride's kin first visit the groom's place (whether they bring *røkndi kng* or not)—in the same way as the bride's kin think of the large wealth they will draw from the groom, the groom and his kin are conscious, one is told, that the bride is a "strong" thing, who will bear children and work for them, so they are impelled to cook pig for the guests. This initial stage (1) may be omitted altogether; it shows the goodwill affines-to-be intend towards each other, and depends partly on their respective wealth.

The shell (occasionally more than one) is both to make the groom's father "feel good", and to impress him. It is always a very large, fine specimen, and the bride's father hopes one of equal splendour will be set aside from the main bridewealth gift in return for it. If the return shell is not judged its match, the original may be demanded back. Since these solicitory items are either returned early in the proceedings, or no return is expected, they are not reckoned as outstanding in the event of a divorce.

The bride is decorated for the visit and, most importantly, is oiled. The oil is sometimes applied by a female ritual specialist (*møn amb*) who recites a spell (*møn*) to secure a generous bridewealth; in any case it is read as an omen (*temal*). Oil running freely down the forehead and nose signifies that gifts will not be stinted; but if it clogs and dribbles to one side, her kin are warned not to proceed. Omens are also interpreted from the cries of certain birds, which may be heard at any point during the transactions. Whether they are heeded depends largely on people's feelings at the time. Clansmen of the groom who do not favour a particular match may take the bird cry to prove their point; but other factors may prevail. One bridewealth at Kelua in 1964 was given for a couple who were "strong" to marry each other, though the girl's kin had doubts. The marriage went through in spite of the warning of the *kot* bird (? a wren). "I can't think why the bird should cry, since the two themselves are so set on the marriage", was a wry comment.

The bride may stay to make the acquaintance of the groom's female kin while her own parents return home. She is escorted by female companions (*røp amb*)—usually an unmarried sister or cousin, occasionally a (clan) sister already married into the groom's group. They remain with her until the final stage. The bride herself supposedly feels ashamed in front of the groom's people if she brings no gifts for them, because they are soon to part with so many valuables on her behalf.

2. The next few days are spent in direct discussion between the parents of the bride and groom over the amounts of bridewealth to be given; prior to this, negotiations were conducted through intermediaries. Depending on their state of readiness, the groom's kin then announce when they will make the formal display.

3. The bride returns home to accompany her own kin for the main display (*amb kuimø*). It is held at the courtyard of the groom's homestead or settlement, attended by the lineage and sub-clan kin of the couple, along with interested clansmen and matrilateral relatives. Shells and money are shown to the bride's male kin in the men's house, but as the discussion shifts from these to pigs, women take an interest. The beasts themselves are brought out for all to see and the men move into the open to continue their talks. For the first time the bride's father is faced with a specific number of items which he must allocate among his watching relatives, whose hopes are always too high. It is under this pressure that the bride's kin negotiate for more. Their tactics of attrition are recognized in the phrase *amb pek rui* ("to scrape or peel (as of sugarcane or a tuber) for the woman")—in pressing for extra valuables they gradually wear away the opposition till the groom's side yields. The main speechmakers are the fathers (or other senior men) of the bride and groom and male kin who have contributed or hope to receive some of the wealth.

Items are not distributed directly by the groom or his father to the bride's menfolk; this is up to the bride's father. He depends on the generosity of the display to be generous in turn, and his own embarrassment may add to the tension between the two sides. He is especially embarrassed if bold promises, such as to provide a cassowary, have not been met. A payment not up to expectation can in the end only be accepted or rejected—the defaulter cannot be brought to court for not having kept his word. But disappointment at this stage may lie behind bitter and mean wrangling should the bridewealth subsequently have to be handed back at divorce. If agreement is reached, the groom's people withdraw a little to let the bride's father make the allocation of valuables. Theoretically, the former should know only the recipients of the items for which immediate return is to be made, but in fact both sides are likely to have a shrewd idea of the structure of contributions and distributions. Nowadays a Local Government Councillor is present as a witness. Amid apparent confusion her kin hurry away with their valuables, while the bride stays behind.

The shells at this stage are not yet divided into those which "die" on the bride (*peng pokla* , "head cutting," the shells that sever her from her kin) and those to be returned, known by a range of terms in some cases also applicable to pigs, e.g. *raka kin* ("shells scraped together"), *anmbile kin* ("tongue shell", see below). It is left to the bride's father to make what return he thinks fit, and the same is also true of money. As far as the pigs are concerned, however, it is of paramount importance that everyone knows to which categories they have been allocated. In the number and quality of pigs offered in bridewealth lies the true generosity of the groom's side, and on the bride's side people with claims to them are always of some importance. Usually more shells than pigs are shown (20–30 on an average as compared with about 15 pigs; see Appendix VI), and these go to more distant connections in ones and twos; as single units, nowadays they are worth much less than pigs.

There are four main categories to be decided upon. These are basic to most bridewealths and could be considered the essential components of the display at this stage.[1]

---

[1] In recent years, however, there has been a move (encouraged by Councillors) which began in Temboka, has spread to some Central Melpa groups and is talked about among the Northern Melpa, to eliminate the final category (4). Complications over this category are said to give rise to severe problems when bridewealth has to be returned at divorce. These were more manageable in the past when the total size of the gifts was smaller.

Main categories of pigs at initial display given to bride's kin

(1)	*mam peng kng* mother head pig	set aside specifically for the bride's mother
(2)	*kem kng* vagina pig *keta kng* mouth pig	given for no return, to "die" on the bride
(3)	*anmbile kng* tongue pig *kokla kng* ? exchange pig *rarop kng* purchase pig *rundukl kng* rubbish pig *kelanda rop kng* joining pig *raka kng* scraped-together pig	live pigs for which return is expected in kind
(4)	*tembokl kng* (killing-) stick pig	live pigs taken by the bride's kin; pigs of equivalent size the groom's kin kill and cook

---

(1) See text

(2) *kem kng*: in obvious reference to the bride's sexuality, is heard at Buk, *keta kng* at Kelua; the latter reference is to the mouths of the bride's kin who will consume the pigs.

(3) Alternative terms for the one category.

anmbile kng: the pig is exchanged for an equal, similar in all respects, i.e. "tongue to tongue". The term may stand for the whole category of pigs which exchange is made. The tip of a shell is also known as *anmbile*.

kokla kng: used generally of the exchanged pigs, particularly of live pigs provided in return by the bride's kin. (When a woman visits home, her husband retrieves her with a gift for her kin known as *kuimø*; they may send her off to him with return gifts, *kokla*.)

rarop kng: cf. the phrase also used of the "exchange of women".

rundukl kng: can refer to any of the exchange pigs or to a particular sub-category: the groom's kin mark one of their live pigs for which they hope a live one will be given in return (also *rundukl kng*); the return animal is then killed and shared among those who helped raise the bridewealth, including the new husband and wife. In the past such a pig was sacrificed to the groom's clan ghosts—for having helped the groom and his kin to raise the many pigs now handed over to another group, so that they will continue to bless the new husband, and his wife will have healthy children. It carries the connotation of "scraping together", i.e. giving all the wealth that can be found. Some people associate it with *rundukl*, the carpet of sugarcane shavings and dried rubbish in a house. The *rundukl kng* replaces the pigs which have left the household, the in-coming pig carrying floor shavings on its back as did the groom's pig going.

kelanda rop kng: when stones are heated for an earth oven, a trestle of firewood is constructed on a square frame of four strong staves. The phrase refers to the points where the staves meet: "as two stakes at right angles meet together in a single join, so the pigs to be returned will match those given". Sometimes *kelanda rop* singles out a specific pig, one which signifies the general intentions of the girl's kin to make an adequate return, and the promise that they will send further pigs in later endowment of the bride.

raka kng: *oka raka rui* is to tear out old sweet potato beds so that no plants remain: in the same way, the bride's kin have returned all they can.

In a display of 15 pigs, these categories might be divided as follows: (1) one pig; (2) five; (3) six; (4) three. Each of them gives rise to discussion.

Invariably the most controversial is the large pig which the groom's kin intend for the bride's mother. The phrase, *mam peng kng*, connotes that it is regarded as a compensation to the woman who loses the daughter upon whom she once depended. Now she will go to someone else's house, draw water and collect firewood for others. One of the pearl shells may also be set aside for the father under the same rubric (*tepam-nga kin*, "the father's shell"), but this is of less importance. The significance of the mother's pig is shown in further terms for it. *Mindi* or *mundi kng*[1] refers to the fact that the woman bore the bride; *mam ombil kng* ("mother bone pig") reminds the mother that she has eaten her pig, whose bones remain at her house, in lieu of the daughter whom she must let go; as no-one else took the pig away from her, so she must not entice her daughter away from the husband. A similar term is *mam ropa kundi kng* ("mother's killed pig")—to "kill" any objections she might have. (The father's shell may be known as *tepam ropa kundi kin*.) *Mam ombil* may also mean "the mother's bones", i.e. the daughter to whom the mother gave life. Many of these terms are analogous to those used for war compensations; the loss of a woman in marriage is equated to some extent with the loss of men in fighting. The loss is not total, however, for it brings compensation gifts.

All the names signify that the pig is meant in particular for the mother, to please her so she will support the marriage. Brides' mothers themselves always insist strongly on being allocated their pig and men say they ignore the women to their cost. The mother has, however, no public part to play in the transactions; although she may have been consulted privately about the forthcoming event, she does not participate in the

---

[1] *Mindi kng* (with a different etymology) can also be used for the bride's endowment, but I do not enter into the details here.

speeches. This does not prevent her (or other women) from interjecting, though her remarks are likely to be spasmodic protests of annoyance rather than sustained arguments. Women who speak out usually do so only if they disagree with the way things are shaping. Sometimes the mother is forced to concur with her husband disposing of "her" pig to meet a debt—particularly if their son had to borrow such a pig for his own marriage. But the category is a focus of dispute on two other counts, stemming from the fact that the "mother's pig" is always the largest on display.

Among Northern Melpa tribes no return is expected for it: the mother should "eat" it in approval of the marriage. Central Melpa groups, however, pride themselves on the generosity with which the bride's kin make a return for the main gift, and they say that the bride's mother should not "steal" the large pigs of the groom, but show her affection for her daughter by endowing her with one as big. A Central Melpa mother may protest in fact if the menfolk decide to return her pig, especially if she is not given further live ones from the bridewealth. On the other hand, she may be proud to display the huge pig she herself has reared in anticipation of her daughter's endowment; she is in an awkward situation if her own is not comparable to the proportions of the one shown by the groom. Simply because it is customarily the largest pig he has it may be difficult to match. In Northern Melpa this is the most important outstanding category to be handed back at divorce; if the bride's kin have disposed of it and cannot find its equal, there is considerable ill feeling, pressure even being put on them to retrieve the original animal. It is usually male, castrated male pigs growing larger and heavier than sows; if a female substitute of the same size is found the groom's kin will quibble because its growth potential is less.

The second "dispute" is a ploy used by the bride's kin, particularly when they suspect that the groom's side are holding back other pigs, to increase the bridewealth. The pig which the groom's father clearly intends as *mam peng kng*, they allocate to the category of *tembokl kng*, which are live pigs comparable to ones the groom's kin must later kill (with a club, *tembokl*).[1] The bride's people show they are confident that they can find an equally large equivalent to present in return. Having allocated the pigs this way, they then comment what a disgrace it is that the mother

---

[1] They put the groom's kin into the position of giving away the huge pig as *tembokl kng* and having to find an equivalent to cook, in addition to providing a further "mother's pig".

has no pig to call her own, and demand that the groom's kin make good the omission.

Discussion over the second category of pigs ("for the woman's vagina") centres on the fact that these are non-returnable. The bride's father has to weigh two considerations: how generous he can afford to be, and thereby how prestigious, in promising to make a return for many of the groom's pigs—and thus keeping this category small; and the usefulness of having several non-returnable items, since debts arising from previous bridewealth transactions can be met with pigs of this category. This is the main class of pigs outstanding at divorce.

It is clear that competition occurs between the two sides, the one making an impressive display, the other claiming that the display can be matched as impressively in the return-gifts. This lies behind disputes over the third category, pigs to be exchanged. The various terms by which these are known emphasize not only the effort to exhaust resources in making a good display, but also that one side should be able to match exactly the gifts of the other. The prestige of both the bride's father and of his close kin is at issue, for these pigs are distributed out to kinsmen who promise to find comparable animals. The interpretation of comparability is strict. Size, sex and condition are all taken into account,[1] the groom's side being informed at the display if a pig of different sex is to be returned; inferiority in size is unlikely to be admitted. Individuals who have promised to take an exchange pig may be distressed if the quality of the groom's falls below that of the pig they have mentally put aside for the occasion.

The fourth category gives rise to similar discussion. It is hoped that these will be large pigs, since ones of their size are later killed by the groom, and the pork distributed to the bride's kin. A much wider range of people are invited to share in this than receive live pigs or shells and her father is anxious to do things properly. The two to three pigs allotted to this category at the display in fact activate not one but two further identical sets of animals. The live ones are handed over with the promise that for each the groom's kin will cook an equivalent (not displayed). On his side the bride's father allocates these to his more distant kinsmen who find equivalents which are returned to the groom. Like exchange

---

[1] Similar, though rather lesser, concern is shown over the quality of pearl shells; matching takes into account the size, sheen, colour and blemishes of the shells originally given. People like bank notes to be crisp and new, but do not refuse dirty or old ones.

pigs, this draws into the bridewealth a wide circle of kin, who participate in the transactions but at the end have no liabilities. It is the recipients of non-returnable pigs (usually close cognatic kin) who run the risk of first deploying but then later having to return their pigs should divorce follow. On the groom's side, however, the situation is different. The live pigs returned by the bride's people are given by the groom's father to those who contributed the cooked pigs. The donors of the live *tembokl* pigs receive no return. It is the groom's father or close lineage-mates who contribute live *tembokl* pigs. Kinsmen providing the pigs to be cooked do not lose, since they receive live ones in return. To this manoeuvre the bride's kin turn a blind eye should divorce ensue, refusing to recognize any items outstanding. The bride's kin themselves regard their return pigs as for the live ones, pointing out that cooked meat is distributed to all and sundry, the immediate kin receiving little benefit and therefore hardly responsible for any further return. This device, in fact, recognizes the problem of how to organize an exchange of live for cooked pigs when the recipients of cooked pork disclaim individual liability. The tension generated by discrepancies of this order are an important factor in people's attitudes towards bridewealth disputes at divorce. While the marriage lasts, no problem arises, the groom's father deriving prestige from the number of *tembokl* pigs given, for he has enabled the bride's kin to hold the feast that is so important to them.

This account of the *tembokl* pigs has anticipated two further stages in the bridewealth proceedings.

4. Within a few days of the main display (stage 3) the groom's kin kill and cook the *tembokl* pigs as arranged. This is a time of relaxation. While major cuts (legs, backbone and head) are destined to be given away, flesh from the ribs, parts of the intestines and other scraps, along with blood- and dripping-soaked vegetables, are eaten on the spot. Sharing in the small feast are the bride and guests who have come with help in the form of contributions. The bride's people use the interlude to prepare the return-gift.

5. The following morning the groom's party—including his close cognates, and supporting clansmen, along with the bride herself—carry the pork over to the bride's place. After their previous separation in dispute and argument, the two sides meet again in an ordered formal fashion; many of the participants are decorated. The occasion is a public one, often taking place at a ceremonial ground, hence its name *penal kng*,

"pigs of the outside place (*pena*)". The groom's party enters in a body and sits opposite the assembled crowd of bride's kin. The whole bride-wealth gift is displayed again together with the items for return. It is then possible to assess the equivalence of the return-gift. As is appropriate to a more public occasion, the speeches are rhetorical rather than argu-mentative, and the transaction is much less likely to break down at this stage.

Once the groom's party have hurried away with their return-gifts, taking the bride with them, her kinsfolk turn to the important task of dividing up the pork. A wider range of her kin are present than accom-panied the party to the groom's home earlier: members of her clan-section or clan, and their wives, as well as married sisters and sisters' husbands, mother's sisters and their children, mother's brothers, and cross cousins. The bride's father's sister will attend the pork distribution even if she and her husband do not receive separate valuables. Their son (FZS) might be given such an item. Sisters are likely to come without their husbands (unless the latter are also receiving a valuable, as they may), but will take portions of the pork home to them. Wives, on the other hand, do not give pieces to their brothers—but take the meat back to the house, for their husbands and children. For this reason, major sections of pork are distributed in the name of women, to ensure that the husbands will receive shares later. Often there is not enough meat for men to consume much at the occasion itself. All these people come to "eat" the bridewealth. Considerable emphasis is put on the significance of this privilege. In referring to the imminent marriage of a female cognate, people look forward to sharing in the pork, irrespective of whether they hope to receive other valuables in addition. Participation also indicates general approval of the match. Little is left of the pig for the bride's immediate family; it is on this occasion that a side or leg of pork is slipped privately into her parents' house for them alone (see p. 102).

Simply because so much value is placed on the *penal kng*, it may give rise to dissension and bitter feelings within the group of bride's kin. The following stormy occasion took place in 1964.

> The daughter of a Kawelka Membo Oyambo man married into Kendipi tribe. The *penal* pork was brought to the bride's home as usual, and after eating some specially prepared tubers most of the groom's party left to let the distribution proceed. The Kendipi had brought only two cooked pigs, but a further side was put secretly into the bride's mother's house. Some

hundred adults were present. The legs were allocated by the father with the help of a Komiti of the same Membo lineage. One was given to the assembled men of the pair clan Mandembo along with Membo men in general; one to the Mandembo wives, another to the wives of the other Membo sub-clan, Køyambo. There was some fuss because wives of the two Mandembo clan-sections wanted separate shares. Other recipients of legs were: married sisters of the bride, father's sisters, any women from the other Kawelka clan (Kundmbo) who were present or from the pair tribe Tipuka,[1] and so on. A small leg was also allocated to "the two Klamakae women". These were the wives (from different tribes themselves) of a couple of Klamakae men who had come with contributions to the return-gift, a sister's husband and a mother's sister's son of one of the bride's father's brothers. The women themselves were not there, and the men would take the portions home to them. The example is interesting in that it shows the extent to which women are thought of as the primary recipients of pig meat.

At this point the men of the bride's sub-clan, Oyambo, were beginning to appear worried—nothing had yet been given to Oyambo wives, and the men withdrew the leg they first had intended for two mother's sisters of the bride, saying there was not enough meat. They then prevailed upon the father to fetch out of the house the side which had been secreted there. The Membo Komiti tried to divide this equally for the men and women of the Oyambo sub-sub-clans, Oyambo and Roklambo. While women were sitting in small knots at the edge of the ceremonial ground, already cutting up their pieces, or simply waiting, Oyambo men jostled round the Komiti. They protested that there were fewer Roklambo men present than themselves, and the Roklambo would get too great a proportion of the meat. A new person grabbed the knife and began cutting. There was a scuffle, the argument grew heated, and the bride's angry mother bore down on the men to berate them for not giving a share to her sisters. These two had protested vociferously when the leg they were to receive was taken back. The man who was cutting the meat (same lineage as the bride) laughed, and said they should try distributing the pork! Disparaging remarks were made about how little meat the groom's people had brought. The two sisters were told to go and eat with other women; they were fobbed off with the comment that the Kendipi had promised a third pig later, and they could share in this. In the end the men distributed the leg and side together, to all the men and wives of Oyambo and Roklambo, the bride's mother still complaining about the way her sisters were treated. The meat rapidly dis-

---

[1] The allocation to "Tipuka women" was meant both for Kawelka sisters married into Tipuka and for wives of Kawelka men taken from Tipuka. The rationale behind specifying this tribe was that Tipuka and Kawelka are closely intermarried, and the connection should be honoured. The pig given to Kundmbo women was because Kundmbo and Membo are neighbours, and the Membo would be ashamed, it was said, to eat by themselves. A sub-clan daughter is also married into Kundmbo.

appeared, leaving a few scraps for the adolescent boys to fight over. The final scene was the arrival of the Komiti's sister, in a whirlwind of fury, who scolded everyone for not having informed her of the occasion or saved any meat. But the day was not ended: as often happens, advantage was taken of the fact that so many people were assembled there, and the Komiti's brother brought up an old dispute with a sub-clan mate—each was accusing the other of pig theft. The Komiti's brother cheerfully met the challenge by eating some of the divination substance of his tribe (*mi*); his rashness shocked those following the argument. The substance has to be consumed with pork, and the presence of the meat must have excited the disputants into this test of their antagonism. The Komiti himself, along with a big-man from Mandembo, was discussing *moka* plans a little distance away and did not interfere.

6. Although the bride accompanies the groom's party when they leave the *penal kng*, she is not fully integrated as a wife till after a further stage. This is the cue for her kin to make her endowment, and it is after this that the bride is allocated gardens.

The final major transaction is a further gift of pork (perhaps two or three pigs) which is sent some weeks later. This is intended for the bride's parents and their close lineage kin, hence its name, *mangal kng* (pigs of the house, *manga*). The gift as a whole may be called "the pig we give the mother". When a polygynist's daughter is married, it was said, the mother's cowives receive first share of the *mangal* pork to allay their jealousy of her for all the pig she is getting. Among Northern Melpa, a largish cooked pig presented at this stage for the actual parents carries th name *amb kik kng* ("woman ashes pig"), a comment on the bride's transformation from a young girl, whose skin her family annointed with oil, to a wife, whose skin will become dry and dirty with the work she does for her husband. Women tend the fire as they cook, and the idiom of being covered in ashes refers also to a wife's confinement to the house and gardens. No return is formally made for this category. The other cooked pigs are usually returned with live ones by Northern Melpa, although among Central Melpa the whole category may be taken as non-returnable.

Mangal kng is given specifically to soften the blow of a young daughter's departure in her first marriage, and may be omitted at subsequent marriages. The bride herself interprets it as indicative of her husband's generosity to her own parents, and may refuse to sleep with him if the gift is inadequate. Her endowment may also be held up. The dowry, *kng mbo* ("breeding pigs") can refer to three things: all the return-gifts made by her kin may be looked upon as "endowing" the bride, who will receive the goodwill of the husband's people; the return pigs made for the *mangal kng* may be known generally as *kng mbo*, although the husband probably keeps only one, distributing the others to close kin; finally, a separate gift of breeding pigs, from one to as many as four, are sent by the bride's parents some time after this final transaction. These are intended specifically for the bride to care for.

If the bride's own parents, or one of them, are dead, at about this stage a sacrifice is made to the dead parent. This may involve the killing of one of the live bridewealth pigs, which becomes known as *mam/tepam tipu kng*, "pig for the mother's/father's ghost". If the bride has no close female guardian, a pig may be allocated to this category in place of the mother's pig.

7. Any outstanding debt over the return for the *mangal kng* is handed back at divorce, but subsequent gifts of cooked pig (known simply as *kng timb*, "legs of pork") may be considered as "lost" on the bride, although they come under the rubric of *kuimø* ("bridewealth"). As many as ten or twenty legs may be sent to the new affines by the husband and his lineage brothers within a few months of the marriage. These are reciprocated, when the occasion arises (a funeral distribution, a sister's bridewealth, etc.).

As the account has hinted, there are a number of regional differences in bridewealth custom, and I summarize some of these in Appendix V.

The Significance of Bridewealth

Bridewealth, like *moka*, is an exchange of goods; it brings prestige to both sides and has competitive overtones. Like *moka* it is also seen as an investment. In this lies the importance of making an exchange in live pigs. Hageners contrast themselves with people of the Tuman river area (on the Eastern Melpa border) who, they have heard, cook all the bridewealth pigs, to consume on the one occasion. This seems quite contrary; if all the pigs are killed, how can the parties re-establish pig business? In Hagen the bride's kin keep the pigs they receive, their return of live pigs to the groom's kin enabling the bride-takers to continue to rear stock. Since the new affines expect to become exchange partners, it is in their interests to ensure each other's continuing prosperity. The bride's father gives her an endowment explicitly so that later her husband will have pigs to give his father-in-law. Sometimes if the bride's parents are unable to make an immediate return for the cooked pigs (*mangal kng* brought at stage 6) they give the groom's kin a small cut of pork, called *opra kng*, indicating that they do not want their temporary shortage to forestall further exchanges. *Nombokla opra iti* refers to cleaning up a track (*nombokla*) that has become overgrown with weeds and grass—the bride's people keep the way open with the gift and its promise of more to come. A further connotation is that they broaden the path their daughter has already trodden, by following her direction of marriage with exchanges. An alternative term for the pork, and for subsequent gifts in return for the "legs of pig" sent by the groom, is *wal tepa kng*, "pork taken in a netbag". The bride was sent with netbags to her husband's place, and has now brought one back to be filled again with pig meat for her husband.

Bridewealth is said to "make the hearts of the (bride's) people good", *wamb mundmong kae petem*, an attitude compounded of sentiment and pragmatism. Sentiment stems from the new friendship between the affines, from the need to conciliate the parents who have lost a daughter, from the appreciation of what a strong thing the wife-takers have gained in a worker and a mother of children. Pragmatically, a generous bridewealth allays desire on the part of the girl's kin to entice her away from the husband, and helps (as Hageners see it) to stabilize the marriage. Occasionally the bride's father reciprocates the groom's generosity by making a total return of the live *kuimø* pigs, showing his readiness to act as a reliable exchange partner. He also displays his generosity to the world. Typically this is the gesture of a polygynist at the marriage of his first daughter: he hopes it will encourage others to offer well for his remaining daughters.[1]

Two factors in practice work against bridewealth as a stabilizer of marriage and creator of friendships. The first is that disappointment with the goods themselves may lead directly to attempts by the bride's kin to pressurize their affines, which they do through persuading the woman to return home. Persuasion, *kund rui* (Pidgin English, *gris*), "to grease, i.e. make a person act as one wants", can involve tactics of bribery, threat, cajolery and appeal to common values or sentiment.

---

[1] It is not only motives of generosity which produce large bridewealths; a man imputed to be poor or accused of attempting an improper marriage, may be stung into raising a huge bridewealth to silence the bride's kin.

Because the danger of this is openly recognized, it can be used as a lever in the games affines play—one side threatens to withdraw its woman, but the other retaliates in threats to withdraw the bridewealth. The advantage is by no means solely on the side of the bride's people, for it is a matter of prestige to marry off a daughter well, and they need the bridewealth. Their bargaining must not be at the cost of a reputation for meanness which will prevent possible offers from elsewhere. The second factor is that while the bride's female kin may indeed be upset by a poor allocation of wealth to themselves, and mollified by a good one, other considerations may weigh with them. This seems to apply to women more than men. A mother, for example, may have been frustrated in her desire to marry her daughter off elsewhere. Hagen men both try to win over the bride's mother with gifts, women like men being amenable to such influence, and impute a caprice to women in the fear that they will accept publicly only to later wreck things secretly. In fact, the bride's kin as a whole are subject to a double stereotype: they are seen as solicitous for their daughter, providing a good dowry and reminding her of the duties she has towards her new husband, since they have eaten the pigs of her marriage to their satisfaction; at the same time they may be represented as consumed by inveterate greed, with only their own interests at heart, liable secretly to withdraw their daughter because of the lure of better bridewealth elsewhere.

The bride is in an ambiguous position. Success or failure in the exchanges involve her own reputation. But the gap between this and her actual control of events (largely in the hands of men) can lead to strain. She is an actor in the proceedings, at some junctures a central one, but has little control over the actual bargaining for wealth. While her approval for the transactions is sought, a negative answer is often regarded by her menfolk as subversive as flight. A girl may become unhappy or angry if the proper gifts are not made to her relatives; default on her kinsmen's part may put her into a similar position of frustration. Hageners openly recognize this.

*In 1963 a newly married Ndika girl hanged herself. Commentators from her mother's brother's tribe said that the suicide was the direct result of a quarrel between her and her parents over bridewealth pigs. They had promised her a breeding sow (*kng mbo*), but held it back ("the mother wanted to eat it"). She was so wrought up (*popokl*) that she went to her mother's stalls and began untying one of the pigs. Her mother prevented her, and in desperation she killed herself.

Appendix VI indicates the size of modern bridewealths and the structure of contributions and distributions. Over 80% of the contributions to a bridewealth come from the groom's clan, including wives. Wives married into the groom's lineage may be seen as helping in their "own name", with pigs from "their" herds or with money they have earned. Like men, they expect eventual return, either from the return-gift or from the distribution of bridewealths brought in by lineage daughters.

The first wife of Kawelka Unt (see pages 53–54) picked a quarrel with her husband over a contribution she had made two years before (when she still had pigs) to the bridewealth of a lineage son. The husband had promised a replacement on condition she move to his other settlement. When he and the young husband were given pork on one occasion by their affines, she protested angrily at their failure to share it with her, reminding them of her previous, still not replaced, contribution.

A woman looks primarily to her husband to allocate her return-gifts. It is between spouses that bitter public altercations ensue when the wife refuses to fetch an extra pig for the bridewealth display—especially if her husband is raising bridewealth for an adopted son (an example is given in Appendix V). Women who protest in public at the way proceedings are being conducted do so only to their husband's kin; they would never engage in a direct interchange with the other side.

Some 60–65% of the *kuimo* shells and pigs at Buk (40–60% at Kelua) are distributed to the lineage or sub-sub-clan of the bride. A higher proportion of cognatic and affinal kin tend to receive from rather than contribute to bridewealth; but whereas the bride's mother and sisters, like her father and brothers, receive because of the immediacy of their ties, and clansmen of the bride have a general claim on the bridewealths of female clan members, other relatives have to strengthen their claims through specific help given during the bride's childhood. Young girls as they approach marriageability are aware of this: they use the imminent bridewealth to solicit small gifts from various kin. They not only prevail upon their parents to give them money, beads, cloth and other trinkets, and let them off household chores, but go around visiting at their mother's place or where fathers' sisters have married. These are women from whom they hope to receive netbags and aprons, while a mother's brother should be solicitous in making gifts of pork to his niece. A claim to share in the bridewealth does not imply, however, a right to take valuables for no return, and kinsmen may help with the return-gift or else repay the debt later. The exception is cooked *penal* meat (stage 5); here members of the bride's sub-clan and clan, perhaps others of her tribe, eat freely, being under no obligation to make specific return.

A mother's brother, then, can only expect to receive at his niece's bridewealth if he has shown concern in her as a girl or helped the family by (say) contributing to a sister's son's bridewealth. If he lives too far away to visit his sister's people, or if the immediate mother's brothers are dead, probably nothing will be sent. A relative who gives a girl a shell ornament may expect a live pig from the bridewealth; those who give trinkets of lesser value hope for a share of pork backbone at the *penal* feast. Some of the backbone also goes to the women who netted her bags. The maker of the bride's most important bag, the *wal kupin* (see p. 14), should certainly be recognized. At Kelua, where suitable fibres for twisting the string are hard to obtain, the donor may demand a live pig, and if none is forthcoming, take back the netbag. The *wal kupin* symbolizes the whole dowry. During one divorce case, the wife was said to be leaving the husband because of her shame that he had made no *mangal* payments, so that her kin had sent her no dowry of pigs. As a girl she had been given a *kupin* netbag: "she took the *wal kupin* to her husband's place, but he killed no pigs for the bag and in anger she brought it back".

A mother's sister plays a relatively minor part in the affairs of her sister's daughter, and the extent to which she and her husband receive at a bridewealth depends on whether the bride has married nearby, if strong ties have been maintained between them, and so on. The home of her mother's sister may, however, offer a young girl the refuge she could not expect from a mother's brother, for the very reason that the woman's husband has no authority over her. The mother's sister herself, may interpret the relationship as entitling her to consideration at the girl's bridewealth.

Shells may be formally given in a woman's name where she, rather than her husband, is the link with the bride, but women consider it a special mark of recognition to be allocated a pig. Like any extra items given, such as a cassowary, money tends to be kept by the bride's father, although he may distribute small amounts about, especially to his womenfolk. The father does not directly receive great augmentation to his wealth from the shells and pigs, since these are mostly distributed among other relatives. He does, however, increase his overall financial standing, for by the very act of distribution he meets previous debts or places himself in credit. He, in any case, derives prestige from the disbursement of wealth. If the groom is young (in his mid or late teens), he may have contributed nothing at all to the bridewealth, though a man marrying a second or third wife will obtain the majority of items himself. Contributions from clansmen or cognates put the groom under no direct obligation; his repayment will be in kind at the subsequent marriages of clan brothers or their sons. Help from kinsmen is in the first place interpreted as help given to his father, and his father is formally responsible for any debts. The marriages of brothers and sisters are frequently arranged so that bridewealth received for the sister is used to obtain the brother's wife; recipients at one distribution may be called on for contribution to another.

Some prestige accrues to the bride herself from the transactions. A woman who brings in ample bridewealth to her own kin, and who arrives at her husband's place with substantial return-gifts, is called an *amb nyim* (modelled on the appellation for a big-man, *wuᵉ nyim*). One reason, it is said, why return is made at all lies in the fact that the bride's parents are "sorry" (*kaemb enim*) for her. As a daughter, she helped them in small tasks, looked after their pigs, and such like, and they do not want to see her blamed by her new husband's kin for being rubbish (*korpa*), because she has brought them no valuables. Her mother may specifically want a certain pig to go to the bride's mother-in-law in order to make her feel kindly disposed towards the girl. The bride's personal status is thus bound up with the generosity of the gifts. If little is given, then she may be labelled *korpa* by either side. Cowives or other women of the husband's residential group pour scorn on her in the course of a quarrel: so little bridewealth was given for her that she cohabits with her husband and bears his children "nothing", i.e. without proper backing. Her own kin, should she later fall foul of them, may equally take the opportunity of reminding her what paltry benefit came to them from her marriage.

A youth marrying for the first time usually has little part to play. He remains in the background, or may even be elsewhere altogether. To a much greater extent, the young bride is involved in the bridewealth proceedings. She must witness the initial discussions and displays. At the end of these (stage 3) she is asked if she is satisfied with the arrangements. Since indeed she is seen as susceptible to influence, notice must be taken of her disposition. Her affirmative, or her silence taken as such, indicates consent not only on her part but on her mother's too. If the mother has been arguing over the pig allocated to her, a senior kinsman may turn to the daughter to ask if *she* is satisfied. Her consent is understood to contain the promise that she will resist being swayed by her mother should the latter subsequently come grumbling to her. At any stage, the bride is able to wreck negotiations by simply walking away. The prospect of being questioned about her own disposition may precipitate this. She might well, in any case, be in a quandry over her feelings, irrespective of grievances she knows others of her kin to have.

The sequence of proceedings indicates the bride's gradual identification with her husband's group. At the outset she is an emissary for her kin (stage 1) but in the final stages she acts for her husband's kin, returning home at the *penal kng* (stage 5) as a member of the groom's party. By the entrance to the ceremonial ground the party waits for stragglers to catch up, so they can enter in a body. The pork, still on the bone, is packed into a netbag. The groom's kin lift this on to the bride's forehead; an unmarried sister of the groom may help her carry some if the prestation is large. Staggering under the weight, she bears this ahead of her affines, who make their entrance behind her. Helped off by her own fathers and brothers, she lays the pork before them and then retires to sit with her husband's female relatives. Her role as bearer of valuables between the two sets of kin is clearly symbolised.[1] It is also taken as a sign of her own acquiescence in the marriage. The bride who willingly carries the burden of pork will not later run away, but will, one is told, stay with her husband and bear him many children.

Hagen bridewealth can be described as a "means of winning and preserving the good will of those with the power to transfer marital rights" (Fortes, 1962: 10). There is, however, no one to one correlation between individual wealth items or categories and particular rights. No statutory amount confirms an allocation of rights beyond which all is open to bargaining, and thus no single component can be isolated as effecting jural transfer. Bridewealth obtains affines as well as wives, and in terms of the bridewealth components, the transfer of rights in the wife cannot be separated from the creation of affinal goodwill.

They may, however, be separated in other circumstances. I have already noted that in the case of marriage with a previously divorced woman, or a wife captured in warfare, payments are often delayed till

---

[1] In the past the bride publicly carried a digging stick given by her father to symbolize her future importance as a garden worker (Strauss, 1962: ch. 50).

the birth of children. These are not gifts to establish paternity over the children (identity of their *pater* is not in doubt) but to regularize relations with the people who are *pamal* (matrilateral kin) to them. Till this point, the couple will have been bound to each other in the performance of all the duties incumbent on husband and wife, apart from those entailing full exchange relations with the wife's kin. In the case of a woman living separated from her husband, such exchange relations may be maintained although other obligations lapse; there is no question that bridewealth, or a portion of it, be returned because the wife is not fulfilling her household duties. Where bridewealth is given, it thus stands for the total marital-affinal relationship; but it is also possible to create marital ties outside an affinal matrix. It should be added that the wife may dislike an arrangement which does not take her own kin into account, and if there is no sign that her husband intends to embark on prestations to them, her impatience may lead to divorce.

Some statements appear to link bridewealth to specific jural situations. An example is the insult between cowives noted on page 118. But this does not mean that the status of the woman's children is jeopardized—rather that she is having them without the support of affinal exchanges to consolidate her own position. Men sometimes claim that once they have paid[1] bridewealth, this gives them the right to treat the woman how they will. A husband charged by her kin with murdering his wife might even make this defence to them. But it is unrealistic bravado: women never lose the ultimate protection of their kin. Someone who tried to assert total "rights" in this way would be put under considerable pressure by his clan brothers to restore relations with his ex-affines through paying the appropriate compensations.

Subsequent Exchanges

After bridewealth, the next significant formal exchange should be child-growth payments (see above). If any children die, then mortuary payments (*kik kapa*, "brushing off the ashes of mourning") are made to the wife's immediate lineage kin. Pork, and sometimes pearl shells, are handed over at the final funeral feast, which takes place some months

---

[1] The pidgin terms "buy" and "pay" which are nowadays used for bridewealth transactions have encouraged younger men to assert that their "purchase" indeed gives them total jurisdiction over their wives.

after the death. A smaller feast ends the first period of a mourning (a few days or a week) and in expectation of later *kik kapa* payments, the maternal kin may have contributed a small pig to it. If they fail to attend the funeral they receive nothing. A father who has made generous bridewealth and child-growth payments may refuse to pay his wife's kin, protesting that the child died in spite of gifts given to ensure its health.

Kik kapa is paid to maternal kin for either boys or girls. The death of an adult man is the occasion for a more extensive killing of pigs for the mourners by his clansmen, and generous shares comprise *kik kapa* for the deceased's maternal relatives. When a married woman dies, her husband and his clansmen are responsible for killing funeral pigs. Cooked, these go as *kik kapa* to her own kin. At Buk (but not to the same extent at Kelua) the latter are likely to have contributed pigs to the initial feast, although the *kik kapa* will be a return in excess of these. If they come to mourn, they receive whether they make this contribution or not. When a very old woman dies, one who has had few links with home in her declining years, then *kik kapa* may be given to her married daughter by her husband and his sons. If, as often happened in the past, widespread and frequent hostilities prevent much visiting or attendance at funerals, the payment to the wife's people is omitted; it may also be omitted if the lineages of the deceased woman's husband and her brothers are in dispute, although her immediate brother might turn up briefly at the funeral. When for whatever reason her kin receive no *kik kapa* from her husband, they cook pigs privately themselves. As well as making recompense to mourners, the feasts establish the spiritual status of the dead person, and if her kin do not re-cook the *kik kapa* as a sacrifice to her ghost, they sacrifice their own pigs. Depending on the scale of the funeral gifts and the nature of existing relations, the wife's brothers send some of the *kik kapa* to her own maternal kin. Her husband does not make direct payments to these people.

Bridewealth is not returnable at a woman's death, although a husband tries to get it back if his wife was very young and had spent most of her time at her parents' place. The wife's kin may proclaim that the bridewealth has "died" on the girl, dismissing the man's complaints, or alternatively, in lieu of returning the bridewealth, they may make a generous *kik kapa* to him. The implication is that since the girl was so much at home, responsibility for her death lies with them. Where relations are exceptionally good, the husband may promise to return the *kik kapa* later. After divorce, the former husband is no longer responsible for *kik kapa* payments. A woman who dies while separated from her husband will be mourned by him; exchanges are made depending on the degree of separation. Normally *kik kapa* is given to her kin by the husband because of their anger (*popokl*) at her death, but if she has been living with them, assisting them in their affairs, it is her husband who has derived so little benefit from her help and who feels angry. Her kin there will be expected to make payments. In the case of a sick woman being nursed first by her husband and then being brought to her brother's place in hopes that she will recover there,[1] but dies in spite of everything, *kik kapa* payments may be judged out of place. They have both looked after the woman, and which should compensate the other?

> In 1964 a Kawelka Membo woman died. She and her two children had for many years been living with her own clansmen. Her brother and married son had only recently moved to a new area and at the time of her death she kept house with a married daughter and her husband who were themselves uxorilocal residents. Her own husband, Tipuka Oklembo Lawe, attended the initial mourning along with several sub-clan mates and their wives. At the end of the week, when the first feast was held, only he and another wife together with the latter's son, came from Oklembo. He appeared at the settlement rather furtively, carrying two pearl shells. In what seemed to me to be great embarrassment on both sides he handed these to his son by the dead woman and to his daughter's husband. They tried to refuse, muttering that the woman had died of old age and payments were not necessary.
>
> It was afterwards explained to me that the reason for the embarrassment was that the payments should have been the other way round: the son and son-in-law should have given the old man *kik kapa*. His wife had died not at his house but at her own home, which must have made the husband "feel bad"; and she had not cared for the husband, but only looked after her children. In spite of the fact that he lived quite near (Oklembo borders Kawelka territory), the husband did not attend the final funeral feast held some months later (he was described as too "ashamed") and was sent no pig from it.

Women are not actively involved in the organization of funeral payments; their duty is to weep and lament for the deceased. There are few important items of property to be inherited at death. Women's aprons, netbags and oil flasks go to a daughter or sister; pigs are killed at the funeral feasts.

Funeral payments between husband and wife's kin may develop into

---

[1] In the same way as a very sick man may be put in the men's house, or the house where sacrifices are made to lineage ghosts, so that he will recover under their strengthening influence.

moka exchanges. Sometimes bridewealth itself is only incompletely transferred, it being understood that subsequent items will be given in *moka*.

*A generation ago marriage arrangements between Yamka and Elti gave
rise to a dispute. The husband had not given proper bridewealth for his
wife (his second), and her kin expected to receive when Elti as a group
later made *moka* with her clan. The husband should have taken this opportunity of presenting her kin with a handsome gift, but they were disappointed, because all he gave were 16 pearl shells, and no pigs. The wife was
pregnant at the time, and the result was that her angry parents' clan ghosts
killed her in labour. Her own ghost in turn became angry; she had died
because the anger her father had for her husband led to interference from
the ghosts. It was thus her father's fault; she had not wanted to die, and
in vengeance her ghost then killed him.

A full analysis of *moka* partnerships is given elsewhere;[1] here I note
that while his wife's people do not provide a man with his sole partners,
gifts to immediate or classificatory affines always comprise a large bulk
of the exchanges made between the individuals of one clan to those of
another on a group occasion. When he has connections with a clan with
which his own is making *moka*, a man feels under more of an obligation
to include his wife's fathers and brothers in his exchanges than he might
cognatic kin; he may also use the tie to exchange with other men of her
sub-clan. In other directions he invests in sister's and daughter's husbands. The husbands of two sisters are identified with each other, and a
man expects to receive at his wife's sister's bridewealth.

A bride's sister's approval of marriage is supposed to auger well for its
stability, women having an interest in the bridewealth of their sisters,
as they do of their brothers. To a lesser extent they are concerned with
the marriages of the offspring (to whom they are father's/mother's
sisters). But whereas a brother is interested in his sister's and her husband's children, her husband has less contact with his wife's brother's
children. Lack of an enduring interest leads to his insignificant role in
prestations with them. Men establish *moka* partnerships with their fathers-
and brothers-in-law (WF, WB), but this is not continued into the next
generation with the WB's children. Unlike that between ZS and MB,
the tie between WBS and FZH is rarely used in *moka* (e.g. Table 16,
Strathern, A. J. (1971)). A man is much more likely to concentrate on
making *moka* with the children of his ZH (to whom is he MB), his own

---

[1] Strathern, A.J. (1971), especially Chapter 7.

son perhaps establishing a partnership with the WB and the WBS (the son's MB and MBS). The son thus succeeds to his father's *moka* partnerships on his mother's but not on his father's sister's side. (See Fig. 5.)

There is some antithesis between a woman's continuing involvement with her brother's children and her husband's relative disengagement. A husband's exchanges are focused directly on the marriage. From the

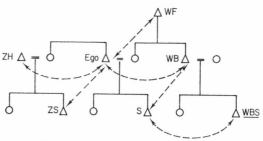

Fig. 5. *Moka* partnerships through time.

S continues his F's (ego's) partnerships with his MB (F's WB); he, but not his F, is likely to make *moka* with his MBS (the F's WBS).

wife's point of view, both her husband and her son activate their links with her kinsmen through her, but it is the son and not the father who has most use for her brother's children. That the fields of kin in which the two men are interested are discrete, if overlapping, lends weight to a distinction between "wife" and "mother" in a woman's roles, a distinction which is also made in other contexts.

Women and the Ghosts

We have seen that women have rights in the wealth of their own lineage and to some extent their clan. They eat at the marriages of their brothers' daughters.[1] Transactions surrounding a marriage—bridewealth, child-growth, *moka*, funeral payments—all indicate the woman's continuing membership in her natal or home clan. In supernatural terms, a married woman remains under the control of her clan ghosts, and at her death in association with them is able to influence her kin. At the same time, she also comes under the control of her husband's clan ghosts and subsequently has ghostly influence as a mother.

---

[1] A woman may be involved in the bridewealths of sub-clan brothers' daughters, but on her sister's side, only the daughters of her immediate sisters.

I have referred to various incidents where dissatisfaction over exchanges has seemingly resulted in ghostly interference. The wife's clan
ghosts take vengeance if their descendants feel cheated in bridewealth.
In a later chapter I consider some of the pressures these people may bring
to bear on the wife and her husband; here I am concerned with supernatural sanctions.

The influence a woman's clan ghosts have over her are strongest when
she is on her clan territory (which is why a sick woman may be carried
home to convalesce and a first child is sometimes born there). Nevertheless, their influence over her persists, though it is weakened, when she is
with her husband. The husband's clan ghosts are generally responsible
for her health, and the husband's as well as the wife's kin sacrifice on her
behalf if she falls very ill. Since she is a potential mother, the interest of
her husband's ghosts focus on sexual faithfulness, and they punish a
promiscuous wife. Like her kin, her own clan ghosts have two kinds of
concern: they ally themselves with the husband's ancestral ghosts to
maintain the marriage, and thus punish her for quarrelling with her
husband, sometimes even for quarrels with a cowife. Or they show
partisan support for their descendants and in the case of disputes with
the husband's kin, use the woman as a point of attack against the husband's clan, by making her or her children ill.

Women are particularly vulnerable to ghostly attack when newly
married, and again at the point of becoming a mother. This is the time
when her cognatic kin may still be harbouring grievances over the bridewealth. A wide range of her kin and consequently their ancestral ghosts
are involved. Ghosts may act on behalf of a woman's mother's or father's
sister and their children, as well as the mother's brother and his children,
and members of her own sub-clan or clan. The culmination of this period
is the birth of the first child; grievances stemming from more distant kin
can endanger the baby's life; if a close mother's brother considers himself
ill treated at the bridewealth, the woman herself may die. Ghosts do not
normally trouble a woman on behalf of her MZ, FZ and MB (though a
MB may send sickness to a ZD in protest against the girl's father),
interfering with her neither as an unmarried girl nor once she has had
her first child. After this period is over, it is only the immediate ghosts of
her lineage who support her close fathers and brothers and demonstrate
their influence. The concern of these is shown particularly in quarrels
between her own and her husband's kin, typically over debts, and a
wife's death as well as sickness may be attributed to their interference.

At the birth of the first child a wide range of the husband's clan ghosts may also be mobilized because of dissatisfactions over the bride-wealth transaction (e.g. if the return-gift or endowment is poor). Norm-ally it is only the close ghosts (on both his father's and mother's side) of the husband who are concerned with the wife's sexual behaviour and obedience. Difficulties in any childbirth may lead to suspicion of adultery.

A dead woman can visit sickness on her own kin, especially if she died young and childless. Her kin only fear vengeance after the death of an older woman if there was some specific grievance at issue. Female clan ghosts act because of a wrong done to their children or to them in their lifetime; they do not otherwise act jointly with their brothers in the exercise of moral control over the brother's children. Nevertheless, sisters are included in the generality of ghosts (*kor kui wamb*) who care for the overall prosperity of their living clansmen. Sanctions operating in respect of male members of a clan also cover females. Thus a boy who steals from his father's sister may be punished by the same ghosts who would act if he stole from a father's brother. The woman's clan status is clearly demarcated here, for such mystical retribution is not normally extended to include wrongs by her clansmen against her husband or her cowives. On the other hand, if she is wronged by a member of her hus-band's clan, she may be supported by their ghosts.

Women are usually buried in the husband's clan cemetery. Their main influence after death focuses on their maternal role. A man's dead mother as well as his father continues to help him; female ghosts can send sickness to both sons' and daughters' children, and there is no dogma that they are less powerful than male ghosts. Although matri-lateral ghosts may be activated over grievances on behalf of a mother's sister as well as a mother, a dead mother's sister herself is unlikely to send sickness to her sister's children.

Whereas a married woman comes under the influence of two sets of ghosts, the husband is not controlled by his wife's clan ghosts (though his children are). It is the wife who becomes identified with the husband, and not the other way round. She may be identified to the point of victimization for her husband's crimes (in one instance by the ghosts of all the angry owners whose pigs had been stolen by her husband; in another case reputedly as punishment for the husband indecently marry-ing a third wife before the mourning period for her dead wife was over). On the other hand, she may suffer directly because of her intermediate position. Ghosts ordinarily control only their own cognates. If brothers-in-law steal from each other, whether it is the sister's husband or the wife's brother in the wrong, the linking woman becomes vulnerable to attack from ghosts from either side who themselves cannot directly influence the affine.[1] The loss of the wife (or the children) is a blow against her menfolk.

A wife's dual mystical status is underlined in the way she is influenced by the totemic-like divination substance (*mi*) of both her own and her husband's tribe. Each tribe possesses a *mi*, frequently leaf varieties, also stones and dogs (Strauss, 1962). A tribe member may swear his innocence if accused of some crime by sucking or chewing on (in Melpa, "eating") the *mi* substance, challenging his clan and tribal ghosts to kill him if he lies. A man normally swears by the *mi* of his father's tribe, but he may on occasion also "hold" the *mi* of his mother's tribe. He is under the influence of their ghosts as well, and while *mi* is said to operate automatically, ghosts support it. Because of this, blood relatives can be used in divination between groups. Although members of a tribe share a common *mi*, if accusations are made between two intermarried clans of a tribe, relatives in one will administer *mi* for relatives in the other, as they also do if the clans are of different tribes. Thus, for example, if an individual is accused of theft by men from the clan of his father's sister's husband, he might give his own tribal *mi* to an actual son of the father's sister. The son eats it on behalf of his mother's brother's son and established the innocence; were he guilty the mother's brother's son's ancestral ghosts would kill the father's sister's son. If the clan making the accusation have a sister married into the accused's clan, they may administer their own *mi* to the sister's son, who eats it on behalf of his agnatic clansmen accused of the crime.

A sister's son may thus be used by either his father's or his mother's clansmen in a test of innocence over a crime which does not directly concern him. His mother is in the same position. A man never swears on his wife's *mi*, but a married woman may swear on the *mi* of both her own and her husband's tribe, and be used in divination tests between intermarried groups.

It is when a wife becomes absorbed into her husband's clan (*rukrung mba pora ndui*, "to have finished going inside") that, as a newly married

---

[1] For a comparable situation in supernatural punishment for incest, see Strathern, A. J. and A. M. (1969:145).

woman cannot she "holds" their *mi*. This is irrespective of whether she has children or not. Thus in a quarrel between two established wives married into the single group, the one may force the other to eat the group's *mi*. Clan ghosts of her husband send the guilty woman sickness. Her own clan ghosts may be said to realise the justice of the prosecution and help the husband's ghosts. If a woman is implicated in some action of her husband's, typically if he is a pig-stealer, and she is suspected of having taken part, she supports her husband by herself swearing on *mi*. In an intra-tribal marriage her own and his *mi* are in any case the same; in an extra-tribal marriage the spouses each eat their own tribal *mi*, or the wife takes the husband's. The few accounts I have of such situations suggest that a wife who eats her husband's *mi* will often include a piece of her own *mi* as well. If she herself is accused of theft by members of her husband's clan, her husband may administer some of his tribal *mi* to her which she eats along with her own.

As an intermediary, a married woman also eats *mi* on behalf of her husband. A man accused of stealing a pig from the lineage or sub-clan of his own wife will have his guilt or innocence divined through his wife eating her tribal *mi* from the hand of the plaintiff. The wronged man might also ask the woman's own father or brother to give her *mi*. I have, however, no cases of a woman acting thus on behalf of an accused brother. Accusations sometimes involve suspicions of poisoning.

To some extent women can manipulate *mi* as a sanction against their own kin. To hold or eat it is a serious undertaking. The person who swears by it runs the risk of death if his words are not true or if his later behaviour belies his oath. But it is for this very reason that *mi* has coercive power. A young wife, dissatisfied with her marriage and not wanting to return to her husband, or a bride at the last stages of wedding proceedings, may use *mi* as a final resort to force her parents to capitulate. The threat is a suicidal one: the daughter declares that nothing will make her go back to her husband; if she does, whether forced to, or herself changes her mind, later the *mi* she ate will "eat" (i.e. kill) her. She thus appeals to her parents to put her life before the marriage, to extend to her sympathy (*kaemb*). However, the same mechanism can be used to opposite effect. It is by marrying that a daughter shows sympathy (*kaemb*) for her parents, since she brings them in wealth. A refusal to marry or an obstinate wish to associate with a man of no means shows what little regard she has for them. Parents may force their will on a disobedient daughter by themselves eating *mi*: if she refuses to obey them, may they be struck dead! Again, the appeal is to her *kaemb*, for would she want her parents to die? We may see this as an extreme form of the threat never to see her again.

*Nerup is the daughter of Kawelka Yura. Her first marriage, in the early 1960's, was to a Romalke man. She had not (according to a sub-clan brother) wanted to marry there, and after a couple of months was home on a visit. After another month or so her husband came to fetch her, and her father and father's brothers told her to return. She obstinately refused. To make her "feel good", a lineage father, Rolta, killed a large pig for her to take back. In return for the four shells and a side of pork the husband had brought with him, Rolta was going to hand over the major portions of this pig and a small live pig, while her father got a pearl shell ready. The pork was cooked at Rolta's place, where Nerup had taken refuge, being afraid to go to her father's settlement. The girl came upon them all opening up the steam oven and about to distribute the pork; some of the ribcage was in Rolta's hand. Rolta explained that her husband had come for her with valuables and they wanted to send her back to him with pig and shells. She grabbed the meat he was holding, slicing a piece off. She said: "From the start I never wanted to marry and I told you not to kill any pig. Now you want to send this pork and the other valuables so I shall not run away again. All right: it is just as well you have killed it—you can return his items and that will be that. I shall not go back. I am going to eat cordyline leaves (the Kawelka *mi*) with this pig. It does not matter what happens to me!" She had the leaves in her hand and her fathers could do nothing but apologize to the husband; they later returned the whole bridewealth to him.

She was then sent to marry a Tipuka Kelmbo man. The same thing happened; she had not wanted to go there and it looked as though she would run away from her second husband. Yura and Rolta took the protesting girl back with them to Kelmbo, presenting her husband's kin with a shell and pig to show they had no part in her recalcitrance. The two of them then deliberately ate cordyline leaves (their own *mi*) so that the Kelmbo and Nerup herself could see what their position was. The woman had run away before and they did not want to have to return bridewealth a second time. Who would know what was going on in her mind (*noman*)? If she listened to them now, that would be good, it would show she thought of them; but if she disobeyed still, that too would be all right, what matter if the *mi* killed them! They would die, and only later when she married someone else would people ask, where is your father?, and then she would be sorry. She was thus persuaded to stay with her Kelmbo husband.

Mi is further used where bad debts lead to a deterioration of relations. Between men, the exasperated party forswears the offender, saying that he will never give anything to the partner again, the *mi* smite him dead if he allows him across his threshold! This may operate against unrelated partners, or against affines.

A woman can set up *mi* against her own kin. She swears they shall not visit her again, may the *mi* kill her if she gives in to them! It is interesting that reasons for a woman's extreme exasperation invariably focus on debts—typically, she and her husband have been constantly giving things to her kin who have failed time and again to make proper return. The wife is ashamed before her husband, and swears they shall not visit her till the debts are made good. She may have been back and forth with requests over the matter, and had to bear the brunt of the husband's annoyance. Ashamed himself to show anger towards his in-laws, he upbraids his wife for the relatives she has. But she is not simply taking her husband's part: the failure has been a personal slight to her as well. The point is that she feels involved enough to risk the *mi* sanction. Although she brings it to bear on her kin in the interests of her husband's good relations with them, at the same time the threat to break off relations is outrageous.[1] She has given in to her anger (*popokl*). Whatever the temporary justification, it is felt that the cost in terms of social relations is too high. Should persons forget their oath, the *mi* retaliates—they may have recovered their temper, but must suffer the consequences of previous rashness. It is feelings of *kaemb* (sympathy and affection) that a woman should really bear towards her own people.

Similar feelings should also develop between spouses. It is interesting, however, that the *mi* sanction is used primarily against a woman's home kin, rarely against her husband. There is one example of a wife reputedly forswearing intercourse with her husband because she was jealous of a cowife. Usually, however, this kind of pressure is not brought to bear against a husband, even if he has debts with her kin. Her sanctions lie in the withdrawal of household services; husbands who have some physical control over their wives, also do not use *mi* against them.

Hageners say that women are "in the middle" (*ruk ile moromen*), they are "between" two sets of people, their own kin and their husband's kin. We have seen that a married woman is doubly vulnerable to ghostly attack and may be the victim of divination tests held between the two sides. Continuing concern of her natal clan ghosts matches the continuing interest of her own kin in her affairs and her welfare after marriage. The woman's reciprocal duty towards them is to support their interests

---

[1] Some of these points are discussed in Strathern, A. M. (1968).

vis-à-vis her husband. This makes the woman in a sense responsible for the exchanges which her marriage brings about. If the husband marries her without bridewealth, it is said, her clan ghosts in anger might kill her, especially if she had acted against her parents' wishes. As a ghost she later takes revenge on the husband. On the other hand, she herself may be resentful (*popokl*) that her husband has made no payments and be killed by her clan ghosts out of pity. A shabby return-gift by her parents might make her equally angry, clan ghosts again killing her in pity for her anger; as a ghost herself, she then takes revenge on her parents.

Women are thus not completely passive intermediaries, being able to manipulate even the extreme sanction of *mi* divination to their own advantage. What is interesting is that their desires often coincide with demands put on them by husbands or brothers. A woman given an item of wealth at a bridewealth distribution is to some extent herself being honoured; at the same time only married women receive in this way. Unmarried girls have no share of the distribution. For the item the woman receives from her kin is also intended for her husband (and vice versa), her own prestige being bound up in the transactions between men. Evaluations which Hagen men make about women, and which women make about themselves, are connected with this.

6

Producers and Transactors

Preceding chapters have dealt with two main topics: first, the economic importance of married women in the agricultural system, and the reciprocal dependence of husband and wife on each other in terms of the division of labour; and second, the importance of marriages to political relations between groups and ceremonial exchange between individuals. Her work in raising pigs, a major exchange valuable, is the point at which a woman's economic role most clearly feeds into her status as an intermediary in the exchange system. The present chapter discusses the relationship between a woman's status as primary producer and her contribution to ceremonial exchange, in terms of Hageners' evaluations of these roles, and the kinds of overall comparisons made between men and women. When men talk about "females" in general they tend to take "wives" as their prototype, although they may modify their attitudes if thinking specifically of "mothers", say, or of "sisters". I therefore take the husband–wife relationship as a starting point.

In his account of male–female relationships in the New Guinea Highlands, Meggitt (1964) describes tension and conflict between the sexes, demonstrated in beliefs about their respective natures and related to the structural concomitants of marriage patterns. For Hagen, the division of labour is also crucial to the way in which male and female "roles" are evaluated. The status of different tasks is a separate issue from what individuals can achieve through carrying them out well or badly, and separate again from whether the tasks are in fact essential or not (cf. Kaberry, 1952:145). We have seen that a married woman may be subject to dual pressures; as far as arrangements between male affines are concerned, this is a matter of competition between parties with common ends, but tension also arises from the different interpretation the sexes put on their own and each other's main tasks. There is a broad contrast between men's and women's activities, which I indicate by the opposing categories, "transaction" and "production". These have no direct linguistic correspondence in Melpa, but stand for a summation of Hagen views, values, attitudes, and treatment of inter-sexual relations. Working in gardens and rearing pigs is productive work; making *moka* with the pigs is transactional work. I suggest that while Hagen men regard themselves as in the main transactors and women as mere producers, women claim some control over transactions made by their husbands on the very grounds of their contributions as producers, even sometimes try to act as transactors themselves.

Producers

I have already referred to claims men may make that they are the owners (*pukl wu^e*) of gardenland. The same is claimed of pigs. *Wu^e-nga mbi morom*, "it is the man's name on them". The wife may care for these things, but in the husband's eyes has no ultimate voice in decisions over the disposal of livestock or how a garden is to be divided for a new season. Men grumble when cowives quarrel over their allocation of plots: "Why should they fight? It is men who clear the gardens, and men decide where the divisions are to be; women should just plant them and harvest the food." Nevertheless, although their work is "just planting", women who devote themselves to gardening and pig-raising are admired by both sexes. Those who apply will and intelligence to these tasks are compared favourably with others who are too slow or stupid or too lazy to achieve much. They are approvingly spoken of as being single-minded (*noman tenda petem*) in their industry. In turn, a woman may take pride in the gardens she has planted, and of her fat pigs and full pig stalls.

Hard work is the mark of a good wife, and young girls are encouraged to show their capacity for work. The mother is supposed to tell her daughter: "You are a girl, and you can never forget your netbag and digging stick. Your father and brother have made gardens and you mustn't neglect weeding them. In the morning you must harvest food for breakfast, then when the sun is warm you can weed the gardens. At night you should bring sweet potatoes back to cook—but you mustn't eat all the tubers yourself: leave some for your father and brothers who will be hungry when they come home. When you have a spare moment, use it to make a head-covering for your father or a netbag for yourself. When the pigs come in, herd them into the house and see they have food. You cannot get up and leave your netbag and digging stick, and go to sit down in the men's house. The men are there talking, and you have no business there. Or if you wander around the paths and roads and neglect your gardens everyone will see, and they'll say, 'Oh, this woman is no worker—never mind, we shall not marry her!' "

Constant concern with the minutiae of food production produces an emotional involvement. The refrains of women's songs hark on themes relating to their garden work. Accounts by some of how their time is spent comprise detailed catalogues of all the crops they grow, and all the names of all the varieties, how they plant them, dig them up, cook them and then share them out. Women emphasize the way they actually hand food over to their dependents, as they also do their participation at special cookings or pig-feasts. The prominence women are accorded on such occasions is summed up in the positively stated desire for children. To have several children, women say, means that they will receive plenty of meat at feasts, for themselves and their offspring together.

Gardens are probably of greater importance to women than they are to men. They spend long hours working there, and the pigs they care for have to be fed with garden produce. Women are sensitive about their control over crops. It is in the disposal of foodstuff that they can demonstrate generosity. The popular woman is one always ready to feed visitors who come to her house, and to invite neighbours to any special food cooking she holds. An Elti man named (to me) eight wives of his immediate sub-sub-clan, of which he singled out two as being generous (kae, "good") women. Of one of them he said, "She gives food to everyone. To anyone passing by, she calls out, 'Are you hungry?' and shares her meal, and talks and laughs (the outward sign of friendly intentions) with us as well." He compared her to others who turn away as one approaches and keep their food to themselves. On another occasion two near adolescent boys (for my benefit) divided up the senior women of their clan into those whom they liked and those whom they reckoned as "bad women" (amb kit). All those outside their own sub-clan fell into the latter category. This was because they were married to men with whom the boys had to maintain some distance, which meant in turn that such wives would not feed them. Since children are brought up to expect food from only their immediate mothers, the boys' complaint that these women never fed them bears no relation to expectations (where they expected to be given food they were denied) but is a manner of evaluation (those are the women who do not give us food and they are therefore bad).

Not only are all women not necessarily generous with their food, but men sometimes talk as though they cannot rely on their wives even for minimum sustenance. The praise accorded generous women would seem to stem partly from the implication that they are paragons of dependability. It is true that a husband may have to fend for himself when his wife is in seclusion, but statements about neglect are also an exaggeration of the commonly drawn contrast between wives and mothers. By suckling her child the mother has proved her care for it; a wife has always to demonstrate her willingness. A man who grumbles constantly about his wife may be met with the same contrast in her retort, "Why should I feed you? I am not your mother!" A wife's irresponsibility is not regarded as shocking as would be a mother's refusal to feed her young children. There seems to be a similar contrast in the fact that whereas a man is at liberty to strike his wife, striking his own mother is taken very seriously indeed.

Men appreciate their general dependency on women in the characterization of females as "strong things" (*mel rondokl*). This refers to the fact that through women food is produced, pigs are raised and children born, and is given as one rationale for making handsome bridewealth payments.

Women value their own contributions as producers, which goes with the admiration an industrious and successful woman is given. To a certain extent we could call this prestige. Yet from another point of view a wife is simply instrumental in her husband's acquisition of prestige. For while they recognize the skill of the successful woman, and the essential nature of female tasks, men evaluate production-activities in general terms as of low status. They are not so worthwhile as making transactions.

Transactors

For a man, his own involvement in production (e.g. clearing gardens) carries relatively little prestige. Industry alone does not lead directly to big-man status. Anyone can make gardens if he applies himself; it is simply a matter of hard work. Renown comes from being able to influence people, demonstrating power over exchange partners and one's clansmen alike. A big-man (*wu^e nyim*) achieves his position because of his oratorical talents, his persuasiveness, his capacity to make people listen to his plans and follow his lead. It is the ability to draw valuables to oneself which makes one wealthy, and these include shells as well as pigs; it is for shell-*moka* and not pig-*moka* that wealth-tallies (*omak*) are worn by men. Shells cannot be grown or reared; they can be obtained only through transactions with others.

Something of the gradation in control which husband and wife have in relation to each other over garden produce, pigs, and shell valuables has been noted in Chapter 3. That women's control over pigs is more restricted than over garden produce is not simply a matter of labour investment, for their work is concerned with both. Rather it is related to the ends to which these items are put. Vegetables are hardly used in ceremonial exchange at all; they may be consumed at public feasts, but the reputation for generosity which the feast-giver acquires cannot be converted into political prestige. Ideal behaviour for a big-man includes such generosity, but it alone does not make him a big-man. Food planted by women is, in the main, for private daily consumption. Pigs, by contrast, like shells, are always on their way between exchange partners. Pigs may be bred and reared by women, but they are also valuables which are the objects of transactions. And it is on the disposal of pigs that many husband–wife disputes focus.

It is my impression that for men, who deal in pigs and shells, vegetable food has minor significance as a category of gift; feeding visitors is seen by them as an extension of domestic hospitality rather than a matter of gift-giving. To women, however, giving away food may have just this quality—it is a means to influence. Because a woman feeds her husband she has a right to his attentions. In a different context women certainly feel that the work they have invested in the care of livestock, primarily the feeding of them, entitles them to some control over the animals.

Women claim such control on double grounds. First, responsibility for the care of stock gives them, in their eyes, a general right to some say in their disposal. In addition, a wife may also feel a proprietary interest in those pigs which were sent by her kin. This applies especially to the endowment stock, but can hold for others that come through subsequent exchanges. Pigs born and reared within a household are spoken of as "of the house" in contrast with others more recently gained; but this is in reality only a relative statement. Animals which a woman may see as having raised herself, her husband may regard as the progeny of some past transaction. Similarly, pigs which a woman sees as having been sent her by her kin, her husband may regard as a return for his original investment. With equal self-justification one spouse can say, "*I* am the owner; you just look after them" (if it were not for the husband's original transaction there would be no pigs in the house), while the other answers, "*I* look after them; you are just the owner" (if it were not for the wife's care, where would the pigs be now?). Most of the time it is assumed that spouses consult each other and agree about allocation, but conflict can arise if the one hopes a pig will be sent as a gift in a particular direction but the other either wants it to be kept or be sent elsewhere. Ultimately, a wife can do nothing if the husband is determined to have his way. He may, however alienate her by high-handed actions (Vicedom and Tischner, 1943–8:2:93; Strauss, 1962:221–4).

If live pigs are to be sent to exchange partners, wives often hope their own kinsfolk, and not other partners, will receive the fruits of their labours, and are liable to put the interests of their kin first. A husband may suspect that her female relatives supply his wife with magic or doctor small gifts of pork so that he will be induced to give them all his pigs and shells. The wife of a polygynist may also be supplied with magic if the husband seems to be favouring a cowife at her kinsmen's expense.

There are situations, however, in which the wife's own interests may clash even with those of her kin: women sometimes express general dissatisfaction at the prospect of their animals being allocated anywhere, to their own brothers or to anyone, because they would rather the pigs were killed and consumed privately. This is a potential area for conflict: whereas the husband is trying to maximize his resources in financial transactions which will yield credit, the wife complains that she thought "the pig was to eat", and that her hard work in caring for it would be rewarded. In fact grown pigs are rarely killed without having passed through many hands, and women are only likely to bring this up in the context of other grievances. The ideal may nevertheless be stated quite forcibly. To me it was put thus: "We women want to rear pigs for eating. If the clan kill pigs together and we all get a share, that is good. But if our husband's individual partners come and pull our live pigs, then we are angry. We look after them. Men only think of shells and money (i.e. things to be obtained with the pigs), but women think they rear the animals to eat them later. We are annoyed with men, because the flesh of pigs is sweet." Or again, "Men walk about and they bring shells and pigs to our house and we feel pleased. We look after the pigs, and we are happy when we can kill and eat them; but when a man (husband's exchange partner) comes and claims a debt and pulls the pigs, we are angry. It may be the man's pig, but we looked after it entirely."

The importance women place on sharing in distributions of cooked pork is partly related to their general involvement with food. Apart from the actual pleasure taken in eating flesh, cuts of pork can always be further distributed, giving women the opportunity to make small gifts in their own name. Food distributions also accord women a recognition of status (cf. page 96),[1] whereas for men these are only one of many occasions on which their various statuses and capacities are acknowledged. Hence it is especially the bride's female relatives who are concerned to "eat the pig of her marriage".

As producers of the pigs women claim rewards for their work. When they claim that pigs they have reared should be intended for their own kin and when they further claim control over pigs derived from these kin, they may be trying to act as transactors.

The archetype of the male transactor is the big-man who commands several *moka*-partnerships. No woman can operate the same political roles, initiate *moka*, settle disputes, plan peace or war and persuade others to follow. I have, however, referred to the phrase used of women which parallels that for big-man: *amb nyim*. An *amb nyim* ("big-woman") has prestige in production—she raises many pigs and her position may be celebrated at dances which accompany pig-*moka*. But in addition an *amb nyim* also participates a little in transactions. A Central Melpa wife defined her as one who has plenty of pigs and who goes and gets pearl shells from her brothers. Her marriage is profitable for both her husband and her lineage kin alike and her own efforts are seen to contribute to the success of the exchange between them: she brings in valuables for her husband and she brings in valuables for her brother. More than just a road for the affines' exchanges, she acts as a go-between. Women, themselves, however, may put a rather different interpretation on their intermediary status than do men. The statement that women are "in between" (*ruk ile moromen*) needs further examination.

In the first place, the phrase is a simple comment on the way marriages

---

[1] The seriousness with which even a young, in this case unmarried, girl may take her position, is shown in this story of a quarrel between two sisters. They were given a share of pork from a distribution, and the elder sister wanted to divide up their portion among their parents' household and neighbours. The younger sister wanted to save the pig so they could eat it themselves. They quarrelled bitterly, with the result that the younger girl hanged herself.

link various groups and individuals. An analogous idiom is that of exchange marriage.

Secondly, it is a compliment men pay to women. The sentimental attachment between brothers and sisters, and the wife's contribution to the husband's efforts, are courteously acknowledged. Even though men see females as having no direct control over the disposal of valuables, a flow of exchanges is one of the benefits marriage brings, and metaphorically a man says he is giving *moka* to his sister, when he transacts with his sister's husband. A woman can thus achieve some prestige as a quasi-participant in the transactions. She is honoured both as a wife and a sister when her husband and brother exchange with each other, and from the point of view of her kin, marriage means not that she becomes less of a sister but that she fulfills her ideal role as a road for valuables.

Thirdly, sometimes women actually carry messages between the two sides. In the past this might mean life or death. A man who tried to maintain connections through his wife with people who were otherwise enemies to his own clansmen, despatched a warning with his wife should his clan have plans to poison or attack his affines. These people might be enemies, but he would be afraid (it was said) that the hostilities would destroy his road (*amb nombokla etek kit iting*). Were his wife's people to die, with whom would he make *moka*, whom would his children call *pamal* (maternal kin)? Such a warning would be sent only when the brothers-in-law were on good terms and there were no outstanding debts between them. It is interesting to note that the sister's husband is supposed to be in a less secure position than the wife's brother: if the wife's kin are killed her importance as an intermediary is lost; on the brother's part, however, if one husband dies his sister can always be married to another. Nowadays women are sent with information about impending group festivals, and requests between the individual affines. Demands made through the woman as a messenger turn into pressure put on the woman herself.

This leads to the fourth point. It is because of her relationship as a sister or wife that she is used as a go-between, and in turn this means that she may herself respond to demands because of the value these relationships have for her. Examples have already been given of the way women are seen as becoming committed to success or failure in the exchanges between her husband and her kin. Bridewealth was cited as the prototype transaction. Instances were given in Chapter 5 of the intermediary woman being manipulated in disputes. Men exploit women's loyalties. Her kin play on her potential involvement as a means of punishment: a bride may be given no or only a small dowry because she married against the parents' wishes. It is not only in bridewealth but also in *moka* transactions that women are susceptible to pressure (see page 130), and their loyalties are also used in the perpetration of hostilities between groups (Chapter 7).

Given these facts it is not surprising that some women perhaps take their intermediary position more seriously than men intend. Over-zealous support of their kin may even lead to the latter's embarrassment.

*A Minembi woman, Kombuklam, is married to Tipuka. She left her husband and returned home with her child because of trouble over a debt. Her father had given her husband four pearl shells, and although he had made several requests to have them returned, the debt had never been made good. Kombuklam was "sorry" (*kaemb enim*) for her father and left because her husband had been so tardy. He followed her but she said she wanted to divorce him. When he came for her a second time, Kombuklam's father stepped in and said that he had had no part in all this—there was no hurry about the shells, they could be returned any time. He had sent his daughter to this man in the first place, and had no intention taking her back. The woman could do nothing: since she had acted out of sympathy for her father, she now had to follow his "strong" words. (1960's: account from Kombuklam's sister's husband.)

Men are ready to recognize the importance of the wife's producer contribution, but while they appreciate links through her with her kin, these are only one of many potential avenues to *moka* partnership. The wife's insistent support of her kin is short-sighted, exchanges with them seeming more important to her than they actually are in the wider configuration of her husband's total network. Ultimately it is to their joint prestige for him to keep open as many contacts as possible. In the same way she may take her own role in his transactions as more important than he would allow is the case.

Women not only see themselves as having a claim on their husband's transactions, but sometimes aver that men cannot make *moka* without their help. A man needs a wife to advise him on how many shells he should return for pork or live pigs, they say. But while a husband may in private grant this, from his point of view internal decisions are a domestic matter: women have no political role in transactions. Since it is through her intermediary position as a wife or sister that a woman acts as go-between, her participation can be assumed to be a structural outcome of this rather than of her own ambitions and political skill. Thus women have few formal acts at public *moka* prestations. They do not participate in preliminary meetings to decide when the exchange is to take place; they lead prized pigs to the ceremonial ground and attend to beasts their husbands are to receive, but do not publicly allocate them; and although husband and wife may openly consult with each other, no man in such circumstances would ask her to come forward and speak. It is in her private capacity, as personally connected to the exchange partners, that her position is used. Above all, women are not speech-makers, and it is their ability as orators which brings big-men promi-nence. We have seen that female relatives of the bride at a bridewealth transaction may grumble openly to their menfolk, but do not address the groom's side directly. Moreover, men tolerate such interruptions only when they are on their home ground: I witnessed one occasion of a groom's mother's open protest about having to provide more pigs; when she carried her complaints over to the discussions held later at the bride's place, she was reprimanded by the men—she should keep her talk for home, they had come to a strange place and what was she doing going on like this? Women are, in fact, often inarticulate in public, and at-tempts made by them to break into the speeches ignored or derided by men.

By herself a woman can rarely initiate *moka* exchanges. She depends on her husband to make transactions with the pigs she raises, to a lesser extent on her brother and other kin. Her own success is immediately de-pendent on male *moka* partners and she cannot by herself become an *amb nyim*. The term is rarely used, in fact, except for the wives of a big-man. Occasionally a widow attempts to act autonomously.

Among several disputes which broke out at the termination of a public *moka* display by a Ndika sub-clan in 1967, one concerned a widow who was seen physically wrestling with a male recipient for a set of pearl shells. She managed to snatch away three, while the man himself, once he had lost them, tried to assume an air of indifference. He was her dead husband's lineage brother. Since her husband's death, the widow's sons had made *moka* with the Ndika and had expected a return, but the only gift was to this man. The sons themselves took no part in their mother's violent defence of their interests.

A separated wife living with her own kin may also assert greater con-trol over her herd than other wives do, perhaps occasionally initiating exchanges herself. Preferring to associate with a successful (*nyim*) brother rather than a less successful husband is an occasional motive for separation. One such wife who lives in her brother's settlement described her husband as a "rubbish man" (*wu^e korpa*) for failing to supply her with breeding pigs; these she obtained from her own brother, and the progeny from them were the basis for payments (under the rubric of childbirth gifts) she made back to him. The sister referred to the fact that she had raised the pigs on her own (*na nanom øit rur*) and described herself as "making *moka*" with her brother. At a later showing of pigs at a public display by her brother, the sister was acknowledged as one of the contributors.

Apart from these exceptional circumstances, men and women alike admit that a woman without a husband is "nothing". A wife married to a weak husband may be led by her ambitions to divorce him in preference for someone of eminence. Men go further and say it is only when they are married that women show any sense of purpose (*noman*). They link it to women having to leave their natal territories, only through marriage acquiring an attachment to (their husband's) land. If her husband dies, a widow is at a loss, it is said; she has promiscuous affairs and runs away. Husbands alone give women pigs and shells and make them *nyim*.

It is in this kind of context that men characterize females as weak (*rondokl tei na tetem*, "they have no strength"), that is, they do not make speeches or influence public events; and as *korpa*, that is, they really own no valuables. Ultimately men see themselves as in control. From this derives the other, rather different, meaning attached to "in between". If a woman's bad behaviour jeopardizes the friendship of two brothers-in-law, the friends supposedly agree, "Let us still make *moka*. The woman has no road—if she wants to run away, we shall not let her! She is between us and cannot act of her own accord. We are two men and she is just a woman." In other words, men claim they can conduct their affairs over her head. It is men who are the transactors, and between them they control women. A wife's father exercises his authority by ordering her to return to a husband she wants to leave, and points out that the latter need have no fear for the future, since he will always send her back. After all, where else can she run but home? (i.e. she is helpless if the refuge she seeks is not granted).

Women's Grievances

The kinds of demands women put upon their menfolk can be illustrated by their complaints.

People harbouring particular grievances (*popokl*) in their hearts may attract the sympathy of ancestral ghosts, who demonstrate this by making the aggrieved person ill. Various examples of people's behaviour, or supposed behaviour, when they are *popokl* have already been given. While the victim looks for sympathy and for appeasement from the person who has made him angry, there is the further sanction that the victim may even die of his *popokl*-sickness. As a ghost he himself then takes revenge. Women quite readily say that their frustrations can lead to this: if their husbands "pull" the pigs they have so fondly cherished to give to some outside partner, this makes them *popokl* and death may be the consequence. It was the opinion of one male informant (in an interview with Andrew Strathern) that women are invariably *popokl* when they die, either because they have not had children or because their children have not appreciated the hard work involved in their up-bringing. Whereas an ageing father gradually hands transactional control of his resources over to his son, a mother continues to rear pigs, and old as well as young women are said to die with *popokl* in their hearts. They still produce for their menfolk and demand recognition for this. These general statements show the serious consequences women may envisage if they are frustrated, almost an admission that women are bound to be frustrated.

Affliction puts the sufferer in the position of soliciting sympathy from other people, so that sick persons may be quite willing to talk about the reasons for their *popokl*; 39 such instances of illness were admitted by 34 different women at Buk and Kelua to have this as their cause. Sometimes more than one reason for being *popokl* was given: the number of grievances amounts to 50; 14 women, not actually ill at the time, also listed for me the total number of grievances and complaints they harboured against others. These two sets of information are distinguished as (A) and (B), respectively. I do not put too much weight on the figures. "Grievances" run into one another, particular ones are subsumed under more general complaints, and since a few of the sick women (A) came with complaints on more than one occasion, some of the grievances are connected and occasionally even repeated; my division into grievance-units is thus necessarily arbitrary.

Reasons for *popokl* bringing about sickness (category A) included: 1. the anger of an old widow with sons of her husband's lineage for not building her a new house; 2. a married woman's complaints that her husband did not help her with garden work; 3. another's that her son had not distributed meat to her when a special feast was held for the young men of his sub-clan; 4. the anger of a young wife against her brother for failing to send endowment pigs so that she could start a herd; 5. that of another with her husband with whom she quarrelled over the allocation of a pig of "hers" provided initially by her own brother; 6. the annoyance of a further married woman that a group with which her husband had been making *moka* (not her own clan) had made a bad return for their investment; 7. of another that although she had helped a man of her husband's lineage with a pig of "her own", to pay a compensation, he had never made good the debt; 8. another's quarrel with her husband because he took away a pig for his own *moka* that had been given to their young son, by her kin; 9. the anger of a married daughter with her father for not allocating her a live pig he had just received in *moka*; and 10. the annoyance of another daughter with her husband over his contributions to her deceased father's funeral.

A young married woman (B) complained about the following: 1. She was *popokl* when her husband hit or remonstrated with her,[1] or when he fetched firewood for her cowives and not for herself. 2. Her husband's brother was an irascible old man, always telling the women to get on with their work, and this she hated. 3. She had a younger sister staying with her who never gave practical help in the gardens or in the house. 4. Her half-brothers do not send her gifts or pork from distributions. 5. She is *popokl* when her own kin are tardy in returning *moka* her husband has given them. 6. Her mother also forgets her at distributions.

Further reasons from other women (B) cover: 7. The wife of a big-man complained that her husband never made adequate gardens so that she could not raise pigs efficiently. 8. A woman fell out with her husband over plans for her daughter's marriage. 9. Another complained that members of her husband's lineage made excessive demands on the portions of bridewealth meat intended for themselves, the bride's parents. 10. Yet another was angry at her husband for not making child-growth payments to her kin.

These statements comprise a rough continuum. Some of the complaints are directly about the failure of others in their household obligations (a husband is lazy, a son does not build a house, e.g. A1, 2; B1, 3, 7). Others seem rather to arise from the woman's desire to assume a quasi-transactional role (as in disputes over the disposal of pigs, e.g.

---

[1] A quarrel may leave either party feeling frustrated; although the one hopes that a show of *popokl* will make the other feel sorry, the latter may in fact react by being *popokl* too.

A 5–10; B5, 8–10). Many are by no means clear cut: for example, complaints that a woman is left out of distributions (e.g. A3; B4, 6) border on both kinds.[1] Disputes over funeral or child-growth payments (A10, B10) involve notions of obligation towards the wife together with her kin; in any interaction between the latter and her husband, a slight may be cast both on the status she has with these people and on her own transactional efforts. In all these cases a woman may feel she is owed rights by her menfolk. A categorization into what could be called "neglect" and "thwart" complaints fits loosely with obligations women see arising from "producer" aspects of their roles, and from their claims to be considered as "transactors".

TABLE X

Proportion of "neglect" and "thwart" grievances given by married women

Type of information	Type of grievance			
	Neglect	Thwart	Other	Total
A	19	20	11	50
B	22	34	18	74
	41	54	29	124

Thwart complaints comprise an appreciable total (43%). An interesting point about them is that they are not couched in terms of generalized frustrations, e.g. that men deny women public life; they are directed to specific contexts, e.g. that a woman is prevented from doing something with her property. Similarly, neglect complaints are directed against specific persons. Provided that their own menfolk help them and individually show them respect, women on the whole do not seem to take much notice of the fact that men disparage females as a class. Thus, in a quarrel, a man may remark to his brother-in-law that all women are "rubbish" anyway, and why should the two men be fussing over nothing? Or when a woman neglects her work, the husband may see this as a typical characteristic: "Women are stupid, what can you expect?" But women themselves tend not to make generalizations of this nature. This partly results from their sharing men's values

---

[1] I choose to regard them as falling towards the "neglect" end of the continuum (see infra).

about exchange, and about what makes a person important. Moreover, on the whole they accept the major domain of their roles as domestic and non-political. They agree that men are strong (*rondokl*)
and this gives them a prerogative over certain activities such as speech-
making and fighting. Nevertheless, women see their domestic (producer)
activities as entitling them to some recognition, so that disputes arise
over particular issues with their husbands, and to a wider acknowledgement of their importance, so that they try to interfere in transactions.
They do not so much complain about males as a class, as demand from
their individual husbands and kinsmen scrupulous attention and consideration.

While this includes some voice in the allocation of valuables, it also
includes demands that the husband be a proper working partner in production activities. A woman's grumbles that her husband does not cut
firewood or make adequate gardens is part of the concern that he should
pull his weight as a producer (whereas men often denigrate these tasks).
"We women, we are not strong—we just work and harvest sweet potatoes; we women stay in the house. Men do good work, they make *moka*
and can earn money from white men, and they talk among themselves.
We are not *popokl* with them for that. But if they don't make our gardens
or cut firewood for us, then we are angry. All day we labour, getting food,
and the baby cries, and the smoke from the fire gets into our eyes, while
the man does nothing. He just walks around and comes home to demand
food and we are cross. *Moka* is a good thing, for we women can join in
the dancing; but we quarrel with our husbands when they do not fetch
firewood."

Women's grievances, then, tend to be particularistic. In cases (A)
over 80% were against men, and of these half against the woman's
husband, the next largest category being sons. Here women were finding
reasons for a specific event; in (B), when they were asked to think about
their overall resentments, complaints about their own kin, as well as husbands, loomed large, while those against sons hardly figured at all. We
may deduce that in speaking abstractly women do not care to admit *popokl*
with their own children, to whom they see themselves in a protective role.
On the other hand, they do think of themselves as still bound up with
their home kin, from whom they demand care and attention. Women
thus tend to perpetuate private notions of *popokl* against their kin, although when it comes to explaining an actual sickness (as in (A)) they
turn to nearer sources of friction, including their children.

Women's dependence on men for prestige and for recognition of their statuses is compounded of emotional and economic factors. A man shows affection for his sister by giving her presents, her husband shows respect by working diligently. We can perhaps regard the incidence of *popokl* as a direct correlate of this dependence (cf. Strathern, A.M., 1968:556). A wife is jealous (*wølik*) of a favoured cowife, but *popokl* with their common husband: it is he, not the other woman, on whom she depends. Sisters are said to be jealous of one another in relation to their common dependence on parents and brothers. They quarrel at the way they are treated at pig distributions, and are sensitive over the crops they have planted on home ground—a woman being very angry if her sister pulls up her plants. The contrast is with their friendly behaviour at their husbands' places. Here they invite each other to feasts, and a woman can help herself with impunity to a casual meal from gardens her sister has planted. When women think of themselves as having cause for anger with their own kin, they are thus expressing these feelings of dependence, the desire for continued interaction, which they hold towards them.

The majority of both (A) and (B) grievances were against husbands. It is on these, rather than a range of people, that a woman's economic activities are focused, close involvement with her mother-in-law lasting for a relatively short phase of her married life. As a woman becomes older this focus is often transferred to adult sons. Sickness-grievances admitted by men show a striking contrast, only a third of these being directed against women (of which about 70% are wives), the rest being against male clansmen, affines, and exchange partners (cf. Strathern, A.J., 1968). This clearly reveals the man's involvement in a wider world.

Of the grievances detailed in Table X, 31% (A) to 36% (B) of "neglect" cases are directed against the woman's husband, the figures for "thwart" cases being 40% to 47%. Of the total grievances against husbands, 50% to 60% are thwart ones. These are mainly concerned with competing control over the joint pig herd. Thwart complaints against other persons, apart from sons, have to do with disappointment in *moka* returns, bridewealth claims, and so on. While widows may try to assert transactional control over their son's herd, or their own pigs whom the son reckons as his, as long as an older woman's husband is still alive it is by him that she continues to feel thwarted; she may, however, come to place increasing reliance on her son's productive help and correspondingly complain of his neglect. A breakdown of grievances by age shows the following broad correlations:

TABLE XI

Grievances of women by age, (A) only

Age bracket	Neglect	Thwart	Other	Total
Under 40	2	10	7	19
Over 40	16	10	4	30
Age not known	1			

By percentage, the younger woman's neglect complaints are roughly 10% of her total, thwart complaints over 50%; whereas for the older women neglect and thwart complaints are correspondingly 53% and 33%. In the younger woman, grievances against her husband and her home kin are roughly matched in number; in the older woman the switch is away from her kin to her sons. The nature of the figures does not, however, allow detailed statistical interpretation.

Particular reasons for *popokl*-sickness may be aspects of wider or more longstanding disputes. The information I have been so far concerned with, (A) and (B), was elicited mainly in response to questions; the following is an example of the multiple and complex issues which may emerge when a woman confesses to her menfolk what is the cause of her sickness.

Kunup, the wife of Kawelka Kipukl, was lying ill in her women's house, her daughter-in-law and a husband's brother's wife keeping her company. Severe dysentery exacerbated a pain in her lower spine which had been troubling her for some time that year (1964). A number of people gathered at the house, including her married son, Mboi, and her husband's brother. Two girls were sent off to find the husband. The general talk was that she and her husband, Kipukl, were always quarrelling and the root of the matter must lie in this. She did not speak herself, however, till encouraged by her son and Kipukl's brother, and after nearly everyone else had drifted away.

She talked with difficulty. Kipukl always picks on her when something goes wrong, though he helps his other two wives. He does not even mend her garden fences but pulls them down to use the stakes for other purposes. She cannot think why he should be like this—she had given him two sons, and they weren't anyone else's sons (e.g. by her previous marriage) but his own. Yet he was trying to get rid of her. He told their eldest son (Mboi) to go and live with his maternal kin (i.e. that he and his mother should leave)! It is true there was trouble over Mboi's pig that had ruined the gardens of Kipukl's other wives and Mboi refuses to get rid of it, but it is unfair the way Kipukl always takes the side of these women in quarrels. He had even brought her son to court. (After having been rebuked by his father, Mboi had killed one of Kipukl's pigs which he had found rooting in his coffee garden.)[1] But she had pointed out that Mboi's troublesome pig, which had come in endowment when he married, was also Kipukl's, and how could he bring his son to court; they all shared gardens after all. She complained that Kipukl had tried to "pull" her pigs in compensation (for the gardens Mboi's pig had ruined, and in return for the one he had killed).[2]

She is *popokl* over this, since he is always taking her animals. She listed other occasions, when her pigs had gone in *moka*, and an earlier dispute in which a cowife had accused her children of stealing, and Kipukl had defended this woman, even though later they found the nibble marks of a rodent in the gardens. Nonetheless, the cowife had demanded one of her pigs in compensation.

After she had finished speaking, the men came outside; they commented that although she had talked about the disputes between herself and Kipukl these were only surface troubles—at the back of it was bad feeling between the spouses for which they did not know the reason. They noted that Kipukl was a somewhat violent man, adding that if he hit his wives alike that would not matter; but he ought not to discriminate against one. They would have to wait till the husband himself came before the talk was really "out". When Kipukl later arrived, he spoke alone with his wife and then called to Mboi to join him. After a while others went back into the house. A cowife had also joined her.

The wife was encouraged to continue talking, Kipukl's brother (who privately had been blaming Kipukl) alternately coaxing her and then Kipukl himself to speak. Kipukl agreed with what she said and admitted that her sickness was because he had wronged her. While he was saying this, the woman vomitted, which was taken as a sign that her anger cannot have been solely against her husband. The others (who afterwards said they were too afraid of Kipukl to blame him openly) turned on her son, Mboi. She had also been grumbling that Mboi had been leaving to her the care of the pig that had been so troublesome. Here was she, all the time not only caring for a pig for which she got no thanks, but being blamed for the consequences of its incorrigible nature. Mboi should get rid of it.

The final judgement of Kipukl's brother, when he left them still talking inside the house, was that both husband and wife were wrong. Kipukl should not quarrel with her as he does, and the wife should not have harboured her resentments so long that she brought sickness on herself. The position of Mboi remained ambiguous.

---

[1] A man has the right to shoot another's pig if it ruins his gardens and he has already warned the owner about tying it up; the carcass is presented to the owner to eat. For a son to kill his father's pig, however, runs contrary to their joint interests.

[2] Compensation pigs had eventually been provided by Kunup's kin and by a younger son.

Women and *Moka*

Hagen women do not participate in a subculture of their own, with its special goals and values (cf. Kaberry, 1939; Berndt, C.H., 1965): rather, they share men's esteem of exchange activities and are almost as concerned with *moka* success. A wife may become embittered about the fact that a husband who once made much *moka* with her kin withdraws from the exchange system to undertake European-style business. The very fact that the spouses to some extent compete as transactors underlines their sharing of these values. Where women say they want to eat pork rather than exchange live pigs, there is indeed a confrontation of values; but claims to participate in transactions brings a confrontation of interests (i.e. competition).

When they are young, boys and girls are equally encouraged to exchange food and small possessions with others, and children among themselves call this "making *moka*". Both sexes may be allocated a pig to call their "own" from the parental herd. On public occasions, however, boys accompany their fathers on *moka* visits and are present at discussions, while the girl's proper place is helping her mother in the garden. When food is distributed girls passively wait to be called out to receive their shares, while boys, much less certain of an allocation, jostle with the men round the ovens and pick at the steaming tubers. In spite of these differences, the diverging interests of boys and girls are not marked by any form of puberty ritual. At the time of marriage, a strong contrast in their roles emerges: while the boy raises bridewealth, in the girl's case it is given for her; yet at the same time there is a congruence of values. The youth who has begun to possess shells in his own name embarks on *moka* exchanges, his success in transactions being displayed in bamboo tallies (*omak*) worn on the chest. His tally gets longer as his exchanges mature. In the past it was at marriage that a girl might also put on an *omak*, in her case made by the groom to signify how many valuables he had given for her (Vicedom and Tischner, 1943–8:2:460). Subsequently, *moka* is made through the links she affords, and thus a woman might later wear her husband's own *omak*. It is said that a polygynist keeps an *omak* for each of his wives, recording his respective transactions with their kin. For all this, many women admit to diffidence (*pipil*, "shame") about wearing the tally, and while nearly all men at sometime sport their *omak*, the majority of women choose never to do so. These are, after all, really things belonging to men.

Women accept, and do not denigrate, the ethos of exchange. But while men may both transact *moka* privately and combine on public occasions as members of a clan or tribe to make prestations, women's major part is a private one. In-married wives may feel a diffuse solidarity at the success of their husband's clan, but little is required from them as a group of women. Each wife makes a separate contribution, through her spouse. This discreteness can be seen most clearly between the wives of a polygynist. I have already noted (Chapter 3) how scrupulous such a man must be towards their claims. They may even demand that he keep a separate axe in each of their houses to use when he cuts their firewood. And we have seen that they are most certainly likely to demand that the return for transactions with "their" pigs are made to them and not another wife. Women list exchanges which have involved their herd as *moka* which *they* have made. Insofar as a husband has over-riding claims on the pigs of all his wives, cowives may have to allow theirs to be used for *moka* to partners in whom they have no particular interest, or to make up a set of gifts being given in the name of another wife. This is one of the few contexts in which cowives are required to co-operate. Such occasions are not, however, very numerous. From a total of 75 *moka*[1] remembered by eight wives of polygynists, 16 concerned exchanges in co-operation with a cowife; the rest were made "by themselves" (i.e. with their own and their husband's resources). In half of the sixteen cases the exchanges were with the other wife's kin, the rest being with unrelated partners. Even the latter were not always called joint *moka* to which both wives saw themselves as contributing equally; rather pointedly, more than one woman commented that her contribution in such cases was not for the cowife but to "help" the husband.

Like men, women may be spoken of as having "good luck spirits on their faces" (*kor kil køi koemb-al morom*). These aid men's success in exchanges, and a woman whose visit home is followed rapidly by an offer of *moka* gifts from her brothers is also said to be helped by the spirits. These are the *amb nyim* (important women).

What envy there is of men seems to come not from the public prestige which men are accorded in *moka* or the renown orators acquire, but from men's greater physical freedom. They are constantly visiting, spending their time discussing *moka* plans, seeing relatives to beg credit, and

---

[1] I do not give details of the different kinds of transaction involved.

so on, and women complain of the contrasting drudgery of their domestic tasks which ties them to the gardens all day. Bitterness may spill over into the sarcasm with which a late husband is greeted: had he such a heavy thing (his penis) to drag around all day that it took him so long to get home? Women who say they wish they had been born male nearly always phrase their desire in terms of the hard work females have to do, not in terms of their exclusion from political life. Exclusion from participation in male cults is ostensibly regretted as a missed opportunity to share in a feast of pork. Men may even go along with this, saying that they exclude women so that they themselves can eat pig.[1] Although these are well recognized attitudes, the extent to which they are held depends partly on individual personality and there are other women who comment that sweet potatoes are their "strong" things and prefer to stay at home because travelling is so tiring. It is a commonplace that women are sad to leave their natal home and think that had they been men they could have stayed behind to support their brothers. The same institution of virilocal residence leads men to say that women are *korpa* (worthless) because they lack the strength of male clan members who stay on their own land all their lives (cf. 142). However individually mobile men are, they have greater stability from their continued association with ancestral territory. It may also lead to disparagement from women. Mothers rebuking their daughters comment that it is not on them but upon their sons they will have to depend in old age.

Male and Female Values

I have been suggesting some of the ways in which Hagen men and women think about themselves and about each other. Whereas men may generalize about all women, and are inclined to dismiss their domestic activities, women share many of men's values, and do not denigrate men's *moka*-making roles. Women do complain when their own interests in transactions are thwarted and the particular males on whom they depend neglect their domestic duties. I would sum up these evaluations in the following way. Men separate out the spheres of activity in which they gain prestige, or interact politically with others, from their domestic contribution to the household: transaction and production.

---

[1] On secular occasions women are foremost recipients of pork.

In some contexts they seem to regard themselves as essentially trans-actors in opposition to women who are essentially producers. Hence women are dismissed as the *kintmant*, the servants, of men.[1] One may suspect innuendo here, for the term refers also to low status male re-tainers attached to big-men, who frequently originate from other clans. Certainly women's clan status is bound up, in Hagen men's eyes, with their minimal role in transactions. Thus women are described as hav-ing no "name" (*mbi*), a phrase also used of fatherless children. *Mbi* itself carries the further connotation of "reputation", as when men of a clan look on their *moka* activities as enhancing their collective prestige (*mbi*).

The contrast men often stress between themselves as transactors, and women as producers, is one which parallels that between wild and planted things, or political and domestic spheres of action (cf. Strathern, A.J. and A.M., 1968). A further contrast between men and women, again from men's point of view, draws the line between men as both trans-actors and producers (i.e. dominant in both external and internal clan affairs) and women as only producers (and of limited importance). Less explicit, and certainly not given the same cultural weight, is what I understand to be the viewpoint of many women, that men and women alike are producers and transactors, even though their spheres of activity are different. Women, moreover, demand that men fulfill their duties as producers, and, while they admit they have no business as major actors in the political sphere, they do themselves to some extent try to take part in transactions. They have their own name to consider. As a producer of exchange items, pigs, a woman feels she has a controlling right in their disposal, and it is through her ties with her husband and her own kin that men are enabled to set up *moka* partnerships.

Women's main contributions as "quasi-transactors" are, we have seen, of a private rather than public nature. A man may give to his exchange partners in the privacy of his homestead but he may also give on a public occasion, in combination with others of his clan or sub-clan. Their concerted efforts enhance their group's reputation, whether they present *moka* to individual partners drawn from a variety of other groups or to members of a single clan receiving payment as allies. In either case they

---

[1] I am reminded by Professor Ralph Bulmer (and see Salisbury, 1962:109–110) that in the past when gardenland had to be cleared with stone tools, a more time-consuming task than it is nowadays, men may not have had such a cavalier attitude towards production. However, even if they saw their own role in production as more important, this does not obviate the fact that political prestige is acquired through transactions.

represent themselves in solitary confrontation against others. Not only are women excluded from being principal actors in the transference of wealth, but their position is logically incompatible with the stance men assume on these public occasions. Women cannot unambiguously participate in the political confrontation of clans, for they represent the interpersonal links between them.

On rare occasions women do dance at *moka* festivals, and the ambiguities of their situation finds expression in the decorations they wear. We have, for example, analyzed women's preference for red face-paint, as opposed to men's for black, as indicative both of the positive blood ties which connect groups and of the danger of affinal inroads into clan solidarity. (Cf. Strathern, A.J. and A.M., 1971.) This and other discussions (Strathern, A.J. and A.M., 1968; Strathern, A.J., 1970a) touch on the use of the male and female sexes as themselves symbols of other things (fertility, clan solidarity, alliance relations, aggression, and so on). Reference should be made to this domain of symbolism, although here I concentrate on beliefs and activities which can be taken as symbolic *of* male–female relations. Thus one may comment on certain aspects of women's participation in dances in the light of the producer-transactor dichotomy.

Women dance chiefly when pigs (not shells) are being given away in *moka*, and in men's eyes their participation essentially celebrates their role as producers. (Married sisters may sometimes be invited to come and help their brothers' *moka* and they dance with the latter's wives, it being acknowledged that had they been men they would have danced as clansmen.) Unlike unmarried girls,[1] however, married women never join the actual line of male performers, but execute separate dances in a distinctive style. When this dancing is over, wives of donors run up and down the line of pigs they have helped to look after, behind the body of men.

This is the apotheosis of the admiration which successful "producers" receive. Although they are splendidly decorated, it would be quite inappropriate for women to participate in the actual counting of pigs or in the speeches made by prominent men on both sides. The very lavishness of female decoration, according to Hageners, explicitly said to emphasize the fact that, unlike men, women are not normally decorated.

------

[1] When men alone dance, unmarried girls of their clan may accompany them. As part of the display of wealth, the clan shows off its nubile women to potential suitors.

Going about their garden and household jobs women have no reason to beautify themselves; men feel sorry for them, it is said, so occasionally allow them to decorate. Ordinarily it is men who decorate and who dance at festivals, and on these occasions women act as *kintmant* (servants) in helping with preparations and fetching at their request. It is so that women's hearts will be good, and they will continue to perform services for their husbands, that they are sometimes given the chance to display the part they have had in looking after the pigs.

That allowing women to dance from time to time "keeps them sweet" is quite a strong element in the statements men make to the effect. While women's role in rearing pigs is the main component of female producer activities celebrated in this way, the associated hard and dirtying work in the gardens and their trouble in looking after children are also rewarded. The formal emphasis is on women's participation as wives. In sacrifices preparatory to decorating the husband prays on his wife's behalf to his own clan ghosts, rather than to hers. The husband's clan ghosts are asked to "help the skin (appearance) of the man and his wife together".

Various aspects of their participation in the dances thus bear out the contrast between men as transactors and women as producers, and these I summarize: 1. Women usually dance only at pig-*moka*, not at shell-*moka* which is seen to derive solely from men's transactions. 2. The exception proves the rule; whereas men often decorate (visits, exchange festivals), married women rarely do. 3. Men (active) supposedly decide when to decorate their womenfolk (passive). 4. Women dance as wives, i.e. their husband's helpers. 5. Women may run up and down the pigs but do not make speeches to the other side. 6. When the dance is over women are divested of their decorations and a payment is made to their kin to compensate them for their return to humdrum household affairs. The very fact that men emphasize how garden and pig work dirties the women draws a contrast with their own more splendid concerns.

What may not be said explicitly is that women dance because of their links with both sides, or because of their active go-between roles in transactions. Nevertheless, certain aspects of women's participation on such occasions are, when taken by themselves, explained as relating to their intermediary position. It is at an implicit level, then, that women dance as quasi-transactors.

Some of the elements suggestive of this are: 1. When only the wives of male donors (and not recipients) dance as a group, sisters of the donor clan married into the recipient clan, and thus roads for the *moka*, may join in the donors' wives' dancing line. Occasionally a sister married into a group due to receive from the present donors at a later date dances "to help her *mønin*" (i.e. BW). 2. The wives of donors may be referred to as "making *moka*" and the sisters or daughters as receiving it. Thus spectators are said to comment, "Oh, the father is making *moka* and giving to his daughter (i.e. daughter's husband's clan), and her heart is good so she is dancing". Such statements belong to the class of compliments discussed in a previous section. 3. The very fact that her kin are compensated[1] when the husband removes her decorations recognizes them as "at her back", for it is on her back that she wears the shell valuable he will present to them. (Cf. pp. 92–93.) Her kin will have helped to provide her ornaments. Indeed, her attire may neatly symbolize her whole intermediary status: on her chest she wears a bailer shell (say) loaned by her brothers to her husband for the occasion, on her back the pearl shell her husband intends to give to them. 4. Finally, when they are decorated for a formal dance, women are said to "become like men". By wearing decoration at all they are displaying themselves in the same manner as men do. The individual ornaments, however, do not imitate men's but on the contrary show several differences. The act of decorating suggests a message to the effect that women are making a contribution to the festival, but it is a different kind of contribution from men's.

In the past wives used to display their husband's wealth at *moka* festivals, appearing swathed in long ropes of cowrie shells and wearing nassa shell "aprons". They did not necessarily participate in the dancing. Vicedom (1943–8:2: Plate 13 no. 2) shows a cluster of women standing at the edge of a ceremonial ground with rows of as many as six pearl shells reaching from neck to ankle. In the past, brides also used to wear some of the bridewealth valuables. Where the shells are intended for recipients related to the women, we can see that wearing them directly indicates the latter's intermediary position. It is illuminating that while between men the gesture of transference is a handing over, or a setting out of valuables for the recipients to pick up, here the woman's person is draped with them. We may take this as symbolic of the fact that women rarely act as negotiators; their intermediary roles are attributes of an interstitial position.

---

[1] Big-men, i.e. those whose wives may be described as *amb nyim*, are most likely to make such payments. Like other gifts to her kin they fall under the general rubric of *kuimø* or *amb peng-al etep ngui* ("to give for the wife's head").

PART 2

The Independent Woman

"How can we know what (this woman) intends: her heart lies within her—how can we see it?"

Elderly wife of a Northern Melpa big-man

7

Pollution and Poison

Relegating women to the sphere of production enables men to claim superiority over them. They say that, by contrast with themselves, females have no "strength" (*rondokl*), are "soft" (*amb wening enem*). Women concur that they do not possess all the capacities which men have, but do not see their interests as so distinct or themselves as totally inferior. They are aware of being physically dependent: as one woman commented, "Women have no bones (*amb-nga ombil ti mon*) i.e. brute strength—men clear the gardens and we are able to eat". But this does not imply a total contrast of abilities. The same speaker also noted, "The bones of men and women are of one kind (*ombil tenda*) i.e. there is no basic difference between us—for men clear the gardens and women plant them". Men for their own part may in any case think of women as "strong things" (see page 135). Their self-estimation as *rondokl*, by contrast with women who are not, represents a dogma to which they can appeal on occasion, but it is not applied with thorough-going consistency. Statements made in different contexts contradict one another. This is partly because "strength" is a highly emotive and generalized notion, and used to give approval (and in some cases disapproval) to a variety of qualities and situations. Some implications of this are explored in the present chapter. It is with male dogma that I have to deal in the main, for men, concerned to establish superiority, are the more articulate and coherent in their statements. Women do not make contrary assertions with the same apparent cogency; they half, although only half, agree with what men say.

The Strong Male and the Weak Female

Capacities and capabilities distinguish the sexes. It is not only in role terms (producers, transactors) that men conceptualize women as different from themselves, but in terms of innate abilities. People are readily categorized as *nyim* (successful) or *korpa* (worthless). We have seen how *nyim* is applied in the context of transactions. *Korpa* describes the very opposite of the successful big-man or -woman, one who lacks wealth or prestige, who does not handle valuables. A husband may accuse his wife's kin of *korpa* behaviour if they are tardy in returning debts, or a wife may call her husband *korpa* for failing to allocate her pigs. The taunt of being rubbish is frequent among the shortcomings cowives viciously detail about each other in the heat of an argument.

> The two wives of a Yamka man were quarrelling over the way he had divided a new garden (1965). With deliberate intent to insult, each included in the taunts thrown at the other: 1. that she had not done a scrap of work in the garden when it was previously made, so had no claims now; 2. she was not a good wife to their husband, staying at home and minding his affairs, but was always deserting him; 3. she had not borne any children; 4. she was old and no longer capable. All these could be described as criticisms of productive activities. But by far the most repetitious was the insult that 5. she had nothing to her name, was an *amb korpa*, a worthless woman. "Who is it that looks after the pigs and shells? You certainly do not—your pig-stalls are empty and you never fetch shells to give to your husband." Or, "You are rubbish! *You* stay on the ceremonial ground and line up stakes (for pigs to be given away in *moka*), do you? No, you have nothing!"

While *nyim* and *korpa* are applied to individuals of either sex, women's *nyim* status is held by men to derive only from their own, and all women may be classed as *korpa*. Their views can make no difference to events, they have no political power, they do not control valuables. This ascription is rationalized in terms of female ability—most women could not be *nyim* if they wanted to be, and women who are in fact exhibit flashes of male qualities (cf. Reay, 1964b: 151).[1]

Thus, there is a contrast between men, forceful in action and cogent in argument, and women, who vacillate and shilly shally. One basis for this lies in the concept of *noman*, "mind" or "heart". Human beings are distinguished from wild animals and adults from children by the pres-

---

[1] Cf. also the fact that women who decorate at *moka* are described as "like men".

ence of *noman*. A person is said to have *noman* when he performs his social roles correctly. But it is more than an index of social consciousness; it also encompasses intention and purpose. Someone who has a single *noman* (*noman tenda*) shows resolution in achieving his ends; these may be admirable (he is steadfast) or not (he is self-willed). In some contexts *noman* may be perceived as divided into upper and lower sections. In the upper section are all the desires and ambitions which plague men and women, pulling them this way and that; but beneath is the single course of action which a person must eventually take. When his desires and actions coincide, then indeed does he have a "single mind". It is a male belief that while adult men have only one lower *noman*, and hence are able to resolve their diverse impulses, women frequently have several. This exhibits itself in arbitrary and capricious behaviour, for women are congenitally unable to rise above their conflicting emotions. Hence females are incapable of the sustained reasoning and single-mindedness necessary for political action; they have no organizational ability. "What woman" mused a young Northern Melpa man, "is ever strong enough to get up and say, 'Let us make *moka*, let us find pigs and wives, let us give our daughters to men, let us wage war, let us kill our enemies?' No, indeed not! *Mel korpa we mangkona ile mint moromen pin'mon*: they are little rubbish things who stay at home simply, don't you see?"

A long-married woman with children, who applies herself to production tasks and the promotion of her husband's welfare, may in her devotion to work reveal a single lower *noman*. But men say that women of exceptional ability obviously started off life in their mothers' womb as male, only happening to be born female.

To carry through resolute decisions and to be able to influence others are qualities exemplified particularly in big-men, but (Hagen men say) males as a whole are inherently more likely to develop these skills than are females. Those who fail are the rubbish (*korpa*) men, who play little active part in public transactions, and are compared to women, covered in the ashes of the fire by which they stay. A clan taunted for not making prestations demanded of them may, in provocative anger, display its wives at another clan's dance—calling them *korpa* was to say they were women. But there are no rigid requirements that a man must conform to an "ideal" of the big-man transactor-type, so that the state of being *korpa* cannot in Mead's terminology really be described as "deviant" (Mead, 1935). The ascription of *korpa* to women as a class is both derogatory and considered appropriate for their situation.

From one point of view, Hagen men set up the oppositions (Meggitt, 1964:219),

strong	versus	weak
nyim	versus	*korpa*
male	versus	female.

But there is a further dimension to be considered. A strong (*rondokl*) person, with a single *noman*, may be contrasted with a weak (*rimb rimb*) one, who has many *noman* or even none at all. Of a woman it may be said: *peng koia rimb rimb nitim, noman mbo ingk pei na petem*, "she has soft brains, there is no true (human) *noman* there". Yet a person who carries his strong-headedness to extremes, the over-violent man, for example, is seen to have gone too far. Unlike a *korpa* man, sanctions may be brought against him. Lacking finesse, he alienates his exchange partners in trying to coerce them; however vigorously he defends his own rights, he finds it hard to attract support. There is an analogous type of female, strong-willed in a perverse way, with only her own interests at heart. Promiscuous women, seeking nothing but personal satisfactions, fall into this category, as do disobedient wives. The obstinacy of a strong-willed woman (*amb kara*) is not, however, quite the same as the aggressiveness of the violent man (*wu^e pundoma*). This kind of strength, also *rondokl*, is not regarded as man-like; rather, it is the epitome of all that is worst in females.

Men's stereotypes of women involve a double ambivalence—not only are their pejoratives balanced by a recognition of women's essential productive contribution, but we see that derogotary statements themselves are internally inconsistent. Women are obstinate as well as capricious, strong as well as weak. While female strength and weakness are both "bad", "weakness" being an inability to act with conviction, "strength" being an egoistic pursuit of ends without regard for others, it is clear that men are both denying that women have any effective power and ascribing such a power to them. These generalizations are heard most frequently in the mouths of men, but women may also describe other women in such terms. The wife who is unable to co-ordinate her actions with single-minded purposefulness is criticized for laziness and thoughtlessness. Obstinacy, on the other hand, is evinced in the behaviour of the wife who suddenly deserts her husband, for no apparent reason, and resists all pleas by her kin to act sensibly.

The stereotypes of the soft-brained and the hard-headed female are not as trivial as they seem. They can be related to certain requirements made of women's roles. As far as the first is concerned, one Hagener (male) put it this way: "A man has a single purpose, to work hard and stay at his place where he will make the name of his clan important. Whatever he does, making *moka*, establishing a pig herd, his thought is directed to this end. But a woman: her thoughts play havoc—she spends her time looking at other men, wondering whether to marry someone else; if her visiting kin are not well received by her husband, she goes off in a fit of anger; all the time she wanders around, visiting from place to place."[1] Such a woman displays only a modicum of commitment to her husband, this partly being due to the ties she also has with members of her own clan. The lack of women's complete involvement in their husband's affairs, so disparaged by men, finds its balance in loyalties to their kin (which actually happen to be important for the husband's own relations with his affines). Since they cannot wholeheartedly commit themselves to one or other set of persons, it is indeed appropriate that women should perpetually be of "several minds". The partial nature of women's involvement in the affairs of their husband's clan is further symbolized in the second stereotype, as a repudiation of all loyalties. They are seen as taking matters into their own hands, and going their own way. From the point of view of men's values, female decisions may appear irrational, and even threatening. Ideally, women are acting, thinking persons who should promote the interests of both spouse and kin in their mutual exchanges. In these terms, women do have "wills" of their own. Along with this, however, goes men's fear that they cannot always be trusted to think of others but will turn strong-willed and act only in their own interests.

Throughout the Highlands of Australian New Guinea (e.g. Read, 1954; Allen, 1967) varying emphasis is placed on antagonism between the sexes; one element of this is mystical antipathy, often expressed in the danger attributed to menstrual blood or semen out of place. It is particularly women's powers to pollute[2] men which are the subject of rituals and taboos. In Hagen such beliefs involve the same ambiguous attitudes towards female strength and weakness that are articulated in other contexts. They are shared by men and women alike.

---

[1] Compare previous statements that women are worthless because they "just stay at home".
[2] "Pollution" should perhaps refer strictly to the transference of ritual uncleanliness, as when persons of lower status contaminate those of higher (e.g. Yalman, 1963); but its use has become accepted in Highlands ethnographies to describe the harmful consequences of contact between males and females under certain conditions; e.g. Meggitt, 1964; Langness, 1967; and see Douglas, 1966: Chapter 9.

Contact with women is said to weaken men, since women are themselves weak; in addition women can pollute men through their menstrual and sexual fluids. Hageners look upon the latter capacity as a specific power, since its harmful consequences are under women's control; further, there is an equation between a woman's polluting powers and the fact that women (as well as men) handle poison. These are not always linked in the Highlands (Mae-Enga women are polluting but not poisoners (Meggitt, 1964, 1965)); it is a significant attribute of volition. In both contexts, the person a man has most to fear is his own wife.

Pollution

Sexual intercourse may be spoken of by either men or women as *ukl kit* ("a bad activity"),[1] male and female genitalia being *mel kit* ("bad things"). Thus it offends if either sex is caught exposed. But whereas for men this is just a matter of personal shame, women can actually harm the opposite sex and are required to be circumspect. In addition, then, to rules which delimit general sexual activity, there are rules specific to women. Necessarily specific to them are further rules concerning their dangerous menstrual fluids. Injunctions which exclude women from men's affairs (such as religious ceremonies) may be based on fear of contamination either from women's present sexual or menstrual condition, or, irrespective of this, because of their general association with sex and menstruation. Men's avoidance on such occasions may be summed up in a third concept, that women are weakening. This in itself has a double derivation; sexual relations are held to be debilitating, so that men lose their strength through too frequent sexual contact with women; and since women in any case are not strong, their presence threatens men's strength. Attitudes are thus compounded of various notions impinging upon one another, although I separate these to some extent in the following description.

A.   Sexual Relations

Men in particular are weakened by frequent indulgence in sexual intercourse, a dogma which perhaps encourages the observance of the long

---

[1] Though *kit* is also an affectionate epithet e.g. *kang wu* *kit*, "the young rascal". On the one hand, both parties are supposed to spit privately after intercourse, expressing distaste for the emissions; on the other hand, value is put on mutual gratification in the act itself.

post partum taboo (see below). The analogue for women is their labour in childbearing and suckling. But in addition to making men grow old before their time, frequent intercourse has the specific effect of causing the flesh to fall loosely—a tight, bulging skin being an indication of good health. In spite of this, the act is one to be enjoyed; both sexes employ love-magic to allure partners, and magic also exists for making a husband or wife sexually faithful. Men do not take any particular measures to protect themselves from immediate contact.

Intercourse may harm external objects, especially new things, and should therefore be restricted to certain times and places. A man making a new garden should avoid women (although he may have coitus afterwards) else the odour (*elkⁿeka*) would ruin the subsequent crops and for the same reason intercourse should not take place inside a newly planted garden. This refers most strictly to mixed-vegetable gardens with their male crops of bananas, sugarcane, and taro, but also to new sweet potato fields. There is some feeling against intercourse in a men's house, although it is not forbidden, the most appropriate places being women's houses, old gardens or nearby bush. Certain special crops also have to be protected from the odour of coitus on the day of their being harvested and/or cooked: taro, fruit pandanus and winged beans.

B. Women's Sexuality

Taboos on intercourse at special times, as when preparations for a dance festival are under way, stem from the fact that qualities associated with females oppose the very ones desired. Thus, a man with a new axe eschews sexual intercourse because women's private parts are "soft" and his axe blade would likewise become soft (blunt); or when he is making a drum, for then it would be like them and "silent". While these are partly rationalizations for why women are avoided, it is also held that outside coitus women's genitals may be harmful. Anything belonging to a man which comes into contact with them is contaminated. For this reason he would never touch a woman's skirt, although it is not harmful for other women or for children. If a female is careless about where she leaves her aprons, she may be severely reprimanded.

> *One woman, instead of wrapping up her apron in its usual bundle and putting it away in the women's house, left it lying around in the sleeping compartment of the men's house. In a rage, her father-in-law threw it out; the wife went home in a high temper, taking this as sign that they wanted to be rid of her. But as her father-in-law observed, she had left it near to

where men lie down to sleep, and were their heads to touch such a thing?
(Northern Melpa, 1960's.)

A woman who takes a spare apron with her (she may wear more than
one) should be careful to carry it in a separate netbag from the one
containing food. Food which has touched her aprons cannot be given
to men without making them sick.

A woman has to take care where she walks. Were she to step over food
or cigarettes prepared for a man, they would have to be thrown away.
Even if it were by accident, she would be upbraided. Exposing herself
by stepping over people's legs is generally impolite, but by men is
taken as a serious insult. If she does this to a relative stranger, her husband may have to pay him compensation. Occasionally such an offence
is committed deliberately: a woman roused to anger in a quarrel may
demonstrate her emotion by stepping across a food oven. It is not pleasant if a man steps over other people, but his action leads to little more
than jokes: does he think he never defecates that he takes such liber-
ties! The particular unpleasantness of a woman doing so is related to the
fact that, men say, women do not wash themselves and there may always
be spots of menstrual blood on them. It would be unthinkable for a
woman menstruating at the time to behave in such a way. Fear of sexual
intercourse is partly based on the supposition that women's private parts
will be dirty with old blood and semen.

C.   Menstruation and Parturition

Womb blood which combines with semen to form and nourish a foetus
is "good" (*mema kae*), and is compared with breast milk which also makes
a child grow. Blood which is not mixed with semen but turns rotten (*pokl*),
to be excreted in menstruation or with the birth of the child, is bad
(*mema kit*). It is interesting to note that semen out of place can be as
dangerous to men as womb blood (one woman reputedly killed her
husband by mixing his own semen in with the food she gave him to eat),
although this does not seem to preoccupy men to the extent that female
emissions do; I have not heard of women being poisoned in this way.

The commonest phrase to indicate that a woman is menstruating
simply describes her as "sleeping in the seclusion hut" (*ui manga penem*);
other terms are more sinister, mainly variants of *rᵉng kit kotimin*, "they
cook bad food". Menstrual blood itself may be referred to as "carelessly
given food" (*rᵉng lil, rᵉng wokelik ngonomen*). This draws attention to the

stringent taboos that forbid a woman who is menstruating from preparing food for men. The victims would fall very, if not fatally, sick.
There is an equally stringent taboo on sexual relations at this time; sexual
intercourse is also "food" (a couple who stay away from the cooking of
one of the crops mentioned on page 165 admit to having "eaten r*eng*
klawa, wrong food"; adultery is *wan r*eng, "stolen food"). Hageners say
that men can absorb menstrual blood through the penis, as well as by
mouth. Blood ingested over a period of time would gradually rise up in
the victim's ribcage in two columns which meet at his neck: this is the
danger point; some sudden exertion easily snaps the columns and he dies.
A nose-bleed at death is symptomatic of pollution. In addition, a menstruating woman cannot go anywhere where her blood might fall and
damage things. She should not enter a newly planted garden of any
kind, although she may walk in a mature banana garden where the
fruit is above her head; she collects food for herself and the pigs from
old sweet potato patches. Affected plants would not only have an unpleasant odour but be poisoned for any male who later consumed
them.

For these reasons a menstruating woman lives secluded in a specially
constructed house or in the rear compartment of a woman's house forbidden to men, for the duration of five days; she cannot cook or handle
food to be given to any male till the 6th or 7th day (there are slight
variations bteween men's personal stipulations). Other adult women
share her meals with impunity, but little boys, once they are fully
weaned, and some say little girls (before they are "like women"), cannot
eat their mother's food. A menstruating woman is not completely excluded from social life—she is able to walk about and go into ceremonial
grounds (but not into cemeteries) and she attends public occasions,
though she would sit to the side of the assembly and not mix with the
main body of men and women. In the past, she could share in the meat
of sacrifice, but would have to remain outside the sacrificial house. She
is not allowed to help her husband decorate for a dance festival, nor
would she dance herself, for her condition is antithetical to the shining,
healthy splendour aimed at on these occasions. Finally, women should
not enter men's houses at this time, and a man may have to compensate the owner if his wife trespasses, irrespective of whether the place was
soiled or not.

A woman who has recently given birth must observe the same range
of restrictions. The after-birth is equated with menstrual blood, and for

this reason men avoid both mother and baby. Only women are usually present at the birth itself,[1] although the husband nowadays may see his offspring within a day or two. In the past the interval may have been rather longer (Vicedom and Tischner, 1943–8:2:231). But he does not touch his child till mother and baby have left the seclusion hut and no longer have "bad blood on the skin". She remains confined for up to two months; from the 6th day after giving birth she can harvest her own food and feed pigs, but cannot cook for any male, and avoids gardens where male crops (bananas, sugarcane, taro) are growing. She washes herself thoroughly on leaving the seclusion hut, but undergoes no ritual cleansing.

During this time she does not copulate with her husband. Sexual abstention encompasses a longer period, however, than the duration of her seclusion. This is the result of a further factor, that semen can pollute the young child. While frequent coitus in the early months of pregnancy ensures that the foetus will be properly formed, after about the fifth or sixth month (by which time it has acquired a *min*, spirit) semen ceases to be beneficial and would only harm the child, perhaps killing it. The mother now becomes solely responsible for moulding its limbs and features: bathing in running water or in the vicinity of a waterfall (both are associated with life) is said to aid this. Throughout the period of breast feeding (usually $2\frac{1}{2}$ to 3 years) the couple should continue to abstain from sexual relations lest the milk become contaminated with semen, and destroy rather than nourish. It is scandalous for a mother with one child at her breast to become pregnant with another. Hageners are aware of the biological importance of the *post partum* taboo in spacing children. The occasional cripplingly under-nourished and retarded child is pointed out as the product of its parents' appetites, for it had to be forcibly weaned when the mother became pregnant again.

A pregnant woman observes a few, not very important food-avoidances, magical precautions rather than rites to demarcate her status. Thus she should not eat dog lest her child be born hairy (and see Vicedom and Tischner, 1943–8:2:238). There do not seem to be any food-taboos imposed on a menstruating woman. This is consonant with the relative lack of ritualization these conditions receive. No specific cere-

---

[1] In one rare case of a mother being aided by a brother, she compensated him handsomely for his trouble; women in any case may give small gifts to female helpers who have "touched their blood".

monies accompany childbirth or a girl's first or any of her subsequent menstrual periods, and their termination is not marked by ritual cleansing or magic to protect the menfolk with whom she resumes contact. It is said that menstruating women might in the past wear cordylines, although nowadays their appearance is rarely modified in this way. This must be one source for men's stated fear that they will come across some strange woman whom they do not know and be enticed into accepting food from or having intercourse with her, only to discover afterwards that she was menstruating at the time. Men have to rely on women's honesty in the matter. While it is acknowledged that they sometimes ignore women's warnings, responsibility rests largely with the latter, and a wife who gives contaminated food to her husband may have to ask her own kin to compensate him.

D. The Weakening Influence of Females

Although the fact that females produce substances harmful to men is not adduced in direct explanation for their general exclusion from major political and exchange activities, it supports the notion that female influence is antithetical to male success. In cults, from whose ritual women are emphatically excluded, the proposition is stated explicitly.[1] The *Amb Kor* or *Kor Nganap* (Female Spirit) cult is an example: men express a degree of antagonism towards women by withdrawing themselves from the contaminating influence of human females and claiming their own exclusive control of fertility. The fact that the female sex may be used as a symbol of fertility does not require the actual participation of women (contrast Dupire, 1963:85–6). A Kelua woman observed that men tell their wives that they are off to sleep with another woman, but it is only stones which they paint to resemble females.[2]

Outside the cult context, women, and likewise children, should not go near the tub of trees (*poklambo*) at the head of the ceremonial ground when these are freshly planted: else the plants would become stunted in

---

[1] Accounts are to be found in Vicedom and Tischner (1943–8); Strauss (1962); Strathern A.J. and A.M. (1968, 1971) and Strathern, A.J. (1970a).

[2] Cf. Bulmer (1965:151). Women themselves may say that men perform the *Amb Kor* because they are afraid of pollution when women menstruate, and one old Elti man compared the secrecy which surrounds its performance with women's seclusion. In the *Kor Wøp* cult women play a limited part in the final dancing, but none in the esoteric ritual. An Elti wife commented, *Kor Wøp* is "good" because women share some of the pig meat cooked by the men, but *Amb Kor* is "bad", since men keep it to themselves.

growth like little children, while their explicit purpose to attract wealth and valuables to the ceremonial ground is contrary to female concerns. Women, it is explained, do not make speeches, do not draw in shells and cassowaries (a prized bird), but look after pigs and sweet potatoes and just stay in the house. *Poklambo amb rakl ik parambil*: "*poklambo* and women are antipathetic, lit. quarrel"; the *poklambo* might even kill a trespassing female. Although she would not die, a woman should also avoid a sub-clan's main men's house, at the time of it's being built on the ceremonial ground, for fear it become like a woman's house, empty of valuables. Ordinary men's houses do not involve the same restrictions. Women's presence near a very sick man can prevent his recovery (Vicedom and Tischner, 1943-8:2:262-3), women also being thought weak-minded enough to gossip and thus spread the news of the man's sickness to his delighted enemies. While women can normally enter the sacrificial house (*kor manga*), they do not themselves ordinarily transact with the ancestral ghosts. The sacrificient holds the rope of the pig about to be slaughtered as he makes his prayer and one of the few occasions on which a woman joins in and holds the rope too (while her husband speaks) is when ancestors of the husband and wife are together invoked to send the couple a long-waited for child. It is also said that sometimes a woman prays for a child to her own clan ghosts, while her husband kills the animal. An old widow, moreover, might cook some pork (although she is un-likely to kill a whole pig) on behalf of her children, in the name of her own and her husband's ancestral ghosts. Although women as well as men are spell practitioners, sacrifices prepared to accompany a successful recitation are conducted by men; and women do not approach the special cemetery head shrines (*peng manga*) where skulls of big-men are kept. These are often the heads of men who died by enemy poison or in battle, and other males are strong enough to come near since they too engage in wars and will be the ones to avenge the deceased; but females do not fight, and the dead man would visit sickness on them. Other activities that are only the concern (*kongon*, "work") of men include dealings with the wild spirits (*kor wakl*) that inhabit the Wahgi flats: here again intrusion would lead to the women's ill health, in this case taking the particular form of madness.

E.   Discussion

Women's weakness (*wening enem*) is the explicit reason behind their exclusion from sacrifice ("we men are strong, we stay at our place (clan territory), while women leave their homes; they are weak, they only look after men's things; it is men who make prayers, while women look on"); moreover, it is apparent that women themselves can provoke attack from things especially thought of as repositories of male power.

Strauss (1962:127f) records a myth which attributes the origin of death in the world to the hasty acts of a woman.

> An old couple bore a boy who defecated on the woman's lap; faeces contain spirit material (*min*),[1] and the man went away to find the right leaves and bark with which to wipe them and thus ensure everlasting life. But he was too long gone, and the old woman, becoming offended at the smell, wiped them away with the leaves nearest to hand. They happened to be those corpses are wrapped in, death-bearing, not life-bearing. When the old man returned, he was so angry he threw away the life-bearing leaves he had brought, with the words that henceforth men would always die.

An interesting element of the myth is the fact that the woman was offended by the odour, reminiscent of the way men find offensive the odour of women. The smell of menstrual blood and of faeces are both *ele*e*ka*. Had she not been disgusted she would have waited till the old man came back with his rejuvenating leaves. But her remedy was the wrong one. What is clear is that the old woman acted in a weak-minded, unthinking way, with destructive consequences for which (in the myth) she was blamed.

A woman is always responsible for the effects of her powers, and is consequently roundly blamed for any carelessness which endangers her menfolk. Although she cannot help her powers, she controls the extent to which they are actually dangerous, by observing or not observing the rules. It is interesting that men suspect women know spells to prevent menstruation, although the only ones told me by women had limited ends: to stop an excessive flow of blood or enable a woman to miss a period, so that she could participate in dancing or escape the boredom of seclusion. Men also suspect that women have all kinds of magical devices to make them infertile or able to terminate pregnancies. The ability to pollute as a power more or less under conscious control contrasts with women's weakness, which, though debilitating to men in certain circumstances and powerful in this sense, is not one they accuse women of deliberately manipulating. They do say, on the other hand, that women may use their menstrual powers to suit their own ends,

---

[1] Not a belief we came across.

as when a wife introduces into his food scraps of menstrual blood or string from her aprons in order to get rid of her husband and marry someone else. Not only may women's carelessness have dangerous consequences (which perhaps contributes to men's obsessive characterization of women as "mindless"), but they may destroy men through deliberate acts. Such volition is tied to role situations.

While all adult females are potentially polluting to males, women in different relationships are expected to behave differently. A man has most contact with polluting women in the roles of mother or wife; sisters more often than not will have left the domestic group to marry elsewhere before their first menstruation. It is sisters who will help to gather food while the mother is in seclusion; and in the past when men readied to fight and were afraid to eat from the hands of married women, it was children and young unmarried girls who brought them their meals. For the most part, however, men depend on their mothers and wives for sustenance. Thus the very persons who nourish them are also those who may contaminate the source of nourishment. But although Hageners see wives as developmentally replacing mothers in the domestic unit, they distinguish clearly their likely motivations. Mothers are not feared for their innate capacity to harm to the extent that wives are. With his wife a man runs a double danger for she may kill him through sexual intercourse at the wrong time as well as through contaminating food. Hagen men say, "Women (= wives) give us polluted food and kill us"; but also, "My mother looks after me and protects me". By having brought up her children, the mother has demonstrated her good intentions—the fact that they are alive and well attests to her care in protecting them. But wives have to prove that they will protect their husbands, in the same way as they have to show their dependability as food-providers.

Women accept the cultural designation that at certain times they are unclean (elk^{e}ka ronom, "bad odour arises"). They may be personally ashamed about their condition, young girls being particularly sensitive when they first begin to menstruate. Women regard the taboos which they observe not as an oppression but as the means by which they can protect their menfolk (sons, husband), as they put it: so that "the good work of the men" is not spoiled. It is a bad, careless, lazy woman, they say, who does not pay proper attention to the rules.

This has a bearing on the way children are taught to regard their mothers and on attitudes to the weaning away of male children from the mother's influence. A growing boy (at the age of eight or ten onwards) is encouraged to sleep in his father's house rather than with his mother as he has been doing, though he is lured there by the promise of a share in the wild foods men collect and hunt or participation in men's talk, rather than forced. This is so he will associate with strong men and thus himself grow strong. In addition, he must scrupulously avoid contact with his mother when she is menstruating. He does not, however, have to make a permanent residential shift to ward off pollution, but must simply keep away during her periods of seclusion. This starts much earlier. Once fully weaned of drinking milk (at about three) he may no longer accompany her to the menstrual hut. But when she comes back into the domestic circle, he resumes his dependency; the periodic withdrawals thus do not affect the whole relationship of nurture. In addition, a positive attitude is imputed to the mother's withdrawal. One of the few contexts in which parents automatically slap a child is to turn him away from following his mother into the hut. The boy learns later that this was for his own good, his mother out of her kindness protecting him from herself. Children do not have to outwit female malevolence.[1] The fear of wives by husbands, on the other hand, is bound up with a further aspect of their role, namely their potential as carriers of poison.

Poison

An explicit association is made between menstrual fluids and poison. Men emphasize the disgusting nature of the menses (women say men tell them their skin smells).[2] Small boys, instructed to avoid their mothers at these times, are informed that the women are smeared with faeces, or have poison (*kopna* or *konga*) on their bodies. Danger rests, they learn, particularly in ingesting contaminated food, which leads to sickness, and children probably associate menstruation with poisonous things long before they become aware of women's physiological condition. Some men relate how they did not discover that women retire to the seclusion hut because of bleeding till some incident occurred—such as an overheard obscenity referring to menstrual blood or an argument among

---

[1] Pollution is tied to the woman herself: little children still at the breast accompany their menstruating mother in seclusion during the daytime and sleep with their fathers at night; there is apparently no fear of contagion in this context (that the child will convey sickness to his father).

[2] Kaberry (1939) gives an example of menstruation being thought dangerous without being disgusting.

adults over traces of blood found in a house. Further parallels between poison and menstrual blood lie in the means of administration (introducing substances into food) and in the likelihood that men, primarily husbands, will be the victims. Poison differs in that it always implies deliberate intent, and is not attributed to carelessness as menstrual pollution can be.

When a person conveys poison on someone else's behalf, or with another's connivance, it is sometimes feared that his or her original willingness may evaporate. The supplier of the poison then secretly applies a magical substance which renders the poisoner-to-be insensible to anything but the task he must carry out. At the moment of actually giving poison to her husband, therefore, a wife may be described as "out of her mind" from the influence of the magic. This in no way diminishes her responsibility; it does to some extent provide people with an explanation of how an individual at once so intimate with the victim could yet commit such a hostile act.

In the past poisoning was believed to occur constantly between major enemies and accusations also sprang up between minor enemies during bouts of hostilities. Nowadays groups suspect that their past major enemies in particular, with whom they no longer come into open conflict, still contrive to send them poison. Clans keep away from pig distributions at cult performances conducted by their major enemies because of this fear. An enemy may bribe a relative of theirs who has some link with the intended victim; since the most frequent and direct contacts with other groups are through women,[1] in-married wives are a prime target for accusation. In the past death or sickness attributed to poisoning led to divination procedures and open charges. Public accusations are rarely made nowadays; people simply whisper their suspicions, and those who suspect they may be sought for revenge avoid possible dangerous encounters with the kin of a sick or dead man.

Men are the chief victims of poison. Poison is regarded as an inherently toxic substance[2] (unlike menstrual "poison" which affects males only),

---

[1] One Northern Melpa youth (born c. 1940) was of the opinion that in the past only men [*sic*] handled poison; it is nowadays, he said, since girls are married from long distances away that poison "walks about" in the hands of women.

[2] "Poison", as distinct from female fluids, and various kinds of magic, here refers to material substances made out of such items as snake skin (because of the deadliness of a snake's attack), rotting corpses (because of the association with death), powder scraped from stones near which dying plants had been observed, and so on. Vicedom, who notes that Hagen poisons probably have no naturally toxic properties, illustrates poison packs (1943–8:1:136).

and in theory anyone eating it would sicken and die. In actuality, it is rarely directed at women. Occasionally husband and wife both fall victim to poison from the husband's enemies. A women can succumb to poison intended for a man, and some say that on occasion cowives use poison (*kopna*), as well as cowife magic (*wølik*), against each other.

Either men or women may be accused: likely suspects would be distant kinsmen or affines who had had recent contact with the victim, poor rubbish men (*wuᵉ korpa*) motivated by jealousy of the successful, and women, especially wives. Wives have ample opportunity to tamper with food. Much less pronounced than poison, is a form of sorcery (magical disposal of exuviae) (cf. Strauss, 1962:132); their intimate relationship enables wives to get hold of hair or pieces of clothing belonging to their husbands, and again they are prime suspects. Divination procedures centred on discovery of the identity of the agent responsible for causing sickness or death.[1] The initial guess as to whether the ailment was due to pollution from menstrual blood or to poison was made on circumstantial evidence (recent deaths, status of victim, local politics), and would be tested by the application of remedies. Someone whose sickness persisted after he was "cured" of poison might then suspect blood-pollution.

When poisoning suspicions fell on living men, divination techniques were resorted to in framing the accusation. But of women, wives were invariably suspects, and might immediately be subject to violent retaliation. Not only did torture force them to confess, but the spectacle was intended to teach other women. Methods included dragging the bound victim over rough ground, roasting above a fire and putting splinters under fingernails. If the accused heeded promises of release and confessed her responsibility, torture was likely to end in summary execution. Both sexes speak with contempt of someone proved to have administered poison and, as with the effects of her menstrual fluids, the woman herself is held responsible. Even though her kin may have supplied the poison, they would rarely come to her aid; and she would be tortured irrespective of whether further action was to be taken. Retaliation on a poisoner was an end in itself, as expressive as it was punitive (Beattie, 1964: 178–179).

The outrage felt against wives has at least three origins. First, the

---

[1] In the case of sickness attributed to ghosts, the name of the individual ghost responsible* Although certain symptoms indicated whether ghosts or the work of poisoners had caused the misfortune, diagnosis was not automatic. Some details of divination procedure appear in Strathern, A. J. (1971:83–4).

woman has betrayed a dependency relationship. As a regular food-provider, the wife should nourish, not destroy, her husband. Perhaps the fear that women will poison food is related to a reluctance to admit such a dependency on them. Any woman might be afraid of accusation when her husband died, and for this reason widows were in the past meticulous in the performance of their mourning duties; a proper display of grief and a willing submission to a long and onerous mourning period, was protest of their innocence. A woman who ran away at her husband's death or who, home on a visit, failed to return was immediately suspect. Wives are suspected of having personal motives for wanting to be rid of their husbands (e.g. a desire to marry elsewhere); however, suspicions do not fall on them simply as persons involved in disputes or known to cherish grievances, but in addition because of their tribal origins. Wives' loyalties lie partly with other groups. Of all wives it is those from or who have links with major enemies who are most vulnerable.

A second cause for outrage, then, lies in the fact that the friendly relations which ties through marriage have supposedly brought about instead have soured, themselves affording a route for poison. Her cognates might supply a woman with poison to kill her husband's clansmen or the husband himself. Women are thus regarded as open to suggestion, and one who administered poison on her kinsmen's behalf is simply abandoning her more recently acquired loyalty to her husband's people in favour of her own kinship ties. The reverse rarely occurs, that a woman takes her husband's part and conveys poison to her kin.

The outrage expressed against an exposed poisoner is related, finally, to the clandestine nature of the act. Whereas a clan might rejoice as publicly at the death of an enemy killed by poison as at a death in battle, from the point of view of the victim's group, there is a considerable difference between open warfare and secret poisoning. Warfare is primarily a male activity. Women did not participate in the fighting. Mention has already been made (Chapter 4) of the fact that marriages were used to cement friendships following peace. And this is the point: what is true for public exchange occasions was also true for warfare, that women could not act as group members in confrontation against the clans with which they themselves afforded links. Their role was limited to carrying messages between the two sides. At the outbreak of hostilities most women remained in their houses. Ideally they should stay with their husbands, and some men were said to forbid their wives from travelling about at such a time lest they brought poison back. If the war was with their home kin they would be in no danger of attack themselves, for sisters and daughters would be spared. In an attack from an outside clan, on the other hand, a woman could be killed if they succeeded in over-running her husband's territory, as a wife of the defeated group. Under either circumstance, some women preferred to flee to their own kin, who might even encourage their return home, saying they did not want her to bear enemy children. Such an action sometimes resulted in permanent divorce. But if she had children she would, it is said, feel sorry for them and return to her husband after the fighting, or if he had been killed marry a husband's brother. Here, then, the wife is seen to have conflicting loyalties: she is safer with her own clansmen in times of fighting, but she is attached to her husband's group through her children and feels impelled to return, even if as a widow. These are, of course, simplified (and ideal) reconstructions of considerations which may actually have underpinned behaviour in the past.[1]

While the wife may re-establish ties with her husband's group, or a marriage cement a new peace, it was often avowed to be too dangerous to marry into a group with which one's own had been recently fighting. Deaths give rise to vengeance-anger (*popokl*), and the revenge may be taken through poison.

*In the 1930's a Kawelka Kurupmbo man married a woman from a traditional enemy clan. Her father had been killed by the Kawelka in a recent fight, but the husband was not aware that she had been sent deliberately in order to contrive revenge. She bore him a son. On one occasion the whole family went to her home on a visit, and this was the opportunity for her brothers to kill the husband with poison. His corpse was returned to the Kawelka, while the woman and her son stayed with her kin. (Account from a clan-section contemporary of the victim.)

Poisoning is thus associated with treachery. It is the more to be feared because unlike open warfare it is secretive. When men fight as a group they respond to the call for solidarity;[2] when women give poison it is always a solitary act and is often because they are subject to hidden influence. It is noteworthy that women rarely kill men through direct physical violence, although instances are readily recounted of the several husbands who have murdered their wives. Because of their susceptibility to persuasion, women's connections are feared.

---

[1] Thus women, in fact, most probably took their young children with them as they fled home, rather than leave them behind.

[2] Men also kill secretly and employ poison, but women can never do more than this.

*During fighting between Kawelka Kundmbo and Minembi Papeke clans, in about 1935, a Kundmbo wife was accused of hiding a bamboo poison container which was found near the hearth. She was tortured and made to confess that three Papeke men, including her own mother's brother, had sent the phial to her; she was released, however, on the plea that she had not actually used the poison because she had been overcome by pity (*kaemb*) for her husband. (From a big-man of the sub-clan she had married into, then a youth.)

Often women suspected of poisoning are those whose own close relatives have been killed. They may be supplied with poison by kinsmen anxious for revenge; but sometimes are seen to act on their own initiative.

*A Penambe woman was married to Kope, traditional major enemies of her tribe. In the 1920's, men of her husband's clan killed a lineage brother of hers in battle. Sorry (*kaemb*) for her dead brother, she herself obtained poison and killed her own husband. At the time she was an old woman with already married daughters: her youngest daughter she brought back with her to Penambe, where she reported the death to her jubilant brothers. (Account from a Penambe tribesman, a young man when it happened.)

Loyalty to the home clan can, consequently, be regarded as leading a woman to act and herself take revenge on its behalf. Sometimes women were said not to have revealed, ever under torture, that their kin had given the poison, thus protecting them from retaliation. The connection between poison and menstrual fluids is a sinister one, for a woman does not have to depend on supplies of poison from her relatives; she may equally well use her own menstrual blood, and there are stories of women avenging dead kinsmen by resorting to just this.

The ability of women to take independent action can be related to a further characteristic: while many stories of poisoning depict them acting out of loyalty to kinsmen, some describe simple motivations of self-interest.

*In the 1920's Oma married Penambe Wiya Muri. Muri's other three wives were jealous and subjected her to cowife magic (*amb wølik*). A Kope man, from Penambe's major enemies, took advantage of the situation and approached her, promising to marry her himself if she poisoned her husband. Muri sickened and died; the Kope man, who was also a BWZH (sub-clan brother's wife's clan sister's husband) to Muri, had been visiting there, and was summoned to the divination which followed the death. The test indicated him guilty, but he jumped up and told the men that it was Oma who had poisoned Muri, and already she would be trying to escape. They did indeed catch her in flight and executed her, the Kope dealing the fatal blow to save his own skin. But he was a marked man and was later killed in battle. (Account from an Elti woman married into Penambe Wiya clan, corroborated by her husband.)

Poisoning was a fairly frequent cause of male deaths; 11 out of 37 deceased men of his clan were reckoned by one Kawelka big-man to have died in this way, a further nine having met their deaths in battle. In few of the poison cases, however, had public identification and accusation of the poisoner been made. There was always more speculation about possible sources of poison than resulted in firm convictions. The following table sets out information on 18 stories from both Northern and Central Melpa, in which women are the chief suspects of poison; the time span is roughly 1910–1950. Death had resulted in 10 cases, in two the victim fell ill but did not die, and in 5 instances the poison was discovered before it could be administered; in a further case these circumstances are not known.

TABLE XII

Females involved in poisoning
(numbers of women)

Victim's relation to woman	Woman is suspected privately	Woman is accused publicly	Poison given on her own initiative	Poison supplied by another
Husband	5	3	3	2[a]
H along with HBs	1	2	0	3
H clan B	0	3	0	2[b]
H's extra-clan kin or affine	1	1	0	2
clan B[c]	0	1	0	1
sub-clan Z ch.[c]	0	1	0	1
	7	11	3	11

[a] 3 cases no information
[b] 1 case no information
[c] Two very unusual instances. The brother who accused his sister of having been supplied with poison by her mother's kin (traditional enemies) was described as an over-violent man (*wuᵉ pundoma*). He came from a section of the clan which had long been residentially separated from hers.

In five of the instances where women were openly accused they were tortured and released, in four further cases they were killed; in two the matter was settled with compensation payments. Of the women under private suspicion, one was apparently summarily killed on little evidence, three others were thought to have brought poison but no action was taken, and three women revealed their guilt by running away. Although these accounts by no means comprise a sample, the preponderance of husbands as a category of victim is striking.

Women are not generally feared by their own brothers as poisoners, but if her husband or men of her husband's clan themselves poison her kin, then, because of her link with the enemy, a woman might suffer. Her own clan ghosts would make her barren or her children sick, perhaps even killing them or herself to take revenge on the husband. It is also thought that the same calamity would befall a wife who brought poison to her husband's group, the angry ghosts of his clan striking her dead. As we have seen, however, the living members are likely to intervene and despatch her first. Childlessness has already been noted (Chapter 5) as implicating young women in particular.

The following circumstances were related about a Northern Melpa death which occurred in 1966. The narrator is a mother's brother's son to the dead man's clan-section.

*Before the arrival of Europeans, A had killed the father of M, a major enemy; anger over the death still persisted. A, now an old man, on one occasion went to stay with X who had married his daughter, B. At that time X's other wife, N, was spending much of her time with her home kin, where X also sometimes lived, maintaining dual residence. There was considerable friction between the cowives, B and N. N was persuaded by her father and brothers to administer poison to A, now that she had the opportunity; N is supposed to have agreed that since her father's father was killed by this man A she would now kill him. A died. His corpse was brought back to be buried on his clan ground. At the funeral, and apparently in front of X, A's clansmen hinted that N had been the source of the poisoning, although nothing was openly done about it. They did, however, say among themselves that N would not escape unscathed, and pointed to subsequent illnesses of hers as being sent by her husband's ancestral ghosts as a sign of her guilt.

Sometimes women were said to disobey kinsmen's warnings, and out of their own strength of mind desire to marry a man from a group which had caused deaths in their own. Such a woman was supposedly asked if she really meant to be a good wife and had no hidden intentions of poisoning her husband. Even if against their better judgement others allowed the marriage to go through, the ancestral ghosts of her clan might show their disapproval by making her fall ill. In particular, the spirits of those who had died could "come on her". The husband would then provide a sacrifice for the dead men, to "make the talk go straight" (*ik kwun iti*).[1] When the innocent intentions of both sides were made clear, the marriage was supposedly safe from further ghostly attack.

The possibility of women taking revenge leads to a ramification of inhibitions against marriages being contracted between hostile groups who have directly inflicted deaths on each other (see Chapter 4). For example, a man would not marry the widow of an enemy he or his clansmen had killed, and would furthermore avoid this woman's sister. In the years immediately following the death, the whole of the killer's clan would be debarred from marrying the widow and her actual sister, although only his immediate sub-sub-clan or lineage would eschew other girls of her natal sub-sub-clan. Similarly, while the whole clan of a killer avoids the victim's clan for two or three years after the death, if the group are not major enemies, the further away in time the incident becomes, the narrower the range of restrictions. After a generation (it may be said) the killer's own son can marry into the victim's lineage if they are otherwise friendly. Women are believed to seek revenge for deaths of sisters as well as brothers, so that a man would never marry the sister of a woman he had killed. The consequences of women's deaths are interesting. If a wife married to an enemy group, though herself not necessarily of enemy origin, was killed, intermarriage between her natal clan and that of the killers would be initially barred, the restriction applying after a while only to the immediate lineages concerned. The enemies would also avoid the woman's husband's clan, for they would be told, "You have slain the mother of our children!" Similar restrictions apply to the natal clan of an unmarried girl killed in war, the vengeance of her uterine sister being especially feared. Some men assert, however, that killing a woman is much less serious than killing a man, and that such restrictions apply only to the girl's or woman's sub-sub-clan, whereas a

---

[1] Similarly, if political relations have improved between ex-major enemies to the point of intermarriage, the ghosts must be informed of the changed circumstances.

man's death affects the whole clan. Clearly these are not just rules but also summaries of attitudes liable to vary with the circumstances of particular cases. Two points can be made. First, there is likely to be a difference between the concern of a woman's close lineage or sub-sub-clan in her death and that of her clan; insofar as a clan estimates its strength in terms of male members, men may not consider the loss of a distant female member quite the injury a man's would be. On the other hand, since women are regarded as actively involved in revenge procedures themselves, marriage with females related in any way to killed persons carries some danger.

The Independent Agent

We have seen that Hageners contrast the sexes as "strong" and "weak". Women cannot participate fully, as men do, in corporate displays of strength. Further, from the point of view of group well-being, incoming women are intruders, their links with other groups creating points of vulnerability.[1] Here men are threatened not by an absence of strength but by positive malevolence: women are credited with powers, the ability to pollute and to poison, regarded (by the victim) as deliberately subversive.

In discussing types of male domination, Douglas suggests that where principles of superiority are not elaborated "absolutely consistently", they may "run into trouble" in relation to other principles, for example, those which accord women protection as minors. Thus Lele men define their dominance by exercising rights of bestowal over females, and yet this itself enables women to play off men against one another (1966: 149). In Hagen, females are both excluded from public political life and also seen as politically committed persons, ready to use their destructive powers, as they use their domestic influence, on behalf of men. I use the term "political" here to emphasize the way women are seen to respond to group loyalties similar to those that bind men. It is certainly true that a sister is more likely to avenge the death of a close (lineage or sub-sub-clan) brother rather than a distant clansman, and that her allegiance is not openly demonstrated in public combat, but surreptitiously as she goes about her domestic tasks, yet her loyalty nevertheless

---

[1] Some implications of concern with group boundaries are discussed in Strathern, A. J. (1969a); and see Strauss (1962:310).

possesses something of the same character. The taking of vengeance has implication for group relations. Women, furthermore, are credited with wills of their own. Thus while their power to destroy through menstrual fluids arise from the simple fact of feminity, Hageners believe it is subject to partial control (cf. Berndt, R. M., 1962: 402). Women have the choice of whether to kill or to protect those under their care. This attribution of positive motive is echoed in the Hagen equation between menstrual fluids and poison, a substance employed usually for political reasons.

Apart from the fact that some marriages are made with major enemies, the political situation of Hagen wives is in any case ambiguous. Wives are drawn generally from a range of clans who are alternating allies and minor enemies to one's own. Micro-political relations can change over a short space of time from amity to enmity. Individual male affines can try or pretend to preserve their friendships, whatever their secret grievances or the wider conflicts of their respective clans. But there is the additional factor of the woman's own loyalties to be reckoned with. She may take the initiative for revenge herself. A wife puts her own interpretation on her obligations to her husband or brother and is the closest potential enemy with whom a man comes into regular contact. A man's clan as a whole will have drawn some wives from friendly groups, some from major enemies. Someone with a wife from a major enemy group was said in the past to warn his fellow clansmen not to eat at his house; even though he thought his wife would not poison him, they might be attacked. Mothers as well as wives are drawn from the same range of clans, but to an individual his own personal blood ties with his mother's kin are secure; he does not regard himself as in danger from that source. His relationship with his wife's kin is much less secure.

Pollution and poison are both weapons open to manipulation. The extent to which women in the past deliberately used these weapons is almost impossible to establish; it is clear, however, that men suspected women of doing so and women admitted the correctness of men's suspicions.

In the absence of open warfare today, women's dual loyalties are played out in the context of ceremonial exchange. Poisoning is sometimes committed in retaliation over a debt. In one instance (not included in Table XII) a man died after eating pork sent him from his wife's kin, and the wife was made to admit that she knew her brother had poisoned it because he was angry over pearl shells the husband owed him and had failed to return. Since her folk had been responsible for the death, his clansmen killed her. Such treatment is relevant to women's jural status; as I discuss later, her kin normally demand compensation if a sister is attacked or killed on her husband's territory. Support for a poisoner, however, would implicate them. Indeed, when a woman is accused of poisoning, her brother, far from coming to her aid, may denounce her and even publicly concur in the execution, saying she has proved herself *kara* ("wayward", "wild") and beyond control. Against this background of doubtful female loyalty, men sometimes react violently when wives betray them in the sphere of exchange transactions.[1] Various details about the following incident were in circulation at Buk in 1964–5.

> *A Kombukla man recently quarrelled with his wife: her brother had come to claim a pig which he refused, on the plea that he had none of suitable size to give him yet. However, his wife spoke up and said her husband was lying, of course he had pigs. After the brother had left, the enraged husband demanded what the woman had been thinking of; in the course of a violent quarrel she provocatively revealed that he had had intercourse with her while she had been menstruating. In a fury he killed her and then gave himself up at the District Office.

Hagen ideas about pollution and poison contribute to notions of female unpredictability. A woman is able to attack anyone, anywhere: poison can be carried around, sent to other people. Even when the poison is supplied by a man, there is no guarantee that she will not use it for her own ends. In order to employ their sisters as roads for poison, men have to admit the possibility of their own wives being likewise committed to their brothers; and since poison operates in secret, they can never be sure of the route it will take. Perhaps some of the anxieties which men display about women stem from misgivings that they have transferred too much power to them.

Poison, in particular, is a most apposite weapon to place in female hands. It is closely associated with food, and it is the wife as producer who gives food to her husband; but coming from an outside source, it is also like an exchange object given in transactions. It is the destructive, impoverishing counterpart of nourishment and of wealth.

---

[1] Ryan (1969:173) reports a Mendi instance where a wife overstepped the pressure she put on her husband to make payments to her (her kin) and was killed.

8

Marital Stability

A *rondokl* ("strong willed") woman is one who assumes initiative. The most frequently cited example (by Hagen men and women alike) is the "typical" divorcee: the wife who has left her husband, against the wishes of menfolk on either side, for some private reason of her own. Given the way in which women are regarded as intermediaries and the importance of marriage to affinal and group alliances, it is not surprising that considerable agitation accompanies the termination of a union. It is well enough recognized that divorce, or the threat of it, can become a strategy in affinal competition. Nonetheless, disputes arising from divorce procedures, and accounts of such events in the past, tend to focus on the behaviour of the wife. There is an antagonism between men and women in their roles as husband and wife which is not so marked in the mother-son or brother-sister relationships. As we have seen, it is wives rather than mothers or sisters who a Hagen man most fears will pollute or poison him. This antagonism is replicated in the context of divorce and its entailments; divorce, like women's powers to kill, touches directly on an attribution of volition.

Concern over Divorce

Men display concern[1] about the stability of marriage. During the early months of fieldwork at Buk three sets of apparent facts were impressed upon me: courts spent all their time hearing disputes over women,

---

[1] Whether or not individuals actually feel anxious is another matter; I am describing a set of socially expressed attitudes.

especially marital disputes and divorce cases; women were always "humbugging" (*kara pi*) and leaving their husbands for no reason; many women never settled down in marriage at all but were constantly on the move from man to man. These were views mainly of men. The persistent theme of women's irresponsibility, and the "trouble" they cause by leaving their husbands, I take as a significant exaggeration of how women actually behave, and an indication that Hagen men do indeed regard divorce as "an index of social pathology" (Marwick, 1965: 180).

Some individuals are categorized as sexually promiscuous, *amb wapra*; but the number so designated form a minute percentage of the total population of married women; circa 2% (Kawelka) to 5% (Elti) in 1964/5, although their very characteristic of mobility may have led to an under-estimation here.[1] While few in absolute number, they are, nevertheless, targets for bitter invectives. Such women, who may have had four, five or even more "husbands" in succession, fulfil their proper roles neither as wife nor as sister/daughter. Cowives who in the heat of quarrelling accuse each other of neglecting wifely duties may also use *amb wapra* as a pejorative. Often *wapra* women have no children, and this infertility is attributed to ghostly displeasure. Women divorced more than about twice can expect no further bridewealths to be paid for them by subsequent husbands till they bear children, so they cannot bring in wealth to their kin. This is supposedly as humiliating for the woman as it is disappointing for her lineage. If they are constantly moving, no satisfactory exchange relations can in any case be created by their unions. *Wapra* means not only promiscuous, but in other contexts "unproductive" and "desolate" (as of waste land). The *wapra* woman is the very antithesis of what a wife/sister should be. Her liaisons are of little importance for affinal alliances or group relations, and hence she is represented as consumed by nothing but sexual appetite.

One of the reasons why parents discourage a daughter from experiencing pre-marital sexual relations is to curb any tendency towards promiscuity, although no great emphasis is put on virginity as such. Sometimes men insinuate that all females are *wapra* at heart. Their fears are revealed in the violent treatment which was in the past, and notwith-

---

[1] Figures are based on histories of women married to Elti or Kawelka or who have married and since left. Whereas "traditional" *wapra* women moving about in short marriages within the tribal area are likely to be included in my figures, others in the vicinity of Hagen town who have drifted out of traditional networks will not be indicated unless they have also contracted some local unions.

standing the sanctions of administration courts, is sometimes today meted out to women caught in adultery or to runaway wives. Often the retaliation itself has sexual overtones,[1] and a girl punished initially for some other reason may be forced into becoming an *amb wapra*.

*Before the arrival of Europeans, a marriage was arranged within the Penambe tribe. A sub-clansman of the groom related this incident. The bride was oiled and sent to the groom's place, where four pigs were put out for bridewealth. Her parents insisted on twice that number, while the groom grumbled that the girl had been married and divorced once already, and he was not prepared to give a large bridewealth. With the bride's side saying they would take her back, and the groom's side saying they had given enough a fight broke out and the bride herself was tugged and pulled this way and that. The groom's side overpowered her while her parents were put to flight and her brother wounded with an axe. Several of the groom's clansmen then had intercourse with her. They kept the woman, under the threat of death, for about a month and continued to use her, then finally dispatched the girl back to her parents. Branded an *amb wapra*, she bitterly accused her parents of being the cause of the trouble by wanting more pigs and resolved not to marry again. It would serve them right if she never brought wealth in for them.

Women fleeing home from their husband's clan, especially in times of warfare and if they were related to enemies, might in the past be caught and raped. A husband who was afraid that his wife would run away and estimated that he was unlikely to obtain a bridewealth return, or out of anger threw the chance of this to the winds, occasionally anticipated the event by inviting his clansmen to plural copulation before getting rid of her. Even someone anxious to retrieve a runaway wife might nevertheless punish her severely. Several stories from the past describe how a husband with supporters from his sub-clan would bodily carry the protesting woman back to his place, trussed up like a pig, and set on her; kicking the genital area or perhaps stuffing her vagina with an irritant[2] such as a mass of ants. Usually, however, the accounts end with the comment that the husband was afraid to take too drastic measures lest the wife run away again. Much clearly depended, as it does now, on the husband's disposition. For occasional adultery he may simply collect compensation from the lover and not punish his wife at all; more per-

---

[1] Cf. Reay's suggestion (1964b: 150) that an imputation of lasciviousness to women on the part of men may derive from the latter's wishful fantasy.

[2] *Wapra* women are caustically asked if they are impelled to lead the life they do because their sexual parts are so irritated with desire.

sistent adultery may lead him to tear off his wife's ornaments and slash her ringlets, for she had no business as a married woman to dress up and carry on like a nubile girl. Sometimes retaliation taken on an adulterous wife was as severe as punishment for female poisoners (see Vicedom and Tischner, 1943–8:2:143–4).

> *About thirty years ago an Elti man, notorious for his violence, a *wu^e pundoma*, crippled his young wife by shooting at her ankles and then cutting the tendons with his axe. She was nursed back to health by a cowife. (Account from her cowife in a subsequent marriage, and others.)

Evidence of *wapra* tendencies remains today one of the reasons for which a husband might murder a wife. Should this lead to enquiries from her parents they may be told that the woman was *wulya* ("mad", "wayward") or *kara pum* ("she was a humbug"). A woman's male kin may in any case be reluctant to interfere if she is accused of *wapra* behaviour, their response to the news that she has run away being *amb elim pum*, "she went herself", i.e. on her own accord, an attitude which parallels their embarrassment should she be accused of poisoning. Sometimes men suggest that it is as dangerous for their health to have intercourse with a *wapra* as with a menstruating woman. A wife irresponsible enough to desert her husband for another man may be described by observers as "going wild", *amb timbi ponom, rakra ran^{e}m* ("she has become like a wild animal, turned into a savage thing").

Langness (1967) has suggested that former conditions of warfare among the Bena Bena of the Eastern Highlands encouraged there the development of an aggressive male personality type ill-adapted to the kinds of interaction between the sexes which focus on sex and dependency needs. Some of the violence shown to Hagen wives in the past (trussing up a runaway like a stolen pig or spearing her) and some of the terminology associated with coitus (to have intercourse (man-speaking) is "to strike a woman"; the same phrase, *amb rui*, being used for rape) may indeed have military overtones. Such behaviour also perhaps expresses anxiety over the recalcitrance of women.[1] If the women *are* treated as enemies, it is because they threaten the institutions which depend partly on stable marital alliances.

The apparently exaggerated attention given to *amb wapra* is paralleled in the strenuous complaints which Councillors and Komitis among

---

[1] One young man suffering from a temporary fit of madness was said to have been possessed by wild spirits because he was so angry over the alleged promiscuity of a newly-acquired wife.

others make—that all troubles which erupt in court disputes stem from women, especially those who are always embroiling their husbands and their own kin in lengthy divorce procedures. At Buk and Kelua alike, about 15% of the cases heard by Councillors and Komitis formally concern divorce, although a further 25% deal with adultery and husband-wife disputes, and another 10% with cowife or in-law relations. Thus about half the cases actually involve women and their marital relationships, the rest dealing in the main with pigs ruining gardens, and theft. Clearly, such figures are determined partly by the jurisdiction of the courts, there being categories of dispute which are usually settled outside the court context or are frequently shelved and not settled at all (e.g. *moka* debts). What is interesting is that disputes concerning women, like theft accusations, are considered appropriate for interference and judgement by a third party where, by contrast, many complaints over matters such as debts in ceremonial exchanges are dealt with privately by the partners themselves. On the other hand, there are more chances for disputes to arise between spouses, of which only a fraction will reach the courts. For whatever reasons Hageners (men in particular) see women as responsible for much litigation, it is true that cases concerning them tend to be the most drawn-out and time-consuming.

The Frequency of Divorce

A comparison of Hagen divorce rates with those reported from other Highlands societies does not suggest that Hagen rates are particularly "high". The definition of divorce, however, has been pointed out by many writers to involve difficulties, primarily in the assessment of what constitutes a marriage. Where major bridewealth gifts are usually delayed till the birth of children (as among the Kuma, Reay, 1959a; and Manga, Cook, 1969), annulment of an initial contract may be quite informal. Or again, where second and third wives are acquired informally, even though bridewealth is paid for a first, it may be difficult to distinguish between casual liaisons and regular unions (Langness, 1969). Dissolution may occur before the spouses have begun to assume full marital relations with each other ("annulment", Reay, 1967:15; Glasse, 1968:75). Quite different factors can vitiate comparisons, such as the high incidence of marriages terminated by death among the South Fore (Glasse, 1969) connected with an apparent stability in surviving marriages. Finally, the type of information on which figures must be based is historical, and for

Hagen at least I am not sure that the analysis can ever finally be accurate. My own impression was that the longer I was in the field the more likely I was to hear of past marriages contracted and dissolved.

The majority of marriages in Hagen are initiated by bridewealth payments, and most or a proportion of the wealth is returned should the woman leave her husband. Nevertheless, unions can be contracted outside the context of affinal prestations (see Chapter 4) and particular circumstances, especially warfare in the past, might mean that even when bridewealth has been paid a marriage can be effectively terminated without formal return of the outstanding items. My assessment of what constitutes a "marriage" is based therefore on informants' evaluations of different unions. I include informally established arrangements in which the affines on each side anticipate eventual exchanges; casual encounters with *wapra* women are thus excluded (although women so-called may also have contracted more stable unions), but any woman who remains long enough to become involved in the household, have gardens allocated to her, be recognized by her mother-in-law, I count as married. A double subjectivity is involved, on the part of informants and on my own part. While these considerations should qualify the figures, it may be remarked that the most dubious category of divorce cases (marriages casually initiated and casually terminated) form only a small proportion of the total. In sum, I count as divorce: (1) marriages initiated by bridewealth and terminated by its return; (2) marriages initiated by bridewealth but return forfeited or otherwise not made; (3) marriages casually initiated and casually terminated. Whether bridewealth is returned or not has no effect on the woman's divorced status, although it modifies relations between the husband and her kin (whether they wish to contract a further marriage, as sometimes happens, and so on).

Meggitt (1965:140) and Ryan (1969:172) both make a contrast between *de jure* and *de facto* divorce.[1] The former involves a bilateral abrogation of the marriage tie, while the latter is made by one side only, the husband typically not recognizing the wife's re-marriage to a second man. In Hagen, however, it is rare for a permanent situation to develop whereby the husband regards himself as still married to a woman who is living with another sex partner. Divorces are commonly preceded by

---

[1] I do not note all the usages of different writers on the Highlands; comparisons clearly call for a standardization of terms.

a marginal period in which the wife stays with her own relatives and the husband attempts to persuade her to return, perhaps supported by some of her kin. I do not call this *de facto* divorce since the wife herself is often unclear as to what her final intentions will be, these in turn depending partly on how the husband has reacted to the situation. Their relationship is in a state of flux. It is relatively unusual for a woman to run away to a third man. Sometimes her brothers or father encourage her to do this if they are anxious that the marriage should break up and want to bring the matter to a head. Not only may such devices be ploys which the bride's kin use against the husband, but going or pretending to go to another man may be a ploy on the wife's part. One or two cases of this recounted to me gave as the wife's motive her anger (*popokl*) with her husband—it is, in other words, an extreme form of protest against him (for his failure to act as a "husband") rather than evidence of a simple desire to leave. Such situations may follow the husband's failure to come for his wife when she returns home (cf. Brown, 1969:94). Occasionally a girl runs away to someone she knew before the present marriage; the husband makes strenuous efforts to retrieve her, but if these fail, quickly displays his pique by denying that she is any sort of wife to him and pressing for a return of bridewealth. Even where none has been paid, or the husband is in a weak bargaining position with her kin, pride will lead to his rejecting her. Whether the supposed divorce is a gambit in the strategies of marital relations, or whether a woman is really seeking another husband herself, the period during which the first husband continues to claim her is in most cases short.

Table XIII puts divorce rates (Barnes, 1949, 1967; all ratios expressed as percentages) for Kawelka and Elti tribes in the context of quantitative information for the frequency of divorce in some other Highlands societies. I consider from the societies of the region between the Markham headwaters to the Strickland gorge (Glasse and Meggitt, 1969:2) those where substantial bridewealth payments are paid at the initial marriage contract, as in Hagen.

Divorce rates for Kawelka and Elti men are based on the total number of marriages (330 and 173, respectively) contracted by living members of clan groups[1] (204 and 94 once-married or currently married i.e.

---

[1] Clan group= "agnatic" and "non-agnatic" clan members in September 1965 resident on clan territory; there are two cases in each tribe of a woman who left her husband and then returned to the same man: total number of women involved = 328 and 171.

TABLE XIII

Divorce frequencies for some New Guinea Highlands societies[a]

| Society | Barnes' ratio C as % | | | % wedded persons divorced once or more | | % all marriages contracted by men of one group ended in divorce |
	Men	Women	Both	Men	Women	
MAE-ENGA[b] Meggitt (1965)			7·2	6·5	7·7	
MENDI[c] Ryan (1961)						6·6
SOUTH FORE[d] Glasse (1969)	12·7	15·1		7·3	18·5	
HAGEN Kawelka	19·5	18·4		21·0	16·7	17·0
Elti Strathern, A. J. and A. M. (1969)	30·7	26·3		34·0	24·7	24·4
RAIAPU ENGA Waddell (1968; personal communication)	35·6	27·0		27·4	28·2	
KYAKA ENGA Bulmer (1960)	35·7	10·9		29·0	11·9	
HULI Glasse (1968)	38·0	28·0		48·0	28·0	
BENA BENA[e] Langness (1969)				60·9		

[a] Figures are in some cases adapted from original citation by authors. I am grateful for permission to quote from unpublished theses.

[b] Including both *de jure* and *de facto* divorce; the 540 marriages "among the Mae" (Meggitt, 1965: 149) are presumably based on the past experiences of both men and women.

[c] Ryan (personal communication) notes that this figure is based on a definition of divorce which gives the impression of a lower rate than might otherwise be computed.

[d] The high incidence of *kuru* deaths among women is a factor here (see above); Glasse remarks (1969: 27) that were marriages not so often terminated by these deaths the divorce ratio would probably be higher.

[e] Bena Bena spouses do not embark on full marital relations till the groom's age-mates have acquired wives, which is followed by a final ceremony; the figure here refers to men who had gone through this ceremony. If termination of less formal unions are included, "almost every middle-aged Bena has had one or more divorces" (Langness, 1969: 49).

wedded men). Rates for women are based on the numbers of marriages (299 and 140, respectively) made by current wives of Kawelka or Elti men (221 and 93), excluding widows who have remained with their husband's group but have not remarried.[1]

Hagen rates seem to fall into the middle range of frequencies for Highlands societies.[2] The first marriage of some 71% of Kawelka wives is still extant, this being true for 65·5% of Elti wives. The proportions of these extant first marriages to the total contracted by men give respective percentages of 47% and 35%. There is a significant difference here (at 1% level) between Elti and Kawelka, a difference also borne out in the contrast between their C ratios (Strathern, A. J. and A. M., 1969: 153). No significant difference is revealed within each group between men's and women's ratios; the difference between the male Kawelka and Elti ratio C is consistent with a comparable divergence between the same female ratios. I would relate this in part to some differences in the emphasis placed on women's roles in exchanges; these points are discussed in Appendix II.

Divorce Rates: developmental Aspects

Relatively high or low rates of divorce may co-vary with certain points in the life-cycles of the spouses, and for this reason should be time-specific (Goody, E. N., 1962:28). In Hagen there is a high likelihood that divorce will involve women in the early childless years of their marriage.[3] Out of 102 marriages contracted by Kawelka men and their wives which ended in divorce, in only fourteen had children been born to the terminated marriage. In ten of these cases there was only one

---

[1] Excluded here to render Elti data, where I have little information on marriage histories of widows, compatible with Kawelka; Kawelka ratio C for women excluding widows is 18·43%, including widows whose marital histories is recorded, 18·15%. The Kawelka figure of 221 excludes 9 married women for whom information is uncertain; the Elti figure of 93 excludes two for the same reason. Elti figures do not include the small number of men and women resident in Temboka.

[2] Mae-Enga rates are described by Meggitt as "low" (as is also implied in the discussion of South Fore divorce); Huli marriages are said to be "terminated without any great difficulty" (Glasse 1968:75); Bena Bena rates are "high" (Langness 1969:51). Craig (1969:196) considers ratio C for Telefolmin, 14·5%, as low; O'Brien (1969:227) on the same ratio for Konda valley Dani takes 44·7% as indicating "common" divorce.

[3] Lloyd (1968:71) notes that the divorce ratio may be an unreliable indication of general marriage stability when most divorces are the result of particular marital arrangements (such as trial unions).

child.[1] Childless marriages terminating in divorce tend also to be short-lived and the wife to be still a young woman (typically the marriage is her first). Information on half (52) of these cases illustrates the interrelation of these factors. Short-lived marriages are those estimated to be of less than three years' duration; young here refers to women under their mid-twenties at the time of divorce.

TABLE XIV

52 Divorces: childlessness, duration of marriage and age of wife

| | MARRIAGE | | WIFE |
	Short-lived	Long-lived	
With children	1	2[a]	Young
	1	6[b]	Not young
Without children	33	3	Young
	5	1	Not young

[a] In one case children probably not surviving at time of dissolution
[b] In two cases children probably not surviving at time of dissolution.

Young, childless women who leave their husbands after a short time account for 63% of these cases.[2] At this stage it is not possible to isolate any one factor as more important than the others. (The total of young wives is 39–52, of short marriages 40–52 and of childless marriages 42–52). As wives grow older or their marriages longer, the factor of childlessness predominates. Hageners themselves regard this as the most critical feature, not because barrenness *per se* is grounds for divorce (which it is not) but because having children fosters a woman's allegiance towards her husband's group. Occasionally a divorced woman is forced by circumstances to abandon her children, and if they are fairly

---

[1] This is not a properly based sample, the data referring to (1) the total of 56 divorces experienced by living Kawelka men (from which the male divorce rate is calculated); plus (2) 16 other divorces by these divorced women before or after their marriage to Kawelka; (3) 30 divorces from 49 experienced by wives and widows currently married to or associated with Kawelka. Any bias will be in favour of divorcees with children, since their marriages are more likely to be recalled. Some of the divorcees had had children by previous marriages, but the table refers to the state of the terminated marriages under consideration.

[2] Here demonstrably weighted in favour of marriages with children, the proportion of without-child unions being 19%, whereas in the 102 cases it was between 13–14%.

old the former husband will almost certainly try to persuade them to stay; nevertheless, women with children are as likely to take them off as leave them motherless with their father. This is a source of non-agnatic affiliation (Strathern, A. J., 1965; 1971). Inhibitions a mother feels about deserting her husband stem partly from a stated reluctance to cut children off from their father's clan, and partly we may deduce from the fact that by the time a wife has borne children she will have been married long enough to have developed some personal commitment towards her spouse. Even in subsequently stable unions a couple often do not have their first child till the third or fourth year of marriage. The early years bear the character of a trial period. Having a child is as much a sign that initial uncertainties have been overcome as it is a means of overcoming them.

The trial nature of this early period is one which Hageners recognize. Although bridewealth proceedings are conducted with an air of finality, there actually is no great surprise (however much opposition) if an incompatible couple part. The frequency with which young wives visit home helps to ease the transition in status; but at the same time, the very demonstration of the fact that they are not wholly committed to the marriage leads to friction—disputes tend to escalate, and the threat of divorce to hang over every quarrel between the young spouses or the wife and her in-laws. Rather than settling their grievances privately, women who are newly married and without children seem to have recourse more frequently than others to Councillors and Komitis.

These features of divorce have several implications. First, the majority involve a woman's (and often a man's) first marriage, and for these bridewealth is invariably paid and must subsequently be returned. Secondly, after only a year or two of marriage it is unlikely that the brothers-in-law or respective fathers-in-law will have become heavily engaged in reciprocal *moka* relations. Usually they wait till it appears that the union will be stable. On-going *moka* partnerships between affines do not normally survive the dissolution of marriage, but in most early divorces this is not a serious personal issue. Even if the affines themselves have not embarked on *moka*, however, from the point of view of their clans the relationship is a potential road for exchanges. The dissolution of any marriage can be taken as a general threat to the system of alliance and ceremonial exchange. In sum, while least is lost in a marriage terminated within a few years, the termination may yet become a vehicle for the expression of anxieties about the stability of other marriages upon which more may depend. This partly accounts for the tension generated over returning bridewealth, and men's public intolerance of divorcees. Finally, relatively frequent divorce among childless women focusses attention on women who are wives and not yet mothers; while the fact that all marriages must go through a childless stage may afford individuals some personal concern. Men's experience of divorce is also somewhat different from women's; polygynists in particular are likely to lose wives in the middle as well as early years of adulthood.

From a woman's point of view, marriage can be characterized as relatively unstable in the early years, but stable in the middle and later years. One locus of instability in middle- and old-age seems to be widowhood.

Ideally widows should, after the period of mourning is over, take a further husband from the deceased's man's clan or else remain with the clan unmarried. The latter course is attractive if they have children old enough to help support them. The choice to remain is formally a decision on the widow's part, although considerable pressure may be put upon her by her former husband's brothers. She may also marry a close cross cousin of the dead man, for while he is not of the same clan, he contributed to her bridewealth.[1] Should the widow leave the deceased's clan and return home or marry elsewhere, either abandoning or taking her children, bridewealth is not returned. If she married her husband's relative, however, it is on the strength of the original bridewealth payments, and any further small payments made to her kin by the new husband are a matter of goodwill which signify his own responsible intentions towards them. Some discussion has already been given of the accompanying sacrifices (Chapter 3).

While widows usually marry men of about their own age or a little younger, there is no particular rule which prevents them from marrying junior men ("sons"), and this occasionally even happens within the deceased husband's lineage. Where a clan is divided into clan-sections, almost all re-marriages take place within the section. The majority of Kawelka widows, from those who re-marry into their former husband's clan, in fact choose second husbands from his own sub-clan or lineage. In the case of Elti, which as a tribe is exogamous, re-marriage is within the sub-clan or sub-clan pair, the most prominent units to take joint

---

[1] This is a piece of dogma, not a principle which establishes a right, for a cross cousin may claim a widow even if he did not in fact so contribute. Such marriages are not very common, but fall within the range of ideal choices.

action on public occasions. There is a statistically significant difference (at 5% level) between Elti and Kawelka in the proportion of widows who initially elect to stay with their husband's group, whether they re-marry or not, over 91% of known cases of Kawelka wives doing so by comparison with 77% Elti.[1] However, of those who re-marry into the clan, approximately 20% of Kawelka widows subsequently divorce their second husbands, while the Elti proportion is half this. Some of these women take a further husband from the same clan or choose to remain there unattached; others move away. If these subsequent divorces are taken into account; the long term redistribution of Elti and Kawelka widows in fact shows no statistical differences. Of known cases some 75–85% of the women in total remain with their husband's clan (more than a third of these taking second spouses from it) while most others return home to live with a kinsman or take up residence at the home of a married daughter. A small number (4%) re-marry outside the clan. The preference for remaining with the former husband's clansmen is not a direct outcome of the control these men assert over the woman, for they cannot strictly prevent a widow from leaving; rather it is probably re-lated to the way relatively old women will have become established within the group and prefer to remain there for some of the same reasons which have contributed to the stability of their marriage up to this point. Among the Elti, a higher overall divorce rate allows personal adjustments to take effect at an earlier stage in life by contrast with Kawelka where widows, after submitting initially to the ideal require-ment that they re-marry their husband's kinsman, are subsequently more likely than Elti women are to divorce the second husband.[2] The initiative in such cases seems often to lie with the widow.

Of those widows who do divorce subsequent husbands, a number are women formerly married to big-men. Such wives were probably

---

1 If marriages with the deceaseds' cross cousin are included, this latter figure rises to 83%.

2 Elti widows in any case are more likely to leave the clan before contracting a second marriage. Clearly widowhood provides an opportunity to annul a previous association with a particular group, and is a factor which should be taken into account in assessing rates of divorce. It is interesting in this regard to compare Mae-Enga (Meggitt, 1965:133–4) who have a low divorce rate and no trial period of the kind experienced in Hagen: although 71% of widows remain under the control of the dead man's agnates, 13% nevertheless re-marry outside this group, a figure significantly high in relation to the comparable Hagen figure (4%) and the low incidence of divorce in Mae society. The 4% may, however, be an under-estimation in that women "lost" to the clan on widowhood are less likely to be remembered than those who stay.

prominent both locally and in relation to their husband's exchange networks; their total position as married women is difficult to re-create in a
second union.

The Stability of Marriage

Among general factors contributing to the relative stability of marriage,
we may consider the manner in which the roles of husband and wife are
presented to the actors. Since marriage sets up an alliance between male
affines who may use the relationship in *moka* exchange, kin on both sides
acquire a vested interest in its continuity. Pressures are sometimes put
directly onto the wife to remain with her husband in order that exchanges can continue. The explicitness of such tactics is illustrated in two
reports of reactions on the part of the wife's kin.

> *A woman returned to her parents to be met by an angry father, who ex-
> postulated: "No! You must go back to your husband! I do not want to
> have a divorce and lose his goodwill—he is a neighbour and 'inside us'
> (the marriage was between two pairclans) and he is a big-man. I want to
> make *moka* and be friends with him."

Marriages sometimes provide links between groups otherwise in
little contact.

> *In the case of such an alliance between affines belonging to clans which
> had scarcely intermarried before the advent of Europeans, a father sent his
> daughter back to her husband, supposedly saying to the husband: "You
> are afraid she will run away again, but I shall not take her back. Before
> we were not allies, but now white men have come we travel around and
> we can exchange women and make *moka* with you. The woman does not
> realize these things—I am her father and where else can she go? I can
> always send her back to you."

Other considerations put to a woman contemplating divorce might
include: the fact that a good bridewealth was paid for her; that there are
no outstanding debts, and so she has no cause for grievance; that her
husband's kin have always been staunch allies to her natal clan; that
she has no reason to listen to (for example) her mother who is only greedy
for pig (and entices her daughter home in order to obtain further gifts);
that the woman must not break up a marriage which sets the seal to
peace between the clans, and that particular *moka* plans are imminent
which would be upset by her divorce. The strength of this interest in
exchanges may be something of a stabilizing factor (cf. Meggitt, 1965:
155–161). In the next chapter I turn to the way these interests are brought

out in the handling of divorce in courts. The way actors react to these pressures indicates the degree to which the values are internalized.

Since public values to do with alliance and exchange are supposedly in the interests of men, husbands are presumed to share them, although in the early years of a first marriage the groom's father probably has a greater interest in this aspect of the union than the young man himself. Wives are also seen to be committed to the success of affinal transactions, there being a congruence in the formulation of the spouses' roles at this ideal level. Both are thus likely to be responsive to generally voiced approval or disapproval at the prospect of divorce, and to the pressures put on them by parents and other kin. A man with any *moka* aspirations depends on a wife to assist, among other things, the development of his wealth. Women also depend on their husbands. A girl's first marriage does not give her "uxoral status" (Fortes, 1962:8) independent of subsequent unions. She needs to remain married: a single woman cannot be an intermediary. In the context of ceremonial exchange the combination of wife/sister roles is put to positive use, and ideally conflicts arising from dual loyalties need not arise.

But pressure may also be brought to bear for opposite reasons: in support (or threat) of divorce. The women who were in the past used as intermediaries to cement military alliances, were also suspected of turning against their husbands because of their contacts with enemy groups. In the same way their part in ceremonial exchange exacerbates conflicts where relations are *not* ideal. They may appear to compete with their husbands, for example, over the disposal of wealth. Enough has been said to indicate that high expectations of exchange can lead directly to dissatisfaction. If it is to their gain, the wife's kin persuade her to leave her husband. The stability of individual marriages thus depends in part not only on its *moka* potential, but on the actual successes or failures of demands made of it. Accounts of the manner in which couples were in the past persuaded by their kin to maintain their marriage emphasize the importance of clan interests as well as those of the individual affines. These might either be in having a military alliance in a particular direction, or in maintaining friendships with otherwise distant groups. The actual stability-rate of any clan's marriages is, then, an amalgam of personal factors[1] and the balance between wider clan interests and the narrower concerns of immediate affines.

---

[1] Some are considered in the next chapter. Personal grievances may of course find other outlets than divorce.

Where group alliances support marital alliances, it is possible that unions are more stable than when established independently; in turn, where extensive exchanges take place between affines related by the marriage (e.g. *moka*) the union will perhaps be more stable than where transactions concentrate on the initial bridewealth payments (see Appendix II). Wider interests might prevail upon too narrow an interpretation of grievances. But at the same time, the more people who are brought into interaction through a marriage, the more vulnerable it is to disputes and conflicts arising for a wider miscellany of reasons. While Hagen wives have the opportunity in *moka* exchanges of constructively combining loyalty to their own and to their husband's clans, on occasion they may be put into the position of having to decide which has the greater weight. Not only warfare but deteriorating affinal exchanges impel women to leave their husbands. In short, where marriages are important affinally, they will, in this respect, be as stable as the affinal alliances; and where to women as well as men marriage has some political significance, political grievances are doubly likely to be factors in divorce.

9

Focus for Blame

Irrespective of factors such as exchange relations set up between the linked affines, husbands and wives have specific duties towards each other. I stressed earlier the extent to which spouses are interdependent; and among the causes of divorce, as Hageners see it, is failure to meet domestic obligations. The relationship between dereliction of duty and the possibility of divorce is, however, a complex one, and it is questionable to what extent Hageners go so far as to classify particular delicts as grounds for divorce. Certainly in public court hearings the manner in which divorces are handled tends to emphasize the disruptive consequences of the impending dissolution rather than notions of redress. Such hearings are revealing as to the nature of jural relations between husband and wife. Furthermore, courts and other procedures for settling disputes are mainly in the hands of men, and provide a context in which public attitudes towards women are displayed.

Reasons for Divorce

People with an intimate knowledge of a case will be aware of the several factors contributing to a divorce. But those less familiar with the circumstances pick on the most obvious reasons or may just offer conjecture. In addition, people make statements about the causes of divorce in a general fashion, without reference to specific instances. Quite separate from the appreciation of reasons, blame for the dissolution may be directed by one party against the other, or by outside observers against those involved. There is certainly no "unwillingness to judge" in such matters (cf. Ploeg, 1969:138, and citing Read, 1955). However accept-able private motives appear, as a public issue divorce meets with dis-approval. The desire to blame seems to be associated with the concern over divorce that men show. Women not directly involved in a particu-lar issue share these attitudes.

When speaking generally, men sometimes deny that other men can ever have motives for initiating divorce: they say that it is women who are responsible. The typical phrase on people's lips is that the wife has "abandoned" (wak rui) her husband.[1] This is partly a comment on virilocal residence, since in most cases it is the wife who usually leaves the husband's place rather than vice versa; but the phrase refers to moral as well as physical abandonment, and some very specific atti-tudes are involved here. The argument is that a man has little advantage in ridding himself of his wife; he has paid bridewealth, and can change her unsatisfactory ways by a beating, or just find an alternative in a second wife. However much he dislikes the woman herself, links with her kin may still be of value. It is said that if the husband openly makes it clear that he wants divorce, his ex-wife's kin jeer at him for his foolish-ness in relinquishing a profitable road when their groups come together subsequently at some moka festival. The institution of polygyny, along with the use of women as roads for exchange, thus render divorce against a husband's ostensible interests. His loss is duplicated in the stipulation that one who himself initiates a divorce forfeits part of the bridewealth return. If the fault lies with the wife, on the other hand, the whole outstanding amount may have to be given back by her kin. The only circumstance under which men taking the initiative successfully claim back the total amount is the discovery that the wife has been administering poison or has been careless over menstrual taboos, or is of promiscuous (wapra) character. Sometimes this leads the husband to inflict violent reprisals on the woman herself as a recognized substitute for the bridewealth return, which is thereby forfeited. In any case, these are admitted reasons for which men indeed may get rid of their wives. Women, by contrast, are said to initiate divorce over the most trivial domestic or personal issues, thereby penalizing their kin, since if the fault lies solely with the woman, they may have to provide an extra item in addition to the returned bridewealth as acknowledgement of this. Women are prone to deserting their husbands at whim; they are

---

[1] The same phrase is used of men when their initiative is admitted.

said to take affront at some slight, or inclination leads them to another man.[1]

In the discussion of particular marital histories, however, people are more ready to acknowledge that husbands might have a wide range of grievances. It is openly recognized that a man who finds his wife lazy or unwilling to support him in his enterprises pretends that she has neglected to observe the proper menstrual taboos. Her kin are supposedly taken in by the accusation, exclaim that she is a rubbish woman (*amb korpa*) to want to kill her husband, and return his wealth. The wife herself may try to deny the accusation, or she may take it as a sign that she is not wanted and let her folk make the return. Nevertheless, outsiders tend to ascribe initiative first to the wife and secondly to her kin. The stereotypes here are the capricious woman who lightly abandons her husband, and her grasping kinsmen who persuade her to return so they can obtain better bridewealth elsewhere. The former stereotype is the most frequently enunciated.

The extensiveness of my own information on reasons for which divorces occur varies considerably from case to case; perhaps it need not be stated that there is a direct correlation between the more people asked about a divorce and the wider range of factors adduced to explain it. In addition, one type of reason (e.g. complaints about neglect of duties) may have its origin in another type (e.g. basic incompatibility). The actual motives held privately by the parties concerned are a further matter, involving psychological considerations which lie largely outside my purview. I briefly describe a divorce which took place in 1964 to give some idea of the complexity of contributing elements. This is an example of a marriage which, *post facto*, neither the bride's nor the groom's side appeared to wish to see maintained.

Nøpil was an Elti girl, perhaps fifteen or sixteen when she married a Tipuka man. The bridewealth arrangements were carried through only with great difficulty and after two attempts, which are described in Appendix V. On the first occasion the bride's mother had seemed unwilling to let her go; the second involved wrangling over the bridewealth, partly on account of differences between Central and Northern Melpa custom.

Within a month of the wedding Nøpil was at home for several days

---

[1] In practice this latter course is rare. Disputes over divorce rarely touch on accusations that one clan has lured away another's wives, but are concerned with the break up of existing ties between the clans of the former spouses. Return of bridewealth is discussed more fully in Chapter 10.

attending a pig festival in a neighbouring tribe. When this was over she was instructed by her father and father's brothers to return to her husband, but she ran away. Her kin began talking of sending back the bridewealth for her, but eventually she was despatched off to her husband with a conciliatory gift. In spite of the distance she had to travel (a day's journey by foot), she kept visiting home, and after four or five unsatisfactory months, the bridewealth was returned.

Nøpil herself said (to me) that her father had sent her off to marry simply because he thought of the bridewealth he would obtain, paying no heed to her own feelings; she had not wanted to marry at all. It was a distant place, she did not like her mother-in-law, or her husband, who were always trying to make her work in the gardens. On another occasion she said her husband was ugly and did not look after her. Her own kin, however, were not altogether unwelcoming when she returned and they imputed to her the motive that she was (as they in fact were) dissatisfied over the bridewealth. The husband's people did not even welcome them with pork when they visited there. Her actual father interpreted her actions solely in terms of the bad bridewealth and her own "will" to leave her husband. In spite of his public protests to the contrary, Nøpil probably sensed that he was not unwilling to terminate the marriage. The groom, a young man who had had little part in the initial transactions, appeared indifferent to what was happening and his own kin apparently made only the most desultory of efforts to persuade Nøpil to remain with him; her mother-in-law was openly hostile to the marriage. They all said that it was the wife's own wish to leave. Her subsequent behaviour certainly revealed a desire to remain at home. She adamantly refused to marry anyone for over three years, in spite of the offers her father had had for her, of which she enumerated 14 in 1967. *Na nanom-nga rondokl-nt pi nø pimb mor*, "I am set against marrying", was her phrase.

Unsatisfactory as it is to treat my cases as though they were based on full information, I nevertheless try to give some quantification to the points I have been making. The numerical nature of the summary should not be taken too strictly. In the following tables, the term "reason" stands for assumed motives on the part of those known to wish for divorce (whether they take the initiative or not). If a man reports that his brother divorced his wife for fear of sickness from menstrual pollution, the "reason" for the divorce is attributed to the husband, though the person "blamed" is the wife. The source of information in such a case is the divorced husband's clansman.

Table XV (a) shows that, on the information which I was given, reasons were imputed to the wife and/or her kin (A, B, C, E, F, G) in the majority of instances (totalling 56-64). It is interesting to add that in half the cases where the husband alone (D) was said to have some reason,

TABLE XV

Reasons attributed to persons in divorces

(a) *64 Kawelka divorces, reasons attributed by Hageners*

Reason attributed to	Number of cases	Total	% cases
A. Wife only	29 ⎫		
B. Wife's kin	10 ⎬	43	67·2%
C. Wife + wife's kin	4 ⎭		
D. Husband only	8	8	12·5%
E. Husband + wife	8 ⎫		
F. Husband + wife's kin	2 ⎬	13	20·3%
G. Husband + wife + wife's kin	3 ⎭		
	64	64	

(b) *Source of information for the 64 cases.* Categories of persons who contributed information on reasons for divorces.

Informant[a]	Attributing reason to						
Men							
Divorced husband	A	B	C	D	E	F	
Subsequent husband[b]	A	B	C	D			G
Divorced H's male relatives[c]	A	B	C	D	E	F	G
Subsequent H's male relatives[c]	A	B	C	D	E		G
Divorced wife's male relatives		B	C		E		G
Women							
Divorced wife	A	B	C	D	E		G
Subsequent wife[b]	A			D			G
Divorced H's female relatives	A		C				
Subsequent H's female relatives					E		
Divorced wife's female relatives			C				

(c) *Assessment of reasons on part of spouses alone.* Comparison between assessment made by Hageners (1) for 64 cases and assessment by author (2) for 24 cases.

Reason attributed to	1. By Hageners		2. By author	
	cases	%	cases	%
Wife alone	33	51·5%	7	29%
Husband alone	10	15·5%	3	12·5%
Husband + Wife	11	17·2%	8	33·3%
Neither	10	15·5%	6	25%
Totals	64		24	

[a] The list is partial, not exhaustive (not everyone related was asked for information on a particular case).

[b] i.e. subsequent spouse of divorced wife/husband.

[c] These were the largest classes of informants.

pollution or poison was specified as was also so in two (F) situations (husband along with wife's kin), making a total of 6 out of the 21 instances in which the husband was said to have a motive. The 64 cases are based on 38 divorces of the wives of Kawelka men and a further 26 divorces experienced from previous marriages by current Kawelka men's wives. Information was collected from a variety of sources, as summarized in part (b). It should be emphasized that where multiple reasons are given, the total number may have been contributed from different sources. Thus in one case entered under E (reason on part of both husband and wife), the divorced husband, along with his male clansmen, said he had his own reason (he was afraid of the woman's former husband's ghost); the divorced wife had her own reason (he was always neglecting her), and this her husband's clansmen corroborated, with the added point that the husband had a further motive (he was afraid his wife was polluting him). In another case, entered under G (husband + wife + wife's kin), the wife's kin said that it was the wife herself who did not care for the husband; the divorced wife gave this and a further reason, that he would not sleep with her. Men of her subsequent husband's clan also gave these as motives on her part; in addition they noted that her parents had wanted her to divorce the husband, and that the husband let her go because she was always disobedient and "humbugging".[1]

In gross terms, the major categories of informants (husband and his male connections, wife and her male connections, subsequent spouses) all found reasons for divorce on the part of wife, husband and wife's kin. Nevertheless it is possible to discern some bias in the information, as I illustrate in part (c) of Table XV. Here I make my own assessment of where reasons probably lie for 15 accomplished divorces and 9 attempted divorces on which I have fairly full data; they include some of the Kawelka cases and others drawn from Tipuka, Minembi and Elti tribes. I limit judgement to a particular aspect, the involvement of the spouses, although other persons in addition may have had reasons. Simple indifference on the part of one or other spouse I do not count as a motive or reason, although it may certainly aggravate their partner's discomfort (as in Nøpil's case, which is entered in Table XV(c) under *wife*) and it is my impression that wives are most open to persuasion from

---

[1] Chowning (1969:248-9) has remarked on "how significant diversity of opinion (in accounts of cases) may be", of which these are an apt illustration.

others when the husband affects lack of interest. Certainly, quarrels with her parents-in-law or others of the husband's residential group usually do not lead to divorce if the wife is cushioned by her husband's support. A show of indifference from a young husband may arise, however, as much from embarrassment over the difficulties which have to come under public scrutiny as from a genuine but unexpressed desire to be rid of the woman, and I ignore it as a positive factor in my assessment.

While motives are overwhelmingly attributed by Hageners to the wife by comparison with the husband (column 1) my own assessment of the facts (for a partially different range of cases) suggests a more even spread of reasons for divorce between both spouses (column 2).[1] The husband's kin usually have motives for terminating a marriage only in the context of a general deterioration of relations between affines (and do not figure in Hageners' attribution of reasons given in Table XV(a)). It is not always a certainty that they can recover their bridewealth, the traditional attitude being that the woman's kin by contrast can always obtain new bridewealth in a fresh marriage. Taken literally, Hageners' view that husbands and their kin are not responsible for terminating marriages so often as women and their kin is largely correct, but it also glosses over the frequency with which both spouses hold reasons for wanting a divorce. If women are seen to be less responsible in these matters than men, it is also true that sinister motives are imputed to their kin. This must be partly because very much more is at stake for the husband (his wife is a producer as well as a transactor) than for the wife's brothers. To them disputes over exchanges in particular may assume grave proportions, whereas for the husband similar grievances can become submerged in other aspects of his relationship with his wife. Sometimes husbands send the wife home with complaints about her kin specified in no uncertain terms, but the threat of divorce is not bandied about so easily nor are examples of actual divorce following such a move so common, as when a brother persuades a sister to come back for a while.

In order to describe the content of the reasons given for the 64 Kawelka divorces, I make a rough division into categories (not explicit as categories in Hagen), presented in order of frequency, highest to lowest.

---

1 The "neither" category of 6 is probably large because of the attempted but not successful "divorces" (3 such contributed to the 6, in which kin and affines were the ones anxious for dissolution). The heterogeneous nature of the examples considered here is forced upon me by the quality of information necessary as a basis for "judgement".

1. Private inclination of wife, who leaves her husband by her own will, *noman*.

2. Personal incompatibilities between the spouses, involving:
   (a) physical dislike,
   (b) old age of one of the partners,
   (c) refusal by one to sleep with the other partner, or deliberate repulsion.

3. Dissatisfactions over affinal exchanges, especially bridewealth (same frequency as 2), e.g.
   (a) wife is angry/hurt because bridewealth not paid for her,
   (b) wife is persuaded by her kin to return home or herself returns home because she is annoyed about debts on their behalf.

4. Allegation of neglect (a reason Hageners appreciate may also lie behind other reasons), e.g.
   (a) husband fails to make gardens for his wife,
   (b) wife does not stay at home as women should, but travels around and neglects her household tasks (an allegation which may be combined with the clinching complaint that she is careless over menstrual taboos (8)).

5. Wife's initial reluctance to marry present husband or desire for further partner, e.g.
   (a) she is attracted to another man elsewhere,
   (b) she was forced into the marriage,
   (c) her husband gets rid of her as a *wapra* woman.

6. Political relations between affines and conditions of war, including
   (a) mutual fears of poisoning on part of husband and wife's kinsmen, husband's fear of wife,
   (b) warfare between husband's and wife's clans, or general hostilities, so wife runs home or is abducted by enemy.

7. "Quarrelling" (same frequency as 6), e.g.
   (a) with in-laws, especially wife and her husband's parents,
   (b) between cowives, or with husband planning to marry a further wife.

8. Wife's malice in neglecting menstrual taboos and endangering husband.

9. Other reasons, e.g.
   (a) wife thinks of children left behind from previous marriage and
       returns to their father,
   (b) husband is afraid of ghost of clansman whose wife he has inherited.

These reasons are found in varying combinations, often overlapping in actual instances. Further reasons cited in cases other than these include: husband's suspicion that his wife has killed their newborn baby; maltreatment of child by other spouse; husband's neglect coupled with long absence in European employment; severe jealousy between cowives which leads husband to abandon one wife; and husband's refusal to have a "church wedding" (wife a Roman Catholic).

The status of a woman in developmental terms (age, number of children) does not seem to affect the allocation of responsibility for divorce; it does, however, affect the content of posited reasons. Divorcees with children, or who are old and have been married for some time, are ascribed reasons mainly to do with sex (5), accusations of neglect (4) and personal incompatibility (2), and their own *noman* (1). The focus is on the husband–wife relationship alone,[1] rather than also on relations between affines over bridewealth or political issues, as are imputed to young spouses involved in short, childless marriages. Internal factors thus become more important with advancing age, duration of the marriage and birth of children. The seeming paradox, that the more involved a woman herself must become in her husband's enterprises and consequently exchanges with her kin, the less frequently disputes over these lead to divorce, is discussed in chapter eleven.[2]

An accusation which specifies a particular complaint may be symptomatic of a more general grievance that a person's status is not given sufficient recognition. Thus a wife left out of a distribution of pork takes this as a sign that her husband wants to be rid of her. Anything may be made an issue for complaint if relations between the spouses have deteriorated, in the same way as almost anything can be tolerated if relations are otherwise satisfactory. It would certainly be misleading to think of all these reasons as constituting "grounds" for divorce. One might call them "provocations". The appreciation of motives for divorce, is quite distinct from the allowance that persons have a right to sue for

---

[1] The older woman tends to go off to another man rather than simply return home.
[2] I have not heard of divorce through failure to make child-growth payments, except when these are also a bridewealth substitute.

it. The publicly most acceptable and in that sense legitimate reasons for divorcing a spouse lie with a husband who finds his wife is a poisoner, has polluted him or is behaving like an *amb wapra*. If her desire to kill or repudiate him in these terms is acknowledged to exist, then the husband is seen as acting correctly in getting rid of the woman. Other reasons he might have, or reasons on the wife's part, can receive private or partisan support, but the intent to divorce will meet with general censure. Even those reasons which rest on complaints themselves recognized as legitimately made (e.g. a spouse's laziness) do not if they are proved, necessarily lead to an automatic allowance that divorce is the appropriate form of redress. There are, in short, few offences on the part of husband or wife to which absolute liability for divorce is attached (Gluckman, 1965:224f.).

Blame for Divorce

The most generally vaunted reasons for why marriages break up appeal to the disposition (*noman*) of the spouses, particularly that of the woman (1, 2 and cf. 5). People often ignore the possible provocations behind female attitudes of mind. Even where it may be obvious that a dissolution has been precipitated by a mutual deterioration of relations, the full force of criticism is frequently directed against the wife. The context of court hearings or informal discussions is one in which censure is freely expressed. Hearings are usually held in public; anyone interested may attend, although the bulk of the audience is always male. This publicity undoubtedly constrains the manner in which the male affines present themselves. In some cases demonstration that the trouble is caused by the woman may be near the truth; but in others it represents a shift of blame[1] from diffuse sources on to the wife. This shift may be achieved quite deliberately, or it may emerge from what appear to be less conscious intentions on the part of the men.

Hageners recognize that the husband and the wife's male kin alike may have reasons for putting overt blame on the wife herself, rather than admitting their own responsibility. A husband, motivated to prove that the fault lies with his wife so that he does not forfeit a return of his bridewealth, may provoke her to leave him without actually telling her to do

---

[1] By "blame" I mean that the cause of the trouble is attributed to a person, not that the person stands necessarily to be punished. Men hope women will feel some shame for the upset they have caused, so blatantly showing no sympathy for their menfolk.

so. Considerable argument in court cases turns on proof of who initiated the disruption; but the fact that the woman has run away is invariably taken as a sign that she wanted to leave. A husband deliberately rouses his wife to this, or with less planning simply finds it convenient not to overcome his indifference and retrieve her. The woman's male kin also wish to deflect possible accusations away from themselves and onto the woman. They are always very sensitive to the charge that they have exerted undue influence over her; it may be the case that some dissatisfied relative has persuaded her to leave her husband, while others of her kin are pleased with the match. Even if they have secretly influenced her, they do not necessarily want this made public. So they are likely to protest that the woman acted independently, of her own free will (*elem-nga rondokl-nt*). The sister or daughter herself often connives at this, making a public denial of any part they might have had, saying it was entirely her own volition (*noman*). Men particularly suspect that women under the influence of their mothers are too loyal to reveal this. Although one or two specific accounts of a mother greasing her daughter were given me, most instances concern a father or brothers.

*Perhaps a decade ago there was a quarrel between a Tipuka man and his Kumngaka wife. The husband's father had died and he had asked her father for a pig to kill at the mourning feast. This pig he had never returned, although his father-in-law was willing for him to make the debt good with pearl shells if he had no pigs. On one occasion when the father-in-law came requesting a return of his pig, he invited his daughter to go back home with him since it was the season of fruit pandanus and there was plenty of pandanus to be cooked. Off the wife went, but after three weeks had not come back, and her husband went to find her. Her parents disclaimed knowledge of her whereabouts. But on the road home, the husband heard the rumour that his wife had run away to a Nølka man. The Nølka, whom he accosted, said that her kin had promised they would hand back the bridewealth and marry her to them. The Tipuka husband protested that he had no intention of losing her and demanded of her parents what was the matter. They were ashamed (it is said)[1] and just replied that they had no idea what she had been doing. The husband returned, along with a party of men from his clan-section, to fetch the girl back; in two days she had run away to Nølka again. Then the Tipuka clansmen stormed over to her parents' home and demanded of her mother and father whether she herself had wanted to marry the Nølka man or whether they had "pulled" her. Her father denied that they had any influence over her and said that she did it "of her own accord". However in his reply he hinted that per-

---

[1] The account is from a Kawelka man not closely related to any of the people in the case.

haps she had run away because she knew he was so angry (*popokl*) over his pig. In spite of the public agreement that it was the wife's own doing, the young husband realized her father's part in the affair, and retrieving his wife, promptly made good the debt.

There are many permutations in the precise relationship of a divorcee to her kin. For each of the following, with a partial exception, both recent and accounts relating to the past were told of divorces carried through successfully, and of threats to divorce which came to nothing.

Circumstances of Persuasion

1. Initiative of wife's kin + concurrence of wife
2.   ditto   + protest of wife
3. Initiative of wife   + concurrence of wife's kin
4.   ditto   + protest of wife's kin

The exception here is (3) in that reports of a woman's kin acting in her support invariably involve accomplished divorces. Examples have already been cited of a wife and her kin conniving to persuade the husband to make good his debts or pay proper bridewealth. It would be incorrect, however, to give the impression that women are always responsive to pressure from their kin. As (2) suggests they may resist, successfully or not, the desire of their kinsmen to break the marriage, being as "strong" (*rondokl*) to remain with their husbands as they may have initially been in marrying against their parent's wishes.

While the manoeuvres of persuasion are well known, those trying to settle a divorce dispute may not bother to sort out the contributing influences beyond a superficial consideration, and will be ready to accept a final dictum that it is the woman's mind (*noman*) or strength (*rondokl*) at issue. This tends to present itself as a solution even where the husband or wife's kin perhaps have no conscious desire to blame her. Three unofficial court hearings witnessed in 1964–5 (all concerning young, childless women) illustrate the point.

1. The Unco-operative Go-between

Ndangmba, from Tipuka Kitepi clan, had married a second wife, Eng, from the far end of the Meka valley; she belonged to a clan of the Kendipi tribe, some 3½ hours' walk away. Kitepi neighbours of Ndangmba's had already made a couple of marriages with Kendipi. In the past Tipuka and Kendipi had combined once in warfare to crush their common enemy, W^{e}lyi, and in 1964–5 the two tribes were contemplating large scale ally payments to each other; thus the links which Kitepi already had in that direction were potential roads for the forthcoming exchanges. Nevertheless, there was some anxiety over the prospective *moka*, for they were not close and heavily intermarried allies; the total number of affinal links were few. Some of the tensions evinced in the following case may have arisen from this.

Eng had made several visits home in the first half-year of marriage, eventually refusing altogether to return to Ndangmba. His clansmen assumed that she had gone of her "own will", while the husband seemed to be ambivalent about her departure, most of the time appearing indifferent to the fact. Finally, a court was held at the wife's home. Kitepi men set off to it in an aggressive mood, asserting that they were going to claim back the bridewealth, and were joined by supporters from their pair clan, and its Councillor, who were hoping (they said) to join in the consumption of the additional item (which is usually pork) that they anticipated her kin were going to have to provide on top of the returned bridewealth. On arrival, however, they behaved in a friendly way towards the assembled Kendipi and the young men embarked on a joint gambling match.

The wife's father prevaricated, and tried to put off the discussion, protesting that he would see to things later. After an hour or so of desultory conversation, the court began in earnest with the arrival of a Kendipi and two further Tipuka Councillors,[1] who said that they should find out if the wife really intended to leave her husband. Eng had to be found, and until she arrived at the courtyard where the hearing was to be, the senior men fell to talking *moka*. I sketch the most important stages of the proceedings.

Men on both sides discussed the fact that Eng herself had run away, and no attempt was made to cover up the desire of the Kitepi to retrieve their bridewealth. But the woman's close kin were unwilling to admit that any situation existed at all, especially as their Councillor reminded them that (under the Dei Council rulings, cf. Appendix II) they could not hope to obtain a second bridewealth for her. The Kendipi Councillor asked Eng directly whether she wanted to remain with Ndangmba.

---

[1] One from Ndangmba's clan, and another from a third, neighbouring clan—a personal friend of the Kitepi Councillor, he had come to "help his talk".

After considerable difficulty he forced her to make a reply: she denied that she was being "greased" by anyone and affirmed it was her "own wish" to leave him. She refused to say more. But the Councillors and others present[1] did not accept this at its face value, and told her to confess who indeed must have greased her. Her father eventually spoke, "There has been too much talking—only the parents of the couple should talk. All right (addressing his daughter): now you must speak out. I cannot look inside your *noman* and see what your desires are—I let you marry where you first said you wanted to, and now you have come back! I don't know what you want. But I am certainly not going to return the bridewealth!" Eng, a slip of a girl probably no more than sixteen years old, watched with an intent expression on her face but said nothing.

Everyone from the two groups of men tried to make her speak, to say what was in her *noman*. Councillors became threatening. The Kendipi Councillor walked over, made her stand up, and pulled off her head covering. They said they would beat her and send her to jail.[2] This provoked the sullen response that Eng did not care if she were beaten or jailed, and she wanted an administration officer to hear the case anyway. The Kitepi Councillor took the cane which his Kendipi colleague was holding, flourished and snapped it, with the assertion that the girl was "theirs" and her father could not object if they beat her; but he did not actually use it. She eventually murmured that she was not going back to her husband, and they (i.e. her kin) could hand back the bridewealth. The moment of tension passed, but the men were not satisfied. If all that were the matter was her desire to visit her parents and see them often, then the answer to this was that she should come to some arrangement with Ndangmba; for instance, she could come home every Saturday and Sunday. She apparently agreed to this proposal. Ndangmba himself had been present throughout the proceedings, but had contributed nothing to the speeches, beyond his initial response to a question from the Kendipi Councillor that he indeed wanted his

---

[1] The chief Councillors (of her own and her husband's clan) were seated in front of a men's house, near the husband, Kitepi and Kendipi men intermingled in a rough semi-circle at their back. Her own father was among them. Eng faced the men, two boys (younger brothers) sitting with her. To one side was a knot of Kendipi wives.

[2] At that time persons committed by local administration officers who held courts in the Dei Council chambers might have to serve sentence there; prisoners were usually engaged in weeding the precincts or helping to keep the buildings in repair. Councillors sometimes themselves "jailed" convicted persons, setting them to enforced labour on the roads (whose maintenance is the responsibility of local clans).

wife back. He did not make any public comment on her apparent agreement.

Talk at once switched to *moka*. Men on both sides began saying that they should not quarrel over a woman, for they were after all due to make *moka* with each other soon. A Kendipi big-man (who was also the father-in-law of one of Ndangmba's clan brothers) addressed the girl, saying that she should attend to her husband's affairs and then they could make *moka* well. Her own father nervously swore, putting a finger to his forehead,[1] that he had not influenced her to return. And the young Kitepi Councillor sagely remarked that when bridges are down one cannot walk about. He congratulated the woman's kin for their decision to send her back to her husband. Eng was sent off to collect together her possessions, and food was prepared for the Tipuka guests.

Eng was a long time in making a re-appearance, and after about an hour had passed came the discovery that she could not be found, she had run away. The Kitepi abruptly said that they would claim back all their bridewealth, and there was general confusion. Most of them made plans to stay there overnight so that they could discuss the payments in the morning.

This case has several interesting aspects. First, the bride's father was extremely reluctant to contemplate a return of the bridewealth. I have not perhaps emphasized sufficiently the difficulties which actually reckoning up the debts brings. All such discussions I have attended have been long, drawn-out, exhausting and argumentative; rarely is there initial agreement on the outstanding items to be returned and both parties tend to become fractious and heated in defence of their position. This unpleasantness is the immediate trouble which women are held to cause. Not only does divorce break up a relationship that held promise of profit to both sides, but it puts the two parties into a debt situation which has to be immediately remedied. Reluctance to return bridewealth on the part of the wife's clansmen, as well as fear on the part of the husband's clansmen that their claims to the outstanding items will not be recognized, are both factors which can encourage men to try to stave off dissolution. Secondly, in spite of the aggressiveness of the husband's clan-mates, both sides seem positively to have wanted the marriage to continue in the light of their *moka* plans.

The wife herself had no defender, or anyone to profess an intimate

---

[1] This is referred to as a *mi*; it demonstrates that the speaker is telling the truth. Probably the head is indicated because of its association as a lodging place for ghosts.

knowledge of her affairs or a willingness to speak out on her behalf. (This is typical of such hearings.) Her male kin gave her little support, and the few women present were silent spectators. Eng's mother was in hospital. Some of the older men tried to tone down the discussion, but this was all. Finally, although Eng was given the opportunity to make explicit any grievances she might have had, she did not use it. Angered by her unco-operativeness, the Councillors refused to accept her statement that she did not want to stay with Ndangmba, and began arranging her return to him. Hence her resort to subterfuge, slipping away when everyone was talking about business. Subsequent versions of the affair from Tipuka men alleged that her father had indeed greased her (for motives they did not specify).

2. The Politics of Silence

The second court hearing concerns a widow, herself of Tipuka Kitepi clan, who had returned home before the final funeral arrangements had been completed for her deceased husband. It has divorce-like aspects in that the husband's clan were trying to activate their claim that she should re-marry one of their men; such claims are fundamentally moral rather than jural ones (for widows cannot be forced to act thus against their will) and must rest on appeals to the friendship between the two groups. Observers commented that the husband's brothers could not pull the girl like a pig; they could only talk and persuade her to go. Nevertheless, there were suggestions that she had been persuaded to leave her husband before his death, and she was currently having a tentative affair with another man. It is noteworthy that little public attention was paid to this. Men of the second man's clan were present (they in any case belonged to a pair clan of the Kitepi, and might be expected to come in support of Kitepi on these grounds) but were not openly challenged with abduction. All the attention was on the widow, Pamnda, and her relations with her deceased husband's group, Minembi Kimbo. (I learnt much later, in 1967, that she had been implicated in his death. Blood had welled up in his nose, and this was taken as a sign that Pamnda had incited him to have sexual relations while she was menstruating, with fatal result. She denied she had intended any such thing and asserted that she had tried to prevent her husband from approaching her while she was menstruating, but he had insisted on intercourse. She was apparently believed, as the dead man's brothers wanted to have her back. Since they came to this decision, the matter was not brought up when her case was heard.)

Politically, Kitepi and Kimbo were in an uneasy relationship. Their clans belonged to tribes allied to each other's major enemies and effectively enemies themselves, but Pamnda's father, a man of importance, was contemplating *moka* with a Kimbo big-man. This was not to be a group prestation, but a publicly transferred gift between the two big-men. Their ties were thus independent of Pamnda's marriage. Nevertheless it was implied that their transactions depended upon her; the Kimbo big-man was among the most vocal for her return. Pressure put on the girl thus did not stem from an immediate threat to the exchanges, but from a general threat to the hoped-for cordial relations between the two clans. Counter-threats were hinted at. The Kimbo were going to claim retrieval of a part of their bridewealth if she would not return to them, on the grounds that she had effectively left her husband before his death (she had been greased while on visits home). Kitepi men feared that the Kimbo might retaliate with poison if they did not get satisfaction. If the Kimbo went away disgruntled, they had a road along which they could send poison, for Pamnda's brother had married a wife whose mother herself happened to come from Kimbo clan.

The court was heard on the ceremonial ground belonging to Pamnda's father. It was the culmination of some weeks of private discussion and negotiation. Men on both sides appeared anxious that she should return. All the sub-clans of Kitepi, it was agreed, receive pigs and shells (in *moka*) from the Kimbo, and what was she doing refusing to go back? Her male kinsmen denied all responsibility for having greased her, turned on her several times to urge that she must go, and commented to the court at large that it was her own obstinacy (*rondokl*) which made for the impasse. She was reminded that in the bad days people fought and there was no law, and explicit references were made to past hostilities between their tribes, Tipuka and Minembi; but this was over now, and why should their affairs be upset by this woman? Of all the men there, only a full brother, who as a Councillor took a prominent part in the speeches, attempted to defend her. He pointed out that her husband in his lifetime had spent time away on plantation work and not looked after her well; but he concluded by ordering her nonetheless to go back. Others told the girl that she could expect no active support from her brother, since he was a Councillor and Councillors "hear law"— they do not pull their sisters away from other men.

Her own father stressed that it was Pamnda's personal inclination (*noman*) to leave Kimbo, and he had had no part in influencing her. A number of other Kitepi men accused Pamnda's mother, who was present, of having enticed her daughter home, and she was reminded how she had done this on a previous occasion. The mother bitingly and vigorously denied this. She said the whole thing lay with Pamnda herself. Most of the time Pamnda had been sitting silently, her back half to the gathering.[1] Throughout three or four hours of discussion she uttered only one statement (that after the first funeral and before the final funeral had been held, it was the Kimbo themselves who had told her to go home).[2] Ostensibly the court had been called to try to see if she would return, and she was commanded to get up and go time and again. Her brother's exhortations grew more imperious, but she refused to budge and, in the end, got up only to wander away from the ceremonial ground.

The final verdict among the men was that she was just strong-willed and that they were not responsible for the way in which she behaved. A group of Kimbo wives (who had come since they would have led back any pigs the Kitepi might have paid) agreed with the men in censuring her. This also seemed to be the attitude of the few Kitepi wives present. One of her clan fathers had said during the proceedings that she should not disobey her father's wishes that she return, and added that it was clear from her obstinate behaviour that she had been formed from the very beginning in her mother's womb an out and out female.[3]

This example very clearly shows how events may be attributed to the woman's disposition, in a context, it so happened, of mutual suspicions between the men. While the husband's clan (Kimbo) suspected both her parents of pulling back their daughter, the widow's male kin (Kitepi) openly turned on the mother, the mother in turn protesting it was all in Pamnda's own mind. Her behaviour (in not wanting to stay with Kimbo) was partly explained in terms of the treatment she had received there, but neither was this seen as good enough reason for breaking off

---

[1] Seating arrangements at courts are not rigidly structured. People sometimes gather in a rough circle, the two sides more or less facing each other, but small knots of men often sit apart, perhaps round a fire or engaged in conversations of their own; Pamnda was showing no disrespect, but using an accepted informal posture which seemed to communicate her desire for withdrawal. She appeared unhappy and disconsolate, at one point hiding her face in a cloth, at another sitting partly out of sight behind the *poklambo* tree.

[2] Perhaps a hint at the pollution accusations which had apparently been made against her. She left once during a lull in the speeches, but was fetched back.

[3] Cf. pp. 160–1

relations, nor did it affect the final judgement that it was her own *noman* at issue. Pamnda's tactics of withdrawal were relatively successful. She escaped having to go back with the Kimbo men on that occasion, although subsequently she did re-marry one of her deceased husband's brothers. Within about three months, however, the second husband himself got rid of her, openly saying that she had tried to kill him, as (in retrospect) it was now apparent she had killed her first husband, by inciting him to intercourse while she was menstruating.[1] Since he had inherited her there was no question of returning any bridewealth, and no further court case arose. Her Kitepi kinsmen were supposed to have welcomed her back with the comment that now her husband had himself divorced her she was free to marry where she liked. Bridewealth was eventually paid for her by the young man of the pair clan with whom she had previously been associating.

3. Reasons for Reasons

The third example is one in which male affines on both sides certainly seem to have had private motives for wanting to dissolve the marriage, although this was not openly admitted in the court situation. There had been long-standing grievances over the bridewealth: the groom's father, Elti Kui, had not sent cooked pig (*mangal kng*) to the bride's kin after the wedding, and one of his brothers had furthermore seized secretly and by force a pig which he claimed was due to him as part of the initial return-payment, and which the bride's kin said was a "theft". Kui was indicted privately by his clansmen for precipitating the divorce since he had not lived up to his promises of a large bridewealth. This ill-feeling between the affines cut across the politically friendly relations between their clans. The two clans were from Elti and Yamka tribes, long established neighbours and allies.

A hearing was arranged to settle the disputes. Two Yamka and one Elti Councillor, along with several Komitis, sought to establish where motives lay: did the wife's father want her back? did her husband and her father-in-law want to let her go? what were her own feelings? The woman, Rang^em, was unusually vocal; she came out straight with her

---

[1] A commentary by a young Kawelka man said that she had no deliberate intent to kill her first husband in order to re-marry, but had simply been overcome by desire for sexual intercourse. We may take imputation of lust as an example of the way "uncontrollable" women are branded *wapra*.

complaints. Her main quarrel was with her father-in-law over the cooked pig that he had never sent to her kin. Even when he received pork from a pig festival he did not forward any to them. Once she and her mother-in-law had begun cooking preparations, but Kui had stopped them; out of shame and *popokl*, Rang*e*m had then come home. Kui had lied to her all the time. The Councillors pointed out to Rang*e*m that she was not married to Kui, but to his son; if her father-in-law were to make good his obligations the very next day, would she return to her husband? She replied that her mother-in-law had teased her over the situation (because full bridewealth had not been paid) and several times she repeated that she would not go back.

Kui defended accusations of meanness by protesting that he had no pigs available, and that his wife (who was not present) had been the cause of all the mischief by telling Rang*e*m to go. He had never been angry with the girl. Rang*e*m at this point roundly declared that Kui was a liar: first he did not keep his promises, and now he was lying in court! She was asked again (by the Elti Councillor) whether she would return or not, and was she ashamed over the poor bridewealth and thinking of her parents, or was it simply her own *noman*? She replied that she had been assuming that she was married, but when had she been treated as a proper wife? That was why she had come home. Her father followed this speech with protests that they must not think he had been enticing her—the daughter had thought of this herself. It was true that the bridewealth had not been as promised, and he pointedly enumerated all the items involved, but denied his own influence over her. He also said it was true that Kui's wife had been instrumental in persuading Rang*e*m to return; after quarrelling herself with Kui over the pig cooking, she had gone off to her own home saying Rang*e*m could do as she liked (i.e. an effective suggestion that she too leave). One of her husband's clansmen commented that she had never settled down well with her husband, but for all that they wanted her back. Kui promised to find the appropriate pigs.

Again the Councillors, and other prominent men, asked Rang*e*m if she was satisfied, and again pointed out that the dispute was not with her actual husband. But she stolidly said she had no intention of returning, whatever the arrangements. Her mother-in-law had suggested she come home and that was that. Her own kinsmen tried to cajole her: had her father kept the bridewealth intact in his house that she was so easy in her replies—did she think he could muster it just like that! Her *noman* was not "straight", the Elti Councillor said, she thought only of payments and not of her kinsmen, whose words she was not heeding. Each time she replied, no.

In the end, saying it was Rang^{e}m's wish[1] to leave her husband, the men began arguing how return should be made for the bridewealth. The discussion was conducted with considerable rancour, and as things became involved, no more notice was taken of Rang^{e}m.

Here Kui's behaviour was elucidated as the reason for Rang^{e}m's running away. The suggested solution was that Kui make good the payments. But as soon as the young wife said that this would not satisfy her, the men fell back on the judgement that it was her own *noman* at the root of it all. The particular dispute (the debt between men) could always be patched up; they wanted to establish *her* will. And if she was adamant to remain at home, they could do nothing. What the men did not discuss as a possibility was that Rang^{e}m's shame at the way she had been treated *entitled* her to divorce. To them the alternatives were simply (1) a genuine dispute over bridewealth which could be rectified; (2) hidden motives, i.e. she must be using the dispute as a cover for her own personal wishes. They concluded that it was the latter situation they were dealing with. It should be added that there was some initial mention of the fact that the husband was not present and they should delay proceedings till he could attend (he was staying with a brother employed in Hagen town)[2] since his inclinations should be also considered; it became clear, however, that this was far from the central issue, which was to establish what Rang^{e}m's real motives were. Rang^{e}m's father at one point said that all he was doing was "following the talk of the girl" in conceding divorce. It would be no use making her stay because she was a "humbug" and would only run away again.

A multiplicity of motives and reasons seem to lie behind the disputes in all three of these examples; the tendency to represent divorce as due in the final outcome to the wife's disposition simplifies situations which are actually complex and glosses over the ambiguous position of affines in hostile confrontation. The woman herself may be indifferent, or be anxious for divorce, but what is taken as relevant is her state of mind,

---

[1] An Elti Komiti adduced the fact that he knew Rang^{e}m had earlier stated she had wanted in any case to marry a man younger than her present husband, though the girl herself stuck to her points about the bridewealth and her mother-in-law.

[2] An example of the "indifferent husband". He had apparently told his father, "If you want to hear the court, go on; if she wants to leave. I've nothing to say."

her inclination, not the reasons which provoked her into wanting it. It is thus not a matter of what she can claim, whether in the circumstances she has a right to divorce, but how she feels.[1] This in turn obviates much necessity on the part of the husband or the kin concerned to examine closely the root of the trouble when there is one. Once it is clear that her *noman* is set (*rondokl*) upon divorce, there is little seemingly to be done; the situation is beyond the control and responsibility of everyone else.

Such manoeuvres serve to protect marriage values, especially those contingent on exchange relations. Blaming the wife enables divorce to be achieved without challenge to the value which men (and in abstract, women) place on enduring alliances. It is men who are in charge of court hearings and they who do most of the speech-making. Female spectators only occasionally interject comments. Although Councillors often make an effort to appear to act in concert, other men frequently behave according to their immediate interests. Affines are in an awkward position, for they are potentially friendly and it is not until agreement to hand back bridewealth is reached that they can oppose one another in a simple fashion. A conclusion to be made here is that the nature of court hearings is itself a variable and these points cannot be expounded properly without some reference to the judicial system.

It is partly because of the nature of the judicial process, then, that advantage lies in asserting that the trouble is not really a failure in the way the affines have conducted their relationships but a trivial matter (however grave the consequences) to do with a stubborn woman. One effect of this is that although conflicts over rights and duties between husband and wife may be recognized elements in a divorce case, they are not so often made the central issue. Divorce is not treated as a simple jural correction to or penalty for breaches of norms.[2] It is as though the structural importance of marital alliances, and it is this which the speech-makers frequently emphasize, over-rides consideration that the satisfactory performance of domestic tasks or conjugal duties could con-

---

[1] Professor Epstein has since drawn my attention to the fact that some African customary courts of law may be guided, not by a limited and specific concept of "grounds for divorce" but by the more pragmatic consideration (based on the total quality of the marital relationship) of whether a couple can live together in harmony (cf. Epstein, 1954, 1967a). The legal assumption in Hagen is that in most circumstances the husband will want to maintain his marriage (cf. Colson, 1958:182) so proof of the capacity to live in harmony lies with the wife.

[2] Cf. (Bohannan, 1957:91) Tiv wives may sue husbands for neglect.

trol the stability of marriage. In the third case, which touched directly on complaints over affinal payments, it was quickly pointed out that (with the assumption that these were in the long term interests of men on each side) they would be easily rectified. Men's manoeuvres are not of course entirely unrealistic. That a woman's father or brother can protest his innocence by saying that the wife is responsible for her own actions is possible in light of the generally accepted fact that women may take the initiative in helping their kin. An ambiguous situation is the result: on the one hand, women may be actually motivated to participate in exchanges; on the other hand, motives of this kind can be imputed to them by men, even where they are not held or are not the crux of a conflict. Under their cover, however, a woman can indeed go her own way.

As one man pointed out, even though siblings are born of common parents they all have different *noman*. One cannot see into the *noman* of others, and this is as true of women as of men. Mental disposition can only be gauged by watching behaviour. Thus "it is up to the woman" (*elemnga noman-nt*) to show pity for her parents or concern for her husband. Or she may "go off on her own bent" (*amb-e-nt rondokl mondopa purum*) altogether. This possibility of independence we have seen foreshadowed in the way the accused women were prepared to accept the fact that it was indeed their own disposition, their own *noman*, at the root of it all.

10

Settlement of Disputes

Hageners had no indigenous system of courts or other bodies with specialist judicial functions. Disputes were settled by force or agreement. Peaceful settlement could be agreed upon privately or be negotiated in public. Grievances were brought up when people were assembled for other purposes (a feast, a bridewealth, an exchange display) or the dispute itself might bring the parties concerned into confrontation (Vicedom and Tischner, 1943–8:2:57; Strauss, 1962:chs. 27, 34). The term for "hearing a case" was specific to the dispute at issue, thus, *amb yoka ik* ("talk over returning bridewealth"), *wuᵉ kumøp ik* ("talk over settling a man's compensation"); or more generally, *ik pukl-i nimb mukli* "to find out the root of the discussion". In a sense, these ad hoc assemblies were antecedents of the present courts.

The Introduction of Courts

As instruments in pacification, the Australian administration appointed "headmen" (Bosbois, Tultuls and Luluais)[1] from clan groups. They were responsible for carrying out Native Regulations, executing orders from the District Office, and generally seeing that the peace was kept. With the establishment of Local Government Councils, Councillors have taken over many of the functions of these officials. In Dei Council there was direct continuity of personnel at the initial elections, two Luluais,

---

[1] For accounts of these officials elsewhere in the Highlands see Bulmer (1961); Berndt, R. M. (1962:313f.); Brown (1963); Reay (1964a); Salisbury (1964). The attitudes I describe here were those current in 1964–5. For a comment on the changing roles of Councillors see Strathern, A. J. (1970b).

12 Tultuls and 13 Bosbois being among the 40 Councillors first elected. Councillors themselves, and their helpers (*Komiti* or *Memba*), interpret the hearing of disputes (Pidgin English *kot*, "court") as one of their most important responsibilities. Certainly it is the most time-consuming, and is an aspect of their work (*kongon*) which most frequently brings them *qua* Councillors into interaction with their clansmen and people of neighbouring clans.

In 1964–5 the only court officially recognized by the administration at this level was the Court of Native Affairs[1] under European magistrates, often local Patrol Officers. The Councils themselves were regarded by the administration as "self-supporting units of area administrative machinery" (Ordinances, N.L.G.C., 1946–60), with legislative and executive but no judicial powers. In fact, however, there is a tacit recognition that the Sub-district Office in Hagen lacks the staff to deal with all the disputes which arise, and individual Patrol Officers may even direct cases which are brought to them back to Councillors' arbitration.

Hageners themselves regard the settlement of disputes by Councillors and Komiti as similar to settlement before a Court of Native Affairs. Cases which cannot be handled by Komiti are referred to Councillors, and those the Councillors cannot conclude satisfactorily are referred to Kiaps (Pidgin English, administration officers). There is a perceived gradation in the amount of power these officials wield, but it is this rather than any sense of their alien character which distinguishes the Kiaps' courts from those heard by Councillors or Komitis (cf. Fenbury, 1966). Since Councillors' courts are unofficial, they can make no direct use of the sanctions (e.g. jail under police supervision) which Kiaps have at their disposal. One of the sanctions they do use is the very threat to take a dispute to the Kiap's court, and cases in deadlock are often brought to a head in this way. Councillors and Komitis see their role in courts as making them somewhat "like Kiaps", and consciously draw upon behaviour which they think would meet administration approval. In the third of the hearings described in Chapter 9, the Councillors from the girl's clan had commented at the beginning that if they later had to

---

[1] Replaced in 1966 by the Local Court, staffed initially by the same persons, usually expatriate Administration officers, although these are gradually being replaced by indigenous full-time magistrates (Barnett, 1967:96–7). The jurisdiction of the Local Court is described in Mattes 1969.

take the court to the "Office" (the Sub-district Office in Hagen town) then the Kiap would ask the husband if he wanted to keep his wife or not, and for the same reason they ought to establish this too. Kiaps and the precepts they follow thus provide models for the Councillors.

But at the same time, the very fact that they lack the power of administration officers puts them into a different situation. Councillors and Komitis frequently complain that people do not heed their words and look back to the days of Luluais and Tultuls when everyone was intimidated by their authority. They have to resort to persuasion, and negotiate rather than adjudicate settlement. The skills they need are those which, above all, big-men exercise. In the past big-men sometimes became mediators between parties in conflict, and present-day Councillors in fact act out similar roles. They also depend heavily on the traditional structure of compensation payments and norms encompassing the definition of wrongs.[1] But this continuity with the past tends to be ignored. The single consequence of the coming of Europeans which most impresses Hageners is the cessation of warfare. In their minds, warfare is associated with violent practices such as extortion in bride-wealth payments, unrestrained thieving between enemy clans, an insidious spread of poison. It is the difference between "now" and "then" that they stress (cf. Reay, 1964a:243), and one of the characteristics of "now" is that "courts have come up". Thus one meets with statements such as, "In the past there were no courts, we only fought each other over troubles." What has happened is that with the ban on warfare, a whole element (comprising redress through self-help, force and reprisal) has dropped from the judicial system. Peaceful agreement, which along traditional lines is achieved largely through material compensation, has become the only feasible manifestation of settlement.

Apart from appeal to Councillors or Komitis, grievances are resolved informally; while these may amount to no more than verbal placations, compensation can also pass privately between the contenders. Debts with affines and exchange partners are often settled away from the public eye. Disputes most frequently brought to the notice of Councillors (see page 189) involve divorce and bridewealth matters, adultery, quarrels which have led to one party striking another, damage to crops, and theft. Homicide comes immediately under the jurisdiction of the Court of Native Affairs. Most of the following discussion concerns the unofficial

---

[1] Similar situations are reported elsewhere, e.g. for Matupit (Epstein, 1969:262-3).

but formal courts[1] heard by Councillors and Komitis. It should be stressed that norms relating to compensation which these persons recommend in particular cases are generally and widely known, and applied to disputes settled without their help.

Some of the changes affecting judicial behaviour are directly relevant to women's treatment in courts; it is this, however, and not the judicial system as such with which I am concerned, and I do not discuss in detail the conduct of court proceedings or the roles of those who act as mediators or conciliators. My treatment of cases is thus little more than illustrative, since I attempt no procedural analysis (Epstein, 1967a). Nevertheless, like men, women are involved in compensation payments and mention of the traditional forms of these must be made.

Traditional Means of Dispute Settlement

With clans of one's major enemies any dispute might precipitate serious hostilities; but between minor enemies/allies there were expectations that fighting would be limited, and agreement without recourse to fighting was a possibility. Fights were likely to have the character of unpremeditated brawling or to involve sticks rather than more dependably lethal weapons. If a battle erupted, persons were less likely to be killed in minor engagements, and the mutual interests of each side could find eventual satisfaction in exchanges and compensation payments. Whereas hostilities arising over disputes between major enemies contributed to a perpetual confrontation, between minor enemies/allies limited force could secure redress for specific wrongs. The payment of compensation was, however, always seen as an alternative to such force; it had a positive value since profitable transactions between both sides re-affirmed their relations as allies. Disputes could end in unilateral compensation, but often good feeling was restored through reciprocal exchanges. Sometimes, however, it was agreed that the original issue had been submerged in the general combat, which equalised (made "equiva-

---

[1] Reay (1964a:246) and Berndt, R. M. (1962:318) use "informal" to contrast courts heard outside the jurisdiction of the C.N.A. with "formal" C.N.A. courts. My own terminology is as follows:

	Official	Unofficial
Formal	C.N.A.	Councillors' courts
Informal	advice from administration personnel	Private settlement without reference to Council or Komitis

lent", *kapokla*) the disputants' claims. Go-betweens who carried messages of peaceful intentions, or who exhorted each side to cease fighting, were called *ik ning kwun mondorong wu^e køkl* ("those men who saw that the talk was straightened") and the modern gloss for this is given retrospectively, in a mixture of Pidgin English and Melpa, as *kot wu^e* ("court men").

Many offences were (and are) defined in terms of the appropriate named category of compensation payments. But there was no simple contrast between disputes settled by such payments and those settled by recourse to violence. Delicts themselves were not classified: the mobilization of a fighting force might be provoked by any act which could also be settled peacefully. Relations between the parties concerned was the chief factor. Thus quarrels between members of a single clan or sub-clan involved a range of sanctions different from those between allied clans and different again from those between members of major enemy groups.[1] In addition, compensation itself was not always obtained peaceably. If negotiations failed or if the two sides could not be brought together to discuss the matter, the victim might seize his recompense by force. It was generally recognized that he had some right to do so if he did not take in excess of his losses. Men in any case would often go armed to claim compensation, even if they did not actually come to blows.

> *An old Tipuka Oklembo man recounted how, twenty-five or thirty years ago, he and two of his clan-mates killed and ate two pigs which they found; as they discovered afterwards,[2] the animals belonged to a big-man of one of their ally clans (Minembi Yelipi) and had wandered over the borders into Tipuka territory. The owner's clansmen armed themselves with bows, spears and axes, to claim redress, and some of the Oklembo readied to fight in defence. But Oklembo big-men urged that compensation should be paid without the two sides fighting, and a young Yelipi big-men reminded the thieves that he was their sister's son (an actual ZS of the storyteller), and how could they fight since they were *pamal* (matrilateral kin)? The thieves returned an equivalent pair of pigs to the owner, along with a further one "on their back," i.e. an addition to demonstrate they were not to be thought mean (*korpa*).

The securing of compensation was always open to bargaining. For this reason a wronged person would try to mobilize support among his

---

[1] Self-regulation (Lawrence, 1969:32) was least prominent in the latter situation, most prominent in the first (quarrelling between close kin bringing sickness on their heads). Supernatural sanctions, which I cannot discuss here in detail, are referred to in Chapter 5

[2] In such cases persons accused of theft always protest they had no idea that the pig was owned by anyone they knew.

clansmen and the accused do likewise. Threat of force thus often lay at the back of "peaceful agreement". In the past a husband might have to manoeuvre a return of bridewealth, for example, his success depending on the strength of his bargaining position as much as entitlement to it. Vicedom makes this point clearly (1943–8:2:105–6). Bargaining on terms for compensation is still an element in the modern court situation.

The value of reaffirming amity (where appropriate) is explicit in the structure of compensation payments: in addition to those made in restitution of a loss, further gifts repair damage done to a relationship. In the case just cited an extra pig of this latter category was given. The payment may be unilateral, or may consist of mutual exchanges. I refer generally to all payments as compensation. The terminological contrast between restitution and reconciliation items, is, however, made mainly in the context of property disputes. Quarrels, homicide and sexual offences involve damage which cannot be rectified with an equivalent gift, and payments here have an overall reconciliatory character, intended to "make good the feelings" of the injured party.

Table XVI gives a selection of terms (there are further synonyms or descriptive phrases) for different categories of compensation payments. Alternative phrases may be used of a single category, and personal idiosyncracies as well as dialect differences affect actual usages. One young Northern Melpa man constructed the following neat distinction between reconciliation payments which are given after a theft. *Ki titimbil* ("the pair shake hands"), he said, is given when a theft had disrupted relations between close kinsmen, e.g. brothers within a sub-clan or clan-section. Between sub-clans or clans the theft has the character of trespass, an intrusion into the territory of another group, which has broken down the fence between them, and here the payment given in recognition of this is called *pakla pan*. He also noted that within the sub-clan *ki titimbil* is paid when general quarrels have occurred, and any kind of theft should be followed by reconciliation payments. But with outside groups reconciliation payments (*pakla pan*) are made only when major valuables (pigs, shells, cassowaries) have been taken, not for minor stealing (of bananas or sugarcane). This is consonant with the fact that the more distant the group, the more permissible it is in the eyes of his own clan-mates for a man to make raids and forays. Between closely related clansmen theft is an offence to their joint solidarity as well as a damage to one of them.

Similar distinctions appear in the terms for compensation following

TABLE XVI

Some compensation terms[a]

A. *Property offences*

Offence	(i) Restitution payment	(ii) Reconciliation payment
THEFT or DAMAGE TO PROPERTY	*kumøp* ("restitution"), also used of debts (*pund*) make good *yoka* (same meaning)[b]	*mbukl-øl* ("item on the back") *ki titimbil* ("the pair shake hands") *pakla pan* ("fenced area" i.e. territory has been violated)
BRIDEWEALTH (when returned at divorce)	*amb yoka* ("wife restitution"), compensation to husband, especially full return of bridewealth	*amb yoka*, also used of additional item given on top of the return *mel lip* ("slippery thing, valuable" i.e. wife's kin have smoothed off all outstanding items with the addition of one more)

B. *Other offences*

Offence	Compensation
ADULTERY or INCEST	*amb noimb nggo* ("pulling out the penis") *amb nggil kan nggopa* ("[re-tying] the knot in the woman's apron")
QUARREL or INSULT	*ki titimbil* (see A)
QUARREL or ASSAULT (especially if blood drawn)	*mongaemb ropa* ("spilt blood") *mema kil* ("blood wiped off") *mema mondoromen* ("they caused blood [to fall]")
HOMICIDE	*wu[e] peng* ("man head"), generally including military payment between allies; also *amb peng* ("woman's head") *on kum* ("funeral bundle"), payment to kin or ally for killing a connection of theirs *peng nggoa* ("broken head"), after own kin or ally killed, payment to their connections for "severed link" *kik kapa* ("brushing off funeral ashes"), where death payments can also subsume compensation (see Chapter 5)

POISONING ACCUSATIONS	*kopna mi* ("to forbid [future] poisoning")

MARRIAGE CHOICE DISPUTE	*amb mon, ndip nomboklal* ("woman road, fire [literally] on the road") (see Chapter 4)

[a] Many of the terms are regularly part of phrases (e.g. *pakla pan rapendoromen*, "they broke into the fenced area"), or are qualified by *kng* ("pig", as in *amb nggil kan nggopa kng*, "pig to tie up the knot in the woman's apron"), where it is the customary item of payment. For brevity I give truncated forms.

[b] I do not consider general differences in terminology between Northern and Central Melpa, except to note that *yoka* seems to have a wider distribution in Central rather than Northern usages. N.M.: *yoka* mainly refers to return of bridewealth plus other outstanding debts at divorce; C.M.: also used of additional item on top of the return, and generally for compensation payments in theft and adultery cases.

quarrelling and assault. Between most classes of relatives,[1] including affines, who wish to patch up a quarrel, a payment may be made under the rubric of *ki titimbil*. It is commonly said that such payments cannot pass between cowives or spouses because the expectation is that "they will always be quarrelling, there can be no end to dispute. Sometimes "blood" payments (*mongaemb* etc.) follow a verbal quarrel; this may involve spouses if the wife's kin have reason to press for payment. It is given as though she had indeed been wounded, and not for "shaking hands". Normally such payments are made when quarrelling develops into brawling, and blood (whether profuse or not) has actually flowed. *Mongaemb ropa* is used casually to cover circumstances involving close cognatic kin, affines and spouses, while payments between allies wounded in a common fight, or men of ally or friendly clans who wish to restore relations after coming to blows over a dispute, are called *mema kil*. A further refinement was suggested by the informant quoted above. *Mongaemb* he referred to as appropriate for contexts where eventual settlement can be reached, as between siblings of a sub-clan or clan-section, matrilaterally related lineages and close cognates in general. *Mema kil* is used for payments between allies, between friendly pair clans, distant cognates (e.g. matrilaterally related clans) and affines. He adduced a third term (*mema mondoromen*) for assault payments between cowives or between husband and wife (or wife's kin), where, he added, reconciliation could be of no more than a temporary nature.

Such terminological distinctions throw light on how compensation is

---

[1] But see below (p. 251).

regarded; they do not structure the size or content of the payment. With the exception of death payments and bridewealth return, none of these need entail gifts of any magnitude.[1] One or two pigs, perhaps other valuables instead or in addition, are likely to comprise the maximum amount. They are thus within the resources of the culprit (or his father or immediate brothers), and liability is not regularly shared among others of his clansmen. The situation of women is described in a later section.

Where the payments include a pig, it was frequently shared in the past among those who had helped a property owner recover his assets or otherwise given assistance; nowadays it is cooked and eaten by the men who assemble to hear the court. Women usually do not partake of it.[2] The persons providing the animal, along with their immediate associates, would usually be ashamed to join in, and leave before the cooking begins. Reconciliation in such circumstances is not expressed in commensality between offender and victim: it lies rather in the generosity which the offender shows in his gifts. Reconciliation is also effected between the living and the disturbed ghosts of the victim, to whom the pigs are killed in sacrifice. Pigs demanded in payment thus signify a grave situation, and are appropriate for sexual offences, assault which draws blood, and homicide. "Shaking hand" gifts are often minor; they may include a piglet or shell valuable, but equally items of no great significance as wealth objects.

While it was always possible in the past to use force for claiming back stolen property, for taking revenge for a death inflicted upon the clan, or for gaining redress in some other way,[3] reconciliation only made sense in a peaceful context. Even if the actual thief had to be intimidated into giving an extra reconciliation item, his clansmen might, in the interests of their general friendly relations, see this was done. It thus sometimes happened that the thief fled when the owners came demanding recom-

---

[1] Under certain circumstances larger gifts are made, e.g. if a theft has led to fighting and two clans settle their differences in mutual exchanges. Here the original offence has been transformed into a more general rupture.

[2] The cooking is likely to add perhaps two hours to the court time, it usually being evening before it is ready to be eaten, by which time any women present have long since dispersed to the gardens. The pig is also regarded as the particular reward of those who helped settle the dispute with their speeches, i.e. the men.

[3] Theft, rape and adultery were all themselves means of retaliation for injury or damage. Reprisal might or might not be accepted or suffered as making the parties equal (*kapokla*) (Cf. Bohannan, 1957:151).

pense, and his lineage brothers would take it on themselves to remove an appropriate pig from his herd. To settle things peaceably was an indication that one did not want to disrupt relations. Here lies a contrast between the traditional and modern systems. Previously, payment of compensation and peaceful agreement over an issue were one end of a range of reactions to offences; at the other end were self-help and reprisal through force. The value placed on solidarity within the clan meant that most disputes between clan members were settled peacefully, while traditional enemies were constant targets for aggression. Between these extremes, among friendly clans of the minor enemy/ally category, settlement might be achieved through either peaceful or violent means. But nowadays all disputes have to be resolved peacefully; under the present administration it is difficult to resort to force-using self-help, whether for recompense or retaliation. Peaceful settlement in the past was often motivated by the desire to resolve quarrels in the specific interests of friendship or kinship,[1] and this ideology of reconciliation has been absorbed into court dealings.

Councillors and Komitis are strongly committed to the new system. Their speeches often turn on the desirability of observing the law which the Australian administration has brought. In an effort to achieve reconciliation between persons in dispute, they may be perturbed at any indication that after an apparent agreement has been reached, hidden grievances still exist. Councillors regard courts as partial failures if they have not eradicated the desire for revenge. Some of the concern over finding out the state of women's *noman* (mind) can be related to this, and it is a concern that applies to men as well.

*In 1964 a long-standing dispute between a Minembi man and his Tipuka wife came to a head. The wife had wanted to send a pig to her father which the husband refused to agree to. They quarrelled, but the husband further refused even to pay any compensation to the wife's kin for having struck her (see below), and she returned home, reporting that he desired to get rid of her. She herself would not go back to him and threatened suicide when her brother tried persuasion. General opinion censured the affair as scandalous, for she was suckling a child at the time. But the wife insisted that she would only return if the husband paid compensation for having

---

[1] This no doubt simplifies actual attitudes held. Ploeg (1969:152) reports how sceptical Wanggulam Dani are towards the efficacy of settlement through compensation. By "reconciliation" I refer not so much to changes in personal feelings on the disputants' part (though Hageners hope for this), as the willingness to resume relations. A person may grumble at having to pay compensation while agreeing that things have been patched up.

hit her. Eventually a court was held, and he was persuaded to hand over a pig (for *mongaemb*), but apparently did so with such ill grace that he was asked outright whether everything was now all right. He expostulated that he was having to pay compensation and that was why he was angry (*popokl*)! The Councillors were agitated that his *noman* should still be full of *popokl*, for this would lead him to take revenge, and lectured him on the fact that he had gained back his wife. The Komiti, from a pair clan to the wife's natal clan, who attended and subsequently told me about the court, added that the dispute was not really settled. They had never got to the bottom (*pukl*) of the quarrel since neither husband nor wife would co-operate in coming out with their true grievances.

Court and Anti-court: the Problem of Divorce

A ceremonial ground is a favourite site for holding courts, but for small hearings the courtyard of a house suffices. Depending on the importance of the matter, there may be several or only one Councillor or Komiti present. Disputes between two clans (e.g. theft or adultery) usually bring Councillors (or Komitis) from both sides, while others of neighbouring or friendly clans may come to "help the talk" of their fellow-Councillors. Anyone may attend, but only interested parties or big-men participate in the discussion. The principal disputants are both urged to speak and will be heard out, but if the court becomes a scene of general bickering the Councillors (or Komitis) will try to intervene, and they usually sum up the case. Their interpretation of the decision reached is regarded by most people as final, although they have little power to coerce the disputants to heed them. If compensation is to be paid, this is handed over in the Councillors' presence, or maybe given to a Councillor a day or so later to take it to the injured party.

Divorce cases and disputes over bridewealth differ in character from others handled by the courts. In instances of theft or adultery, the offence itself is disruptive, and the transfer of goods which follows—the compensation—repairs the relationship, signifying the ideal attainment of recompense and reconciliation. But quite the opposite happens at divorce. There is no fresh transfer; rather, a previous contract has to be undone. Returning wealth may be referred to as *mel na mbθ akopa ngui*, "to dig up and give the valuables". This does not re-activate amicable ties, but is a clearance of debts which breaks off a former intimate relationship. Public jokes[1] are made about thieving—people say they are "glad" they

---

[1] When the theft is among neighbours or people otherwise closely connected, embarrassment may enter into the situation.

were stolen from because they have received such handsome compensation!—but divorce is rarely the subject of such bravado in the presence
of ex-affines. Disruptiveness is its most salient feature.

The main bridewealth items due for return at divorce are the "mother's
pig" (Northern Melpa) and the pigs which originally "died" on the
bride, along with shells or other items for which return was not made at
the time. Various factors modify this. If the fault is the groom's he cannot, as we have seen, claim back all the outstanding wealth, and may
even forfeit any return at all. If there are children to the marriage, the
wife's kin are likely to say that all or at least some of the payments have
died on them. This is so whether the children remain with the husband
or whether the wife takes them off—for in the latter case the husband may hope that his offspring will eventually come back to him and
to demand his bridewealth would be tantamount to a repudiation of
claims. Childbirth payments are not relevant here. Whether or not
there are children, if the marriage has lasted for some years the wife's
kin will be reluctant to return wealth items, on the grounds that the
husband has had enjoyment of her services and labour. A groom is most
likely to be able to recuperate his bridewealth if the marriage is of short
duration, childless, and the blame for divorce lies with the wife.

Further, much depends on the cordiality existing between those trying
to reach agreement over which items are outstanding. If both parties are
interested in maintaining fairly amicable relations, in spite of the divorce,
then the groom's people may not push for the return of items they might
otherwise demand. The cooked *mangal* pigs, or gifts of pork made after
the marriage, may or may not be settled upon, and in order not to
appear too mean the bride's kin sometimes forgo their claims to a return
of the endowment pigs. These can in any case be counted as part of the
initial return the bride's people have already made to the groom. It
might be in such a spirit of reconciliation that the wife's father (who
is chiefly responsible for the return) adds to the assembled goods an
extra pig (*amb yoka*) to be eaten by the husband's clan, irrespective of
where the fault lies. But while there is this possibility of asserting that
friendly relations can endure beyond the break up of a marriage, it is
much commoner for the wife's kin to make the return only grudgingly,
and be shamed into providing the *yoka* pig because the proof of blame
was with their side.

As long as the marriage lasts, disputes arising between affines over
debts or other matters can lead to hostility, but are not usually brought

to public notice. Dissatisfactions are sorted out in the idioms of generosity and reciprocity rather than in terms of formal rights and claims. Effective pressure can be applied, threats of termination depending on the supposition that in the end continuity on friendly terms will be more highly valued. However, as soon as termination becomes a reality, efforts to maintain friendship are frequently abandoned, and people display more legalistic attitudes to their claims. Where the divorce itself is the culmination of unsettled grudges, these contribute to the bitterness with which the parties usually contend over the items due to them. The nature of the issue—returning a heterogeneous set of valuables given on several different occasions, contributed by and distributed to diverse persons—gives ample scope for conflicting interpretations of what would constitute a settlement. Not least are the differences of opinion which frequently exist over assessing equivalence between the size and quality of the valuables which each side asserts they gave in comparison with those offered in return.

It is highly likely that a divorce dispute which ends in agreement to hand back bridewealth will be anything but conciliatory in atmosphere. The following points summarize the way in which such proceedings differ most from other dispute settlements.

1. In other cases the offence can often be separated from the continuity of the relationship; but even where brothers-in-law stoutly maintain they will continue to be friends, divorce dissolves affinity. (*Moka* relations in practice rarely persist after the marriage is broken, though occasionally the wife's kin send another woman to the ex-husband.) It is not just that norms have been ignored, but the link itself is severed.

2. The return of bridewealth dislocates the network of donors and recipients involved in the original payments, rather than bringing them together in affirmation of their ties.

3. Unlike most agreements on a compensation item, the decision to return bridewealth is likely to be the start of hours of discussion rather than the end of it. Even if the bride's kin offer the extra pig, this rarely stops disputes developing over individual valuables. Moreover, in spite of a possible desire on the part of the principal male affines to maintain amity towards each other, they have the claims of other donors and recipients to consider. Discussions often display tension, expressed in antagonism against the opposite side.

4. When people face one another with accusations and denials of theft or adultery, the court has to ascertain who is guilty and deliberate on the

appropriate compensation; the accused may offer extenuating circumstances as reasons for avoiding payment, but there is no argument as to the permissibility of theft or adultery. These are actions which are condoned only in private and when committed against persons with whom face to face relations are not regularly maintained. But the values placed on marriage and affinal alliance militate against public assertions that divorce as such is desirable. Divorce is both the outcome of offences and itself has the character of an offence.

A divorce court is concerned with relationships between spouses and between their respective kin; that it is held at all signifies the extent to which these relations are under strain. Those hearing the case try to assess the actors' behaviour, but are aware that people can be provoked into acting reprehensibly. There is often no clear locus of guilt on this score. Yet divorce can never be a proper solution, however inevitable it turns out to be; and Hageners tend to seek a cause for the total situation, by finding someone to blame for it.

Courts aggravate rather than minimize some of the conflicts which attend the dissolution of a marriage. In pre-European times, hostility between affines could be absorbed[1] into more general hostilities expressible between their respective clans. If a woman was married to a major enemy group her kin were able to refuse a return of the bridewealth, high-handedly exploiting the situation by declining to enter into negotiation. They might throw out the challenge: "If you want your bridewealth, come and get it!" The husband had the choice of giving up, or retaliating by an attack on his ex-affines. Full-scale fighting might break out over such issues, even between groups who were not out and out major enemies.

*A big-man from Kawelka Mandembo clan (a slightly different version coming from an Oklembo informant) recounted what happened when a girl from his pair clan, Membo, divorced her Kundmbo husband, also of Kawelka tribe, sometime during the 1920's. A man from Membo's ally clan (Tipuka Oklembo) had earlier been wounded in a battle fought on its behalf, but had received no compensation for this. In anger, he and other Oklembo began to attack their property—stole pigs, raped wives—and Membo decided they had to make good their debt with him. So it was they who persuaded the girl married to Kundmbo, with whom political relations were uneasy, to leave her husband and go to the Oklembo ally in-

---

[1] Though this was not inevitably the outcome: good relations between them could over-ride group confrontation. The point is that group hostilities provided cover for affinal antagonism when relations were not good.

stead. They accepted bridewealth from the second man but did not bother to return any to Kundmbo, on the grounds that Kundmbo had fought along with their major enemies against them in a previous engagement. This first husband and his Kundmbo clan-mates were furious at this treatment and a war party set out to kill one of the woman's Membo brothers. They came across a man from Mandembo, whom they murdered instead, precipitating a war involving all three Kawelka clans and their respective allies.

While the woman's kin might refuse to negotiate with the husband, there was always the possibility that he could seize items by force. But frequently in the past bridewealth was not returned at all, this being so for about half the cases which I have recorded as occurring before about 1940. Now that the majority of divorces filter through courts there is greater security that in the end return will be made, and this has perhaps encouraged the rise in total amounts given in bridewealth, a trend which Hageners regard as inflationary. Thus, there has been a transformation from small bridewealths, returnable often only through self-help, to large ones where return is more or less guaranteed by the court system. But the increase in valuables has meant an increase in the numbers of people involved as donors and recipients (a large proportion of the pearl shells are collected from contributors singly or in twos or threes). The effects of rupture are thus wider. Moreover, divorce through court hearings means that the rupture has to take the form of protracted face to face "peaceful" arguments. While the court allows people to state their precise claims more easily than was often the case before, it has probably led to more insistent demands of an exact and strict return of the goods. Withdrawal or open aggression are no longer available paths of action. The rupture has to be negotiated; whatever their private feelings, the men of both parties are forced to take a public stance over the dissolution.

Blaming women is one way in which the men protest their innocence; the non-participation of the husband himself on some occasions also makes it easier for the other affines to assert *their* friendly intentions. They defend themselves against the charge of responsibility, and may even appear anxious for reconciliation. As long as no decision has actually been reached, it is always possible that divorce will be prevented and affinal relations re-assumed. Putting the blame onto the wife, or perhaps total blame where her motives are only partly the cause, makes her a scapegoat. There are witchcraft elements in such "blame-pinning . . . explanations of misfortune" (Douglas, 1967:73). Divorce is regarded particularly as "helping" women; at the same time it is an affront to male solidarity to let women have their own way. Thus females are seen to be hostile to male interests. Frustration and dissatisfaction over the marital alliance may lie with the men, but it is the women they accuse of wrecking the system. This is even played out between the spouses themselves. A husband who wants to be rid of his wife may not bring himself to actually tell her to go; he may (with more or less deliberate intent) begin to neglect her, favour another wife or seek another woman, be idle in his household tasks, let transactions with her kin lapse, till she is provoked into running away. He then accuses her of desertion.

The manner, then, in which women sometimes receive treatment in divorce cases brought to court stems partly from the latter's relationship to the rest of the judicial system. Divorce is settlement in reverse. The final handing over of goods breaks affinity instead of bringing an abused relationship back to equilibrium, and in dissolving a marriage it is as though the court were condoning an offence.

Women and the Compensation Nexus

Jural status is an important factor in women's treatment in courts. This may determine, for example, the extent to which women are held responsible for their actions, are liable to pay compensation or are entitled to receive it. My discussion is based largely on contemporary arrangements, but accounts of pre-European settlements and the descriptions of Vicedom (1943–8:2:52, 82, 87, 223 *et seq.*) and Strauss (1962: chs. 34f.) indicate how closely these follow the traditional system.

Women not directly involved in a case contribute little to hearings. If they are gathered for some other purpose (e.g. a bridewealth function or Sunday church meeting) they will listen in on a dispute, and local wives in any case usually make up part of the audience. But, unlike men, they do not often travel to attend courts held away from home, and rarely participate in the discussion. Their presence is tolerated rather than welcomed by men, who become restless as the day wears on, for the wives are not seeing to their proper work. As a body, men may turn on the women and tell them to be off to the gardens. Hearing courts is essentially male business, and women do not question this. Women may be required to act as witnesses in cases otherwise not concerning them, or in offences in which they are held guilty but not liable to provide compensation.

When disputes involve men alone, payments are usually transferred quite straightforwardly, e.g. from the guilty man to victim. Offences involving women are more complicated. In some situations, females appear to act autonomously, both giving and receiving wealth; in others, transfers are made on their behalf either by or to their husband or their kinsmen. In some instances the payments are not even credited as on their behalf but simply pass between men.

Adultery accusations often fall into this latter category. Invariably the wife's lover is required to compensate the cuckolded husband; the man's usual stance is that he was enticed by the wife, but he is still made to pay for his weakness in not having resisted her offers. The wife in turn pleads that she was enticed or overpowered by the lover, but this will be met with scepticism, even sarcasm, if she did not resist, struggle or cry out at the time. In the majority of cases, however, nothing is required of her, although attendance at the court is necessary to prove the lover's part, and she will be harangued by the Councillors; she is in the wrong and thus far responsible, but not liable to pay compensation (Epstein, 1967b). (The lover's own wife, on the other hand, is regarded as neither wronged nor as able to place any claims.) Interestingly enough female non-liability is not a rigidly adhered to principle. Councillors not only often debate whether to beat an adulterous woman in public (although nearly as frequently they desist, with the axiom that it is up to husbands to control their spouses), but on rare occasions may actually demand that the woman produce a payment.

> *One such case (Central Melpa), heard by a former Bosboi perhaps fifteen years ago, ended in the latter's recommendation that the lover pay one pig to the husband (who was of the same sub-clan) and that the adulterous wife should ask her kin to provide another pig, also for the husband. The wife prevaricated, pointing out how distant her home was and what a long way she would have to go, and the injunction was not pressed, for fear that if she did go she would take the opportunity to run away. The Bosboi (who recounted the event) instead gave her a beating.

The male lover is frequently accused of responsibility in adultery cases, there being no attempt to pin blame entirely onto the woman.[1] Nevertheless, females are specifically excluded from a share in the com-

---

[1] Sometimes, however, a man sends report to the husband that his wife had approached (or even had intercourse with) him, and in agreement that the fault was the woman's the husband may reward him for his honesty.

pensation pig: men say that if women tasted the meat it would encourage them to seduce men all the time.[1]

Circumstances in which women are both responsible and liable include the following three.

1. Sexual offences: if relative strangers of opposite sex insult each other through accidental exposure, or are seen urinating or defecating, they make amends with small private payments. Such issues are never the subject of courts. Both sexes pay and receive compensation.

2. After a quarrel, reconciliation payments may be exchanged publicly or privately "because of the cross words".

*About 1960, Punggi, who was married to a Kawelka Kurupmbo man, accidentally broke a pearl shell belonging to her husband's brother. In anger, the man insulted her by saying that she was a rubbish woman and never brought shells (in exchange) to their clan. All *his* shells had gone in raising bridewealth for her, and now she had broken even this one! Had she been angry as though no bridewealth had been paid that she wanted to "eat" this valuable? What did she bring from her kin? Her parents were equally rubbish since they had made such paltry return-gifts at the marriage. She did not reply. Punggi's father was apparently present when he said this, and because he was afterwards ashamed of his hasty words, the husband's brother gave a small pig to him. (He might otherwise have given this to Punggi's husband.) The father returned a pearl shell *via* his daughter. In handing it over, Punggi said to her husband's brother that her father was keeping the pig because of the quarrel with her, but she could now give him a shell to replace the broken one (as *kumøp*). In addition she presented him with three pounds of her own money as a reconciliation payment. Separate, then, from the transaction between her father and her husband's brother, was the gift which the wife made of her own accord, so that they could "shake hands" (*ki titimbil*). The relevant tie was the wife's own with her husband's brother, a resident of the same settlement, and the second gift re-established this. The man himself is reported as saying that Punggi was not his own wife but his brother's wife, and so he would give another pig to her to make amends. No court was held; the husband spread the tale around, which was how my informant, a member of his clan-section, heard of it.

Such gifts are often made outside the courts.

3. Women also have ties with persons completely independently of their husbands. If two sisters, or a brother and sister, or cross-cousins, quarrel, they may settle this with *ki titimbil* payments. Often these are reciprocal

---

[1] Andrew Strathern points out that Christians (who disapprove of most pig-killing occasions) say that if men eat the animal, it encourages them to prostitute their womenfolk.

exchanges so that the husband does not lose by his wife's paying compensation, although he expects to be informed of her actions.

*The same informant (as in the previous case) told of what he had heard befell a girl of his sub-clan who married into Roklaka tribe, some fifteen years ago. As a young bride she was taking a leg of pork from her husband to her parents, and on the way was accosted by a cross cousin (FZS) who laid claims to the meat ("Give it to me—if it is for your father, then I can share in it as well. I am not a Seventh Day Adventist who is forbidden pork!"). They struggled over it, the girl gave in; her cousin then said he did not want it since she had not willingly given it to him first of all, but she was already away. So he took it off, and later sent her a pearl shell and a small piglet. She gave the pearl shell to her husband, since this was in return for the pork, but the piglet she kept herself as *ki titimbil* and sent her cousin a piglet of her own as a sign that their relationship was back on good terms.

Wives are often allowed to have more control of the disposal of piglets they have reared themselves than over full grown pigs. Along with netbags, aprons and head coverings (all manufactured by women), old flasks of oil and some ornaments, these were the items which women used in the past for minor compensations. The woman could dispose of them without informing her husband. But most ornaments incorporating shells were too valuable to be lightly given away, and a woman could use her pearl shell pendants or cowrie necklaces (and similarly newly filled flasks of oil) only with the husband's agreement. On the other hand, the husband would not himself use such articles without asking the wife; stone axes, salt bundles, plumes, grown pigs and major shell valuables were the main components of compensation payments between men. Women were thus most free to use minor items in the settlement of minor disputes. Nowadays they regularly employ money, earned in small amounts by themselves, and which is regarded as their own. The divisibility of money makes it eminently suitable for minor payments. A man who has received cash in compensation for a ruined garden may keep some for himself but also parcel small sums out to his wives whose crops have been spoiled. When a woman is told to hand over a cash payment, men add that this is to make her feel (*mindil indi*, "to cause pain") and thus suffer for her wrong. While some husbands are known to help their wives in disputes with women of the neighbourhood, others assert that these affairs are nothing to do with them and tell a wife to find her own means of compensation. To stop a wife from stealing in the future a husband may, on the other hand, threaten that *he* will send away in compensation all her little ornaments, netbags and aprons, so she will have nothing. Access to money has undoubtedly encouraged women's participation in these payments,[1] although it did not create it.

Some details of cases in which women give or receive compensation and further cases where others make payments on their behalf are given in Appendix VII. I summarize the points here. A husband is liable to compensate the owner if his wife steals or pollutes property, in the latter case even if it is property belonging to men of her own clan. For minor thefts, especially of food from other women's gardens, we have seen that the wife may settle the issue herself. Her husband steps in to pay compensation, however, if a major wealth item is required for damages, or he may step in because his wife's actions have threatened his own relations. This is open to idiosyncratic interpretation. If his wife steals from a brother's wife's gardens, the two brothers may take the matter out of the women's hands altogether and settle the case between themselves, with the payment of minor articles belonging to men (such as bushknives). A husband can thus be indemnified on his wife's part for the depleted gardens, as he may also be if her woman's house (which he built) is burnt down. Following quarrels, reconciliation payments are usually handed to the aggrieved woman herself, although again if major items are involved these may go to the husband. Whereas small thefts of food can be met with food (*kumøp*), if proper reconciliation (*ki titimbil*) is to be made, wealth items are needed (e.g. shells or pig), and to pay these a woman depends on her husband's help. In a quarrel between a wife and her husband's brother, the latter may pay her a pearl shell which she hands over to her husband.

A woman's kinsmen also retain some liability in respect of her. This applies mainly to her lineage kin, particularly her own father and brothers. Attacks against her husband, such as pollution which injures the man himself, arson which destroys the husband's men's house, or a violent physical assault on his own person, may be met by compensation from them. Poisoning, however, puts themselves in a very ambiguous position, as was pointed out earlier, and they are more likely to acquiesce in retaliation directed at their kinswoman than make payments on her behalf. If the wife herself has been the subject of assault, her kin are indemnified. This is true whether the attack is from her husband or (a much more rare occurrence) someone else of his clan; in the latter case

---

[1] An examination of the cash component is given in Appendix VII.

items might be channelled through the husband, who retains some of the payment. If a wife is struck by her parents-in-law, however, she often keeps the payment herself. Such contexts in any case merge with those where a reconciliation gift is appropriate, and is due to the hurt woman.

A wife's kin receive payments at her death (see Chapter 5). Should a husband actually kill his wife he gives *kik kapa* gifts to her lineage, unless she was a suspected poisoner or other circumstances intervene.[1] The gifts are also known as *amb peng*: for "the woman's head". If she is very old, and her kin dead or are far away, he may pay her children. Women killed by others of their husband's clan were usually suspected poisoners or *amb wapra*, and their kin would forfeit compensation. Occasionally a sister or daughter is murdered by her own brother or father (for incest, or from the man's outrage that his married kinswoman constantly returns home, putting him in the position of having to placate the husband with presents or return the bridewealth). Here payments (*kik kapa* or *peng nggoa*) are due in the first place to the girl's maternal kin; relations might already be bad with the husband and no further adjustment made in that direction, or his bridewealth may be returned. *Kik kapa* is in any case due to the husband when a woman dies on her home land. If an unmarried girl is killed by a close kinsman, then the latter makes payments to his clan brothers as well as the matrilateral lineage. Should a wife die from poison intended for her husband, he ought to compensate her clansmen. He also gives them *kik kapa* should an outsider kill his wife, and claims *amb peng* for himself from the killer. Sometimes the husband made *kik kapa* to them were she killed by an enemy, although attacks were inflicted most frequently by major enemies, which excused the husband from individual liability; he and his defeated brothers might be dispersed, perhaps permanently, as refugees with other groups, and would in any case be in no practical position to raise the requisite wealth. Women's deaths are occasionally acknowledged in retrospective war compensations between allies or minor enemies, being included with those of men also killed in battle; here the deaths are often a pretext for rather than cause of the transactions. A major enemy would not be called upon to pay, although, in the heat of fighting, the death of a wife was sometimes avenged by the husband or his lineage-mates killing an enemy wife. Funeral payments were

---

[1] Often in the past when the wife's and husband's clans were major enemies or actively fighting, these (like all other transactions) were suspended.

in any case likely to be omitted for any women who died while the men were involved in fighting.

In the case of a married woman guilty of homicide, compensation is usually her husband's liability. In one story, a man's married sister fell prey to poison which his own wife had brought with her, and he paid handsome *kik kapa* to his sister's husband, while slaying the poisoner, whose kin were too ashamed to claim compensation. The circumstances in which a woman might poison or pollute her own husband have already been noted; should she kill him directly she may be killed herself by his brothers, or her kin would be liable for compensation (*wu^e peng*). A unique incident in which two cowives, in their mutual exasperation, turned upon their husband and clubbed him to death, was settled by their kin returning all bridewealth. Should a woman kill a wife of an ally clan, her husband's clansmen would pay the latter *amb peng*, who in turn would give *kik kapa* to the victim's kin. The killer's kinsmen might contribute to the *amb peng*. If one cowife herself kills another, again the husband gives *kik kapa* to the dead woman's people; he may claim payment from the killer's clan. This and his own payment might be presented jointly to the victim's clan, or he might keep it himself. Instances of such actions on the part of women are few. Death by suicide, however, is relatively common. Payments for the wife's death here follow other death payments and are subject to similar vicissitudes; the fact of suicide only affects them insofar as it suggests a direction of blame. If as often happens it is at her own home that the woman hangs herself, then her kin will make the initial *kik kapa*; if at her husband's place, then he is liable.

We may summarise this by saying that *kik kapa* usually passes between the kinsmen and spouse of a dead woman, while *amb peng*[1] payments settle compensation due between her husband's clan and others. If a woman commits homicide, then either her husband or her kin, or them both jointly, are responsible for payments (*wu^e peng* or *amb peng* depending on the sex of the victim).

While the husband is indemnified by the lover if his wife is accused of adultery, kinsmen are involved should she have illicit sexual relations with cognates (incest), and consume the pig provided by the male partner as a sacrifice to the outraged ancestral ghosts. Which of her

---

[1] Through his bridewealth payments the husband has already "acquired" the woman's "head" from her kin: see p. 99. However, it should be emphasized that, as with all these compensation terms, people's individual usages vary.

kinsmen share the meat depends upon the relationship between the incestuous pair. For example if a man entered into illicit relations with his MBD or FZD he would have to compensate his own agnates along with the woman's. Relations with a sister, on the other hand, would involve chiefly their clansmen, although payments might also be made to the girl's matrilateral kin. We may define incestuous relations in Hagen as those which bring rapid punishment (e.g. sickness) from the ancestral ghosts (Strathern, A.J. and A.M., 1969: 144–5); often there are violent consequences. One father killed the daughter with whom he had copulated; madness inflicted a man for sleeping with a lineage sister. Often the deed is not discovered till ghosts have killed one of the offending parties. Without entering into details, one may note that such consequences often affect the manner in which compensation is or is not paid. In addition, there is a range of kin with whom sexual relations comprise an affront to their common relatives, although ghostly reprisals are not so automatic. For example, intercourse with a lineage sister will bring rapid supernatural retaliation on the heads of the guilty pair, whereas involvement with a clan sister would not, although sickness would eventually demonstrate the ghosts' displeasure, if the act was not brought to light. The latter relationship still trespasses norms of clan solidarity, and members of the man's clan would expect to share in compensation. Such offences are the more likely to be atoned for by direct compensation, without the complications which often accompany full incest. In the case of intercourse with a clan sister, the man's own father and mother might provide the pig and be precluded from sharing in it, as would also the guilty pair themselves; it would be consumed by the girl's parents and brothers, and members of the clan in general. If the girl were a classificatory MZD, he would indemnify her parents and his mother's clansmen; his immediate MB stands between them and might either claim compensation or help him raise it. It is noteworthy that even where the offence is contained within a lineage (for example, illicit relations between a man and his FBW), if a compensation pig is given, then the whole clan and not just the lineage concerned eat it.

The latter is an example of "group-spouse adultery" (Goody, J.R., 1956). Relations with such women within the sub-clan entail rapid sickness of the kind otherwise diagnostic of incest. The offence, however, does not involve the woman in her status as a member of her natal clan but as a mother married into the offender's own clan. Women are sometimes beaten for their part in such affairs, but it is the man typically held responsible and blameworthy. Compensation payments do not concern her kin at all (unless for adventitious reasons, e.g. if they were present at the court discussions). As a husband of the woman, the FB is among those indemnified, although the man's own father is likely to stay away for shame or because he provided the pig on his son's behalf. Depending on the distance between the brothers, a man who copulates with a BW may provide compensation for the husband alone (as in adultery) or for the clan at large (as in cases of incest). Intercourse between a man and married sister is rare; the husband as well as her kin would be indemnified, and he would probably also claim back his bridewealth. Compensation does not, however, rigidly discriminate categories here. A pig given in a straightforward case of non-group adultery may be consumed by the husband's clansmen for their part in hearing the dispute; members of the woman's natal clan may also participate for the same reason. There is no difference in the designation of payments made for sexual offences.

It is in disputes between spouses that the wife's kin become most often involved in her actions. A woman who behaves with deliberate aggression against her husband has to ask them for the valuables with which recompense is made. The wife cannot use the husband's property here; although after a quarrel between cowives which led to bloodshed, one of them may transfer a pig of her own, i.e. from the portion of the husband's stock which she cares for, to her cowife's stalls. Part of the intent in demanding that a woman fetch a compensation valuable from her own kin is to "make her feel". If she has to go to them too many times she puts herself in bad odour with them. But it is also the case that they have some responsibility for her. Sometimes they are blamed should the woman turn out to be *wapra* ("promiscuous"), *kara* ("disobedient") or *wulya* ("half-witted"), or worst of all, a poisoner. Hence, also, a husband may demand indemnification if they "allow" her to be raped while she is on a visit home. In one case a man wanted payment from his wife's father because his wife was "mad" enough to run away and desert her dependent infant. Their responsibility shows further in arrangements for compensation between married sisters who engage in a violent quarrel. If the quarrel occurs at the place where one of them is married, the husbands may help with the compensation payments; but if (as probably happens more often) they are both at their natal home, then a father or brother, anxious to settle the dispute between them, may provide the valuables; major ones the sisters then give to their respective husbands. While a woman's kin are liable for her behaviour in relation to her husband, her husband is responsible to others of his clan, hence his involvement in payments to his own brothers or their wives. Sometimes brothers absolve each other of such a responsibility, one handing back in embarrassment an item the other gives him, saying the quarrel was not between themselves, only with the wife. Solidarity between brothers can over-ride separate liability for their wives' actions. The definition of liability thus depends partly upon the goodwill or otherwise existing between the parties concerned, in the same way that mortuary payments are contingent on the circumstances of the death or homicide. Recognition of liability is not a simple matter of legal status, but open to a certain amount of manipulation.

In spite of this, a woman tends to see as absolute her kinsmen's rights to indemnification if she is assaulted. She may make this an issue even where they do not press for payment. Most frequently this is so in husband-wife quarrels. Stress is put on the fact that blood has been spilt (and severe injury may be symbolized by a demand for blood payments). Systematic and regular beating of wives is uncommon, so that most blood is actually spilt in mutual fights or by the husband blindly striking out, perhaps punching his wife in the nose. By spilling blood, however, the husband has done injury to a substance which the wife shares with her kin (though I never heard it put quite like this). Certainly Hageners entertain the notion that when a wife is killed her kin as well as her husband have suffered a loss. The husband may hand an assault payment over to his brother- or father-in-law directly, or put it into the hand of his wife to take to them. In either case the woman regards herself as compensated. Her own uniqueness is represented in her clan affiliation and it is this which the payments make explicit. Thus a wife will protest if the husband tries to pay her with a pig that originally came from her kin or which she has been looking after. Pearl shells or money do not present the same problems. Should the amount be made up of part shells and part money, the wife might keep the money herself. If the payment is a pig, the wife is invited to share in it when it is killed and cooked by her parents or brothers. The woman's mother, we may note, as well as her father, is regarded as being compensated for injury to the daughter.

Occasionally a woman alone (and not also her kin) receives compensation from her husband. Thus it is said that a father who beats his child may give a small present to the child's mother for having hurt it.

Old women, whose close kin are long since dead or whose links with them have effectively lapsed, may also be the sole recipients of compensation items. Only immediate members of a woman's lineage are likely to give support or make claims on her behalf, and older wives may have no one to take this interest in them. The following case relates to a middle-aged wife whose parents are dead, and has no close siblings; in spite of the fact that she came from a clan some of whose members had settled near her husband's territory, these people were not concerned in her affairs.

> An oldish Yamka polygynist was finding difficulties in giving up all but one of his three wives, as is the ruling for persons who wish to undergo a full conversion to Christianity. One of the discarded wives, Monge, accused him of still following her, and in 1964 a court was heard over the brawl between her, the husband, and the wife he had officially chosen to keep. The third wife, prematurely senile, did not figure in the dispute. Monge was badly knocked about and sat nursing a hand, swollen from where her husband had bitten it, black with blood now dry and clotted. The blood was deliberately not washed off but left as evidence of injury. She was awarded a compensation pig for the blows the husband had given her. The pig came from their joint herd, that is, it had been one she had been caring for, but the husband now made it over to her entirely, an arrangement feasible in the light of their supposed intention to separate. It was felt to be an inducement to leave him, and also some kind of compensation for the fact that she had not been chosen as her husband's Christian wife. Monge had protested strenuously when her husband brought up "one of her own pigs", and tried to get the court to say that she should be awarded one of her husband's animals (i.e. from her cowife's stalls). The Councillors supported her and told the husband to produce a second pig, but the one he eventually fetched out, with great reluctance, was also from her own stalls; but then the Councillors said that since the trouble partly lay with her for not having moved away as she should,[1] they would consume the second pig on the spot. The husband (who had provided the compensation) and his other wife stayed away, but the injured Monge joined with the men who had been present at the hearing in a hurried cooking and eating of the pork.

Further instances of payments passing directly between husband and wife are described in Appendix VII. It is pertinent to add that there are examples from the past of women receiving compensation in their own right.

If her close kin are alive, the wife has the right to demand protection

---

[1] Given that she as well as her husband and the second wife had chosen to become Christian, the Councillors upheld the desirability of their establishing separate residence. From this point of view the case has very non-traditional aspects.

from them. She goes home (especially if they live nearby) with her complaints of neglect or persecution, in the hopes of a sympathetic reception. They may then accompany her back to her husband's settlement and fuss about the way she has been treated. But such support is not given automatically. To begin with, her kin (and it is her father or brothers rather than her mother or sisters who can give effective and open help) are likely to have interests in the marriage separate from her own, and may not wish to antagonise the husband by behaving too aggressively over her complaints. Women probably see themselves as counting on their male kin to a greater extent than the latter agree to implement their duty to defend. The men may be afraid of the charge that they have enticed her away from the husband. Thus it is usually the woman who takes the initiative in running home. Her own kin rarely assume the onus of interference, except when she has been severely wounded or actually killed. Her brothers may then come demanding compensation or take their revenge, and in the past might be ready to kill in turn.

> *About a generation ago, two Tipuka Oklembo brothers with sticks beat to death the wife of one of them. They were enraged at her constant promiscuous wanderings. When her clansmen (neighbouring minor enemies, Tipuka Kengeke) came to demand what had happened, themselves armed with fighting sticks, the brothers protested they had beaten her because she was a *wapra* woman, and they had wanted to mend her ways, not kill her. Her kin were satisfied with a pig, which they ate among themselves. (Account from a middle-aged man who was an unmarried youth at the time, and a brother-in-law to the husband's clan.)

The support a woman can hope to receive over minor issues depends largely on the quality of existing relations between the male affines. Sometimes a husband takes the initiative in paying blood compensation (*mongaemb*) to her brothers because the latter are diffident about pressing him over his quarrel with the wife. The husband fears they harbour bad feelings in their hearts. Nevertheless, it is also the case that her brother or father will demand compensation for a minor injury done to their daughter or sister if they have reasons of their own to be angry with the husband, typically over a debt. Support given to the wife may thus be an extortionist ploy (cf. Vicedom and Tischner, 1943–8 :2 :82).

Interference usually becomes appropriate only under certain circumstances; men do not care to fuss over the small domestic incidents, which can in the wife's mind loom large. There is a "judicial tolerance" in the marital relationship. By this I mean that husband and wife exercise considerable latitude in their behaviour towards each other; notice is not taken by others till a certain threshold is reached.

Husband and wife do not normally compensate each other for verbal quarrelling, for neglect of their duties, the wife's laziness, the husband's defaulting in exchanges with her people, for beating or striking unless blood is drawn. This is not because the spouses' joint estate makes compensation between them meaningless in property terms; we have already seen that a husband can transfer an item over to his wife, perhaps collecting a pig from his sister, or compensating his in-laws on her behalf, while a wife has a lien on her kinsmen's resources. Rather, it is to do with the nature of relations between spouses, in some respects similar to those of close cognatic kinsmen. Although recompense is given for material damage and theft, close kinsmen[1] need not pay compensation for simple quarrelling and may even strike one another (if no blood is drawn) with impunity. Unless the squabbling is felt to be accompanied by malicious intent (which may be revealed subsequently if the ghosts demonstrate unresolved *popokl*, by sending them sickness), then it means nothing. Similar disputes among more distant kin and affines, on the other hand, necessitate compensation payments. Likewise, quarrelling between husband and wife is said to be "for no reason".[2] The comparison is mine; Hageners compare spouses and cowives (see page 231), for between cowives final satisfaction is impossible; their natural state is one of antagonism. Compensation is paid only in the context of a specific physical injury, and discussions following cowife accusations tend to concentrate on the details of the actual dispute, who hit whom, when and how, rather than enquire into larger issues in an attempt to repair the whole relationship. Between husband and wife, then, compensation is unrealistic, either because the quarrelling "means nothing" or because "there can be no end to it". Of them it is said, *ik eta pei na petem* ("the talk lacks the straightness of an axe shaft").

Routine performance of marital duties thus falls below the compensa-

---

[1] I do not specify the range of kin here since the definition varies from situation to situation, but people say that immediate siblings or cousins, or MB-Zch, FZ-Bch, do not make payments after verbal quarrels. (Recorded examples in fact include instances of this; clearly such statements are theoretical comments on the intimacy of these ties, and in practice much depends on the actual state of relations.)

[2] Contrast Barotse (Gluckman 1965 e.g. 223–4) for a case where relations between spouses are distant in antithesis to those between kinsfolk.

tion threshold. Payments usually become relevant only in situations of outright aggression: a men's house burnt down or a wife wounded. But up to this point there is latitude. A man is allowed, for example, to cuff or beat his wife, it being assumed that this is done only under provocation. It is a very different matter if her husband's brothers or her father-in-law touch her ("So you are the husband are you, and hit this woman?"). This holds whatever the provocation. Since only disputes whose settlement can be marked by material transfers are in fact dealt with by formal courts, simple complaints of neglect or dissatisfaction are unlikely to result in a hearing. In fact women frequently go to Councillors and Komitis with their grievances, but are told to return to their husbands. A woman stands more chance of being heard if there has been damage to property or physical injury. There are accounts of women reputedly turned back by their brothers with the comment, "See what happens; if your husband really draws your blood, then you can come home."

While this judicial tolerance means that Hageners regard the husband–wife relationship as perhaps too intimate to be constantly open to public scrutiny or examination by courts, at the same time spouses are *not* close kinsmen whose ties are given. The continuity of marriage depends in a direct way, as Hageners see it, on the satisfactory performance of roles.[1] Mutual care and concern must be positively demonstrated; yet pressure cannot be put on a spouse through appeal to the courts, or to informal settlement by compensation, for every issue which arises. Alternative mechanisms lie in the mutual long-term advantages to each to remain with the partner, which in turn enable acts of force and protest to be used with coercive effect. Most of the sanctions to which spouses have recourse can thus be classed as self-help.

Recourse to Self-help

If a wife neglects her work, the husband can strike or insult her; or even refuse to provide pigs or make gardens, threats only feasible over any length of time for a polygynist who has other wives on whom he can depend. The wife may well regard such pressures as an indication of deliberate neglect, which means her husband intends to be rid of her. Reciprocally, a woman may refuse to cook his food properly or deliber-

---

[1] These obligations are not as "incident to the relationship" as Radcliffe-Brown observes of marital relations in some African systems (1950:12).

ately go off on visits to avoid household chores. She may show her independence in the huffy manner with which she communicates to him that she is going into seclusion and cannot cook his meals. These are all devices employed in the main to draw attention to grievances in the hope that faults will be rectified. Demonstrating independence contains an appeal for the restoration of reciprocity.

There are other mechanisms by which this appeal is made. Either spouse can be driven by his or her grievances to a state of *popokl*. This may erupt in quarrelling or fighting, or in an extreme situation lead the husband to kill his wife or the wife to commit suicide. The threat of suicide is one which women make much more frequently than men. If, on the other hand, *popokl* is revealed by sickness through the intervention of ancestral ghosts, a return to health must be effected with confessions of what has caused the trouble.[1] More dramatically, the *popokl* person may become possessed by wild spirits and suffer a fit of madness. This tends to be utilized by women, but not men, against their spouses. A specialist has to be called in to cure the sufferer, in the course of which reasons for the *popokl* state of mind are again brought out. Expressions of grievance may take quite different forms; rather than inducing sickness, *popokl*-anger may incite a person to commit outrageous acts. A husband's invitation to his clansmen to have intercourse with a recalcitrant wife falls into this category; a woman employs her power of pollution to render food unfit for male consumption or burns down the men's house, as a slightly milder form of protest.

A number of these sanctions have already been referred to, but others are worth expansion. We may divide them into two classes: acts of outright aggression—beating, homicide, outrage; and injury inflicted on the self, either by a supernatural agency (*popokl*-sickness, madness) or by the aggrieved person's own hand (suicide). The contrasting nature of these appeals should not, however, obscure the fact that in all cases they stem from a condition of *popokl*, and, except in the successful commission of homicide or suicide,[2] are intended to remedy an unsatisfactory situation.

---

[1] Or else death from the illness brought on by *popokl* may result. There are stories of women who died this way because of *popokl* over debts, and others which parallel the circumstances of suicide (see below). In one instance a young wife supposedly died from *popokl* with both her husband and her father, the latter having cajoled her with presents to make her return to her spouse.

[2] And the husband's sexual revenge on his wife, by which he repudiates their relationship. The threat of death is carried in some of the self-inflicted sanctions, e.g. *popokl*-sickness or spirit-possession.

The self-inflicted injuries are no less oblique in their message than others which take a "more direct line of attack" (Lewis, 1966:315). What is interesting is that within the conjugal relationship husbands are more likely to express their *popokl* through inflicting injury on their spouse, while wives more frequently fall victim to self-injury. The forms are, however, by no means exclusively restricted to one or other sex.

Reasons for which women become possessed by wild spirits are similar to those which give rise to *popokl*-sickness. Indeed the mystical agents may be the same. Central Melpa tend to attribute madness (*kupør, kekelip*) to wild spirits, *kor wakl*, while Northern Melpa are more likely to make ancestral ghosts responsible (*kor* or *tipu wamb*). *Kor wakl* also themselves act as agents for the ghosts and inflict sicknesses, including fatal ones, on people. A fit of madness, which makes the victim run amok, babble nonsense, threaten others' lives, or disappear into the bush, sometimes brings to light the person's own guilt, typically an unconfessed act of incest. As frequently it is a revelation of *popokl*, the sick person complaining of a grievance rather than admitting to a sin.[1] Six tales of Central Melpa women's possession by *kor wakl* all revolve round grievances directed against the husband. In three cases the wife was angry over the disposal of pearl shells or pigs; in two the wife, who did not want to leave her husband, complained that he did not care for her and desired a divorce; in the final instance a husband had quarrelled with his wife for visiting home and leaving him the child to look after, the quarrel making her *popokl* in turn. Like *popokl*-sickness, spirit-possession can bring into focus complaints arising from situations where aggressive counteraction might provoke the other party into taking the very steps of which the patient is fearful, for example, that a woman's husband will divorce her. It draws attention to a plight rather than inflicting damage in protest, oriented thus to excite sympathy and avoid conflict. The imputation of supernatural intervention also carries with it the supposition either that the victim was justifiably aggrieved or that a wrong of some magnitude has been committed and must be put right. Cases recorded from the same area of men falling prey to *kor wakl* are not consistently concerned with their *popokl*, and few of them arose because of grievances against the wife.

In committing an outrage, women can exploit their attributes of uncleanliness. They may do so quite deliberately and openly, as when an

---

[1] There are some differences in the forms which madness takes, but I do not discuss the matter comprehensively here.

angry wife steps over a food oven. When a wife desires to drive another woman away she may have recourse to such devices, for to show *popokl* by leaving herself would play into the other woman's hands. An old Penambe man (an adolescent at the time) recalled the following series of exploits, a sequence of mutual reprisals between husband and wife, the relish with which he went over the details indicating some of the amusement men derive from seeing cowives fight for a husband. The story is quite a rough one by Hagen standards.

*The story-teller's "father" (FB) had one wife and tried to obtain a second. The established first-married woman (who had two children) was extremely upset that her husband should want to marry again. The pair quarrelled, the wife asking if all that was going to happen to the pigs she had raised was their expenditure in bridewealth for another woman; the man maintaining that he could take as many wives as he pleased. When she began quarrelling with the bride, who had been brought to his house, the husband intervened on the latter's behalf and broke her head open with a stick. At the time of killing three pigs to take as *penal kng* to the home of the new wife, the first woman tussled with the men in her effort to prevent their departure—whereat her husband struck at her again, this time with an axe. She was left bound and tied up in the house while the party took off the cooked meat. That evening, after she had been released, she turned on the bride and hit her; the new wife threatened to go off to her own place, because she was tired of being the constant target of the older woman's *wølik* (jealousy). The husband said she should do no such thing and grabbed at the senior wife, apparently breaking her arm with a blow from a stake of wood. The husband and his new bride, along with others including the story-teller, were still in the house when the first wife climbed on to the roof, tore a hole in the thatch and urinated on those below. She shouted out that the husband should either get rid of the second woman or she would set fire to the house and kill her. At this point he gave in (it was surmised he feared the wife would kill him as well with poison) and sadly told his young bride to return home. Shame at his wife's actions made him compensate with a pig those who had been insulted by her public exposure.

The example shows how violence may precipitate further violence. A threat lies in the husband's superior strength, which sometimes leads to manslaughter. There are cases of men provoked to lash out at their wives, picking up a weapon lying near by or dealing them a hard blow, with fatal, if unintended, results. However, a husband might deliberately kill a wife whom he suspects wants to leave him for another man, or whose ways are promiscuous, while poisoners were executed with their husband's permission. In such cases the wife has proved herself to be no wife; but murdering her is also a quasi-suicidal act on the husband's part, for he has destroyed something of potential value to himself. Here the distinction between other-inflicted and self-inflicted injury is not an absolute one.

The typical circumstance in which women act on a threat of suicide is dual alienation from both husband and home kin. After a marital quarrel the wife retreats; but far from taking her side, her brother or father try to despatch her back with conciliatory gifts to placate the husband. A wife who is rebuffed in her demand for kinsmen's support against an injury done her by her husband may hang herself out of frustation and for revenge (the *popokl* ghost is able to attack its survivors, it is said). Of 29 cases of accomplished suicide, 22 were of women and 7 of men; the same ratio is repeated in 4 attempted suicides, 3 female and 1 male. These occurrences, which I heard about in 1964–5, span 40–50 years in time. 20 accomplished suicides were of married women and, in eleven of these, the imputed reason was that the wife wanted to leave her husband but was forced to return to him by her parents. Other cases are explained as the result of quarrels with either the woman's parents or her husband, offence at insults, shame at a *wapra* reputation, and inability to endure pain. Women are frequently quite young, while among men imputed reasons for suicide include the frustration of old, no longer fully active men, who are neglected by their sons or close relatives. The theme of impotence and frustration in attributed motives is stated not in general but in specific terms, the suicide being described as *popokl* with a particular set of people, especially those on whom he or she depends for support and recognition.[1] The threat of suicide may be used by a young girl to coerce her parents into allowing her to marry where she wishes or letting her run home after marriage with an uncongenial partner. Eating the *mi* substance makes the same appeal to their sympathy.

All these attention-gaining devices could be classed as acts of self-help. The protest takes the form of a violent attack, or threat of it, about

---

[1] Suicides of this nature perhaps provide a rough index of such dependency relations. In situations where a woman is strongly dependent on her husband, quarrels with this person alone might cause suicide (cf. Berndt, R.M., 1962:Ch. 10); in Hagen it is the subsequent rejection by her kin as well which leads to drastic action (and cf. Brown, 1969:95 on Chimbu). It is interesting to note that whereas in real life suicides (among women at least) may stem from a condition of *popokl*-anger against persons on whom they depend, in the myths recorded by Vicedom (1943–8:3) suicides (here committed almost as often by men as by women) frequently follow the total withdrawal of such a person, and are committed in "grief" (likely to be a compound of *popokl* and *kaemb*) at the death of a guardian or spouse.

which something has to be done. In a sense the acts themselves are all reprehensible: outrage and aggression obviously so, and self-inflicted injury insofar as the person has let his state of *popokl* dominate all else. Along with the withdrawal of services and neglect of duties, however, it is the first class of acts which receives most criticism. While they bring attention to a grievance, they aggravate rather than dissolve conflict.

It is in relation to this that one can place the act of running home. Threats of divorce are commonly made by women, and are implicit in appeals to their own kin or to Councillors. I have shown that in the settlement of disputes, women may take an active part in paying or receiving compensation, or else regard payments transacted by men as on their behalf. I never heard any complaints by a woman that she, rather than her menfolk, should have paid or been paid compensation. It is clear that such transactions enable women to effect adjustments in their social relationships much as men do. Women may even occasionally do a man-like act in being especially generous in payments. One area, however, extremely important to women, in which adjustments cannot easily be reached in such terms is the conjugal relationship. Formal *mi* sanctions are also inappropriate. It takes a deliberate show of violence before rights to compensation are recognised (Cf. Epstein, 1969: 159; Goody, J.R., 1962:53.). Dissatisfaction or disappointment is expressed through economic sanctions (withdrawal of services) and other measures of self-help. Of these, the threat of divorce is a blatant challenge to the continuity of the relationship. It is both an act of retaliation and a display of injury.

The woman who goes home to her kin does so because she feels she has been hurt, their support of her demonstrating how unjustifiably she has been injured. Sometimes women, aggrieved that they have not been treated as a wife, express extreme *popokl* by running off to another man from whom they hope to be retrieved. To the abandoned husband, however, his wife's desertion bears the character of aggression.[1] A woman should think of her husband. A wife too hasty in turning to her kinsmen for support is like (it was maintained)[2] the man who puts his hand to his

---

[1] See Bohannan, 1957:141–2: what an initiator considers reprisals for an injury, the other may take as aggression.

[2] The Hagen contrast between the (admired) men of peace and the (criticized) men of war is commonly made. Self-help often leads to an escalation of reprisals, when retaliation is "more serious than the initial breach of norm" (Ploeg, 1969:133). Strauss (1962:240) comments on the criticism a man receives from his clansmen for acting so hastily over a crime that he jeopardizes his chances of compensation.

weapons as soon as a quarrel comes up. Such a man makes a fight of the most minor issue. In the same way, a woman who jumps to her feet and rushes home lacks self-control (she is "mad, or unreliable, in her mind", *noman oronga wulya purum*). One who stays and straightens things out with her husband is, on the contrary, like the man who is ready to discuss matters and accept compensation.

There are various reasons why threats to divorce may appear aggressive to men. Since failure in the performance of domestic duties does not constitute standard grounds for divorce, dissolution is readily related to the disposition of the spouses, especially that of the woman. While she may use the threat to coerce her spouse into paying her attention and so adjusting his behaviour, the husband is hurt by the provocative suggestion that his interests are not really her concern. Her *noman* is not set on helping him. Another factor is the whole relationship of divorce disputes to others. Difficulties for the men involved in confrontation over a bridewealth return leads them to pin blame on the wife. While these difficulties were always present if peaceful settlement was desired, the modern court system has probably sharpened and exacerbated them. It has also thrown into relief the high-handed nature of self-help. In the past, women's actions in running home would have been congruent with the manner in which men sought the support of their clansmen or seized wealth they felt was due. Their behaviour encompassed aggressiveness of the same order. To the injury which husbands feel as the victim of such acts, is nowadays added, we might surmise, a measure of frustration, insofar as women's recourse to extreme self-help (e.g. desertion) cannot be met by unrestrained self-help on the part of men. Most people see themselves as following "law"; and while middle-range acts of self-help (e.g. economic sanctions) are in practice still taken, overt violence has been constrained. This shows, it would seem, in the way in which men in the 1960's provoked into killing a wife frequently followed the deed by giving themselves up to the administration. Yet at the same time, in order to have her complaints heard by the court a woman must help herself by instigating serious conflicts. In resorting to such means she is putting herself into a blameable position.

11

Judicial Status

Mae-Enga women are described by Meggitt as jural minors (1964:220–1); without title to valuable property and rarely participating in public affairs, they remain the wards of males for life. But he also depicts male–female relations in power terms: Mae-Enga men have "won their battle", whereas Kuma men, on the other hand, "continually strive to dominate women". A contrast can perhaps be made between "jural" and "judicial" status. Rights and duties entailed in various roles may receive general acknowledgement; but the extent to which rights can be exercised is another matter. Courts illustrate the point that for Hagen women their political status has an effect upon the settlement of issues which concern them.

Fortes' discussion of familial and politico–jural domains in the realm of kinship is relevant here. He argues, "the rules and sanctions that lie behind kinship relations and institutions . . . cannot be understood without regard to the political and jural constraints that are generated in the extra-familial domain of social structure" (Fortes, 1969:71). In Hagen, conjugal rights and duties have a public legitimacy in that they are upheld in open discussions, one arena for these being dispute settlements. Spouses, it is reiterated, with reference to various specific examples, should care for each other. The value put on marital stability is supported by sanctions derived from the political framework of society (marriages and transactions associated with them being a dimension of inter-group relations). Obligations inherent in the husband-wife relationship are thus indeed related to the politico-jural domain. This is particularly so as far as positive pressure encourages spouses to perform their duties and maintain their marriage; but in situations involving breach of duty or threat of divorce other issues become relevant. Women have status not only vis-à-vis their particular husbands but vis-à-vis men in general. In a society where political activity (including the establishment of alliances through marriages ties) is seen to be largely the concern of males, political values may be used to confront females. Hagen women cannot really be called jural minors, that is, as having no responsibility for their actions, but the extent to which they themselves can make claims, their judicial status, is related to the fact that they are in a way "political minors".

Property and Oratory

While women have an important contribution to make towards the accumulation of wealth, by and large effective disposal is in men's hands. I earlier pointed to the existence of an implicit dichotomy in what Hageners regard as major attributes of male and female roles, to which I gave the terms transactor and producer. Many disputes which concern women, whether handled privately or in courts, are resolved through the payment of compensation, made in wealth objects (pigs, shells) as well as smaller articles (female clothing, bags or ornaments). Thus women's participation in the transactions must be bound up with their ability to dispose of wealth goods. Liability to make (or ability to obtain) compensation is an aspect of property-owning status.

That people give and receive valuables on behalf of a woman does not, however, come simply from her lack of complete control over these items. One old Penambe man, it is true, commented that while if a father hits his child the wife may persuade him to give them (herself and the child together) a present, should the mother strike him or her, "there is no road" for compensation because women are rubbish (*korpa*). Yet a woman is not exactly like a rubbish man, or even someone temporarily without valuables seeking a loan; rather it is the case that certain categories of persons have liabilities to provide for her or the right to receive on her behalf and may do so independently of the woman's participation. Here we must distinguish between payments involving her kin and those involving her husband.

When her kin are awarded compensation for injury done her, this is because of their rights in her as a female clan member, comparable to their rights in male members to whose defence they also come. Payments on her behalf to her husband recognize the accompanying obligations. But although a married woman has identity as a clan member, much less than a man is she herself able to mobilize persons in her support from outside her closely related set of fathers and brothers. This in fact modifies the strength of a clan's obligations to its female members. While a woman in a sense has a general right to help from her clan, it is likely to be activated only at the instigation of her own father or brother. Conversely, it is only where she has kept in touch with the latter that they and others of her clan will claim rights to indemnification. These people are the ones primarily concerned in her affairs. Often the span of such persons corresponds to a *tepam-kang^emal*) lineage group, and I have used the phrase "lineage kin" to indicate a woman's close fathers (father and father's brothers) and brothers. It would be misleading, however, to give the impression that the lineage is a group definable in terms of its jural control over members. When the lineage is a large one, for example, more distant members may be no more supportive than others of a woman's sub-sub-clan.

The rights her close kin have to share in compensation which is also seen to include the woman herself (as for assault) comprise some kind of return for their support; but she cannot return their support in kind—because she is a woman she does not fight or speak on behalf of others. Her help is covert: putting pressure on a husband to make good his debts, purveying poison for them, and so on. There is a further factor: that in some contexts a woman is felt to be compensated only when her kin also receive compensation, and even when they alone may be paid. A sister, on the other hand, is not usually a recipient of dispute compensations paid to or made on behalf of a brother. She may seek revenge for his death (through poison), but does not, as some of the men of his clan do, stand to be indemnified if he is killed in war, hurt, insulted, and so on. And while she may be the target of attack, she does not pay out wealth. In short, women cannot participate to the extent that men do in the affairs of their lineage or clan and cannot represent it by giving or receiving compensation for other members. Although they may suffer moral injury when damage is done to a clansman, they are not jurally injured. A simple designation of jural minor, however, does not quite cover their status for in respect of themselves they do receive compensation (as well as their kin), and when payments are made to them alone they are in a sense representing the claims of their kinsmen. The situation is further complicated if we consider wealth transactions outside the context of dispute compensations, for in bridewealth and funerary payments they do have claims as lineage and sometimes sub-clan or clan members. Here, payments made to them are often merged, depending on context, with gifts intended for their husband/brother. We may summarize this by saying that a woman's jural status differs from that of male members of her natal clan in that for many payments which accompany the settlement of disputes she is not liable on their behalf as they are for her, while her judicial status as a female who cannot fight or come to the open assistance of her brothers means also that she cannot count on mobilizing more than a small segment of her sub-clan or clan in her own defence. It is these persons who in practice carry most liability in respect of their daughter or sister.

The rights and liabilities of a husband differ from those invested in a woman's kin. Spouses have a joint household and joint interest in property, so that damage done to a wife is also damage to the husband. A woman contributes her labour to the raising of pigs and has limited claims on their bestowal; if a third party is demanding compensation for a wrong for which she is responsible, then the husband's liability to provide payment is partly an outcome of the fact that some of his property can also be defined as hers. Husbands manage, however, to contest both liability for all their wife's acts (as over petty thieving, when a woman can use minor female articles) and the wife's ownership of major valuables. It must be noted again that often compensation claims are paid directly to the husband. Since a woman cannot in turn dispose of valuables without her husband's consent, he may be seen either as helping his wife to raise the requisite wealth or as taking charge of the transaction. While, then, the wife has certain moral claims on her husband to use what she may regard as their joint property, the husband can act as the ultimate possessor, so that she is in this sense under his jural authority. The politico-jural value upholding such a relationship is indeed that which designates females as propertyless (*korpa*), although evidence has been given of the extent to which women themselves dispute its relevance or men fail to apply it consistently.

Quite separate from the transfer of wealth is the allocation of responsibility. Women are held both to be responsible for their own actions and to be persons who can suffer injury; there is no question, for example, that they are regarded as young children, blameless because they lack understanding of the consequences of their acts. The concept of injury is "bound up with assumptions about the nature of the human person"

(Epstein, 1967b:382), adult women like adult men having *noman* (social consciousness, conscience). They do not retain the status of a child. The notion that women are responsible persons, and may be both blamed and offended against, has been encouraged by the absorption of money into the compensation system. Far from resisting the idea that women should be made to suffer for what they have done, men may require them to express this responsibility by paying with resources of their own.

It is not sufficient, however, to deduce areas of jural responsibility from the structure of compensation payments. The making of such payments did not in the past take place in exclusively judicial terms and today in the courts such payments do not flow automatically from legal proof that an offence has been committed. The position of women in disputes makes little sense without a consideration of the fact that compensation procedures are part of the political system;[1] in other words, they are bound up with the kinds of relations and attitudes generated in the confrontation of groups (clans, tribes). These affect a woman's participation vis-à-vis men, and make relevant her group membership to the outcome of a dispute.

When men go over the heads of the women concerned and pay compensation to one another, they are conducting a transaction. Women do not normally make exchanges with men and their partial exclusion from the compensation nexus is one aspect of this. I have already referred to the element of bargaining, and to the implication that compensation peacefully agreed upon should reconcile the disputants. Thus, in spite of the fact that proof of a wrong-doing may be established in court, the guilty person sometimes, aggressively, refuses to hand over the requisite compensation, either because he feels he has been done down in the argument or because he has no real desire to mend relations; there may be little that Councillors and Komitis can do. Whether or not payments were made in the past often depended upon the relative strength of the two parties brought into dispute (as noted in Strauss, 1962: 254–5). The present unofficial courts also, like traditional modes of settlement, have both political and judicial aspects. Decisions emerge from the segmentary opposition of conflicting parties, and entail assertions of strength which put weak or low-status men at a disadvantage. On these grounds, a woman who cannot readily muster support is at a like

---

[1] Cf. Gulliver 1963:297–8; Pospisil's contrast between political decision and legal judgment (1958:262); Epstein *in press*.

disadvantage. In-married wives are thus in a potentially weak situation, exacerbated when they cannot depend on unequivocal help from their male kinsmen. But women are not only generally weak; they are in a sense regarded as being quite outside the sphere of political action. In addition to the inappropriateness of women taking wholly on themselves transactions of any importance, court situations often require the solidary alignment of group members[1] for one another's support—support which we have noted in other circumstances (e.g. ceremonial exchange and warfare) women are unable to give or be given unreservedly. Disputes directly affecting inter-group relations (such as theft between neighbouring clans) frequently bring about such alignments of men. Those concerning women's marriages are at an opposite extreme, where the whole issue revolves around interpersonal ties across group boundaries. In between fall other disputes concerning women.

When a woman has been clearly wronged—the victim of assault or theft—then her kin or her husband will be anxious to secure damages on her behalf, since their own rights have by implication been violated. On the other hand, the same men may fail to defend women themselves charged with some wrong. An accused wife often has to provide her own defence. But this is not simply a case of men ready to claim where they have interests, but reluctant to defend for fear of incurring blame. A husband, for example, often cannot come automatically to his wife's defence, as he might to a brother's. The contexts in which he is likely to assist his brother are political ones, when some crime has been committed outside the clan, and settlement involves the clan or segments of it as more or less solidary units. These are much more common than acts of overt aggression within the clan. Women, apart from poisoning, tend not to commit politically significant crimes. "Wives do not steal from distant places", it was said. "They steal only from nearby". The thefts and quarrels in which they are involved are with their husbands, husband's brothers and the wives of these men, or with their parents-in-law and cowives;[2] or else with their own close kinsmen.[3] This means that support cannot be given unambiguously to a woman defendant. If she steals from members of her husband's sub-clan or their wives, then her husband is put into a difficult position. While he is partly responsible

---

[1] Big-men have rather different roles.

[2] These account for 18/22 cases listed in Appendix VII, involving persons of their husband's sub-clan or clan-section.

[3] A further three cases.

for what his wife does, he also has loyalties to the persons to whom she has given offence, and may himself be outraged by her actions.

A small court which I witnessed at Kelua in 1964 concerned two brothers and their wives. Makel had a pig which he failed to stall properly, and it went into the garden of his full brother, Kinti. Kinti's wife came to tell her husband, exaggerating the extent of damage with the report that the whole crop was destroyed. Incited by this, Kinti went to Makel's wife and blamed her for having let the pig out. The two began to fight, but this was broken up by other people. Kinti's wife had also been involved in the fighting; Makel's wife reported the incident to the Komiti of her husband's clan. At the subsequent court, the two brothers both blamed Kinti's wife for causing all the trouble and lying about what damage had been done; a woman should not make brothers quarrel. The Komiti said that she should pay Makel's wife some small amount in compensation for having struck her, and Kinti agreed, adding that she could find it herself (meaning from her kin): he would not help her. He protested when the Komiti suggested that he provide the compensation himself so that they could finish the court quickly. In the end it was said that Kinti and his wife should give Makel and his wife £A2, and Makel would return £A1 to show that he had no quarrel with his brother, and in recognition of his own carelessness in letting the pig escape. But Kinti tried to avoid making the payment, saying that the fault lay with his wife and not himself. Finally his wife was sent off to fetch 10/- which she had of her own, and Kinti made this up to £A2. In no part of the hearing at which I was present did Kinti defend his wife by saying that she had been carried away into thinking that her garden was ruined, and Makel was at fault since he was the owner of the pig (the latter argument is heard frequently enough on other occasions). It was left to the Komiti to comment that there was a "little wrong" on Makel's side too.

A few months later (I was told subsequently) the reverse happened—Kinti's pig got into Makel's garden. Makel's wife yelled at Kinti, calling him a *wuᵉ etamb* ("dwarf rubbish man"), like a toad with short legs and a bad skin. Makel, ashamed at hearing his brother insulted, made the woman give Kinti 10/-. If it had been a matter of the garden, simply, then Kinti might have given her a gift in compensation, but he (Makel) was not going to have his brother treated like this, and she must pay for it.

In such cases the attitude of the wife's own kin is likely to be one of careful indifference over issues which they can choose to regard as private affairs of the woman's husband and his kin. Were they to interfere, their defence would at once lend the conflict something of a political character, since they represent the interests of another clan. For reasons of their own, as we have seen, they may decide to give assistance or (equally) to withhold it. Women's crimes are thus frequently non-political, especially when committed against others of their husband's clan; but there is an inherent threat of political confrontation should appeal be made to their home kin, and in these circumstances men tend to take over the business of transactions on their behalf.

Little articulate support can be expected from other women. I noted in the discussion of divorce cases (Chapter 9) that a woman defendant may have no one at all to speak on her behalf. Her menfolk may be liable to provide compensation for her, but they will not necessarily come to her public defence. Responsible for her own actions, she (and not those liable) is usually blamed. This brings out another component of court behaviour.

Oratory in Hagen eyes is a special political skill, one means by which persons demonstrate influence over others. It is through his words that a Councillor not only has to show that wrong has been done but persuade the disputants that they have an interest in coming to a settlement. In courts, as on other public occasions, men make the speeches. Women rarely offer unsolicited comments. They have little actual experience in speech-making, and often appear reticent when asked to talk as principal defendant. This overt reticence is linked to men's suspicions that their arts of persuasion are covert and clandestine; females entice others secretly rather than confront them publicly.[1] They are well known to be less effective in argument than men. Women cry, one is told, when some man has them beaten in an interchange, letting forth a torrent of abuse more forceful and articulate than a woman could counter, so that their only retreat is into tears. Inarticulateness on public occasions is encouraged by the very limited participation demanded of them, usually restricted to direct response following questions. No one expects women to contribute to the general discussion. They thus both lack skill at public speaking and would receive little serious attention if they attempted it.

Women, in short, cannot conduct any but the most minor settlement of grievances themselves. They have to persuade others—their kinsmen, or husband, a Councillor or Komiti—to heed their complaints. This may be hard when the very complaints are against members of their husband's clan or others with whom the men have no wish to provoke a quarrel. Councillors and Komitis can judge a grievance as too trivial for consideration. The frequency with which women resort to acts of outrage or other forms of self-help is some indication of this

---

[1] A similar contrast is found in their actions during warfare—they employ poison not spears.

difficulty. Sometimes women choose public occasions on which they can state their grievances with some drama—drawing on to a ceremonial ground, for example, a bundle of broken sweet potato vines to demonstrate how a garden has been rooted up by pigs, as I saw one woman do in 1964 while her husband's clan were giving *moka*. Obtaining a hearing is, of course, in itself no guarantee of success. There is more than one account of women unsuccessfully causing trouble which they hoped would secure a divorce. In one instance a menstruating wife stepping over the cooking pits indeed brought about a court hearing, but instead of being allowed the divorce she wanted, was made to find compensation for her husband. The over-riding factor in this case was that she had children. In another instance a wife who wished to leave her husband paid innumerable visits home, but was thwarted in her desires by the faithfulness with which her spouse constantly followed her with conciliatory presents.

Women are, nevertheless, in a rather better position nowadays to gain attention for their complaints than was the case in the past. Married women tend to go first to the Komiti of their husband's clan, clearly an advantage if their kin are dead or far away. It is the close kin of their natal clan, however, rather than its Councillor or Komitis from whom they may also seek help, although the latter often come in at a later stage. To some extent Councillors and Komiti see themselves as less partisan in their reaction to crime or other causes of disputes than a woman's husband or kinsmen might be. Women are able to mobilise their support through appealing to this ideal, or under the threat of drawing administration attention to the trouble. Although big-men in the past might also have had more interest in peaceful settlement than in perpetual resort to self-help, apparently they were not persons to whom women felt they could turn, as they do to Councillors and Komitis. The latter may even urge people to bring their disputes to them rather than settle them privately.[1] In divorce cases, however, the desire not to appear too partisan and to avoid accusations of greasing may make a Komiti act particularly sternly towards his own kinswomen; some Komitis, on the contrary, exploit their position, in making decisions (as over the return of bridewealth) in favour of their own clan. The very fact that

---

[1] Women tend to take minor complaints to a Councillor or Komiti, as they do to their father or brothers, whereas men usually go to them when some demonstrable injury as been done, till then handling the matter themselves. Many women's grievances thus do not precipitate formal action, while most of men's do.

Councillors and Komitis do to some extent see themselves as "like Kiaps" has strengthened their hand in one direction. Although they complain of the lack of effective sanctions at their disposal in dealing with offenders, in court cases concerning women punitive intentions are frequently expressed.

Punitive reactions against men in the past mainly took the form of revenge and physical retaliation; an element of this exists sometimes in the imposition of compensation payments, especially when these are also fines to the court (as in the case of the reluctant monogamist, pp. 349). The concatenation of circumstances which often surround women's court appearances lends greater prominence to such an element. A woman defendant may be isolated during the hearing, both hesitant to speak and without articulate support from men. To this is added the fact that she is fully culpable but not necessarily liable to provide compensation. Those conducting the proceedings are provoked into making forceful threats in order to induce her to talk, or recommending that afterwards she should be beaten. Adultery accusations in particular frequently end with the latter recommendation. In the strict sense, the only crimes[1] (as opposed to deliberate pollution and torts) Hageners can be said to recognize are the use of poison, by either sex, and sexual wrongs, especially extreme promiscuity among women. On discovery, these receive automatic and general censure. The distinction is not a particularly useful one, however, since most offences committed within the clan come under the general censure of other clansmen, as well as clan ancestors. But it does lead one to consider whether any offences are conceived of as against society at large, and insofar as this is at all the case poisoning and promiscuity are treated as such. Women accused of such crimes (and low-status men accused of poisoning) invariably put themselves beyond the open support of their kin; the acts are subversive, challenge dominance, threaten values. There is possibly some carry over of fears aroused by such crimes into the revelations made in divorce and adultery cases.[2]

The parallel between these court hearings and the treatment of female poisoners (say) in the past is not of course quite exact. Poisoners

---

[1] A term I have been using loosely to cover offences of all kinds.
[2] Berndt, R.M. (1962:325, 377) suggests that "informal" court procedure among the Kamano and their neighbours highlights violence, for which other outlets nowadays are few, punishment providing excitement and emotional satisfaction for the spectators as well as the complainant.

were tortured with the clear intent that they should be made to suffer for their wrongs, and the resultant maiming or killing was also a form of revenge. But modern court procedure on the whole constrains rather than encourages violence; and in spite of their threats, Councillors and Komitis are often reluctant at the last minute actually to lay hands on the woman they have been promising to beat, even where this would not meet the disapproval of her husband or kin. In most cases they are dealing not with outright demonstrations of un-wifely behaviour, which would forfeit humane consideration, but with indifference or acts of minor disloyalty. It is openly admitted that beating is little cure for recalcitrance. Instead, considerable verbal aggression may be directed at the woman, who is roundly abused for all the trouble she has caused.

From the woman's point of view non-co-operation can be a powerful weapon. In courts men tend to be the more pugnacious, both defending themselves more positively and pressing more forcefully with their charges. While I do not want to overdraw the picture, the sullen, silent female defendant is a Hagen stereotype. From cases I have witnessed apparent withdrawal is a characteristic pose, frequently though by no means always resorted to in divorce and adultery suits. Where open and violent quarrelling has erupted, or the dispute concerns theft or pig trespass, or some issue between women themselves, the disputant women are likely to be much more vocal. Inarticulateness itself frustrates the infuriated men handling the dispute, who are trying in vain to get to the root of the conflict. But a woman who knows that her husband or her own kin will provide the compensation may have little personal incentive to defend her position, although when charged with adultery most wives flatly deny their responsibility. In the court itself, a woman defendant is able to insulate herself, professing that she has no money or other resources, where an accused man, trying to avoid payment, would argue his defence to the end. Personal defences may of course be made in private afterwards. It is my impression that private retaliation, once the court is over, is not often taken on a guilty wife or sister. Men do grumble if too much wealth seems to be being spent in making payments on their behalf.

Several accounts of disputes settled informally suggest that there is a positive value in reticence—a woman who does not answer back her male accuser will be more lightly treated than one who embarks on vituperations. Women who argue with or abuse men are likely to make things more difficult for themselves (as in the instance of the two brothers with quarrelsome wives, p. 265). In formal divorce cases, a young woman wishing to leave her husband may be well aware that in the end the divorce will be attributed to her own disposition, and she has nothing to gain by being explicit in her reasons for complaint. The stubbornness imputed to her is sometimes in fact a real one. Men will be anxious to talk, to discuss, to find out where motives lie and what the "true disposition" of the parties are; but a woman can gain her own way by simply refusing to co-operate in a verbal argument which she knows she is likely to lose.

I have undoubtedly simplified what is a complicated interaction between a woman's own inclination, others' expectations of her and how she pre-judges the situation. But it is suggestible that in this context many women do *not* seem to share male values, and notions of honour or shame do not goad them into public self-justification. Certainly there is an element of vengeance in women's stance of withdrawal.

To summarize; in several respects women are not jural minors: they are responsible for their actions and blamed for what they do; they act as principals in court cases which directly involve them. On the other hand, women negotiate compensations to only a limited extent, since men own the major valuables often needed for payment; their husband and their lineage kin have a liability in respect of them, whereas they do not have reciprocal liability for the men; their chances of convening a court of any magnitude over a dispute without the support of men are negligible; finally, the political aspects of the court situation, with its emphasis on transactions and oratorical skills, place women at a disadvantage. It is useful, therefore, to draw attention not only to women's formal jural status, but to their position within the judicial system; women are political minors, and this affects the chances they have of pressing for claims within their rights. Being able to exploit this position, however, provides them with a degree of personal freedom.

The Factor of Age

It is younger women in particular who appear intimidated by courts and are reticent, if not taciturn, when called upon to speak. Their elders conduct themselves with more assurance. With age, a woman seems to find it easier to manipulate the court system and although older women may not have so frequent recourse to Councillors and Komitis as young women do, they are both able to apply more pressure when aggrieved and are themselves more likely to yield to pressure in the informal settlement of disputes. I would regard this as a direct result of their growing importance and stature. Although there is no change in the jural rights and liabilities carried by their husband and kin, the complaints of older married women will be taken more seriously. Moreover, for various reasons a woman herself rather than her kin may be the recipient of compensation; however fortuitous such reasons are, they affect older rather than younger persons. There is a greater chance that the former's kin will be dead, and age in some cases brings with it gradual dissociation from them. This is one reason why it is useful to keep distinct a woman's ability to act in courts and her power in informal settlement (judicial status) from the formal responsibilities she has or others have in her (jural status). Women's judicial status undergoes some development through time.

I have already mentioned that greater effort is made to ensure that a mother with children does not leave her husband than in the case of a childless wife. Not only does having children result in specific pressures on a mother to remain with her husband, but she herself may be more amenable to pressure, if leaving him means that the children lose a father (or in rarer cases, the mother). As a mother, a woman is under less suspicion from her husband's people as a possible carrier of poison. The actual periods of child-bearing remove a polygynist's wife from direct sexual competition with her cowives, although in fact they may engender equally bitter accusations of more general neglect during the long period of *post partum* taboo. Children are, moreover, a focus of interest on the part of ancestral ghosts on each side, and their illnesses and deaths may heighten tensions between the spouses. By the same token, the danger of putting the children's health into jeopardy operates as a sanction on the behaviour of both spouses alike.

Precipitating factors which lead to divorce—the particular quarrels, conflicts and frustrations affecting individuals—change somewhat with age, and so do the enabling conditions. Although women can always resort to running away, the tacit and much less the open support of her kin is harder to obtain the longer the marriage has endured, and she meets with more general disapproval from people at large. Divorce in effect becomes harder. But the developing stability of marriage over time is probably related also to the fact that spouses acquire commitment towards each other. Moral obligations develop between husband and wife (Fortes, 1949:105). The very fact that a wife has worked for her husband, and tended his gardens and herds, puts her into a position of being able to demand reciprocity in his care for her. Thus a woman who has proved herself a good wife expects sympathy from other people for difficulties she experiences with her husband. Poisoning or promiscuous behaviour by contrast, forfeits such consideration. The satisfactory performance of duties thus becomes to some extent a moral basis on which claims on the other partner can be made. This position is achieved; in practical terms, if the marriage is a first one for both spouses, it may not be reached for some years. (A young man sometimes delays systematic garden work, for example, till the birth of his first child.) Women also gradually acquire knowledge of their husband's developing affairs, and an interest in the disposal of pigs and shells. In this sense the older woman becomes a more genuine participant in compensations given and received on her behalf by her husband.

Although causes for dissatisfaction must multiply with increasing involvement, conflicts as often reach solution. For one, disputes arising from exchanges which a woman's husband and her own kin will have established between themselves may be settled in their own terms, independently of her, whereas in the early years of marriage she is invariably involved. Pressure may still indeed be put on the other partner through the wife, but the more there is at stake, the greater a threat of divorce increases in effectiveness as a sanction—promoting the desired readjustment without leading to actual dissolution.

Women themselves, as their marriage matures, use the same threat with increasing success. The notion of feminine irresponsibility is thereby kept alive, even though actual intention to obtain a divorce lies far from an elderly woman's mind when she goes on a prolonged visit home or badgers a Komiti with complaints. Sometimes a wife arrives at her brother's settlement, the younger children with her, explaining with some explicitness that she will return in a week or two when she thinks her husband has learnt his lesson. With no surviving brothers, she may go off instead to a married daughter. An older woman's resort to self-help need not even be a means to draw public attention to her situation and thus initiate a court. She may simply intend to coerce her husband into acting as she wants or into feeling remorse for his past behaviour. Failing to cook his meals or tend his pigs, perhaps leaving him the care of older children, aside from any threats to his exchange partnerships, are effective pressures from a mature mother and housewife, but of little force from a newly-wed bride. The former's actions of self-help are thus likely to be more calculated, and have less the character of despairing gestures. They are not such an extreme test of her position (Colson, 1958: 143). In talking about divorce (and the same is true of suicide) people tend to imply that actors are oldish, established women whose menfolk are heavily involved in exchanges, whereas in fact in both cases the more established the marriage is, the less likely it is that the threat will be translated into action. From this we can gauge the positive success of the sanctions.

In 1965, a middle-aged woman and her Kawelka husband quarrelled over the distribution of some pork, which he wanted to give to several people and she entirely to an old sick paternal uncle of hers. In *popokl* she abandoned her husband, taking her little daughter with her, and spent the next two months at her brother's place, some two hours' walk away. She returned regularly to her own gardens to harvest food each day which she took off "home" for herself and her daughter. Her pigs were tended by her son's wife, to whom her husband had also to turn for food. She had no intention of leaving him permanently, but would not return till he had realised that he should have taken account of her.

Occasionally, however, threats rebound.

Again in 1965, a youngish-middle-aged man living uxorilocally at Kelua quarrelled with his elderly wife, whom he had inherited as a widow. She accused him of not bothering to put the hens away at night, and he retorted that she had had nothing to do all day (and could therefore carry out this task), whereas he had business talking in men's houses. She had grumbled that she spent all her time looking after the pigs and working in the gardens, but the husband's angry reply was that she was an old woman to be such a humbug. He was a young man, full of "grease" (*kopong*), but she was not of his "skin" (i.e. was lucky he married her). Her threat (made before on similar occasions) to go off to her married daughter by a former husband elicited the easy response that she could go to her own kin if she wanted! He would retrieve a former "wife" (*amb wapra*) of his. The whole matter was a subject of much comment the next day when her two brothers (both unmarried low-status men) were engaged on preparing a joint garden with her husband, along with help from neighbours. Her own version was that of course her brothers would not want her to leave and go to her daughter's place. To me she protested about her husband's willingness to let her go off—what a thing to have said: why should he tell her to go? Were they not husband and wife, who should be together in one place?

An older woman is able to act more forcefully towards members of her husband's community,[1] and assumes initiative in coming to informal agreement over disputes and in making reconciliatory gifts. She is able to bring greater influence to bear on her husband's people, and her own good will in turn is valued by them. We have seen (Chapter 2) that outside the mother-/daughter-in-law nexus wives of a residential group are not forced into close co-operation with one another. The young bride has no easy and immediate basis for solidarity with these people, and friendships are built up only gradually. At an informal, personal level the older woman may expect encouragement from other wives of her husband's lineage and sub-clan, where the new wife encounters indifference. It remains true that in the public arena of a court, her husband and his male kin are not any more likely to come to the defence of an older rather than a younger woman; but there is a greater possibility that the grievance will be resolved before it reaches court dimensions. Although she will never contribute independently to court discussions in the manner of men, the older woman is more articulate as a defendant and more persistent as a plaintiff.[2]

It is perhaps redundant to state this is not a society in which simple seniority carries high status. Old age is accorded some respect, often sympathetic pity (kaemb), but per se little prestige. Once past their middle years most women lose rather than gain stature, and by contrast with the roles of sister, daughter, wife and mother, that of "grandmother" is of little significance beyond intra-familial domestic relations. Few women in any case have living grandchildren of any age, and their important relations are still with their husbands and own children.

Extreme old age brings with it a greater dependency on such persons, as ties with the home kin finally recede. At the same time, beyond the years of child-bearing age, threat of divorce becomes an inappropriate sanction. The old woman in any case is likely to have too many obvious reasons of her own for staying at her husband's place, as the figures on the number of non-married widows who elect to stay on their husband's territory indicate. At the peak years of her contributions to the household, then, at a time when exchanges with her kin are still flourishing, a woman has most sanctions at her disposal. Eventually these decline, and the very old may suffer a position of helplessness, their imminent death alone holding a threat of any power. It was with such an air of helpless-

---

[1] One exception here is the re-married widow who leaves her former husband's place.

[2] I do not wish to suggest that all women acquire "judicial confidence", factors of personality clearly being important here; nor do marriages follow identical patterns.

ness that an elderly and rather feeble Elti woman, recounted to me her troubles.

In 1965 she was lamenting the deaths of all her close kin, for when her husband is angry with her she has nowhere to go and feels very bad. He accuses her of keeping back their daughter from marrying (i.e. to look after her) as they have no sons. She pointed out that she has always concerned herself over her husband's business: for a long time she has had no brothers to come and present him with things—all that she procures is by her own work. It is his fault that they have no sons. Her eldest boy died because of his father's mean ways. This came about through the latter's failure to contribute to a funeral feast for one of his own brother's sons even though he had pigs available at the time. The spirit of the dead boy then seized their own son in revenge. And her husband did not even kill any funeral pigs for his child![1] She was pregnant at the time, and the baby did not survive a premature birth, being killed in turn by its brother's spirit. Still her husband would not sacrifice any pigs. Then her daughter fell sick, from the spirits of ancestral ghosts crying out for sacrifice, and she begged him to kill the pigs now. He pretended to tie an animal up, but never despatched it. So the girl died too. But what can she do? He does not listen to her. *Elem-nga muntmong ku rar^{e}m-nda*, "perhaps his heart has turned to stone?"

Laik bilong Meri

A married woman's increasing involvement in the affairs of her husband's clan is not only a matter of her incorporation but of a more general status as an adult woman. We cannot talk in any simple way of the authority of husbands over wives. In the early years of marriage women may assert a contraposing power (e.g. the ability to simply leave the husband), while in later years conjugal relations are tempered by the development of moral ties.

Many marriages are characterized by disputes which become public from time to time. The frequency of disputes is not, however, a direct register of marital disharmony. Quarrelling allowed to become publicly known arises in a situation in which neither spouse can easily bring the other to court for failure in domestic obligations, and where the threat of divorce is a sanction open to manipulation. It is a means of applying pressure, and not necessarily also an indication that the spouses find each other incompatible. The wife rather than the husband usually

---

[1] The man himself asserted (on a subsequent occasion) that he had killed pigs at the deaths of all his children, although no public second-stage funerals were held.

gains most in publicizing a grievance, for the male image of the latter is of one who controls his wives and settle disputes internally, and does indeed have authority over them. The power of any wife's threat to divorce her husband lies partly in the general concern men have over the stability of marriages and alliances contingent on them, male suspicion of feminine irresponsibility, and the attention which divorce cases receive—in which the wayward-wife stereotype often appears to be validated. These are particular aspects of the fear that women will act with complete autonomy.

Reay describes how nowadays in court settlements Kuma women are often seen to get their way. "A rule known by the Pidgin (English) term *laik bilong meri* ("what a woman wants") prevails in formal and informal courts dealing with marriage and divorce" (Reay, 1966:170; cf. 1967: 16). The rubric derives from Administration attitudes towards marital stability and women's rights. In Hagen, Councillors likewise model themselves on administration officers, and some of the values which Europeans hold concerning women are widely known. However, individual officers vary in their approach (some asserting that marriages should be preserved at any cost, others that women should decide their own future) and there is no evidence that the Hagen administration has clearly encouraged *laik bilong meri* above all other considerations. Some degree of freedom to act independently is also an indigenous attribute of Hagen women's status.

A brief consideration of the possibly contrasting circumstances of Kuma marital stability is to the point. In order to obtain divorce, a Kuma woman was often in the past dependent on a new husband's readiness to go to war (Reay, 1959a:55); or had a struggle to "convince her kinsmen that she has left her husband with a good enough cause . . . to make them willing to terminate their own valued association with their affines" (Reay, 1967:15). It is in spite of men's assertions of control that Kuma women run away from their husbands. There is a crucial difference here between Hagen and Kuma. In Kuma, much of the antagonism in conjugal relations is related to sexual causes (Reay, 1959a:82–84); a woman deserting her husband tends not to return for any period to her kin but go at once to another man, and this often precipitated warfare in the past. Hagen women who take this course are in a minority; we might relate the difference to the initial degree of choice exercised in selection of a spouse. The Kuma preference for sister exchange means that a woman's marriage is critical for the debts her clan has with others with which it is in alliance. To a much greater extent than in Hagen the selection of a girl's husband is in the hands of male kin. Reay comments that the flamboyant "courting" period in which young girls enjoy considerable freedom has in fact little bearing on the realities of marriage (Reay, 1959a: 175–181). Hagen girls seem to have more restrictions on their freedom at this time, but what freedom they have is not totally unrelated to the choices they later make. Acknowledgement of this, however token, is found in the public consent a girl must signify to any choice made on her behalf. This is not all. That Hagen women tend to run away to their kin is directly an outcome of the extent to which the threat of divorce is used as a bargaining weapon in day to day relations. This is of little apparent significance in Kuma.[1] Threat of divorce has a very particular meaning here, since for Kuma repaying bridewealth upsets specific reciprocities established between the clans concerned in a marriage. The main marriage payment is often not made till the birth of the first child. Once bridewealth had eventually been handed over, the husband's clan was in the past extremely reluctant to let her go; effort was made to see that she at least took a second husband from the same clan (Reay, 1967). This is not so in Hagen, where (paradoxically) closely intermarried groups can in fact afford individual unions to lapse, however much protest the prospect of divorce brings. For the Kuma, we should distinguish annulment and divorce.[2] Before full bridewealth was paid, it seems to have been quite common for girls to run away to another man, though this also led to accusations of wife stealing. Divorce was hard to obtain; annulment apparently much easier. In Hagen full bridewealth accompanies the initial transaction; and subsequent divorce is most likely to stem from internal difficulties in conjugal or affinal relations. It is the relationship between the ex-affines which has to be adjusted. The group from which the wife perhaps hopes eventually to take a husband is in most cases irrelevant. The character of Hagen divorce and associated male attitudes towards females is thus different. A woman's kinsmen may themselves

---

[1] Though a Kuma woman retains loyalty to her clan of origin, which may bring her into dispute with cowives and wives of other men of her husband's clan (Reay, 1959a: 80–82). If a wife did run home, her clansmen might use her attempted divorce as a device to bring the husband's payments "up-to-date" (Reay, 1967: 15), the suggestion being that they usually disregard the woman's wishes, rather than encourage her to take such action in the first place.

[2] Reay's contrast between annulment and divorce is specifically in terms of whether a marriage in the full sense of the word has taken place or not: whether spouses have settled down "to performing their usual roles" (Reay, 1967: 15).

have motives for terminating a marriage, whose transactional advantages lie not in the initial settlement of a debt through providing a particular group with a wife, but in the potential of lucrative exchanges. On the other hand, however much blame is put on to them, rightfully or not, the system allows women to secure divorce. If *laik bilong meri* is heard in Hagen courts today it is not as a new principle of rights due to a woman, but rather the well-worn ploy of excusing others when she does get her way.

I do not want to suggest there have been no changes; women probably find it easier to exercise their independence now that warfare does not make the runaway a target for rape by her husband's or own clansmen's enemies, and the violence of the retaliatory measures these men themselves can take is constrained by the administration. It was also probably the case, and this is the way accounts are put, that marriage choices were more closely supervised in the past, when valuables were scarcer and a woman's folk were anxious to secure wealth. The tendency for relatively wealthy families to marry each other may have been more marked then. Thus one hears statements to the effect, "Now they (the women's parents) are afraid of courts and let women marry where they will". While it is certainly true that the court system which deprives men of some of their sanctions also enables women to obtain a hearing for their grievances, accounts from the past[1] dealing with particular incidents illustrate well enough the possibility that women might go their own way, as well as the possibility of their being forced to comply with the wishes of their menfolk. When Local Government Councils were established in the Wahgi Valley and at Hagen, an annual poll tax was instituted (in the region of £2 per man and a few shillings for women in Hagen in 1964–5). Men of the then Minj Council (Kuma) resisted the notion that their women should contribute tax; since females controlled no significant income of their own this was seen simply as a device which would raise men's taxes (Reay, n.d.). It is illuminating that in Hagen there seems to have been no question but that women should contribute their share, although this was never assessed on the same scale as men's.

The notion of women's independence or autonomy (*noman rondokl*) is not tied to the court situation. Although divorce is a striking context in which a woman's *noman* becomes a public issue, the concept that

---

[1] There may of course be some projection from present-day values on to the rendering of these.

females have wills of their own modifies interaction between husband and wife, and men and women, in many situations.[1] Men recognize, for example, that it is not enough to spell out the duties of a wife: a woman must become motivated to work towards their joint prosperity —her *noman* must be set on hard work. This has to be encouraged by the man's co-operation; wives feel let down when husbands are indifferent over their own producer contributions. Penalties for ignoring a woman's *noman*, forcing her against her will or otherwise failing to act as she hopes, include supernatural intervention through the inducement of *popokl* (Chapters 6 and 10). Both a woman's own kin and her husband may fear her *popokl noman*. Not only should her positive agreement to arrangements be sought, but acting contrary to her desires can result in her sickness and death. This theory by no means informs all decisions affecting females, but it is one corollary of letting women go their own way.

The subversiveness men fear in women operates on two levels. With the same interests as men, they compete with them (for example, when they grease away wives because of personal dissatisfaction over a bride-wealth) or they pursue different and contrary interests (as in persuading a girl to leave her husband for some reason such as the man's appearance).

A middle-aged woman at Kelua, now a matron with several children, gave an account of herself as having been very strong-willed in her youth (she was a girl in the 1930's). As an adolescent she spent her time turning head, thereby avoiding the tasks her mother set her (girls tired out by their exertions being usually excused work). She was the eldest daughter of an important Mokei big-man in a large polygynous family. Her father was fond of her, and she played him off against her mother. But when the time came to marry he tried himself to prevent her from attending any more courting sessions, while it was the mother's turn to show sympathy. She refused several presentable suitors whom her father favoured; the gift of a pig with which he tried cajolery she shared with her mother, and promptly went off on her own devices; and once during the middle of actual negotiations walked away. The father was furious, but was forced to comply with her eventual desire to marry an Elti man.

With continuing gusto, she recounted her disapproval of a younger half-sister's marriage to an old and ugly man, whom she (the elder sister) did not care for. At the back of this lay a grudge she held against him, for not

---

[1] Strauss (1962:298): men and women both readily claim equality (*kapokla*) with others; as in Wanggulam (Ploeg, 1969). It is noteworthy that "Wanggulam are inclined to overstate the autonomy pertaining to the members of their society" (Ploeg, 1969:71), a situation that is true of Hagen when men sometimes attribute independence to women who are trying in fact to bring about an alteration in relationships which they do not want to abandon.

having treated her properly at the bridewealth. She had provided a special pearl shell and cooked pig as a solicitory gift for which the groom made no adequate return. So, in *popokl*, she influenced her sister to leave the old man. When the irate husband accused her of this, stalking up to her house at Kelua where the sister was staying, he was told, "If you were bringing to me the valuables which you really owe, I would send my sister back: but I see you come empty-handed!" There was a long court hearing; the wife refused to return, while the elder sister (the story-teller) protested that it was the girl's own desire to leave her husband. Several people accused her of having greased the girl, and her father was very angry; in retaliation she refused to help him in the handing back of the bridewealth.

She spoke with quiet amusement of how afraid her sister's current husband was of her. The sister subsequently remarried, and she and her mother went over to the new place to see about bridewealth. The piqued father professed no further interest in his daughter's affairs. According to her story, the two women refused to budge till the new groom's kin had produced some money. There were grumbles about doing so. "You are only her sister; why should we give you bridewealth? Did you bear the woman that you ask for pay?" But in the end they gave her £40. She brought this back to their father who was pleased, and said to her, "We were not strong, and would not have gone to demand payment—you yourself went, and it is up to you to distribute the bridewealth!" She ended with the observation that when her brothers' daughters and other sisters get married she is always now given a prominent share of the bride-wealth, lest she persuade them to leave their husbands too. The incident of her younger sister's marriage happened about 1958–9. Her husband (from whom she was estranged in 1964–5) does not come into the account at all, and she represents herself as in control of these situations.

Whether or not things happen precisely as is claimed, it is clear that women may look upon themselves as influencing events in the same way as men charge them with doing.

Women in Between

The autonomy which Hagen women show in some of their behaviour seems to be a correlate of certain intrinsic aspects of their roles. It is not simply a function of household status; in addition it has to do with extra-domestic elements in their position, of which the most important relate to the institution of ceremonial exchange. Chapter 6 described how women see themselves and are to some extent seen by men as more than passive links between groups; they are participant intermediaries. A woman's whole devotion to a man's enterprises, even the care with which she carries out her household tasks, has to engage her *noman*, is seen as an act of volition. Whether or not everyone is actually ambitious for success —and while many are concerned to promote transactions between their home and their husband's kin, others lack interest—emphasis put upon women's structural position, their close association with two groups, contributes to their individuation. A married woman is held to have loyalties to both or either sets of people, and furthermore to act on these. It is this potential which possibly sustains the notion that women can behave independently of either their kin or their husbands, for they are in a theoretical position of choice. It is not only in "allowing" women to manipulate poison that men perhaps fear they have surrendered too much control (p. 184); by encouraging them to become involved in exchange relations and motivated to demonstrate loyalty to their own or their husband's clan the third possibility is admitted, that they may entirely go their own way.

Female involvement in politics and exchange does not, however, have the public consequences that men's actions carry. Partial involvement and partial exclusion leads to certain difficulties of the type I have called judicial. A woman's social horizon is relatively narrow, her life being largely focused on her immediate kinsfolk and husband, the members of the small residential unit where she lives, and their close neighbours. She perhaps demands more of relations with her husband and her brothers than they exact from her. For while she is concerned in the success of exchanges and other affairs between these people, if either side fails or defaults, her position in formal terms is nothing. She may apply informal or self-help sanctions, but in the last resort is not the full transactor, only an intermediary. Political pressures of the kind available to men in coping with defaulting partners—such as threatening to hold up a group-*moka* or to carry on without a particular gift—are not available to the woman "in the middle".

Bohannan's suggestion that certain combinations of roles may be suicidogenic (1960:259–260) is pertinent here. A proportion of female suicides in Hagen, as we have already seen, reputedly stem from anxieties over exchange relations, in which women act as both sisters and wives. A young Northern Melpa man, talking abstractly on the topic, gave in this order the following four reasons why a woman might commit suicide:

1. she wants to leave her husband but is forced by her parents to return;

2. her parents refuse to make proper *moka* with the husband;

3. her husband hits her but does not pay compensation to her parents when they come to ask for pay;

4. she is discovered having sexual relations with a close kinsman.

In the first three cases she kills herself out of *popokl* (revenge–anger), in the last out of shame (*pipil*). One of the causes of the woman's *popokl* when her parents go over her head, and collaborate directly with her husband in sending her back (reason 1), must lie in their denial that her positive compliance and agreement is crucial to the perpetuation of the relationship. Similarly, when a wife is nagged because one or other side has defaulted, an element in her *popokl* may be that a failure to honour debts with her husband/kinsmen is a slight on her own status.

*A now old Kawelka Membo man gave this version of why his elder sister had killed herself, an event that happened about the time of the first European explorations in the Hagen area. She was married to a Kawelka Mandembo man, who gave a bridewealth of cooked and live pigs, nassa shell headbands and cowrie ropes, and a single pearl shell. Her parents agitated for more payments, demanding further cowries and another pearl shell—it was especially pearl shells they wanted, for these had "just come up" (i.e. had begun to increase in availability). Her husband refused to send them any, and after a year or so with him she returned home, where she stayed about a month. Her kin went on nagging her, saying how much they desired further valuables. She hanged herself at her parent's place, *popokl* with her husband for not making the payment and *popokl* with her parents for demanding it.[1]

Suicides committed by Hagen women in relation to difficulties over exchanges (e.g. reason 2 in the above list) can be summarized in terms of Durkheimian and similar categories. Apart from the Hagen belief that the suicide's ghosts can take samsonic revenge on the survivors, the act is compounded of fatalism (the woman is all but resigned to her inability to do more), and anomie (she is unable to apply pressures which would coerce the defaulting men into making good the payments). Berndt notes in respect of female suicide among the Kamano and their neighbours how few legal alternatives[2] a woman has if she quarrels with her husband (Berndt, R. M., 1962:205, 400); Hagen women are in a rather different judicial position, but it remains true that they cannot

---

[1] The account should not be taken to indicate that the girl's kin valued wealth more than herself; they probably would not have intended their pleas to have such drastic results.

[2] Brown (1964:355) suggests that suicide is a typical reaction to offence on the part of Chimbu women.

always satisfactorily influence arrangements with which they are yet involved. Their protest also contains an altruistic element (the woman effaces herself before her husband or brothers, it being their values she shares); finally it is an egoistic act (she is in fact allowed considerable personal leeway, her independence is encouraged and she is not so tightly integrated into her husband's group that she can show no loyalty towards her own). The last point needs some clarification. A woman's parents are likely to show initial tolerance, even welcome, when she first comes home, since it may be to their advantage to use the visit as an excuse to press for more goods themselves, and such permissiveness only changes when she appears to jeopardize the whole relationship by a prolonged stay. And this perhaps can sum up the basic difficulty with which Hagen women have to cope: their compliance in men's affairs, their involvement in politics and exchange, is both sought and encouraged on the one hand, but on the other rejected in the ultimate interests of males.

It is necessary to make some distinction between the way in which roles are conceptualized and the actual behavioural situations to which they give rise. In the context of exchange there is no absolute incompatibility perceived by Hageners in the roles of wife and sister, that is, in respective attachment to the husband's and the home clan. Ideally they should equally find prestigeful expression in *moka*. Indeed, when things are going well, the roles are positively reinforcing (the good wife brings in valuables for her husband, the good sister brings in valuables for her brother). But the roles of wife and sister are not totally isomorphic. A wife should not only promote her husband's affairs with her own kin but in general (and his wider interests may overshadow transactions in that particular direction); a greater commitment to her husband's business (*kongon*) is expected of her than she is required to show loyalty to her brother. And although there is an ideal expectation that they can, her husband's and her brother's interests certainly do not always coincide. It is illuminating that men avoid discussing the theoretical possibilities of role-difficulties for women in divorce cases. We cannot say, therefore, in any simple way, that a woman's roles lack overall integration. Some kind of integration is achieved through successful transactions. Yet a woman's intercalary position is effective at one level, and not at another: publicly she is held to have little influence, although privately her loyalties may be important. Strain arises not so much from inherent conflicts in the conceptualization of diverse roles, but from the fact that integration depends on success. One conclusion reached from the studies by Bohannan (1960), is that women of these societies tend to commit suicide in a domestic context, failure to play satisfactorily the roles of wife or mother meaning total failure. For the Hagen woman a crucial source of strain seems to be, and is one tacitly perceived in alleged causes of suicides, her intermediary position. As long as her husband and her own kin maintain reciprocity in their relations with each other, and their interests coincide, difficulties are dormant. But when something goes wrong, when the interests of the men diverge, one or both sides making demands through her, she is not necessarily able to set it right. She can exert various pressures, but ultimately the decisions do not rest with her. And yet the manner in which pressure can be put on her, prototyped from the start of her marriage in blame from her own kin when bridewealth is poor, blame from her husband when dowry is poor, actually exploits her intermediary status, and perhaps makes her think they do.

12

Status, Incorporation
and Commitment

Writing of African descent groups, Radcliffe-Brown comments that "it is the adult men who really constitute the corporate kin group" (1950: 41), for the reason, to re-phrase Lewis (1965:103), that although women may be members of such units, they are generally only second-class citizens. In other words, female membership usually does not entail the same range of rights and duties that would fall on males. What is meant by "women's incorporation" therefore needs to be closely specified. The phrase is used commonly in reference to the status of a wife who takes up virilocal residence at marriage. It may cover a variety of elements: a woman's social absorption into the husband's local community; attachment to her husband's descent group through the subsequent filiation of her children; transference of rights in her at marriage; control over her person. None of these conditions necessarily indicates the nature of a wife's participation in the affairs of her husband's group or the quality of her overall commitments. Where women come under the authority or power of men at the same time they cannot be equal with them, as co-members of corporate groups, "equal . . . in jural status" (Fortes, 1969:304). In Hagen, a woman's political status disqualifies her from acting like a male clan member; nevertheless she exercises membership of a kind. Unlike most men, women regularly participate in the affairs both of a natal kin group and of a second group with which they are associated by marriage.

In a restricted sense women may represent their clan of origin. My account has already indicated that in her internal relations with men of this group a sister has not the same liabilities as her brothers have, and in relation to external bodies she cannot receive compensation on its behalf. Nevertheless, vis-à-vis her husband's kin the in-married wife, from her contacts with her natal clan, may be the subject of attack (physical or ghostly) or the recipient of gifts. She can at least act as a representative of her own lineage-mates, and also of her husband, if not their clans, by receiving wealth in their name. Moreover, she carries about with her the political status of such units, as poison accusations show. As far as her own position is concerned, a woman may interpret association with her husband's or her brother's clan as laying upon her certain duties, such as the obligation to take vengeance for a brother's death (especially when inflicted by a member of her husband's clan) or warn her husband of imminent warfare (especially from her home clan). Conversely she certainly sees herself as having a right to protection and a right to be consulted about exchange transactions. These obligations are at one remove from those defining men's group membership. The point to which I wish to draw attention is that concepts of incorporation, absorption, assimiliation and the like, take groups as the basis for analysis in which men have well defined interests. In relation to these women are unquestionably interstitial (Douglas, 1966) second-class members, with residual rights and peripheral status (Lewis, 1966: Wilson, 1967). But the concept of incorporation is too limited to subsume the totality of a woman's situation in a society such as Hagen, where positive use is made of a her linking roles.[1] Involvement in the affairs of her natal and her husband's clans is the parameter of an intermediary status. Some of the esteem in which individual women are held, of the prestige accruing to women's roles, of their independence, are products of this. Prominence of the intermediary role must in turn be partly related to the quality of alliance relations as they operate in marriage arrangements, warfare and ceremonial exchange.

Exchange institutions, as much as the character of corporate groups, vary between societies in the Highlands (Strathern, A.J., 1969a; 1969b). It is beyond my scope to make a broad survey of differences in female roles and statuses. Nevertheless, a few limited observations may serve to point up distinctive features of Hagen society in this respect. The following sections consider again various aspects of women's intermediary

---

[1] Werbner's comment on Peter's analysis of Cyrenaican Bedouin: "in-marrying women are axial in relationships between corporations" and play "mediatory roles" (Werbner, 1968: 130), citing Peters (1967a; 1967b).

roles in Hagen by comparison with other Highlands systems: first, the manner in which rights in women are distributed between kin groups, and second what can be inferred about women's perception of their attachment to these groups. The degree of authority or control which men exercise over women is a third aspect which cuts across or combines the first two.

Until now, I have refrained from assertions about "women's status" as such, if for nothing else than to avoid the implied assumption of harmony or complete integration between aspects of one role or between the several roles which women might play. Certain combinations of roles may indeed be compatible at an ideal level, as I have argued seems true for the pair wife/sister. Yet here, the very fact that it is limited participation in exchanges which enables women to combine wifely and sisterly duties as an intermediary leads to its own difficulties. Men and women come into conflict over the extent to which the sexes share interests as producers and transactors. However, these latter are not well-defined and recognized roles in the way that relation-specific (sister, in-law) or function-specific (pig-herder, big-man) roles are, and the point need some discussion.

Status may be taken not only as compounded of various roles to which rights and duties are attached, but as stemming also from the way in which roles or combinations of part-roles are categorized and evaluated. Thus the specification that females are polluting defines a role "woman" (women having a duty to observe menstrual taboos) but in addition is an attribute of a category[1] "woman", defined by certain characteristics. Such categorizations in turn influence the way in which woman in particular role-situations are treated (e.g. a husband reacts with indifference to his wife running away because "women" are expected to behave irresponsibly). Conversely, attributes may be modified by the roles relevant in specific contexts (e.g. men may say that all women carry poison, but "wives" and not "mothers" or "sisters" use it against their menfolk). Categorizations are drawn from a range of beliefs and experiences; they summarize social attitudes.

Any account of status has to refer to both role and category. Role specifications would seem to incorporate relatively stable sets of values

---

[1] Like Nadel's "class concept" (1957:24) except that "category" may comprise several (perhaps conflicting) attributes. Cf. Newman (1965:41): "the roles (man) and (woman) are very general . . . being one or the other largely determines a person's total life pattern in so far as it is structured by roles."

which support the norms. Thus, mothers should look after their children (duty); maternal care is indispensible (value). Attitudes held towards a category of persons, however, may partially contradict one another: thus, women are soft-brained; women are strong-headed. Hence, it is that when wives and sisters are seen as of this category, conflicting generalizations are made about them. In one context wives may be praised as good gardeners, in another denigrated because they do not own the soil; praised for the transactions they have stimulated with their own kin, denigrated for having left their clan territory. Unlike the values which support role-norms, there is no requirement for consistency in social attitudes defining a category. Roles themselves may be evaluated, and taken as contributing to categories, as when they are being ranked or are seen as belonging to different domains. The result can affect the relationship between roles any one person may hold (e.g. wife/sister) or between those held by different persons (e.g. wife/husband). "Producer" and "transactor" are categories which thus rank the overall contributions of husband and wife (and persons in other roles) from men's point of view. The categorization is separate from how far ranking is acceptable to women, and separate again from the way individual men and women may be esteemed in their own domain. I have tried to demonstrate equally the formal Hagen specifications of the roles "wife" and "sister", and the kinds of attitudes which are held about "women" in general. Women for their part do not share all the values implicit in male attitudes, yet themselves lack any well defined public stance towards the opposite sex.[1]

My emphasis on attitudes is intended to underline the mythical and dogmatic character of assertions of male superiority (cf. Reay, 1959a: 156). From their actual dominance in the political domain, men claim total superordination in any sphere of importance. In fact, they are aware that they depend on women: for domestic comforts, for children, for the production of food and care of livestock. More than this, they depend also on their wives' general support in all kinds of enterprises, and on links through women to provide roads for exchange. They see exchange networks as, to some extent, hinging on marriages. While in most societies it must be the case that the dominant partner is still de-

---

[1] I noted that women tend not to generalize about men but rather consider their specific claims. Berndt, C. H. (1965) compares ceremonies performed by Aboriginal men and women: whereas male rituals make general statements about inter-sexual relations, female rites are directed to personal ends.

pendent on his spouse for domestic sustenance (cf. Lewis, 1966:321; Langness, 1967), Hageners enlarge the area of dependency in making women intermediaries between sets of men. Perhaps this has something to do with the fact that while husbands often resort to violent demonstrations of control (beating, calling in clansmen to help punish), they also react on occasion to their wives' indifference or independence by displays of peevish *popokl*-infliction, in direct appeal for *kaemb* (sympathy). Admission of dependence on women is not sustained to the extent that male superiority is; but it is to be found in certain dogmas (such that women are strong, i.e. sources of productive strength); and also in attitudes which modify men's behaviour in their treatment of individual women (for example, that a mother should receive care in old age *in reciprocity* for the way she cared for her children).[1]

Treating women as political minors stems from attitudes towards their participation in clan affairs. As a corporate body the clan may indeed be one person; but female members who associate with other clans and wives who come in from foreign places cannot be the same kind of persons as men. The association of male members *qua* members with other groups has the special quality of political confrontation. Oratory and transactions are aspects of this. Quite separate from the issue of whether women are controlled by men or not, is the fact that political activity is inappropriate to the linking functions of women's intermediary status. From this point of view transactions do not typify "women's" activities. I have suggested, however, that "transactor" can itself be treated as a category term. Elements in a woman's intermediary role—her contacts with groups, bringing in of wealth, influence over husband or brothers—can cast wives or sisters into the category of quasi-transactor. Both categories, "political minor" and "quasi-transactor",[2] derive from social attitudes which on the one hand differentiate men and women, and on the other suggest an equation. Keeping discrete public disavowal of women's influence and private admission of their covert importance in exchange affairs glosses over the contradiction to which Hagen values give rise; the non-political person becomes involved in transactions; the transactor has no political standing. Or,

---

[1] Berndt, C. H. (1965:247) raises the question of whether personality variations are allowed freer rein in some roles than in others. It seems true of Hagen that mother–child relations (for example) are in behaviour more standardized than those between husband and wife.

[2] I am not suggesting these are the only categories, but in addition to "woman", these (and their male correlates) have been useful to the present analysis.

it might be stated, women are intermediaries (not the chief actors), but participant (and not completely disengaged).

This attempt to represent Hagen notions points up the impossibility of making a unique definition (e.g. as high or low) of women's status by comparison with men's. As Kaberry notes in her analysis of Aboriginal women, there need be no fixed relationship between the sexes that is relevant for all cross-sexual interaction (1939:276).

Rights in Women

In the contrast between a formal allocation of obligations and an actor's commitments or loyalties to kin groups, one axis of comparison suggests itself: an exclusive distribution of interests, as against interests held non-exclusively. At marriage, certain specific rights in a woman are transferred to or bestowed on the husband and others are retained by her kin, while her own personal loyalties are shared between both sides. However, rights and duties themselves are not in every case allocated absolutely. There are quite important areas in which interests overlap.

Sexual rights *in uxorem* a husband does hold to the exclusion of all others. Rights *in genetricem* are similarly held for the duration of the marriage, but if it terminates in death or divorce, the affiliation of children not yet independent may be in subsequent doubt. Interest in his sister's children, which a wife's brother maintains through their childhood, may, if the woman returns to her clan, become sponsorship of their attachment to it. Hageners explicitly say marriage means that a girl who used to work in her parents' gardens no longer will do so, but will transfer her labours to the husband, his gain being their loss. However, there is always the possibility that she may live separated from her husband and reside and garden at home, in which case she contributes to households there. These are rights in a woman, then, which marriage allocates to a husband, but not permanently; they are contingent upon the conditions under which the union persists. The extent to which a dead man's clansmen have claims beyond the duration of the marriage is in actuality contingent also on the woman's choice (whether to remain, re-marry a brother, etc.), although the clansmen usually try to assert control over her.

There are two areas in which rights broadly defined may be held simultaneously both by a wife's kin and her husband. The first are rights over the wife (*in personam*) as an intermediary. These are acquired by a woman's kin as well as her husband at marriage, with the expectation that the wife/sister will promote exchanges between the two sides. However, the husband's more general demands on her labour and services, which he holds against her kin, may detract from the reciprocal recognition of this right. It is perhaps even stretching the point to regard it as a "right" of the same order as others mentioned here, in that participation in *moka* exchanges is inherently voluntary, and from the wife, it is something to be hoped for rather than an obligation imposed. I return to this in the next section. There are also rights in the woman (*in rem*) which her husband and her kin share, insofar as they have a general interest in her protection from injury, and, conversely, liability for the consequences of her actions. Here, however, there is sociological differentation. The husband's rights are held specifically against persons of other clans (including hers and sometimes his own), while her kin hold this right against her husband and sometimes against relatives identified with him. Circumstances may modify this broad correlation.

It is the nature of a wife's legal standing with her own kin that Lewis (1962) suggests should be considered a crucial variable in the comparative analysis of divorce rates (cf. Fallers, 1957; Leach, 1961; Lloyd, 1968; Glasse and Meggitt, 1969: 7). Lewis demonstrates that low agnatic solidarity or a partial transference of genetricial rights at marriage are not necessary correlates of high divorce. Somali husbands have absolute rights in their bride's fertility, although only for as long as the marriage lasts. Where agnatic solidarity is pronounced the spouses' loyalties may be divided, and this itself undermines the cohesion of marriage (Lewis, 1962: Ch. VIII). A Somali woman is tied but lightly to her husband's group, and divorce is quite common;[1] whatever rights a husband gains in his wife, women remain jurally under the control of their agnates, who are responsible for major categories of compensation payments due in relation to them. Somali is a society in which marriages are important for political alliance, although as Lewis points out such alliances are as fluctuating as the marital unions themselves. As in Hagen, the manner in which alliances are conceptualized rests on the notion that wives never relinquish their "social identity" (Fortes, 1949:98) as members of their natal clans. Women, however, appear to lack active intermediary roles. Where divisive loyalties are channelled into an institution such as that of ceremonial exchange, whose success is seen to

---

[1] Male ratio C as a percentage, 32%.

depend partly on the marriage's success, and through which the discrete ties of husband and wife are publicly utilized, they do not in themselves necessarily lead to marital instability. Much recent discussion on divorce poses an antithesis between stability through the wife's incorporation and instability through divided loyalties. In the Hagen context, where positive requirements are made of a woman's dual commitments, the rights a woman's kin continue to have over her undoubtedly bolster her intermediary position, thus also strengthening her situation as a wife. From her point of view, the right to demand protection from them is the converse of the loyalty she shows them and the same is true, to some extent, for relations between the spouses. Conflicts do arise, however, and partly from the very prominence which her dual attachment receives. Hageners do not have a particularly high divorce rate—but their rates are certainly not among the lowest in the Highlands.

It should be noted that there are systems in which women may experience a conflict of loyalties which has nothing to do with an intermediary position or with extensive exchange relations between groups linked by marriage. Tallensi (which Lewis links with Somali and Soga in this respect) are a case in point. The following (quoted with permission from Professor Fortes and the International African Institute) could almost have been written of Hagen:

> "All her life a woman is subject to the pull of her patrilateral kinship ties. As a wife, however, she must submit more and more to the contrary pull of her marital ties" (Fortes, 1949:90). "The tension due to these opposing sets of social ties appears most acutely in the early stages of marriage, obviously as a result of the fact that marriage is an alliance between two genealogically independent corporate units with rival interests in the protagonists" (1949:91). "And it is not uncommon for men to instigate a daughter to leave her lawful husband for another man . . . as a means of raising what we should call ready cash . . . Thus, observance of the jural proprieties gives a husband a weapon with which he can try to assert his rights to and over his wife. It does not give him an absolute guarantee of these rights nor does it ensure the stability of the marriage" (1949:86). "A wife . . . can be in sympathy with the interests and can respect the values that rule the actions of her husband and her sons as members of their agnatic descent group, while being herself excluded from an effective public role in relation to them. But a cleavage remains. Thus in a conflict between her husband's clan and her father's clan she might very well take the side of the latter, not openly, it is true, but covertly" (1949:99).

In many societies where bridewealth accompanies marriage, the bride's kin use her position to obtain more wealth. "A son-in-law is a bark to be stripped", runs a Kalanga proverb (Werbner, 1964:211). A particular point, however, can be made in relation to Tallensi. Fortes repeatedly stresses how a woman is sub-ordinated to those men in authority over her, primarily her father, relations between husband and wife having more the character of a power-conflict (1949:104–6). Perhaps her overall female status as a jural minor is more consistent with the role of a daughter than of a wife. In general, formal super-subordination in relationships (e.g. between senior and junior lineage members) is not marked in Hagen. With marriage a woman ceases to be a child: she is not tied to her natal clan as a perpetual daughter.

It is because of this that I do not think it appropriate to talk simply about a Hagen woman's status in relation to those who might have authority and control over her. In my vocabulary, she is a political minor but not a jural minor. That a woman always remains at a disadvantage in the courts is because of their political nature. Thus, I hesitate to equate what is upheld in courts with jural status. The nature of rights between spouses is a case in point. Dereliction of duty frequently fails to be rectified through compensation and similar court procedures, not with a denial that the obligation is a binding one, but from the overwhelmingly high value placed upon marital stability which must receive affirmation in public. It is as though confrontation in a court situation is felt to exacerbate or harden existing tensions; disputes must be settled as far as possible privately, courts being reserved for open conflict under threats of self-help. Perhaps also, husband and wife act internally as a production unit which transacts with outsiders, so that it is inappropriate for the one to compensate the other over domestic issues. They can quite easily transact with each other when the wife is thought of in her capacity as a member of her natal clan (e.g. when she is injured).

Rights may, then, be distributed in such a way as to subject women to a conflict of loyalties that has nothing to do with the kind of exchange and alliance system existing in Hagen. Nevertheless, within the restricted context of the Australian New Guinea Highlands these latter factors are perhaps of relevance. In most Highlands societies major rights in a woman's fertility, labour and companionship are claimed by the husband, who expects that she will come to reside with him on his clan territory. But considerable variation exists in the quality of links a woman retains with her kin. It would have been interesting to compare Highlands societies in terms of the degree of jural/judicial control over an adult woman which is vested in her kin: who is liable to pay or receive compensation for her, in the case of injury, death, delicts, and so on; the extent to which, once married, she can be reallocated to another husband without reference to her kin; and her effective claims on their protection.[1] In addition, there is the degree to which informal ties between a woman and her kin are maintained. One assumption behind some of the non-exclusive allocation of rights over Hagen women is that, throughout her married life, a wife will continue to associate with her home clan—she returns for visits, some of the wealth from her labours flows to it, she may seek refuge there, and so on. There are immediately apparent differences between this and descriptions given of certain Eastern Highlands societies.

Langness writes of the Bena Bena, that although "it is widely reported for the New Guinea highlands that women retain rights in their natal groups after marriage . . . a much stronger case (in Bena) could be made for asserting that women at marriage become members of their husband's group" (Langness, 1969:55). He defines membership precisely: women who remain with their husband's clans "and thus indicate they are willing to be members, are members; any loyalties they may have to their natal group are over-ridden. A woman's only security is with her husband, for her agnates cannot or will not keep her" (1969: 55). The commitment Bena women show (as evinced in the possibility of a wife's suicide at her husband's death, since return to her natal kin provides no genuine alternative choice of action) is balanced by the fact that her kin do not necessarily retain rights over her person. Bena brides are frequently allotted "brothers" in their husband's clan to care for them, since there is a likelihood that they will never see their natal kin again. And this has implications for relations between men: "No ties of any real importance are necessarily established by marriage"; Bena brides change group membership (1964:178–9). Thus it is that bride-wealth tends to have the character of a once-for-all transaction, the bride being lost to her natal clan.[2] On the groom's side, the transac-

---

[1] Some of the fuller accounts are found in Glasse, 1968 (Huli); Ryan, 1961 (Mendi); Meggitt, 1965 (Mae-Enga); Berndt, R. M., 1962 (Kamano, Usurufa, Jate, Fore).

[2] The bride's mother and other women of her clan may wear mourning at the bridewealth ceremony. Among the Fore the loss "is expressed by a permitted show of physical hostility on the part of the women" (Lindenbaum and Glasse, 1969:170), as also occurs in other Eastern Highlands societies. A bride in the Kainantu area (Berndt, R. M., 1962:123) may carry an arrow at her wedding which is presented to the groom, "symbolizing her willingness to aid him in fighting—an attempt to avoid the conflict of loyalties which might normally be expected."

tion is a clan-wide enterprise. Corresponding to the relative disregard of individual networks outside the clan is the manner in which many more activities than in Hagen are conducted with reference to group membership. Thus, the assumption of full marital relations between youths of an age-grade and their brides is synchronized; the first garden a pair have is made with the help of the groom's clansmen, and "all gardens are a communal enterprise" (1969:46). It is into a much more tightly knit local community that the bride comes.

A somewhat similar situation emerges from Salisbury's account of the Siane, although the wife retains effective rights of protection in her kin, and the head of a woman's natal lineage remains her guardian (Salisbury, 1962:22, 35, 37). Kin terms employed by the Siane woman (see p. 32) suggest a complete transformation in status at marriage and with the birth of children; from being a non-member of her husband's village, she becomes a full member. A Hagen woman, on the other hand, by no means fully adopts her husband's terminology for his people. I have emphasized the lack of systematic ties between a Hagen wife and others of her husband's residential group, with the exception of her mother-in-law (the very fact that this woman is typically her own husband's mother being an aspect of the exclusiveness of the husband–wife dyad). It would seem to be the case in Siane that wives of a lineage not only live near one another, but cook meals together and work in groups in the gardens (Salisbury, 1962:17–18). Although, in theory, women send individual portions of food to their husbands (1962:58), Salisbury notes that the "elementary family hardly functions as a unit" (1962:17). Households in Hagen are based on the elementary family, the husband having duties to provide his wife with gardens and pigs, the wife having the reciprocal duty to grow and cook food for him and tend livestock. The exclusiveness of this arrangement (cowives being members of separate units, not of a joint household) is accompanied by the often solitary performance of household tasks. Homesteads and settlements themselves are not clustered into villages (as in the Eastern Highlands) but are dispersed over group territories. A factor in Bena and Siane is that in-coming wives may be able to acquire some status as village members, irrespective of clan membership. Nevertheless, Salisbury explicitly states of a Siane woman that "her husband's clan tries to assert she is a member of that clan" (1962:37).

A Bena or Siane woman thus seems to associate closely in the performance of her everyday household jobs with others of her husband's community. In Bena a woman's kin often in effect relinquish rights *in rem*: she looks to others of her husband's community rather than to them for protection. In Siane, her husband's people make exclusive claims to a wife's fertility in the sense of denying the matrifilial uniqueness of children born to the clan.[1]

Bena Bena and Siane boys, like those of other Eastern Highlands peoples, e.g. Kamano (Berndt, R. M., 1962:94), Gururumba (Newman, 1964:266) and Gahuku-Gama (Read, 1954:27), undergo blood-letting rituals, which in the Siane case (Salisbury, 1962:34; 1965:61-2) are intended to remove the spiritual influence of their maternal origin. The mother's contribution to her child must be eliminated, in order that he can grow to maturity on "male food". There is a symbolic attempt to equate, in one respect, the in-coming female with male members, through the denial that their foreign origins can have consequence for the subsequent bodily substance of their offspring; what influence exists is removable.[2] In Hagen, the whole emphasis of inter-clan relations is on keeping marriage links open, as roads for transactions. Hageners delight in tracing out connections through blood. Far from it being purged from her children, the blood a mother contributes to them becomes an idiom for the important extra-clan contacts her marriage also brings.

Loyalties

Jural rights held by Hagen kin groups over their members (*in personam*) shade into political expectations. Men who fail to associate with their clan or its smaller segments on important occasions, or who move away permanently, even perhaps flaunting association with enemy groups, may be considered to have "lost" their clansmen. The same is true for women who in taking up virilocal residence must "lose" their home kin to some extent. A clash of personal attachments is a likely outcome from any virilocal arrangement when ties of some sort are maintained with the wife's people. Where women are further concerned with issues (as in Hagen, warfare, exchange) which bring men into political conflict, the

---

[1] Though Siane mother's brothers maintain interpersonal ties with their sisters' children, which results in an uneasy tension between the mother's and father's clan (cf. Strathern, A.J., 1969a :44 for a review of some of these points).

[2] A Siane wife's natal clan also in a sense deny that they donate their blood when they send sisters and daughters off in marriage; girls' puberty rites celebrate the evidence of agnatic blood ("spirit") at their first menses, but on marriage the bride's spirit emblem (*gerua*) is retained by her natal group (Salisbury, 1965).

possibility of clashes is aggravated. The point is that women are credited with the faculty of loyalty in a political sense (taking sides in a confrontation of groups). Their husbands and brothers expect to be able to influence them. I have suggested that such factors sustain notions about female independence. This in turn lies behind men's complaints of strong-headed women, but equally behind the notion of individual responsibility and the tenet that women should not beyond a certain point be coerced against their will.

Unlike peoples of most Highlands societies, Hageners do not perform regular rituals to cleanse and protect men from contact with women. Their sporadic, ambulatory spirit cults enunciate certain male values, but are not, for example, closely tied to celebrating boys' *rites de passage*. Participation in the cults brings no permanent movement from one status to another. Some of the apparent lack of ritual concern over sexual differentiation at puberty may be related to the very fact that a man's sister is not cut off from him when she marries; her kin wear no mourning. Mae-Enga brides receive constant chaperoning from their groom's kin to prevent them from becoming homesick and to hasten self-identification with the new parish group (Meggitt, 1965:113). As in Kuma, visiting home in the early months seems to be discouraged. But Hagen marriage ceremonies and subsequent visitings and prestations emphasize not a switch in the bride's affiliations but an expansion of them. When a Kuma girl marries, she is decked in her finest ornaments and led by one of her kinsmen to a man from the groom's side, who takes her by the hand into the company of her husband's clansmen. At this point, when her own kin see the girl's retreating back, they may weep (Reay, personal communication). There is little display of such emotions in Hagen. The bride is not literally handed over: she merely stays behind at her new husband's place after the first bridewealth display. Her main symbolic action is quite different. A day or two later she accompanies her husband's kin back to her own home. Here *she* introduces them to *her* kin, by marching ahead of their entry, bearing the pork which she places as a gift from her husband's group before her own clansmen.

Kuma to the east and Mae-Enga to the west are near-neighbours of Hagen. In both societies the transfer of women in marriage is important for individual and group alliances, but women's roles in the arrangements vary. There are differences between Kuma and Mae-Enga (cf. Reay, 1967), and again between these societies and Hagen. I have already, for example, pointed out (pp. 276–7) the practical difficulties which Kuma women seem to have in prevailing upon kinsmen's support for divorce. Whatever their theoretical rights to protection, it is often the case that the mutual interests of brothers-in-law weigh against consideration for the woman. Predictably, this goes with considerable disregard for the woman's personal involvement in her husband's or brothers' affairs with each other. The same seems true of Mae-Enga. Meggitt states that Mae-Enga men allow their women little independence and at the possibility of divorce, a wife's kin are usually anxious to send her back to her husband. Women apparently enjoy little success in taking unilateral action, being forced to return to their husbands if negotiations over return of bridewealth break down. (Meggitt, 1965:147.)

I outline some points of contrast between Hagen, Kuma and Mae. I am not trying to make correlations of general validity; my intention is to suggest limited comparisons in order to better emphasize what seem significant or distinctive features in Hagen. Some such estimate must precede generalization, but the procedures should not be confused. It is here that a danger lies. A summary of the distinctive features of a system is indeed a matter of emphasis, this in turn being derived from personal selection, bias, and so on. One is, to begin with, taking into account different levels of fact. Some cultural details can be established as existing or not—whether it is admitted or denied, for example, that women can handle poison; but there is also the assessment of behaviour—e.g. "the extent to which" women participate in ceremonial exchange. The problem is analogous to the study of such topics as leadership, where the observer is in addition dealing with an institution that is likely to involve or encourage most participation from people of certain personality types. An assessment of women's "participation" would be similar to estimating a big-man's "influence". Nevertheless, one can separate to a limited degree cultural expectations from behaviour evinced by outstanding individuals. Standardized items of custom, such as the symbols which reveal the bride as a bearer of valuables, provide one type of indication; notions about the person provide another, and I have drawn attention to the concept of *noman*.

One emphasis in the presentation of Kuma female roles suggests how much women there are pawns in the games of men, chattels over which men have rights of disposal, in short, a category of valuable (Reay, 1959a:23). This emerges particularly clearly in the manner in which marriages are arranged. As in Hagen there is a preference for marrying into friendly rather than enemy clans, even to the point of avoiding clans with which there have been hostilities (Reay, 1959a:26, 59). This is formalized in the exact exchange of brides, so that one aspect of relations between men is a network of debts in women. In order to maintain exchanges of women with due reciprocity, men have to exercise unqualified powers of disposal over them, and this is incompatible with an allowance that women themselves can exercise choice in marriage. Brides might be carried off in a mock battle and afterwards have to be guarded, in case they tried to escape (1959a:178–9). Relations between friendly clans is marked by competition and rivalry, while clearly can exist outside the context of actual military hostility. Kuma clans are rivals over their exchanges, the allegiance of members, and women. Women are thus an object of competition between clans. They have value as exchange objects as well as being potential mothers. Yet before marriage, Kuma girls are "sexually desirable persons who can confer prestige by demonstrating their choice of partners" (1959a: 22). Men's fear is that they will persist in doing so even after marriage. Hence perhaps the emphasis on the traumatic change of status which marriage must bring, from that of a girl who takes the initiative in sexual adventures to a domestic drudge. Men cannot afford their wives to be sexually desired valuables.[1]

Once married, Kuma women's activities are almost exclusively directed to domestic, household tasks. They do not seem to be acknowledged as making significant contributions to the exchanges conducted between brothers-in-law. A wife may, nevertheless, personally experience a pull of loyalties, although Reay suggests that commitment to her husband's groups is always "relative to the interests of her own clan of origin" (1959a:83, 183). A sister will put her brother's claims first, and apply pressure on her husband to meet his obligations over marriage payments. But a crucial point seems to be that her role here receives little acknowledgement at any level; however loyal she may be, her brother does not necessarily reciprocate. Kuma wives are able to exploit the dichotomy between friends and enemies, since their own clans of origin might have ties with clans enemy to their husband's groups, or they may have had sexual adventures with men of these clans before marriage. The advantage they take of such connections, however, is largely personal in

---

[1] Extreme sexual jealousy between spouses, each fearing the other is seeking further partners, is evinced in the rule that women should converse with other men only in their husband's presence (Reay, 1959a:82–3). I know of no such rule in Hagen.

pursuit of further sexual partners. It is noteworthy that although sorcery techniques are used, it is mainly men who are accused with any seriousness of harming their enemies in this way.

Hageners also stress that intermarriage should bring friendship, but it is one tinged not only with rivalry, but occasional military hostility. Most intermarrying clans are minor enemies to each other, although Hageners do not find it totally paradoxical to take some wives from major enemy groups. When thinking of groups as providing women for one another, and of the reciprocity which alliance entails, men use the idiom of "exchange marriage". But such exchanges do not involve debts in women, and although a girl's senior kinsmen will have their own interest in whom to select as her marriage partner, she is often allowed some choice. Marriage is thus neither the fulfilment of a promise nor the completion of a debt: it is the start of an exchange relationship. While Kuma speak of certain women as roads for the marriage claims made through them, Hageners use the same idiom in reference to the exchanges their contacts bring. One might put it that it is from the day of her wedding that the Hagen girl acquires "value" in this sphere. Certainly marriage is not for her the traumatic break it appears to be in Kuma.

As between their groups, relations between individual male affines in Hagen are marked both by mutual interests and by rivalry. Brothers-in-law may give private support to each other, but in public situations they are often in asymmetrical positions, for example, donors and recipients. Unlike brothers of a clan or sub-clan they do not combine together to give jointly to some third party, although a brother-in-law may help at a dance or in warfare. It might even be that because male affines tend to gloss over potential threats to their relationship entailed in the enmity between their clans, that elements of friendliness and hostility are the more sharply differentiated in relation to the linking women (cf. Brown, 1964; Meggitt, 1964:224). Wives are contrasted with mothers in terms of dependability and commitment, the extreme charge being that they poison their husbands; mothers are never so accused of harming their sons.[1] The latter is virtually true of sisters. Whereas wives and mothers are both food-givers and thus persons on whom men rely for sustenance, married sisters are not. A woman may tend gardens at home but does not *produce* regularly for her home kin, for crops she

---

[1] There is not the same degree of anthithesis between relations with mother's brothers and wife's brothers.

harvests from land given by a brother she brings back to her husband and children; sisters, like wives, on the other hand are thought of as carrying valuables between their husbands and their own kin. In sum, whereas mothers are mainly producers and sisters mainly quasi-transactors, wives are both; and it is about wives that the most conflicting categorizations are made.

Hagen men's general attitudes towards women are, then, modified in respect of women in particular role situations. By contrast, attitudes entertained by Mae-Enga men towards their womenfolk seem to be made in block terms; mothers and sisters no less than wives imperil men. The separation of boys from constant contact with women is very much more formalized among Mae-Enga than among Hageners, and culminates in bachelor rituals (Meggitt, 1964). A Mae boy who does not heed the admonitions of senior men to spend more time in the men's house is beaten and ridiculed; he is told that if he persists in keeping with the women he will become contaminated, simply from female company—for prolonged association with any woman impairs health (1964:207). The Mae boy has to make a permanent residential shift to ensure his safety, whereas a Hagen boy has to avoid only his mother while she is actually in seclusion, danger from her being thus delimited. Maternal concern is ascribed to the Hagen woman who protects her child from undue contact; but the converse of this is that willed malevolence is seen in the action of the wife who does exploit her polluting powers. Hagen men credit females with the will to control their dangerous emanations and add to this fear the further one that they will also manipulate poison, necessarily an act of volition. A point I shall return to is that Mae (like Kuma) women do not use poison.

Meggitt himself links the polluting power of Mae women to the fact that marriage is made with unequivocally hostile groups. There is no mitigation of the hostility as in Hagen, where marriageable minor enemies are contrasted with less desirable major enemies. Although in actuality Mae tend to marry quite heavily within the phratry (32% of all marriages: Meggitt, 1965; 103) and clans of a single phratry should not fight too damagingly (1965:77), from the emphasis given in Meggitt's account (1964:218; 1965:102-3) it would seem that Mae-Enga think of themselves as obtaining women from dangerous foes.[1] More

---

[1] Similarly when Kuma think of clans interrelated through marriage they stress the present friendship rather than possible past enmity between them. These are facts of a conceptual order.

completely stated, his hypothesis is that among the societies of the Central New Guinea Highlands, who share similar beliefs about the nature of females, the extent to which women are regarded as polluting can be related to structural implications of marriage arrangements, and to women's general social status.[1] In inter-sexual conflicts of the Kuma type, women have a relatively high social standing, exercising power to obstruct men's aims; the antagonism is that of competition. While Kuma men share general Highlands notions about female pollution, they tend to be careless in their observance of the taboos, which is related to the fact that Kuma wives do not have hostile origins, but come from friendly clans. Conflict of the Mae type, on the other hand, derives from intense fear of pollution from women who are associated with enemy groups, although as far as their status is concerned "the men have won the battle and have relegated women to an inferior position" (1964:220).

The fact that Hageners intermarry most frequently with groups which are neither entirely friendly nor out and out enemies supports Meggitt's hypothesis in so far as Hagen women seem to be both "more polluting" than Kuma, and "less polluting" than Mae. Hageners do not observe quite as many taboos concerning intercourse and menstruation. For example, men have little inhibition about using female as well as male head hair for making their wigs, as Mae have. A menstruating Hagen woman is forbidden to go into any but old sweet potato gardens, but a Mae woman in addition can enter even these gardens only at night. Nor are the beliefs systematized to the same extent: Hagen women, unlike Mae, do not undergo magical cleansing on emergence from seclusion and men do not regularly employ purificatory devices.[2] Hagen men's aversion to women, in short, does not seem so thorough-going, and like the Kuma they hold flamboyant courting parties and indulge in romantic attitudes towards informal sexual attachments.[3] Nevertheless, they are much more scrupulous than Kuma men seem to be about observing the basic rules with which they do hold. It would be unthinkable for a Hagen man to copulate with a menstruating woman for reasons Kuma give (Reay, 1959a:84).

---

[1] And to a third factor, the presence or absence of male purificatory cults.

[2] Gray (1969) suggests that similar rituals among Laiagam Enga emphasize a redress in the balance between sexual powers, rather than a purification of males from female contamination.

[3] The average Hagen youth probably marries (and always has done) at a younger age than his Mae counterpart. If Mae men are shocked by Hageners' exploits (Meggitt, 1964:223), Hageners nowadays regard the reputation of Kuma women with mingled revulsion and fascination.

Assessment of status does not follow directly from these facts. Meggitt implies that because Mae fears of female pollution are expressed in myriad taboos, these burden women with restrictions on their freedom, and is an aspect of their subjugation. It is questionable how far a plurality of rules can in turn be used as an index of such fear. For an individual Hagener, fear may be as *intense* as for an Enga man, although it is certainly true that Hageners are relieved of ascribing malevolence to women in all role situations. On the other hand, the Hagen combination of powers of pollution *and* the presence of volition attributed to wives, and men's dependence for protection on female good will, could make men seem more vulnerable, and hence to harbour greater fears. Hagen men have no magic of their own to manipulate (except in certain sporadic cult performance) and the taboos women observe do not afford automatic protection. Again, although Mae and Hagen men share similar beliefs about this aspect of female nature and have rather similar rules (though not of quite the same range) to circumscribe danger, yet the resultant attitudes towards women may be very different. There is a significant contrast in what boys are taught concerning menstruation, Hagen beliefs, I suggest, distinguishing women in specific roles. However informal, such attitudes are relevant for any consideration of status.

Much antagonism between the sexes in Hagen can be related to women's attempts to be considered in certain respects as men (transactors). If, as Meggitt posits for Kuma, this means they have a "high status", it is for different reasons. Competition between the sexes in Kuma, as we have seen, seems largely to revolve around the choice of sexual and marital partners. But if Hagen men also characterize women as unreliable and apt to upset male arrangements, the power men try to exercise is not focused so directly on the initial marriage arrangements. Hagen brides do not have to be closely guarded, and Hageners in any case insist that it is folly to force a girl against her will. We could say that the root of the competition lies rather in the fear that a wife will exploit her ties with home or be exploited by her kin against her husband's interests. Mae-Enga women participate little in transactions, although wealth exchanges accompany intermarriage. In Hagen, a single marriage link between groups making *moka* can be used as the basis for exchanges between classificatory affines or cognates, but a man also claims priority on conducting *moka* with his immediate affines or matrilateral kin, which in turn gives the linking woman a position of some uniqueness; hence her concern over the propriety of too close marriages. This does not appear to be the case in Mae (Meggitt, 1965:158). Conflicts between men and women over exchanges do not seem to arise, and there is no suggestion that a bride's kin might persuade her to leave her husband because of dissatisfaction with post-bridewealth exchanges. Yet Mae-Enga depend, it would seem, on marriages for the operation of *tee* as Hageners do for *moka*. Members of Mae descent groups have a common interest in one another's brides, for whom they help raise bridewealth. Further, Mae regard marital and affinal relationships as enduring: divorce is consequently disapproved of as likely to endanger inter-group links. Its rate appears to be considerably lower than in Hagen. Men have clear motives to preserve marriages (e.g. Meggitt, 1965:156–7), and male control over women is such that the latter have small alternative but to succumb to their imperatives (1965:150). If we add that women appear to take little initiative in exchanges between affines, it emerges that Mae arrangements indeed depend on marriages, but not upon women.

Hagen is not a society unique in the importance attached to women's intermediary status.[1] In many ways Mendi women of the Southern Highlands (Ryan, 1961, 1969) play similar interstitiary roles. It is a basic assumption here that ties will be maintained between a wife and her own kin, and the personal exchanges a husband conducts with his brothers-in-law do not outweigh the interests of the wife/sister but are seen to involve them. The existence of friendly ties is an "inducement for him to treat her well" (1969:171).[2] A woman who runs away has a choice of places to go to, and if a husband has been cruel then he forfeits return of his bridewealth. Moreover, wives are direct instruments in affinal exchanges. "(Common) is the case of the wife who returns home because her husband has failed to meet his economic obligations to her or her kin. If the husband fails in these payments, his wife withdraws her services and returns home until he redeems her" (Ryan, 1969:173). Initiative seems clearly attributed to the woman here.

In Mendi, marriage contributes to the alliance matrix between friendly clans, but (unlike Kuma) individuals have considerable autonomy in their choice of spouse. Indeed, Ryan's note that men exercise almost

---

[1] Since writing the present account, I have read Brandewie's paper on Hagen (Western Melpa) exchanges and note his comment on the "position of the woman . . . as go-between" (1968:27).
[2] Contrast Enga: "Any normal husband should be able to thrash an erring or lazy wife into a proper frame of mind" (Meggitt, 1965:150).

complete freedom and women only somewhat less (1969: 175) suggests that this is greater than in Hagen. Independence is shown in other ways and is an attribute of the person made of both men and women. Thus the young groom raises the bulk of marriage payments himself, and the bride is allowed discretion in distributing her own bridewealth. Her kin hand her two shells from the groom's initial display, and her public acceptance of them indicates approval of the transaction. "This action also signifies that the girl herself is the recipient of her own bride price, that it is hers to dispose of as she thinks fit, and that her kinsmen are acting only as her agents. This assumption of her independence is a distinctive and basic feature of Mendi marriages . . ." (1969: 166). It is she who later makes the actual distribution of wealth to her kinsmen, with the power to exclude persons who have failed in their obligations towards her.

The symbol (and the fact) of the bride distributing her own bridewealth suggests that Mendi give more public recognition to women's part in the financial arrangements[1] accompanying marriage than is so in Hagen. It certainly is true that a husband's failure in his subsequent exchanges (*twem*) with his wife's people leads more automatically to divorce. One important difference between Hagen and Mendi lies in the nature of these affinal exchanges. Whereas it is obligatory upon a Mendi husband to make *twem* with his wife's people, all *moka* exchanges are voluntary. Here Mendi arrangements are reminiscent of the formal and mandatory payments that have to be made with Mae-Enga affinal and matrilateral kin, although Mendi formally acknowledge women's intermediary role as Mae do not. The voluntary nature of *moka* partnerships puts emphasis on success and achievement. *Moka* is not an automatic consequent of affinal exchanges but has to be established and maintained. In spite of the fact that divorce seems as easy[2] in both societies its seemingly lower rate in Mendi by comparison with Hagen (cf. Table XIII) may have something to do with this.

The Sex War

Accounts of relations between the sexes in societies of the New Guinea Highlands frequently refer to Read's description: "Sex differentiation

---

[1] Even if they do not permanently own articles of wealth (Ryan, 1969: 167–8).

[2] Mendi women can return home to their patrilateral kin or find refuge with other cognates; and there is a likelihood of their being able to prevail upon the former to return bridewealth.

. . . is more than the simple assignment of different roles and a respective sphere of interest to men and women and the over-all recognition of interdependence . . . The institutionalized pattern of Gahuku-Gama sex relationships prescribes a rigid differentiation of roles based on the dominance of men and the submission and inferiority of women" (1954: 24, 29). But dominance is not unchallenged. Gahuku men, for example, interpret the demonstrable signs of maturation and fecundity in women as threats to their own superiority. In spite of men's dominance, there is antagonism between them and their inferiors. This has been put in more general terms: in societies where men "monopolise the social structure . . . (implying) the subordination and deprivation of women" there is an innate conflict, a war between the sexes (Wilson, 1967:366; Lewis, 1966).

Writing specifically of New Guinea, Allen (1967:65) says, "male dominance is a characteristic feature of all Highland societies but differs in degree." Male–female antagonism itself he relates to the structural exclusiveness of solidary single sex associations, for example, between men of a locality who are united by membership of a corporate and exogamous patrilineal descent group. Such sex hostility, he suggests, exists equally in Enga, where women are in a "subordinate position", and Hagen (Mbowamb) (where "the status of woman is high") (1967:56). What varies are the modes of its expression. Where men are most dominant, his argument goes, and women's status is lowest, antagonism on the part of females can find little expression in either ritual (rites being controlled by men) or everyday activities. Where men are less dominant, but still retain a measure of superiority so that antagonism is combined with women having high status, hostility displayed in male ritual will be reduced, while women may be able to give voice to some of their feelings in secular life. Allen thus distinguishes the contexts in which antagonism appears, e.g. in secular affairs, in ritual. There are several facets to the concept here. Cult performances and ritual may presuppose a formal antithesis between the sexes, in the example of their complementary contributions, or the dangerous influence one has on the other. The antithesis may be perpetuated at a mundane level through the ascription of inherent differences in nature and make-up (women's power to pollute is not confined to ritual context). Cults and rituals are likely to involve at least one sex in collective action against the other; informal but still collectively expressed antagonism may be stated in public confrontations between men and women (as at bridewealth occasions).

Antagonism may also inhere in the confrontation of individuals—not necessarily for personal reasons, but because an individual's actions are felt to be characteristic of his or her sex (for example, "women are promiscuous"). Thus men may feel their collective interests are threatened by the actions of particular women; they suffer from the Delilah complex (Douglas, 1966:154).

The puberty rites by which Gahuku-Gama men achieve and demonstrate their superiority at one and the same time must also make a quite contrary statement: men draw attention to physiological differences between the sexes and furthermore interpret female capacities as a challenge to their own.[1] The same holds for Mae-Enga. Rituals associated with the bachelor cult do not bear out men's victory in secular affairs; rather they represent women as having at every turn the power to endanger their physical well being. Nor does secular dominance go unchallenged. Notions about women's waywardness, fickle nature, perversity and so on, are common place throughout the Highlands, and each derogatory remark must contain the admission that in some spheres men have not in fact been able to impose full control. Hageners say that a woman's mind is like the plume of a casuarina tree: it sways back and forth, this way and that. Kuma use almost the same idiom to epitomise the fickleness of a girl's desires (Reay, 1959a:181). Siane women are capricious and unpredictable (Salisbury, 1965:75); Bena women untrustworthy (Langness, 1967:172), and so on.

Antagonism would seem to be partly an outcome of the idiom in which dominance itself is expressed. The emphasis in some Eastern Highlands[2] societies on violence and physical aggression, which likens encounters between men and women to battles (cf. Langness, 1967; Berndt, R. M., 1962), posits the existence of an enemy. For example the superiority and masculinity of a Fore man is seen as challenged when he is struck by his wife, and age-mates rally in sympathy to take collective vengeance on the woman (Lindenbaum and Glasse, 1969:169). Mae-Enga, on the other hand, stress male jural authority, which depicts women as minors and wards of men, requiring of them meek and submissive public behaviour (Meggitt, 1964:221). Kyaka Enga, who perform a version of the Hagen Female Spirit Cult, believe that the cult

---

[1] E.g. Read (1966:153): the ideal image of the superior, independent, largely self-sufficient male is heavily qualified.

[2] The following elements are found in some combination in the attitudes of most Highlands peoples—too much should not be made of the weighting I give.

not only protects men from women, but keeps the women "in their place" (Bulmer, 1965:150). Although Hagen men like women to be quiet on public occasions they do not exact formal obeisance. If they take a stance, it is as big-men. Hagen males, seeing themselves as transactors, try to act towards females as big-men do towards those over whom they have influence. But in positing that women are amenable to influence, they admit that an individual may harbour multiple, perhaps conflicting loyalties. Choices presented in a woman's intermediary role also lead to the fear that they will exercise choice entirely for their own ends.

Hagen men "compete" with women precisely for the reason that they see them in this way. "Unless men and women have access to the same goals and rewards they can hardly be said to come into competition with each other" (Wilson, 1967:368). Wilson suggests that in societies where women are genuinely (and effectively) depressed then their rivalry is likely to be directed towards other women, who are their equals rather than towards men, who are not. He thus stipulates that the kinds of Somali spirit-possession, analysed by Lewis (1966) as mystical pressures which depressed categories with few other means available can exert upon their superiors in circumstances of deprivation, are better understood as a means to identify status when this is threatened, necessarily by equals. Thus cowives compete with each other, not with the husband (*for* whose favours they are rivals). These points of view are not perhaps so disparate as the controversy (in the pages of *Man*, 1966-8) suggests. Antagonism against a competitor for the same goal can also contain within it protest against the desired person for failing to accord each party the uniqueness of status they claim. In Hagen, the very fact that "each woman takes her social standing from individual males" (Wilson, 1967:373) means that her dependency is likely to appear the most frustrating and herself most subject to "abuses of neglect and deprivation" (Lewis, 1966:314) when threatened by another woman. *Popokl* often afflicts Hagen wives at the news that their husband proposes to marry a further wife, but it may also arise over a variety of other conflicts between the spouses.

Hageners' distinction between cowives who are *wølik* (jealous) with each other but full of *popokl* (protest anger) against their common husband supports the concept that cowives are equals, competing for the superior husband. Nevertheless, in other contexts it seems that competition itself is an element in *popokl*. While *popokl* is most clearly a protest mechanism used to point up a dependent situation, it may also contain an appeal that the relationship be restored to one of reciprocity. Hagen women do not compete with men as equals in every sphere; but in some they demand the kind of equality implied in making mutually acceptable decisions, in the recognition that their labours entitle them to have a say over the disposal of crops and pigs, and that links with their kin should be honoured. This leads to the point that while in any male-dominated society a woman is likely to enter "into relationships more particularly on a dyadic basis within the domestic realm as compared to the corporate or group matrix of her husband's social status" (Wilson, 1967:373),[1] such opposition between the sexes in Hagen is modified in one important respect. Success for men comes from the manipulation of partnership networks, not from attainment of some office within the clan community or from an assumption of rank. While clan and personal prestige are to some extent bound up with each other, it is chiefly from their individual standing that men are accorded renown. There is certainly a contrast in the way a woman's efforts are seen to focus on her husband, while he does not show the same degree of dependency on her. But it would perhaps not be too far off the mark to say that a wife's involvement in her husband's enterprises, while being restricted to only a segment of them, is not of a totally different quality from her husband's own concern with his individual partners.

Hagen women accept on the whole their political inferiority, and do not challenge men's rights to hold *moka* or question the manner in which courts are conducted. Women accept that in public life men are dominant. Competition with men is not to do all that men do, but to draw a recognition from them of the claims they make as women. At particular junctures, acknowledgement of such claims may be against other male interests. Wives in particular demand of husbands a recognition of their intermediary roles; while spouses frequently share similar notions about the prestige *moka* exchanges bring, their actual interests may diverge. A man might construct complicated plans for transactions with a range of partners, but his wife is likely to think primarily of his links with her own clan. She also may lay direct claim to the pigs she helped rear, and try to keep them out of exchanges altogether.

It is considered appropriate for women to cherish sentiments towards

---

[1] Gulliver (1963:141–4) makes a similar comment about Arusha women who are less confident of their affiliations and loyalties than men, and he specifically suggests that their "inferiority is increased because of the persistent ambiguity of [their] status".

their own kin, that they should make visits home, even occasionally setting up permanent residence there. Separation allows compromises to be made without challenging the structural values of marriage; although the husband loses his wifes' immediate services he retains links with her kin. A woman is thus allowed to exercise a certain amount of freedom in her domestic life, and is certainly not under her husband's constant surveillance. It is expected that a number of young brides will not stay with their first husbands. This allows for personal adjustment between the spouses, and recognizes their right to be considered as individuals in spite of the wider significance of marital ties. At the same time, the particular concern which men have in prospect of affinal exchanges colours their attitude towards divorce. The mutual interests of brothers-in-law is expressed in men's tendency to blame the wife when a marriage does break up.[1] A man wishing to be rid of his wife is simply said to display an idiosyncratic quirk; but a woman who deserts her husband exemplifies traits latent in all females. Dissolution cannot be claimed as a right because its consequences are too threatening for alliance. It must therefore be seen as the outcome of violence, and appears as sabotage. By ascribing independent volition (*noman*) to women, men can blame them for divorce. Expectation that women will sometimes "get away with it" both is a result of and results in a certain permissiveness of the part of men or senior kinswomen; in actuality women are sometimes able to push through a marriage or divorce against the better judgement of others. *Noman* has a double aspect: it is both "disposition" and "will". Because of their innate disposition women may be seen to obstruct men's aims, and through independent wills follow their own inclination. The allegation that a wife has been greased by her kin and the assumption that females have inherent promiscuous tendencies neatly epitomizes the double bind; on the one hand, a wife sides with some men (e.g. her brother) to threaten others (e.g. her husband); on the other, she jettisons all advantages men see in stable marriages by appearing to repudiate its values and thereby jeopardizes the entire

---

[1] Mothers are also blamed, probably more frequently than the incidence warrants, for greasing their daughters. Some mothers may find satisfaction in prolonging the period of uncertainty after marriage; during bridewealth proceedings their parental role receives open acclaim but the further away from this point in time affinal exchanges become, the more marked the *moka* element and the less relevant their own position. It should perhaps be added that women are not blamed for all misfortunes—men may be held responsible in adultery, a husband be criticized for not keeping discrete the claims of his cowives, and so on.

system. It is significant that men do not find it inappropriate to attribute transactional motives to divorcees. They expect women to become angry if the proper payments are not made to their kin or debts mount up on one or other side. The correct solution, in men's eyes, however, is for a restoration of relations through settlement of the debts, rather than a termination of them.

The same double issue appears in the way women use poison for political and personal ends. I have more than once referred to the significance of Hagen women being credited with the conscious manipulation both of their innate powers and of harmful external substances. Highlands societies vary in the extent to which females are held to employ poison, sorcery or witchcraft. Sorcery is insignificant in Hagen and there are no witches in the usual sense of the word.[1] Hageners lay stress on poison; Gahuku-Gama women are suspected of helping sorcerers by obtaining semen for them to doctor (Read, 1954:27-8); Gururumba women are witches (Newman, 1964:259). The kinds of attack men expect from women delimit areas of vulnerability. Gahuku men, we might conclude, are concerned about loss of male strength; among the Gururumba it is active, strong or assertive people who become targets for female aggression. Mae-Enga men suppose that women sometimes deliberately pollute their husbands with menstrual blood (Meggitt, 1964:207). That it is poison, as well as premeditated pollution, Hagen men fear, indicates some vulnerability, among other things, to womens' group loyalties. One dimension of such beliefs lies in how far only personal and how far political motives are allegedly involved. In his description of Gahuku sorcery, Read makes it clear that women are feared for their contacts with other groups, particularly their own relatives whose requests are hard to resist. In this context he notes, "Women do not become members of their husband's clan when they marry" (Read, 1954:28) and an immediate contrast with Bena suggests itself. Significantly, Bena women are not suspected of either sorcery or poison (Langness, 1967:166). Whether in-married wives maintain active contacts with other clans seems relevant here. But there is a further factor.

---

[1] The terms need some definition. Strictly, I would use "poison" for supposedly fatal substances administered typically in food, "sorcery" for magic made over the victim's leavings, exuviate, etc., "witchcraft" for internal harmful power (other than weakness or pollution). Some writers would include all such magic under the rubric "sorcery" (see Lawrence and Meggitt, 1965). Hageners certainly operate a host of magical devices (love-magic, increase-magic, magic against cowives) employing spells and objects in a metaphorical or metonymical manner. These tend not to lead, however, to the kinds of accusations that result from poisoning.

Kuma women do not operate poison or sorcery (although like men may be suspected of witchcraft) while Mae-Enga women occasionally have resort to limited sorcery techniques. In both societies, the links women afford with their natal clans are kept open. Since Kuma avoid marriage into hostile groups, wives would not be immediate roads for poison, whereas it would seem Mae women might well be. The circumstances, however, in which Mae women resort to use of menstrual blood (or the evil eye) have little political character at all, motives being purely personal ones (against cowives or because they have been "crossed in love" e.g. Meggitt, 1964:207). More than the simple fact of incorporation is the kind of action of which females are judged capable. Wanggulam Dani believe that women, and only women, use a fatal substance, *mum*, for purposes that include revenge for deaths of close kinsmen, and retaliation for theft or debts. It brings them some prestige. Men are the most frequent victims (Ploeg, 1969:52–54). Ploeg suggests that this in part compensates women for their general inferiority and subordination to men (1969:159). Wanggulam women do, in fact, participate to some extent in public affairs, and Ploeg's account by no means suggests they are completely subjugated.[1] The same contrast between overt and covert influence is made in Hagen, but poison here is a weapon either sex can use. Men's and women's means to covert influence in this run parallel. I would look on female poisoning activities not entirely as a compensation for power Hagen women otherwise lack, but also as an extension of other positive, if partial, sources of influence in spheres including political affairs. It is one which contrasts secret doings unfavourably with the kind of open political activities most characteristic of men.

I might reiterate the point here that female ghosts are as concerned for their descendants' welfare as male ghosts, although their interest is restricted to closely related persons, whereas ghosts of all the clan's past big-men are invoked on major occasions. Again, although it is men who conduct, participate in and officiate at public cult performances, outside the cults women as well as men may be ritual specialists (*møn wuᵉ, møn amb*). Their sphere of action is mainly limited to the recitation of private spells, ones to help an individual's crops grow, remove the

---

[1] As, for example, would seem to be the case for the Havik Brahmin widows described in Harper (1969), whose use of poison is their sole demonstration of power. Perhaps, on the contrary, belief in *mum* and such like gives men themselves a weapon (in the accusation process) with which to control possible insubordination (Lewis, 1966:319).

effects of menstrual pollution, and so on; but there is no suggestion that these are the less effective because recited by a female. There is, moreover, considerable overlap in the types of spells which men and women know,[1] and bridewealths were one important semi-public context to which a woman often in the past was called to act as spell expert. In the presence of the bride's close kin she would divine the success of the forthcoming enterprise.

Investment of female loyalties in the (male) political system has its corollary in the rarity with which women as such ever come together to solidary groups, or even combine on the basis of their sex in the expression of opposing interests. When men see women "going their own way", this is in the context of solitary acts, not in group alignments with other women. While the exclusion of females is ritually enjoined in the performance of certain male cults, no combined action is required of their sex. They have no secret societies, hold no ceremonies of their own, not even rituals associated with menstruation, betrothal or birth. In Hagen it would be meaningless to talk of a female subculture; women's concerns are not systematically directed towards other women, and this would seem to derive from the fact that as intermediaries it is primarily men they link.

The divergent interests of men and women are given public and collective expression in some Highlands societies (e.g. Reay, 1959b; Lindenbaum and Glasse, 1969: 169–70). In Bena Bena (Langness, 1967: 173) and Gahuku-Gama (Read, 1966: 196) women, as a body, attack men during bridewealth ceremonies, and may also express combined opposition to them during the initiation of boys (and see Read, 1966: 136). Only very sporadically, and with little display of seriousness, do such alignments of women occur in Hagen. At the end of a courting session, the senior wives who have chaperoned their daughters throughout the night may combine with them at dawn to pelt the dispersing men with ashes or mud. This sport gives the young men licence to trample over the women's gardens or tear down bananas or sugarcane. Pelting with ash or mud occurs on other occasions when youth and girls from intermarrying clans come together in a crowd. At an exchange festival, separate groups of girls and men may each execute their own dance, flinging out taunts and invitations to the other. All these encounters, in

---

[1] Some details are given in Strathern, A. J. and A. M. (1968: 182–3); a person using his knowledge to help someone else is paid, and women might receive gifts of pork or minor valuables for their services.

fact, express the possibility of cross-sexual links rather than simple male–female antagonism.

Women's challenge to male dominance lies elsewhere: in assertions of independence over marriage choices and sabotage of the exchange system through divorce; both in claims to be treated as quasi-transactors and in manipulating political subordination to their own advantage. These do not involve women in corporate confrontations with men, but as individuals following the dictates of their *noman*. Emerging from particular situations and roles, attitudes are generalized into public notions about men's and women's natures. As often as not the challenge is imagined: the sex war is more a construct of male than of female fears. But the very fact that men think it declared allows Hagen women a measure of genuine independence.

Appendices

I

The Subdivisions of Two Hagen Tribes

Demography influences and is influenced by recent histories of migration and group movements. For sub-divisions of the Elti and Kawelka, I indicate something of the population structure.

Tepam—kang^e^mal (lineage) sets within sub-sub-clans are not given. Population figures for Elti and Kawelka men refer to current members of the clan group (September, 1965), and in the Elti case include those living in the Central Melpa area but not the few still in Temboka. Exogamous groups are asterisked (Figs. 6 and 7).

The Central Melpa Elti tribe were driven out of their former Temboka territory in about 1930 by a coalition of enemies, including the formidable Mokei (6199).[1] They were given refuge at Kelua by clans of the Ndika (total 6749) and Yamka (2281) tribes. Some four-fifths of the Elti (445 people) now live in the Central Melpa area. Two groups of Elti had previously moved northward at some unknown date in the past, one settling on the Wahgi river and the other moving from the Wahgi up to Buk. At Buk they were partly absorbed by the Tipuka (2419). The segment in the Wahgi valley lived with groups from the Elti's pair tribe, Penambe (678), but at about the time of European contact succumbed dramatically to disease and dwindled away to a handful. Under pressure of land shortage on the small strip allocated to them, the recent Elti arrivals at Kelua have since moved out from here to

---

[1] Figures are adopted from Administration censuses (1961, 1962); later statistics for Elti and Kawelka are based on our own censuses (1964–5).

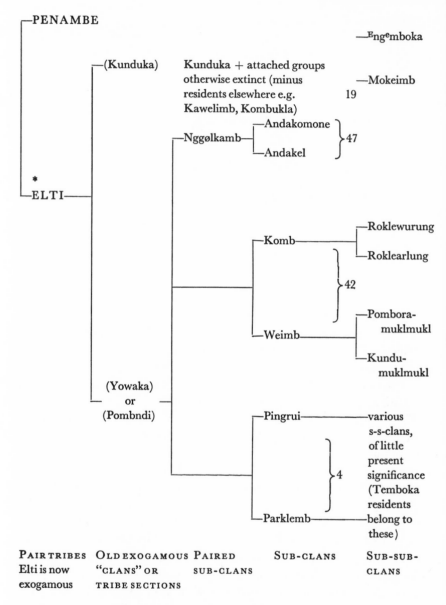

Fig. 6. The Elti at Kelua: numbers of adult men

join the remnants on the Wahgi and to combine with a Tipuka contingent who have come from Buk to settle on the Gumant river. The Gumant and Wahgi rivers are renowned for their pig pasture.

The Northern Melpa Kawelka tribe at Buk, pair to the Tipuka, is of medium size (860 persons). Clans of the Kawelka and Tipuka tribes

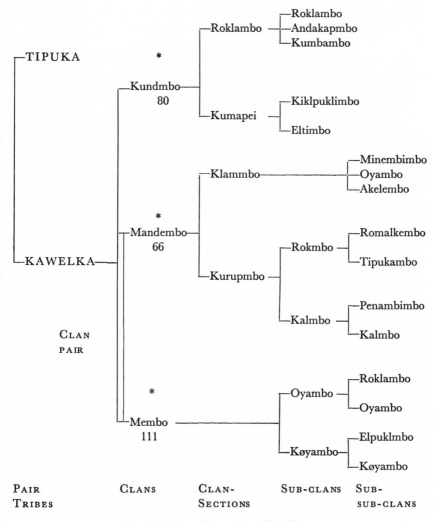

Fig. 7. The Kawelka: numbers of adult men

were allies against their traditional enemies, the Kombukla (1542) and Minembi (2813) pair. Apart from the recent settlement on the Gumant, Tipuka are an example of a tribe inhabiting an uninterrupted stretch of territory. But within a tribal territory, clan territories may alter. Thus one of the clans which now considers itself having a very close association with Kawelka originally lived at the far end of Tipuka territory, from where it was hounded in warfare to be invited to settle on Kawelka's eastern border.

II

Differences in Marriage and Divorce Patterns between Elti and Kawelka

Polygyny and Marital Status

If the category of youths of marriageable age but as yet unmarried is excluded, some 79% of Kawelka and 76% of Elti men[1] are currently married. Previously but no longer married men account for approximately 8·5% of the Kawelka total, and 18% of the Elti; there is a corresponding difference in the proportions of never married (*wangen*) men, Kawelka 13% and Elti 5% (see Strathern, A. J. and A. M., 1969). Vicedom's figures (Vicedom and Tischner, 1943–8:2:23f), for the Ndika tribe in the 1930's compare with those for Kawelka, his categories "married men", "widowers" and "slaves" showing the following approximate percentages: 81%, 4% and 14·5%. Whereas Elti and Kawelka men stand equal chance of being married at some time,[2] Elti are more likely to lose their wives. Some previously married Elti men are now regarded as near-*wangen* or *etamb* ("rubbish").

The difference between Elti and Kawelka here is that among the

---

[1] Figures (rounded to nearest unit) are for clan groups, that is, agnates plus attached nonagnates on clan territory. I note that there is no striking evidence for differences in the adult population ratio between the sexes (see Strathern, A. J., to be published).

[2] There is no statistical difference in the proportions of Kawelka and Elti men once married.

former such men have been able to acquire a wife at some time, even though they have not managed to keep her; whereas among the latter, once beyond the ordinary age for marriage, the chances of ever marrying are weaker. This implies a greater circulation of women among Central Melpa groups. It is the smaller tribes who might be expected to show more losses than gains. There are two points to note here. One: Central Melpa were the first to benefit from the European introduction of vast supplies of shell valuables, and Vicedom comments (Vicedom and Tischner, 1943–8:2:24) that the big-men[1] of the larger tribes were able to attract numbers of women to themselves. Certainly among some of the bigger Central Melpa tribes (e.g. Ndika) polygyny is found on a scale practically unknown among the Northern Melpa. The Ndika sponsor of Elti men who were given refuge on his land himself has had twelve and is currently married to nine wives. The fact that this scale of polygyny is maintained today we may put down to rather different circumstances: Central Melpa groups are more heavily committed to Christianity than their Northern counterparts, and declared Christians are supposedly monogamous; there are thus fewer men, outside the mission system, competing to have more than one wife. At the same time, big-men of the stature of the Ndika sponsor are not found among all Central Melpa groups, refugee groups in particular being historically in a poor position. This suggests that there has been a flow of ex-wives from such tribes to more wealthy ones. The second point is to do with the reputation for promiscuity, which women near Hagen town enjoy; I return to this in the discussion of divorce rates. To a certain extent, there is a greater circulation of women among *all* Central Melpa groups. Thus even relatively less well-to-do individuals can hope for a period of marriage.

In comparing Elti and Kawelka we are thus dealing with several components. Elti are an example of a small Central Melpa tribe which is affected by the greater flow of Central Melpa women by comparison with Northern Melpa. We might expect larger Central Melpa groups to show an apparent stability in their marriage patterns,[2] since their greater power enables them to retain more wives, while Northern Melpa conservatism is a reason for the greater stability of the Kawelka pattern.

---

[1] Most big-men have more than one wife; although not all polygynists are major leaders (*wu^e nyim ou*), many are at least minor big-men (*wu^e nyim kel*).

[2] I have no recent figures for groups such as the Ndika, however.

Divorce Rates

There are no outstanding differences in the personal reasons which Central Melpa men and women advance for divorce (see pp. 208–9). They cover a range of reasons similar to those given by Northern Melpa. In the cases of which I have details, dissatisfaction over bridewealth payments is an issue which turns up frequently, as does cowife jealousy and complaints that the wife is *wapra*, along with the occasional esoteric factor such as a woman's attachment to a policeman (when Hagen was still a small station) frowned on by his superiors.

I cannot fully account for the contrast between Elti and Kawelka (see Table XIII). To some extent it must be related to conditions existing generally among Central and Northern Melpa tribes. Marriage networks necessarily involve one group in a number of others: thus the proportion of past wives which Kawelka men have lost in divorce to other groups is about the same as the proportion of previous divorces which their current wives have experienced. Divorce ratios for female members of two Kawelka clans, most of whom have made extra-Kawelka marriages, are similar to those for Kawelka men's in-coming wives (ratio C: Kawelka sisters 17·1%, wives 18·4%). The ratios for women are in any case based on histories involving previous marriages to other groups. The figures span the personal histories of men and women of all ages, but I have not differentiated age categories in presentation. To take (say) divorces experienced in the first ten years of marriages of men now fifty by comparison with men now 20–30 years old would require a rigour in the assessment of age and chronology greater than my information allows. As they stand, the ratios relate to a forty or fifty year period. Three factors possibly contribute to the difference in the two divorce rates.

Historical events prior to pacification is one. The Elti migration from Temboka was the outcome of perhaps a decade of battles with various of their neighbours, and the probably unusual amount of fighting Elti experienced over this period affected their patterns of marriage and divorce. Undoubtedly Elti lost some wives who ran home at the outbreak of war or who deserted on the travel northward. Elti may, in fact, have been in a worse position than some of their more powerful neighbours, who gained women at their expense. There is no statistically significant difference between Kawelka and Elti in the proportion of men currently married to women whom they took as widows or divorcees. Elti's higher rate of loss, in other words, does not seem matched by a higher rate of acquisition of ex-widows and divorcees from other groups.

I refer again to Central Melpa as the region first to benefit from the new wealth brought in by Europeans. One result I have suggested seems to have been an intensified competition for women, more men being able to offer bridewealths with the prized valuables (see above). Hageners themselves say that European contact has had a direct impact on the stability of marriage. Northern Melpa speak of women near Mt Hagen town as humbugs (*kara*) who are always divorcing their husbands, to an even greater extent than their own women. There, they say, girls have experienced the free life on the government station and profited from business opportunities in prostitution. With the development of roads and transport systems, these opportunities are becoming available to a wider range of women. At the time of my study, however, Northern Melpa had been less affected by processes of change.[1] Central Melpa themselves acknowledge the increase of *wapra* women. As one middle-aged Elti man put it, "Before there were only a few promiscuous women, but now white men have come, there are plenty. We look at their skins (i.e. their outward appearance)—they have breasts and wear netbags (like all women), but what are their thoughts?"

There are more women with a past reputation for promiscuity among current Elti wives than among those now married to Kawelka, although these *amb wapra* do not in themselves contribute to the higher Elti divorce rate. (A significant difference remains in the male divorce ratio C between the two tribes after the exclusion of all marriages made with women who were or who became categorized as *wapra*.) We are dealing with a more general influence in which the particular *wapra* women play an indirect part, their presence perhaps encouraging individuals of both sexes to take their unions more lightly; certainly they present examples of choice apparently freely exercised. While many girls still hope that large bridewealths will be paid for them in the traditional manner, they also show passing preferences for youths who have money, can provide them with European-style clothes, and so on. Education and mission teaching has reinforced the prestige of those who follow European ways. At the same time, young men may find it hard to meet both the old and new requirements, especially when they spend periods away from home in order to earn money in employment. Their absence is likely to be

---

[1] I do not give a systematic account of social change, but simply note that divorce rates often rise in such situations (e.g. Ardener, 1962; Mitchell, 1961).

criticized as abandonment. Younger people, investing their energies in making money and spending it on new things such as the prestigeful trade-store tinned food and clothes, are less able than their established elders to combine this with exchange commitments. Women for their part, if they are not complaining about gifts to their kin, complain that they cannot also go off and earn large sums of money in open employment.

There is, finally, the impression that bridewealth transactions are conducted on a rather grander scale in Central Melpa, especially in relation to shell valuables and the higher proportion of wealth returned by the bride's kin (Appendix VI). To some extent there has been a lessening at Kelua (by contrast with Buk) of extensive individual *moka* networks. Whereas some Elti wives are still involved quite heavily in their husband's exchanges, others are of the opinion that, "Now law has come up, we do not make *moka*". Bridewealth, however, continues to be a major focus of attention and investment.

The Northern Melpa Dei Council early in its history agreed on legislation to standardize and reduce the number of items to be given in bridewealth, but for a long time this was discussed first by the Hagen and Kui Councils, and then by the amalgamated Hagen council, before any decision was made (finally in 1966 although ratification was delayed for another three years). Central Melpa Councillors were reluctant to agree to such a financial curtailment. The deliberate attempts in both areas to reduce the amount of wealth is direct recognition of the fact that while a high premium put on successful exchanges may help support a marriage where transactions are carried out to satisfaction, exchanges may themselves also give rise to numerous dissatisfactions, and be the cause of subsequent divorce. Bridewealth is an initial and crucial context to which this applies. A high bridewealth may demarcate for the wife and her kin her prestigeful intermediary role, but when expectations are geared to a level which cannot be met, there is frequent discontent on either side. Sometimes in the past, men took wives on the promise of payments, and failure to keep their word led to the woman's return home. Bridewealth transactions are indeed trial exchanges. In evaluating this situation, Hageners significantly tend to stress the role of the bride's kin in "pulling" her away from the husband, rather than action on the husband's side. Thus in Dei Council a related move forbad a woman's kin from receiving a second bridewealth for her once she was divorced, lest they hawk her from marriage to marriage in pursuit of bridewealths spiralling ever higher.[1] Bridewealth is not only the first and most likely of all transactions to eventuate between affines, but occurs at a stage when both parties may be uncertain of each other, sensitive over possible slights and liable to precipitate disputes. With greater emphasis put on the transaction, disputes are perhaps more certain to arise. This may always have been a point of difference between Central and Northern Melpa, and it is possibly aggravated in a situation where affines cannot be so sure of post-bridewealth exchanges. One of the issues facilitating the Northern Melpa Council's reduction of bridewealth amounts was the fact that generosity could always be shown in subsequent *moka* exchanges.

---

[1] A ruling which operates in favour of the husband's side, since with his recovered bridewealth he can look for a new spouse, and may even be able to obtain a divorced woman for no initial payment at all. Contrast Vicedom's comment (1943–8:2:432) that (in the past) the husband was more often the injured party—he had to raise fresh bridewealth if none was returned at divorce, whereas the woman could always remarry. As far as I know, these proposals were not initially prompted directly by the administration (as among the Bena Bena, for example, Langness, 1963:165).

III

Separation

TABLE XVII

The situation of nine separated wives of eight Kawelka men,
in September 1965[a]

A. Conditions of separation

Wife	1	2	3	4	5		6
1.	C	A	a	/6	1 (2) Io		?
2.	A	A	a	1/	2 (2) Io		+
3.	A	A	a	/1	1 (2) Io		?
4.	C	A	a	none	2 (3) IIo		+
5.	D	?C	?	(1)2/	2 (2) I≠		−
6.[b]	B	B	b	4/	3 (3) Io		+
7.	B	B	b	4/	3 (3) IIo		+
8.	D	?C	a	(1)/	2 (2) II ≠ wid		−
9.	D	C	c	3/	3 (2) IIo		−

Key

1. Wife's age now:

2. Her age at time of separation:

    A 18–25 young
    B 25–40 middle-aged
    C 40–50 approaching menopause
    D 50+ old

3. Duration of marriage before separation:
    a : under 5 yrs,   b : 5–15 yrs,   c : 15 + yrs
4. Number of children born: by previous husbands (1);
    to the marriage, before / after separation
    (thus 1/3, one child before and three after)
5. Number of wives including subject:
    at time of separation, and (currently)
    (thus 1 (2), one wife then and two now)
    Wife's position at time of separation: Ist, IInd wife
    Her previous marital history:
       o not married, ≠ before divorced, wid before widowed

6. Jealousy with cowives given as specific reason   +
    Jealousy with cowives probably a factor   ?
    Jealousy with cowives probably not important   —

[a] Wives nos 6 and 7 are married to one man.
[b] She had been apart from her husband for most of her married life, but tried living in his settlement again before finally separating from him: I count this final separation.

Although separation is possible throughout married life, we see that a quite common combination (cases 1, 2, 3, 4) is for a young wife (column 2), not long married (column 3), perhaps already with a child or else

B. Current arrangements between separated spouses

Wife 7		8	9	10
1.	Home kin	H	(H) (B)	Inter-visiting; she sometimes sends food to H; he cares for children.
2.	h k	H	(B) (H on B's land)	She makes his aprons, etc.; he cares for child.
3.	h k	H	(B)	Estranged because her kin demanding child payments.
4.	h k	B	(B)	Visiting between H and W.
5.[a]	With son in Xn village	?	(H) (S)	Not much visiting.
6.	h k	H	(H) (S and B)	Sometimes sends H food, says he neglects children.
7.	HB at H's former settlement	no pigs	(HBS)	Little visiting; she says he neglects the children as well as her.
8.	h k and married son	S?	(S)	Occasional visiting.
9.	h k, then ZDH place	S	(S and ZDH)	Little interaction; her son is hardly recognized as of his F's clan group.

Key
7. People with whom wife lives: h k = home kin (e.g. her parents, brothers and their children)
8. Whose pigs she cares for: H husband   HBS husband's brother's son,
9. Who makes gardens for her: B brother   ZDH sister's daughter's husband
                                     S son
    (   ) indicates discrete contributions.[b]
10. Further remarks on interaction between husband and wife.

[a] She is baptised and lives in a Christian (Xn) settlement, where her married son by a previous husband holds office.
[b] Thus in case 6, the husband makes her gardens on his land, while her own son and brother together make further gardens at the place of her domicile.

pregnant (column 4), to leave for reasons associated with jealousy of a new wife the husband marries. (In cases 1 and 3, the first wife moves away before the second actually comes.) If she is suckling a child, the long *post partum* taboo on sexual intercourse allegedly makes the husband relatively indifferent to his first wife's departure. We may note that five are first wives, and seven have been married only to the one husband. Cases 6 and 7 are middle-aged women who separated in anger at their husband's preference for a younger wife; while 8 is an old woman who went to live with a married son by a previous husband; 9 returned home first to look after her brother's orphaned children, and then moved to where the sister's daughter was married and her own son had brothers-in-law: "My husband has other wives to look after him," she commented.

In all these cases, the woman's children live with her rather than their father, so that where S (son) is an entry this implies that she looks after her son's pigs, or he makes gardens for her, independently of her husband.

These examples show the variations which there can be in the mutual involvement of the spouses. In case 1 husband and wife are close, while the spouses of cases 8 and 9 are married only in the sense that the wife has gone to no other partner and occasional visits still take place; the affines, however, remain potential exchange partners.

IV

Exchange Marriage

There is considerable variation in the span of grouping seen to be involved on one or other side of an exchange. For example, someone might say that the marriage of a Kawelka Membo Køyambo woman to a Tipuka Kitepi man was reciprocated when a Tipuka Oklembo woman went to Membo Oyambo, the span on the Kawelka side being a clan, and on the Tipuka side two pair clans from a common tribal section; but another person might allege it was reciprocated by a Kitepi sub-sub-clan sister marrying into Kawelka Mandembo clan.

I illustrate this diversity for 153 exchange marriages described to me by Elti and Kawelka.

TABLE XVIII

Span of groupings between which exchanges are said to be made. Percentage of exchange marriages allocated to unit

A. Unit on Kawelka or Elti side (and including exchanges within Kawelka, or within Elti in the past)

	Tribe	Pair clan	Clan[a]	(Sub-)sub-clan	Lineage
ELTI	55%	—	20%	15%	10%
KAWELKA	—	12%	26%	47%	15%

B. Unit of "other group" marrying into Kawelka or Elti

	Tribe	Pair clan	Clan[a]	(sub-clan, lineage combined)
ELTI	29·5%	18%	34·5%	18%
KAWELKA	4·3%	8·6%	30·2%	56·9%

[a] Paired sub-clans in the Elti case: see Appendix I. The exogamous units are Elti: tribe, Kawelka: clan.

Elti and Kawelka form a contrast here. Kawelka informants tend to single out common membership of a sub-clan or lower level group both in reference to the relationship between the partners on their (A) and on the other (B) side. Elti on the other hand cite their tribe as a whole (A). This is partly a function of its small size and the fact that it operates now as an exogamous unit; but if we look at the groups with whom Elti say they exchange (B), we see that in nearly 30% cases the most inclusive span is the tribe. This is consistent with their recent migration and the immaturity of their marital alliances in a new area. There is an effort perhaps to see themselves in exchange relationships with as many large groups as possible, even where the actual marriages contracted are rather thin on the ground: so that Elti informants were citing as exchanges pairs of marriages where the only common link between the brother–sister on one side was that of tribal membership.

V

Regional Differences
in Bridewealth Custom

Tribes regard themselves as forming regional clusters. Thus Northern
Melpa groups (called by others *Kopon* people) designate Central Melpa
as *Kuma*, and Western Melpa as *Wer*. Within Northern Melpa, Kendipi
and W^{e}lyi tribes may be distinguished from Minembi, Tipuka and
Kawelka as *Melpa*. Differences in bridewealth custom are among the
features which discriminate between such regions.

1. Central and Western Melpa[1] often make a return for "the mother's
pig" (*mam peng kng*), while Northern Melpa (including the *Melpa* tribes)
do not. See Chapter 5 for discussion.

2. Cooked pig set aside for the mother (*mindi kng*) is now omitted among
Central (and Western) Melpa, the live *mam peng kng* replacing it. Some
Kawelka and Minembi informants include themselves here, saying that
only the *Melpa* tribes, W^{e}lyi, Kendipi and their neighbours, still do
this. The omission is traced as having spread from Central Melpa tribes
(Ndika and Yamka) to Kawelka and Minembi, and now further to
include Klamakae and Tipuka. (Cf. Map 1.) The reason for which it is
no longer given is the same as that which has led groups to give up
tembokl kng (see page 104): a cooked pig tends to be widely distributed
and it is unfair, the argument goes, should divorce ensue, for any one

---

[1] Informants from Central and Northern Melpa. Western and Central groups are broadly
classed together in their bridewealth customs, as are the *Kopon* and *Melpa* tribes of Northern
Melpa. *Melpa* groups are also said to be influenced by Wahgi Valley contacts. Clans of the
Minembi tribe may link themselves to either Northern or Central Melpa.

person to assume the responsibility of finding a replacement. Traditionally, the recipient of certain parts (head, liver, etc.) was formally responsible: modern insistence on the difficulties created at divorce must
be related to the higher expectation that bridewealth will be returned,
and to the greater size of the gifts. Cooked rather than live pigs was a
general characteristic of bridewealths in pre-contact days.

3. All the Northern Melpa tribes and the Eastern Melpa Kuli (on the
south east border with Minj-Wahgi) are said to bring raw intestines
(*kitim*) along with the pork for the bride's kin (stage 5); Central Melpa
cook them. The raw *kitim* is carried specially wrapped up in leaves, and
is presented as a delicacy by the recipient (bride's father) to those who
have helped him most in the transactions. The Kuli are said to give it
to the bride's mother. Refraining from cooking this item is a gesture on
the part of the groom's kin: it symbolizes the fact that they have not held
back any of the pork for their own consumption (cf. stage 4) but come
with all the bits and pieces—intestines, liver, heart, kidneys, tail—for the
bride's kin. Presenting titbits indicates that they are the kind of people
who stint on nothing.

5. There are recognized variations in the manner in which the bride's
people make the return gift. Central Melpa claim that they return a
larger proportion of the live pigs that Northern Melpa do (see Appendix
VI). This is an explicit show of generosity. (At Buk, the bride's kin only
promise to hand back the majority of pigs as a contemptuous dismissal
of a small bridewealth.)

6. At the *mangal kng* (stage 6), however, Central Melpa groups may not
return live pigs for the pork, but just a few small shell valuables, perhaps
a little money (or salt in the past). Northern Melpa claim they return
live pigs, although the bride's people may give the bride her own breeding sows at this juncture (*kng mbo*). This is said to happen among the
Melpa tribes who may dispense with the *mangal kng* completely and
simply despatch the bride's dowry in return for "legs of pork". Sometimes
they hand over the dowry at *penal kng* (stage 5). They are said to be
afraid for their pigs (the *mangal kng* may escape return at divorce, so
that it is an uncertain investment). *Kopon* tribes, on the other hand,
prefer to separate the two transactions: they keep the endowment till
later, because the bride's kin want to eat the meat of the *mangal kng*,
for which they make handsome return. The giving of a *kik* pig (see page
112) at this stage is omitted among Central Melpa.

7. There are several terminological differences for the categories of valuables, omitted here since I do not discuss dialect variations in general.

Marriages take place between these regions; the theoretical arrangement is for the groom's kin to follow the customs of the bride's people. This accords with their desire to appear generous in the latter's eyes. It is illuminating that many of the differences in fact turn on local interpretations of munificent behaviour. When Northern Melpa marry a Central Melpa girl they comment on how generously her kin reciprocate their gift at the *penal* (stage 5) but grumble at the poor return for their *mangal* pigs (stage 6). My impression is that in fact procedures in these two regions are closer than people sometimes say is the case. Thus, for example, Northern families often cannot raise enough pigs for a full return of the *mangal kng*, while in Central Melpa live pigs in fact may be given along with other items.

Nevertheless, bridewealth negotiations between people from different regions can founder, it is purported, on procedure. In addition, marriage with far groups can be inhibited by the decision of the groom's kin not to cook *tembokl* pigs (for the *penal kng*) because of the distance they would have to carry the meat. There is also the fear that promises made by relative strangers will not be kept. A complicating factor nowadays are the rules which Local Government Councils give on the maximum size that a bridewealth should be.

A marriage was arranged in 1964: the bride[1] from a Central Melpa tribe (referred to subsequently as CM), the groom an orphan from Northern Melpa (NM), whose bridewealth was being raised by his father's brother. They lived a long day's walk apart.

July 30th: 28 pearlshells, £15 ($30 Australian) and 13 pigs were displayed at the groom's home. Two of the pigs, one proposed by them as the "mother's pig", were quite large, the rest small. The decision of the bride's party to take only two or three pigs for nothing, to have two or three killed and make an exchange for the rest was praised by NM men; the CM, however, were clearly disappointed in the showing. The groom's kin said they were bound by Council "laws" not to give more. (30 traditional items, pigs and/or shells were the stipulated maximum.) CM decided to return the "mother's pig", the three non-returnable ones going to the bride's father's sister and her father (which the mother would of course keep). The bride's mother then suddenly declared that she did not want to lose her daughter and refused the special pig allocated to her. The bride hid herself

---

[1] Nøpil: see pp. 203-4

in concurrence. Transactions could not proceed, and the disgruntled visitors left, the CM blaming the girl, NM men her mother.

August 27th: Another bid to obtain the bride; 16 pigs appeared. The bride's kin complained that one was sick and tried to get it changed, but the boy's stepmother made a great fuss over finding a replacement on the grounds that the groom was not her own son. In the end, CM took 15 pigs; the pearl shells had been reduced to 24 in accordance with Council rulings and the money raised to £20. The CM tried to get the pigs originally marked as *tembokl kng* (for killing) as live animals, calling one of them the "mother's pig". The NM were a little worried that the mother would not have a pig for herself, since the CM said they would make a return for it. Proceedings ended quite amicably, the groom's father killing the sick pig for the guests to eat then.

The *penal kng* was delayed a fortnight. CM returned 8 shells, £15 and 9 pigs. There was considerable ill-humour, however, over equivalences. NM had been unable to find suitable shells to return for the solicitory ones (*rumndi kin*), so the CM took their own back; the NM also seized two of their own shells, and four of their own pigs. The CM said afterwards they were disgusted at this behaviour. When the following gift of *mangal* pig fell below their expectations they privately accused the groom's people of "stealing" the girl for nothing. This led to a general disparagement, each in private commenting on the practices of the other party.

The situation was exacerbated by the unwillingness of the bride to marry so far away. She ran home on more than one occasion; her father tried to patch things up by returning her with shells and money. But the marriage ended in divorce (see Chapter 9). Although differences in custom were by no means the sole factor in the dissolution, the bride's people in particular accounted for some of the difficulties in these terms.

VI

Composition of Bridewealths

Synopsis of 30 Bridewealths from Northern and Central Melpa (Buk and Kelua)

Northern Melpa: 15 marriages, all contracted 1964–5;

in 11 cases these were the first marriages for both groom and bride; in one case the bride had been married before, and in three polygynists were contracting second or third marriages with girls previously not-married;

details for contributors: 10 cases:[1]

recipients: 11 cases;

2 of them Christian marriages.[2]

Central Melpa: 15 marriages, 10 contracted 1964–5 and the rest since establishment of Local Government Councils in 1962;

in 12 cases these were first marriages for groom and bride; in three both parties had been married before, one of these involving a polygynist;

details for contributors: 5 cases;

recipients: 5 cases;

2 of them Christian marriages.

---

[1] The bridewealths of four grooms (3 Northern Melpa, 1 Central Melpa), men of non-agnatic status, who were being helped in the main by their matrilateral kin, are excluded from the analysis of contributions, although they are included in the total number counted for size etc. A comparison of bridewealths for agnatic and non-agnatic clansmen is given in Strathern, A. J. & A. M. (1969).

[2] Christians consciously give smaller bridewealths than non-Christians, this being one interpretation of the law they should now be following. Bridewealths for re-married brides may also be smaller; but the Buk and Kelua cases seem fairly evenly balanced both as to Christians and as to second or third marriages.

TABLE XIX

Comparative size of bridewealths[a] at Buk and Kelua based on 30 cases:
total number of items

	Initial display of items (stage 3)				Return-gift (stage 5)			Final prestation of cooked pigs (stage 6)
	Pigs	Shells	£	Other	Pigs	Shells	£	
BUK:	260	303	765	8 cassowaries 1 tube of tree oil $+$[b]	95	42	160	42
KELUA:	213	483	320	3 cassowaries 1 tube of tree oil $+$	101	93	110	45
	Average bridewealth							
BUK:	17·3	20·2	51	0·5 cassowaries	6·3	2·8	10·6	2·8
KELUA:	14·2	32·2	21·3	0·2 cassawaries	6·7	6·2	7·3	3

[a] This tabulation of items omits solicitory gifts and the extra legs of pig sent privately to the bride's parents.

[b] $+$ plus minor items, e.g. shells as longer in fashion, bird of paradise plumes, which are given "on top."

TABLE XX

Proportion of bridewealth returned (stage 5)

	Pigs	Shells	Money (£)
BUK:	95/260 35%	42/303 13·8%	160/765 20%
KELUA:	101/213 47·4%	93/483 19%	110/320 34·3%

Comments

1. Fewer pigs but more shells seem to characterize modern Central Melpa bridewealths by contrast with Northern Melpa.

2. The relatively low proportion of money as an item in the Central Melpa examples can be partly accounted by the more numerous demands on money made among groups living near Hagen township. In 1964 apologies were explicitly given for the small sums offered because clans were saving up to buy trucks.

3. Central Melpa people seem to live up to the characterization made by Northern Melpa, and recognized by themselves, that they return a larger proportion of the bridewealth. This holds for all categories of items.

4. Casowaries figure more in Northern bridewealths, groups here having easier access to one of the habitats of these birds in the Jimi valley.

TABLE XXI

Contributions and distributions

Contributors and recipients are divided into three categories by their relation to the bride/groom:

(a) self, parents and lineage kin, sub-sub-clan kin;

(b) sub-clan, clan kin and other distant agnates, e.g. of pair clan;

(c) other cognates (matrilateral and sororilateral, e.g. MB, MZ (and MZH), FZ (and FZH), cross-cousins, ZS); and affines (ZH (and Z), DH, BW + BWB).

Comments

1. Involvement of category (b) men may come from particularistic loyalties that arise through neighbourhood or co-residential ties, but I do not take these into account here.

2. It is sometimes ambiguous the precise point at which a person is regarded as having contributed (or received) an item in his own name. Thus several of the items which the groom's father raises in fact will have come from other people at some time in the past. But at the time of the bridewealth he will say they are all "his".

3. Husband and wife may act as a corporate pair in giving to and receiving from bridewealths, so that gifts phrased as "for" the FZ will also go to her husband, gifts "from" the Z are also from the ZH.

A. Proportion of bridewealth items contributed by categories of kin, Buk 10 cases and Kelua 5 cases

| | Initial display | : | % of items | |
	Pigs	Shells	Money	Cassowaries
Northern Melpa				
(a)	74·4%	70·1%	62·2%	80%
(b)	17·9%	19%	18·1%	0
(c)	7·7%	10·9%	19·7%	20%
Central Melpa				
(a)	64%	69·6%	39%	100%
(b)	22·7%	22·4%	24·5%	0
(c)	13·3%	8%	36·5%	0

B. Proportion of items received at bridewealth by categories of kin, Buk 11 cases, Kelua 5 cases

| | Initial display | : | % items | |
	Pigs	Shells	Money	Cassowaries
Northern Melpa				
(a)	65·4%	62·8%	92·7%	100%
(b)	14·4%	18·8%	3%	0
(c)	20·1%	18·4%	4·3%	0
Central Melpa				
(a)	59·2%	40·6%	72%	none
(b)	18·3%	29·7%	11·8%	none
(c)	22·5%	29·7%	16·2%	none

Comments

1. Affinal and cognatic kin (c) seem to receive rather more in shells and pigs (20%) than they contribute (10%).

2. However, the majority of items are given by or to clansmen (a) and (b): with the exception of the money contributed to C. Melpa bridewealths, 80–90% of all items are contributed by clansmen of some degree; while they receive 70–80% items.

3. The number of cases analyzed from Central Melpa is really too small for meaningful comparisons; but there seems to be a higher distribution of shells to extra-clan kinsmen (nearly 30%) than appears in the Northern Melpa examples.

VII

Compensation Payments

I examine 56 cases in which married women were involved directly in compensation. I omit certain categories of dispute, mainly those with which they are only indirectly concerned, or which are discussed in detail elsewhere. These are: occasional adultery, homicide, bridewealth and disputed marriage agreements, and poison accusations.

The cases refer in the main to the period 1960–5. They cover disputes over theft, other property losses (e.g. breaking the pearl-shell (p. 241), and pigs ruining gardens), assault (e.g. instances in which two people come to blows or the one party is beaten by the other), setting fire to a house (which may be accidental or deliberate), quarrelling, insults (verbal abuse, indecent exposure), pollution (as when a menstruating woman enters a man's house), and sexual offences. These last include, on the one hand, wilful and persistent adultery by a woman who may therefore have to compensate her husband; and, on the other, sexual intercourse between people related by kinship in which the kinswoman might be regarded as the victim (as when a man has intercourse with his "mother") or as a wrongdoer (as in one case between a man and his MZD): I loosely call these incest. The cases are divided into two series: A, where the woman is felt to be a wrongdoer, and she or someone on her behalf has to compensate the injured person; and B, where she is the victim and she or others receives compensation. Eight cases in which women both give and receive compensation overlap between the two series, and thus appear twice.

I first of all demonstrate the extent to which either women themselves may provide or be paid the compensation, or, if this is done on their behalf, the relationship of the category of person receiving or making the payment. This is then summarized in terms of relations between women and women or between men and women. The nature of the goods involved in making payments bears out the suggestion that use of the easily divisible Australian currency facilitates the transfer of small amounts of cash between women or between men and women. In certain major disputes, however, cash is not regarded as an adequate substitute for the traditional shells and pigs.

TABLE XXII

Relationships of persons involved in compensation

A. Woman responsible as a wrongdoer; number of cases

Injured person (relationship to woman)	Woman herself pays	Paid on her behalf by:		
		Husband	Lineage kin[a]	Other
Men				
Husband	2	—	5	1[b]
HB	2[c]	—	—	—
HBS	1	—	—	—
"B"[d]	—	1	—	—
BSS	1	—	—	—
Stranger	—	1	—	—
	6	2	5	1
Women				
Cowife	2	—	—	—
HBW	1	2	—	—
SW	1	—	—	1
Z	1	—	—	—
	5	2	0	1
TOTAL	11	4	5	2

[a] In all these cases her parents or brothers.

[b] A son and MZS.

[c] In one case the HB and woman's own F also exchanged goods.

[d] A clan-brother in this case. I indicate relations outside the lineage as "B", "S" etc.

B. Woman as injured person; number of cases

Compensation paid by	To woman herself	On her behalf to:		Both to her plus:	
		Husband	Lineage kin	Husband	Lineage kin
Men					
Husband	3	—	6	—	1
HB	1	1	—	1	—
HMB, HZS	—	—	—	2	—
S, "S"	5	—	—	2	—
DH	1	—	—	2	—
HF	1	—	—	—	1
F	—	—	1	—	—
B, "B"	1	—	2	—	—
ZH	—	—	1[a]	—	—
Stranger	1	1	—	—	—
	13	2	10	7	2
Women					
Cowife	2	—	—	—	—
HBW	2	1	—	—	—
HM[b]	2	—	—	—	—
Z	1	—	—	—	—
	7	1	0	0	0
TOTAL	20	3	10	7	2

[a] This was a complicated incest case in which the two parties were related in several ways and the man had to pay the woman's husband as well as his own clan brothers.

[b] Including one case in which the husband also helped the HM (i.e. a son his mother).

In half the cases (31/64) women give and receive themselves. For 15 only her lineage kin are concerned, and for 7 only her husband. We may note that in 5 instances compensation passes directly between husband and wife, and it is of some interest to examine the circumstances of these.

One of the two cases in which a woman paid compensation to her husband was for persistent adultery: its final exposure ended in a fight between the husband and lover in which both were nastily wounded. Because the woman was known to have been adulterous several times, she was publicly blamed for causing the trouble. She denied the charges, but the lover was anxious to prevent the case being taken to an

Administration court, and said he would pay compensation. The Councillors hearing the court in addition made the woman give a pig to her husband. She brought one which had been sent her earlier by her father. In effect, it thus belonged to her husband as well, but this and the other compensation pigs were eaten at the end of the court by the husband and his clansmen along with all those who supported his case. From the point of view of the woman "her" pig was thus lost, i.e. consumed without her participation.

The other case was much less serious. A big-man and Councillor had two wives who squabbled over the allocation he made of a taro and maize garden. The wives attacked each other and then turned on the husband who was responsible for their dispute, and hit him with sticks. He called in a Komiti of his own clan to hear the case, and the Councillor of his pair clan also came. Because they had refused to accept the authority of their husband in making garden allocations, and for attacking him so violently, they were told to pay him £1 or £2 or else a pig.

Cases in which the husband handed over compensation to his wife include one already described (p. 249). The second case concerned a wife who had no effective kin nearby. She was a Mendi girl, from the Southern Highlands, who did not get on very well with her Hagen husband; they bickered constantly. He came home one morning after an all-night session turning head and gave some peanuts, which he had bought on the way, to his wife to cook for him. When he woke he found she had not done so and hit her with the flat of his hand. She returned with a stick and the husband put his arm up to shield his face so that the stick came down on his wrist. The watch he was wearing was smashed and in anger he punched her on the nose and mouth so that she bled. News of the commotion reached a Komiti who went to investigate. The Komiti said that he would have told the husband to pay his wife £3-4, but as he had suffered the loss of his watch, he made it only 10/- This he did. The Komiti was afraid that the wife might run away if the matter were not settled, as she had done in the past.

In the third case the wife was also awarded compensation because everyone feared that she would divorce her husband. There was a long standing quarrel between them and the wife had several times made complaints to her Komiti that her husband did not look after her properly, which the husband met by saying she never cooked for him. When a brother's son of her husband was being married, she made an open fuss over having to provide further pigs. They scrapped in public

TABLE XXIII

The kinds of disputes for which compensation was given

A. Woman responsible; number of cases

| Payments made to | By woman herself | Payments made | | |
		Husband	On her behalf: Lineage kin	Other
Men	Property loss 1 Assault 2 Insult 1 Adultery 1			
		Pollution 2	Pollution 2 Arson 3	Incest 1
	Other 1			
	6	2	5	1
Women	Theft 1 Assault 3 Quarrel 1	Theft 2		Theft and assault 1
	5	2	0	1

B. Woman as injured person; number of cases

| Payments made by | To woman herself | On her behalf to: | | Both to her plus to: | |
		Husband	Lineage Kin	Husband	Lineage kin
Men	Theft 1 Property loss 1 Assault 7 Insult 2 Quarrel 1	Property loss 1	Assault 7	Assault 1 Quarrel 1 Arson 1	Assault 2
		Arson 1	Incest 3	Incest 4	
	Other 1				
	13	2	10	7	2
Women	Theft 2 Theft and assault 1 Assault 3 Quarrel 1	Theft 1			
	7	1	0	0	0

and then that night quarrelled again and hit each other. There and then they went to wake up the local Komiti. He did not want to settle the case in the middle of the night, and said briefly it was the woman's fault: they should go back to sleep. The next morning they discovered she had gone, taking the children with her. The husband feared that she would either commit suicide or not come back. She returned within a few days, however, and the Komiti heard a small court. The husband handed his wife £1A, paid *via* the Komiti, and she kept the money herself.

TABLE XXIV

The medium of compensation

I briefly state here the proportion of payments which are made in Australian currency. Others involve mainly pigs but also shells. †Indicates payments which are a compound of cash and one or other or both of these further items.

In payments *between women*, money was used in 6/8 cases or 75%

In payments *between men and women*, . . . 10 + 2†/19 cases or 63%

In payments *between men*,ª on behalf of women, . . . 3 + 3†/29 or 20%

ª For example, between woman's husband and her kin; I ignore here the fact that a woman's mother as well as her father may sometimes be regarded as receiving compensation if the daughter is assaulted. These 29 cases also include those where a woman as well as her kin or husband may receive compensation but I do not distinguish out that category here.

We may draw the conclusion that payments to or from women are more likely to be of cash, while those between men in cases concerning women are less likely to be so. For assault, incest, and other serious offences such as pollution, pigs are the most appropriate category, and it is for such offences that payments tend to be made most on the woman's behalf.

Bibliography

Allen, M. R. (1967). "Male cults and secret initiations in Melanesia." Melbourne University Press.

Ardener, E. (1962). "Divorce and fertility: an African study." Oxford University Press.

Barnes, J. A. (1949). Measures of divorce frequency in simple societies. *Jl R. anthrop. Inst.*, LXXIX, 37–62.

Barnes, J. A. (1962). African models in the New Guinea Highlands. *Man*, 62, 5–9.

Barnes, J. A. (1967). The frequency of divorce. *In* "The craft of social anthropology" (A. L. Epstein, ed.). Tavistock Publications, London.

Barnett, T. E. (1967). The courts and the people of Papua and New Guinea. *J. Papua and New Guinea Soc.*, 1, 95–101.

Beattie, J. (1964). "Other cultures." Cohen and West, London.

Berndt, C. H. (1965). Women and the "secret life". *In* "Aboriginal man in Australia: Essays in honour of Emeritus Professor A. P. Elkin" (R. M. and C. H. Berndt, eds.), Angus and Robertson, Sydney.

Berndt, R. M. (1962). "Excess and restraint: social control among a New Guinea mountain people." University of Chicago Press.

Bohannan, P. (1957). "Justice and judgement among the Tiv." Oxford University Press.

Bohannan, P. (1960). (ed.) "African homicide and suicide". Princeton University Press.

Brandewie, E. (1968). Reciprocity, exchange and social structure in the Central Highlands of New Guinea. *In* "Anthropica: Gedenkschrift zum 100 Geburstag von P. Wilhelm Schmidt". St. Augustin bei Bonn, Verlag des Anthropos-Instituts.

Brown, P. (1963). From anarchy to satrapy. *Am. Anthrop.*, 65, 1–15.

Brown, P. (1964). Enemies and affines. *Ethnology* 3, 335–356.

Brown, P. (1969). Marriage in Chimbu. *In* "Pigs, pearlshells and women", (R. M. Glasse and M. J. Meggitt, eds.). Prentice-Hall, New Jersey.

Bulmer, R. N. H. (1960). Leadership and social structure among the Kyaka people of the Western Highlands District of New Guinea. Unpublished Ph.D. thesis, Australian National University.

Bulmer, R. N. H. (1961). Kyaka bossboys: post-contact leadership in a New Guinea Highland society. Paper delivered to ANZAAS.

Bulmer, R. N. H. (1965). The Kyaka of the Western Highlands. *In* "Gods, Ghosts and Men in Melanesia" (P. Lawrence and M. J. Meggitt, eds.). Oxford University Press, Melbourne.

Chowning, A. (1969). Review of "Sorcery in its social setting," M. G. Marwick. *Oceania* XXXIX, 248–9.

Colson, E. (1968). "Marriage and the family among the Plateau Tonga of Northern Rhodesia." Manchester University Press.

Cook, E. A. (1969). Marriage among the Manga. *In* "Pigs, pearlshells and women" (R. M. Glasse and M. J. Meggitt, eds.). Prentice-Hall, New Jersey.

Craig, R. (1969). Marriage among the Telefolmin. *In* "Pigs, pearlshells and women" (R. M. Glasse and M. J. Meggitt, eds.). Prentice-Hall, New Jersey.

Douglas, M. (1966). "Purity and danger. An analysis of concepts of pollution and taboo." Routledge and Kegan Paul, London.

Douglas, M. (1967). Witch beliefs in Central Africa. *Africa*, XXXVII, 72–80.

Dupire, M. (1963). The position of women in a pastoral society. *In* "Women of tropical Africa" (D. Paulme, ed.). Routledge and Kegan Paul, London.

Epstein, A. L. (1954). Divorce law and the stability of marriage among the Lunda of Kazembe. *Rhodes-Livingstone J.* **14**, 1–19.

Epstein, A. L. (1967a). The case method in the field of law. *In* "The craft of social anthropology" (A. L. Epstein, ed.). Tavistock Publications, London.

Epstein, A. L. (1967b). Injury and liability: legal ideas and implicit assumptions. *Mankind* **6**, 376–383.

Epstein, A. L. (1969). "Matupit. Land, politics, and change among the Tolai of New Britain." Australian National University Press.

Epstein, A. L. *In press*. Law, indigenous. *In* "The encyclopedia of Papua and New Guinea" (I. Hogbin, ed.).

Fallers, L. A. (1957). Some determinants of marriage stability in Busoga. *Africa*, XXVII, 106–123.

Fenbury, D. (1966). Kot bilong mipela. *New Guinea*, 161–66.

Firth, R. (1957). "We, the Tikopia." 2nd edn. George Allen and Unwin Ltd., London.

Fortes, M. (1949). "The web of kinship among the Tallensi." Oxford University Press.

Fortes, M. (1962). Introduction *to* "Marriage in tribal societies." Cambridge Papers in Social Anthropology No. 3, Cambridge University Press.

Fortes, M. (1967). Totem and taboo. *Proc. R. anthrop. Inst. 1966*, 5–22.

Fortes, M. (1969). "Kinship and the social order. The legacy of Lewis Henry Morgan." Aldine, Chicago.

Glasse, R. M. (1968). "Huli of Papua. A cognatic descent system." Mouton, Paris.

Glasse, R. M. (1969). Marriage in South Fore. *In* "Pigs, pearlshells and women" (R. M. Glasse and M. J. Meggitt, eds.). Prentice-Hall, New Jersey.

Glasse, R. M. and Meggitt, M. J. (1969). Introduction *to* "Pigs, pearlshells and women." Prentice-Hall, New Jersey.

Gluckman, M. (1965). "The ideas in Barotse jurisprudence." Yale University Press.

Goody, E. N. (1962). Conjugal separation and divorce among the Gonja of Northern Ghana. *In* "Marriage in tribal societies" (M. Fortes, ed.). Cambridge Papers in Social Anthropology No. 3, Cambridge University Press.

Goody, J. R. (1956). A comparative approach to incest and adultery. *Br. J. Sociol.* 7, 286–305.

Goody, J. R. (1962). "Death, property and the ancestors. A study of the mortuary customs of the Lodagaa of West Africa." Tavistock Publications, London.

Goody, E. N. and Goody, J. R. (1967). The circulation of women and children in Northern Ghana. *Man (N.S.)* 2, 226–248.

Gray, B. (1969). Aspects of male/female relationships in myth and ritual amongst the Yandapu Enga. Unpublished seminar paper, University of Sydney.

Gulliver, P. H. (1963). "Social control in an African society. A study of the Arusha." Routledge and Kegan Paul, London.

Harper, E. B. (1969). Fear and the status of women. *S.W. J. Anthrop.* **25**, 81–95

Heider, K. G. (1969). Attributes and categories in the study of material culture: New Guinea Dani attire. *Man (N.S.)* **4**, 379–391.

Hiatt, L. R. (1965). "Kinship and conflict. A study of an Aboriginal community in Northern Arnhem Land". Australian National University Press.

Kaberry, P. M. (1939). "Aboriginal woman, sacred and profane." The Blakiston Company, Philadelphia.

Kaberry, P. M. (1952). "Women of the grassfields. A study of the economic position of women in Bamenda, British Cameroons." H.M.S.O., London.

Langness, L. L. (1963). Notes on the Bena Council, Eastern Highlands. *Oceania* **33**, 151–70.

Langness, L. L. (1964). Some problems in the conceptualization of Highlands social structures. *Am. Anthrop., special publication on New Guinea* **66**, 162–182.

Langness, L. L. (1967). Sexual antagonism in the New Guinea Highlands: a Bena Bena example. *Oceania* XXXVII, 161–177.

Langness, L. L. (1969). Marriage in Bena Bena. *In* "Pigs, pearlshells and women" (R. M. Glasse and M. J. Meggitt, eds.). Prentice-Hall, New Jersey.

Lawrence, P. (1969). The state versus stateless societies in Papua and New Guinea. *In* "Fashion of law in New Guinea". (B. J. Brown, ed.). Butterworths, Sydney.

Lawrence, P. and Meggitt, M. J. (1965). *Introduction to* "Gods, ghosts and men in Melanesia. Some religions of Australian New Guinea and the New Hebrides." Oxford University Press, Melbourne.

Leach, E. R. (1961). "Rethinking anthropology." University of London Athlone Press, London.

Lewis, I. M. (1962). "Marriage and the family in Northern Somaliland." East African studies, **15**, Kampala.

Lewis, I. M. (1965). Problems in the comparative study of unilineal descent. *In* "The relevance of models for social anthropology." A.S.A. Monographs 1, Tavistock Publications, London.

Lewis, I. M. (1966). Spirit possession and deprivation cults. *Man (N.S.)* **1**, 307–329.

Lindenbaum, S. and Glasse, R. M. (1969). Fore age mates. *Oceania* XXXIX, 165–173.

Lloyd, P. C. (1968). Divorce among the Yoruba. *Am. Anthrop.* **70**, 67–81.

Maddock, K. (1969). Alliance and entailment in Australian marriage. *Mankind* **7**, 19–26.

Marwick, M. G. (1965). "Sorcery in its social setting. A study of the Northern Rhodesian Ceŵa." Manchester University Press.

Mattes, J. R. (1969). The courts system. *In* "Fashion of Law in New Guinea" (B. J. Brown, ed.). Butterworths, Sydney.

Mead, M. (1935). "Sex and temperament in three primitive societies." Geo. Routledge and sons, London.

Meggitt, M. J. (1964). Male–female relationships in the Highlands of Australian New Guinea. *Am. Anthrop., special publication on New Guinea* **66**, 204–224.

Meggitt, M. J. (1965). "The lineage system of the Mae-Enga of New Guinea." Oliver and Boyd, Edinburgh.

Middleton, J. and Winter, E. H. (1963). "Witchcraft and sorcery in East Africa." Routledge and Kegan Paul, London.

Mitchell, J. C. (1961). Social change and stability in African marriage in Northern Rhodesia. *In* "Social change in modern Africa" (A. Southall, ed.). Oxford University Press.

Nadel, S. F. (1957). "The theory of social structure." Cohen and West, London.

Newman, P. L. (1964). Religious belief and ritual in a New Guinea society. *Am. Anthrop., special publication on New Guinea* **66**, 257–272.

Newman, P. L. (1965). "Knowing the Gururumba". Case studies in cultural anthropology. Holt, Rinehart and Winston, New York.

O'Brien, D. (1969). Marriage among the Konda Valley Dani. *In* "Pigs, pearlshells, and women" (R. M. Glasse and M. J. Meggitt, eds.). Prentice-Hall, New Jersey.

Paulme, D. (1963). "Women of tropical Africa." Routledge and Kegan Paul, London.

Peters, E. L. (1967a). Some structural aspects of the feud among the camel-herding Bedouin of Cyrenaica. *Africa* **37**, 261–282.

Peters, E. L. (1967b). Sex differentiation in two Arab communities. *In* "Masculine and feminine" (J. Peristiany, ed.). Social Science Centre, Athens.

Ploeg, A. (1969). "Government in Wanggulam". Martinus Nijhoff, The Hague.

Pospisil, L. (1958). "Kapauku Papuans and their law." Yale University Publications in Anthropology, **54**, New Haven.

Pouwer, J. (1966). Towards a configurational approach to society and culture in New Guinea. *J. Polynes. Soc.* **75**, 267–286.

Radcliffe-Brown, A. R. (1950). Introduction *to* "African systems of kinship and marriage" (A. R. Radcliffe-Brown and D. Forde, eds.). Oxford University Press.

Read, K. E. (1954). Cultures of the Central Highlands, New Guinea. *S.W.J. Anthrop.* **10**, 1–43.

Read, K. E. (1955). Morality and the concept of the person among the Gahuku-Gama. *Oceania* XXV, 234–282.

Read, K. E. (1966). "The high valley." George Allen and Unwin, London.

Reay, M. O. (1959a). "The Kuma: freedom and conformity in the New Guinea Highlands." Melbourne University Press.

Reay, M. O. (1959b). Two kinds of ritual conflict. *Oceania* XXIX, 290–296.

Reay, M. O. (1964a). Present-day politics in the New Guinea Highlands. *Am. Anthrop.*, *special publication on New Guinea* **66**, 240–256.

Reay, M. O. (1964b). Review of "Excess and Restraint", R. M. Berndt, *Oceania* XXXV, 149–154.

Reay, M. O. (1966). Women in transitional society. *In* "New Guinea on the threshold" (E. K. Fisk, ed.). Longmans, London.

Reay, M. O. (1967). Structural co-variants of land shortage among patrilineal peoples. *Anthrop. Forum* II, 4–19.

Reay, M. O. "Multi-racial elections in New Guinea."

Ross, W. (1936). Ethnological notes on the Mount Hagen tribes. *Anthropos* XXXI, 341–363.

Ryan, D. J. (1961). Gift-exchange in the Mendi Valley. Unpublished Ph.D. thesis, University of Sydney.

Ryan, D. J. (1969). Marriage in Mendi. *In* "Pigs, pearlshells and women" (R. M. Glasse and M. J. Meggitt, eds.). Prentice-Hall, New Jersey.

Salisbury, R. F. (1962). "From stone to steel: economic consequences of a technological change in New Guinea." Melbourne University Press.

Salisbury, R. F. (1964). Despotism and Australian Administration in the New Guinea Highlands. *Am. Anthrop.*, *special publication on New Guinea* **66**, 225–39.

Salisbury, R. F. (1965). The Siane of the Eastern Highlands. *In* "Gods, ghosts and men Melanesia" (P. Lawrence and M. J. Meggitt, eds.). Oxford University Press.

Scheffler, H. W. (1965). "Choiseul Island social structure." University of California Press.

Strathern, A. J. (1965). Descent and group structure among the Mbowamb. Fellowship dissertation, Trinity College, Cambridge.

Strathern, A. J. (1966a). Despots and directors in the New Guinea Highlands. *Man* (*N.S.*) **1**, 356–367.

Strathern, A. J. (1966b). Ceremonial exchange in the Mount Hagen area. Ph.D. thesis, University of Cambridge.

Strathern, A. J. (1968). Sickness and frustration. *Mankind* **6**, 545–551.

Strathern, A. J. (1969a). Descent and alliance in the New Guinea Highlands: some problems of comparison. *Proc. R. Anthrop. Inst. 1968*, 37–52.

Strathern, A. J. (1969b). Finance and production: two strategies in New Guinea Highlands exchange systems. *Oceania* XL, 42–67.

Strathern, A. J. (1970a). The Female and Male spirit cults in Mount Hagen. *Man.* (*N.S.*) **5**, 571–585.

Strathern, A. J. (1970b). Kiap, Councillor and big-man: role-contrasts in Mount Hagen. *In* "The politics of Melanesia". (M. W. Ward, ed.). Australian National University Press.

Strathern, A. J. (1971). "The rope of moka: big-men and ceremonial exchange in Mount Hagen." Cambridge University Press.

Strathern, A. J. "One Father, One Blood." Australian National University Press. To be published.

Strathern, A. M. (1965). Axe types and quarries: a note on the classification of stone axe blades from the Hagen area, New Guinea. *J. Polynes. Soc.* 74, 182–191.

Strathern, A. M. (1968). Popokl: the question of morality. *Mankind* **6**, 553–562.

Strathern, A. M. (1969). Stone axes and flake tools: evaluations from two New Guinea Highlands societies. *Proc. Prehist. Soc.* 35, 311–29.

Strathern, A. J. and Strathern, A. M. (1968). Marsupials and magic: a study of spell symbolism among the Mbowamb. *In* "Dialectic in practical religion" (E. R. Leach, ed.). Cambridge Papers in Social Anthropology No. 5, Cambridge University Press.

Strathern, A. J. and Strathern, A. M. (1969). Marriage in Melpa. *In* "Pigs, pearlshells and women" (R. M. Glasse and M. J. Meggitt, eds.). Prentice-Hall, New Jersey.

Strathern, A. J. and Strathern, A. M. (1971). "Self-decoration in Mount Hagen." Gerald Duckworth, London.

Strauss, H. and Tischner, H. (1962). "Die Mi-Kultur der Hagenberg-Stämme im Östlichen Zentral-Neuguinea." Cram, de Gruyter and Co., Hamburg.

Vicedom, G. F. and Tischner, H. (1943–8). "Die Mbowamb. Die Kultur der Hagenberg-Stämme im Östlichen Zentral-Neuguinea." 3 vols. Cram, de Gruyter and Co., Hamburg.

Waddell, E. W. (1968). The dynamics of a New Guinea Highlands agricultural system. Unpublished Ph.D. thesis, Australian National University.

Werbner, R. P. (1964). Atonement ritual and guardian-spirit possession among Kalanga. Africa. XXXIV, 206–223.

Werbner, R. P. (1968). Spirits and the sex war (correspondence). Man (N.S.) 3, 129–130.

Wilson, P. J. (1967). Status ambiguity and spirit possession. Man (N.S.) 2, 366–378.

Wurm, S. A. (1964). Australian New Guinea Highlands languages and the distribution of their typological features. Am. Anthrop., special publication on New Guinea 66, 77–97.

Yalman, N. (1963). On the purity of women in the castes of Ceylon and Malabar. Jl. R. anthrop. Inst. 93, 25–58.

Subject Index

like low-status men, 160–162, 260, 263, 268

narrow horizon of, 137, 140, 147, 281, 309

as "political minors", 161, 169f., 182, 260, 263–266, 270, 285, 289, 293

as responsible for actions, 164, 166, 169, 173, 262f.

secret acts of, 176f., 312

as "servants" of men 152 154

sharing men's values by, 131, 150, 270, 283, 309

as "strong" things, 102, 114, 135, 289

as "weak", 142, 160f., 168f., 307

us without "name", 153

see also Attitudes, Independence, Virilocal residence and Wife

Women and men, inter-sexual conflict of, 305f., 313

Women's house, 10, 11, 53, 165, 170, 243
divisions of, 47, 57

sharing of, by women, 56–57

Work,
of councillors, 225
of men, 13, 45, 172
of women, 13–16, 27, 83, 153f., 235
and evaluation of, 92, 133–135, 151–152
and relevance of to women's status, 132f., 235, 290
see also Division of Labour

Y

Yamka tribe, 4, 123, 160, 219f., 249, 317, 331

Young women,
as liable to seek divorce, 97, 195–196
grievances of, 147f.
position of, 34, 37, 99–100
recourse of to councillors, 195, 270f.
as wives dependent on husband's mother, see Mother-in-law